Balfour and
the British Empire

Balfour and the British Empire

A STUDY IN
IMPERIAL EVOLUTION
1874–1932

Denis Judd

Macmillan
LONDON · MELBOURNE · TORONTO
St Martin's Press
NEW YORK
1968

To My Parents

© Denis Judd 1968

Published by
MACMILLAN AND CO LTD
Little Essex Street London WC2
and also at Bombay Calcutta and Madras
Macmillan South Africa (Publishers) Pty Ltd Johannesburg
The Macmillan Company of Australia Pty Ltd Melbourne
The Macmillan Company of Canada Ltd Toronto
St Martin's Press Inc New York

Library of Congress catalog card no. 68–20708

Printed in Great Britain by
ROBERT MACLEHOSE AND CO LTD
The University Press, Glasgow

Contents

Part 4—The Indian and Colonial Empires

Part 5—The Colonies of White Settlement

List of Illustrations

PLATES

All the photographs are reproduced by permission of the Radio Times Hulton Picture Library

CARTOONS

The cartoons are reproduced by permission of Associated Newspapers

Preface

THIS book has grown out of a Ph.D. thesis submitted to the University of London in 1967, and sets out to examine the attitudes and policies of Arthur James Balfour towards the British Empire. It spans the years from 1874 when Balfour entered the House of Commons, to 1932, two years after his death. The study has been extended to 1932 in order to deal with the Ottawa Conference of that year and to incorporate the Statute of Westminster of 1931. Moreover, it has been necessary, for a better understanding of the subject, to give an account of some aspects of imperial history before 1874.

Within the context of the book the term 'British Empire' includes the self-governing colonies (called Dominions after 1907), the Indian Empire, the crown colonies, protectorates, protected states, chartered territories, mandated territories and condominiums. Thus both Egypt and the Sudan are treated as part of the Colonial Empire, as are the mandates of Iraq and Palestine. Ireland, despite Balfour's Chief Secretaryship there between 1887 and 1891, has been taken to form part of the United Kingdom until the formal independence of the Irish Free State renders this unacceptable. Furthermore, Balfour's interest in the Anglo-Saxon world in general and in Anglo-American co-operation in particular, has meant that in Part 5 of the book the United States has (temporarily) rejoined the Empire. This is a matter of scholastic convenience only, and need cause alarm in neither Washington nor Whitehall.

Other terms employed require explanation. To begin with, 'Imperial' refers to the policy or action of the British government; 'imperial' to the policy, action or problems of two or more components of the Empire. 'South Africa' is used to describe the area including Cape Colony, Natal, the Transvaal and the Orange Free State. The term, though not a precise one prior to the establishment of the Union of South Africa in 1910, was extensively used in official and private documents before that time. Balfour's contemporaries spoke of the 'Near East' rather than the 'Middle East'. To avoid confusion the text keeps to the former term throughout. Also, for the greater part of the book, 'Unionist' describes the party which was born out of the Irish Home Rule crisis of 1886 and comprised the Conservatives, the Liberal-Unionists and the Chamberlainite Radicals. With the Anglo-Irish Treaty of 1921, and the independence of the Irish Free State, the Unionists become the Conservative and Unionist party.

It may seem as though excessive use has been made of Balfour's speeches in both Houses of Parliament. There are two reasons for this. Firstly, Balfour was a man who frequently thought while on his feet. He rarely made copious notes for speeches, and those he did produce were often scribbled on the backs of envelopes. Therefore, the real Balfour regularly emerges from the pages of Hansard. Secondly, Balfour's correspondence on imperial affairs grew increasingly sparse after the First World War. Hansard is once more a most fruitful source of information. Finally, the book does not claim to be a comprehensive and exhaustive analysis of sixty years of imperial history. It is firmly linked to the career of one man who, throughout these years, occupied a position at the centre of the political stage. If it is myopic as a result of this, the blame should fall on the author, rather than on the statesman whose sight was mostly sharp and sometimes penetrating, and who saw so many years of imperial evolution.

The writing of both the thesis and the book have left me with many debts of gratitude to discharge. In the first place, the Earl of Balfour has allowed me to consult the Balfour Papers at Whittinge-hame, and has furnished me with certain pieces of vital information as well as the most delightful hospitality. The British Museum, the University of Birmingham, the Public Record Office, the

India Office Library, the Bodleian, and Christ Church, Oxford, have been good enough to let me use documents in their possession.

Dr Mary Cumpston, of Birkbeck College, who supervised my thesis with endless patience and critical care, has contributed immeasurably to whatever proves worth while in my book on Balfour. Two postgraduate seminars (one at London chaired by Professor R. Robinson, and one at Oxford under Professor J. Gallagher and Dr F. Madden) helped to destroy my wilder fancies. My friend and colleague Dennis Dean has read the book and criticised it. Brenda Bolton and David Carlton have checked all or part of the proofs. Some research assistance was given by two of my students, John Aldridge and Edgar Buckley. Kenneth Young's *Arthur James Balfour* has provided me with information and stimulation, and its author gave me early encouragement. Lastly, I owe a special debt of gratitude to my wife Dorothy for designing the book jacket and also for allowing me so many hours of peace.

DENIS JUDD

London, August 1967

A Select Calendar 1848–1932

1848   Balfour born at Whittingehame, East Lothian.

1861   Goes to Eton.

1866   Goes to Trinity College, Cambridge.

1874   Elected M.P. for Hertford. Conservative election victory. Disraeli Prime Minister.

1876   Queen Victoria proclaimed Empress of India.

1877   Transvaal annexed.

1878   Balfour accompanies Salisbury to the Congress of Berlin as his Parliamentary Private Secretary. Afghan War.

1879   Zulu War.

1880   Liberal election victory. Gladstone Prime Minister.

1881   Battle of Majuba Hill, Transvaal subsequently regains independence.

1882   British occupation of Egypt begins.

1885   Death of Gordon at Khartoum. Gladstone's government resigns. Salisbury Prime Minister.

1886   January, Salisbury resigns. February, Gladstone forms third administration. Introduces Home Rule Bill, June; defeated in Commons. Salisbury becomes Prime Minister, wins general election. Balfour made Secretary for Scotland. Gold discovered in Transvaal.

1887   Victoria's Golden Jubilee. First Colonial Conference, London. Balfour becomes Chief Secretary for Ireland.

1891   Balfour made First Lord of the Treasury and Leader of Commons.

1892   Liberal election victory, Gladstone Prime Minister.

1894   Rosebery succeeds Gladstone as Prime Minister. Colonial Economic Conference, Ottawa.

1895   Unionist election victory. Salisbury Prime Minister. Balfour First Lord of Treasury and Leader of Commons. Joseph Chamberlain Colonial Secretary. Cabinet Defence Committee established. Jameson Raid. Venezuela crisis.

1897   Victoria's Diamond Jubilee. Colonial Conference.

1898   Battle of Omdurman, and Fashoda crisis. Anglo-German agreement over Portuguese African colonies. Curzon becomes Viceroy.

1899   Outbreak of Boer War.

1900   'Khaki' election keeps Unionists in power.

1901   Death of Queen Victoria. Edward VII succeeds her. Australian Commonwealth created.

1902   Anglo-Japanese alliance. Peace in South Africa. Colonial Conference. July, Balfour succeeds Salisbury as Prime Minister. Defence Committee reconstituted by Balfour.

1903   Tariff reform controversy splits Cabinet, Chamberlain resigns.

1904   Reports of Elgin and Esher Committees. Fully-fledged Committee of Imperial Defence established. Younghusband Expedition reaches Lhasa. Outbreak of Russo-Japanese War. Entente with France.

1905   Climax of Kitchener–Curzon dispute. Curzon resigns. Japan defeats Russia. Anglo-Japanese alliance renewed. December, Balfour's government resigns. Campbell-Bannerman takes office.

1906   Landslide Liberal election victory.

1907   Colonial Conference. Entente with Russia.

1908   Asquith succeeds Campbell-Bannerman as Prime Minister.

1909   Lloyd George introduces the 'People's' Budget. Morley–Minto reforms in India.

1910   January, Liberals retain office after general election. George V succeeds Edward VII. December, second general election. Liberals stay in office. Union of South Africa.

1911   Parliament Act passed. Balfour resigns as Unionist leader, succeeded by Bonar Law. Imperial Conference.

1915 Balfour made First Lord of Admiralty in Asquith's wartime coalition government.

1916 Dublin Easter rebellion. December, Lloyd George overthrows Asquith. Becomes Prime Minister. Balfour Foreign Secretary.

1917 Balfour Declaration. Imperial War Conference and Cabinet.

1918 Lloyd George coalition wins general election.

1919 Dominions and India sign Peace Treaties separately. Government of India Act embodies Montagu–Chelmsford reforms. Balfour becomes Lord President of Council.

1921 Imperial Conference. Balfour leads British Empire delegation at Washington Conference, 1921–2.

1922 Balfour receives Order of Garter. Created Earl of Balfour and Viscount Traprain. Chanak incident. Lloyd George coalition destroyed. Bonar Law Conservative Prime Minister. Formal independence of Irish Free State.

1923 Baldwin succeeds Bonar Law as Prime Minister. Imperial Conference advocates preferential tariffs.

1924 First Labour government. Ramsay MacDonald Prime Minister. November, Baldwin and Conservatives return to power.

1925 Balfour Lord President of Council.

1926 Imperial Conference. Balfour chairman of Inter-Imperial Relations Committee.

1929 Baldwin government resigns. Balfour surrenders his last office. Ramsay MacDonald leads second Labour administration. Conference on Operation of Dominion Legislation and Merchant Shipping Legislation. Irwin Declaration promises India Dominion status.

1930 Balfour dies, 19 March. Imperial Conference.

1931 Statute of Westminster. Ramsay MacDonald heads national government.

1932 Ottawa Imperial Economic Conference introduces imperial preference.

1 Balfour and the Empire: an Introduction

> We have been making, at first half-consciously, the most novel and the greatest experiment in Empire-building which the world has ever seen. It is vain to think that so great an undertaking can be carried to a successful issue without earnest effort.
>
> BALFOUR, 1926

FOR one who appeared so unwilling to exert himself, Balfour's life was full of accomplishment. Admittedly he was born in 1848 with considerable advantages. His father was from an old-established Lowland family which traced its descent back to Robert Bruce, and his mother was a daughter of the 2nd Marquis of Salisbury. His Cecil blood and the close relationship that was to develop with his uncle Salisbury (the 3rd Marquis, and three times Queen Victoria's Prime Minister) proved invaluable in carrying Balfour almost effortlessly to the highest political offices and eventually to 10 Downing Street itself.

But Balfour was not merely well-born. He was also fortunate in possessing a formidable and original intelligence. Although at Eton he 'did nothing worth describing',[1] at Trinity College, Cambridge, he came under the influence of Henry Sidgwick, the philosopher, and read for the newly-instituted Moral Sciences Tripos, gaining a second class degree in 1869.

Balfour thus acquired an enduring taste for speculative thinking. He published two philosophical works during his lifetime: *A Defence of Philosophic Doubt* in 1879, and *The Foundations of Belief* in 1895. He therefore carried into his political activities a philosophical detachment which frequently infuriated both friends and enemies. Balfour was perpetually able to see both sides of a problem. Unfortunately, he was not always ready to make decisions.

Moreover, although his love of toying with ideas and words could stimulate those of equal intelligence, he all too often confused dullards. There was perhaps something to be said for conducting Cabinet or committee meetings as if they were seminars, but less so if the plodders were left gasping for breath.

On the other hand, Balfour's donnish exercises at least encouraged an adequate and rational debate of issues as complex as that of the *uitlander* problem, and also served to focus attention on the intricacies of imperial defence. His contemporaries, however, often failed to detect the firmness of purpose beneath his dilettante methods. They took his debating skill and word-jugglery to be the essence of the man; they confused political tightrope-walking with lack of principles; they failed to appreciate that a philosopher could also be a dour realist.

Balfour was often accused of lacking deep political involvement, but in fact politics was the greatest passion of his life. It is certainly true that he was capable of abandoning causes and personalities when it became expedient to do so. Although an aristocrat, and fundamentally opposed to Joseph Chamberlain's attempts to democratise the Unionist Party before 1906, he eventually refused to support the diehard peers against the radical Parliament Act of 1911. Later, in December 1916 Balfour, the last of the Athenians, refused to sustain Asquith, the last of the Romans. Instead he took office under Lloyd George, the first of the Goths. In both cases, Balfour would have argued that the national interest had dictated his course of action.

Nor can his fundamental loyalty to the Conservative and Unionist party be doubted. Although in 1922 he bitterly deplored that Bonar Law and Curzon had seen fit to smash the Lloyd George coalition, his resentment was based chiefly on the belief that the coalition was an invaluable and 'historic party'.[2] Without doubt there was also an appreciation of the lucidity and energy which Lloyd George had brought to the task of government. Of course, Balfour enjoyed public office inordinately (no matter what impression he gave to contemporaries) and, despite his own lackadaisical airs, the efficiency of Lloyd George's wartime administration had been much to his taste.

But then, Balfour was content to serve different masters, although he was happiest of all with his 'Uncle Robert'. Even after the loss of the Unionist leadership in 1911 he held office quite contentedly under Asquith and Lloyd George, in coalition governments, and finally under Baldwin in a Conservative administration. All in all, Balfour's political career lasted fifty-five years, and for twenty-seven of these he was a minister of the crown.

As if this was insufficient occupation, Balfour's life was otherwise extraordinarily full. Although he never married, women were not unknown to him, and one affair, at least, ran a lengthy and occasionally hazardous course. But perhaps he valued women as friends rather than as women. Balfour had an abundance of friends and delighted in conversation and company. At the same time his friends were not always convinced that he would be greatly moved if death were suddenly to strike them down.[3] Yet his cold Cecil temperament and his philosophic detachment contrasted with his passion for music and his interest in the visual arts. But Balfour's life abounded in paradox: the logician who dabbled in spiritualism; the landowner who preferred tennis and golf to hunting and fishing; the Victorian aristocrat who advocated scientific research; the apparently lazy man who could, on occasion, get things done.

It is tempting to see Balfour as a rare hot-house plant nurtured in the late-Victorian sun, beautiful but useless, or to argue that beneath the glittering exterior there was merely a man of straw. However, Balfour's attitude towards imperial problems reveals that such an analysis is some way from the truth.

In this field Balfour was consistently practical and occasionally ruthless. Refusing to be wedded to theory, he sought for empirical solutions instead. Seeing that there was little natural harmony in the Empire, he chose to swim with the course of imperial evolution rather than attempt to create an artificial harmony. Here his methods contrasted violently with some of the more forceful, hasty and basically unsuccessful measures proposed by Joseph Chamberlain. Balfour did not believe that the colonies of white settlement would submerge their new-found identities for Britain's benefit. He was sceptical as to the value of tariff reform,

and fought a long rearguard action against it, aided by those melli-
fluous but almost meaningless phrases he could employ so well.

Set beside Joseph Chamberlain and the great proconsuls, Balfour seems cast in an unheroic mould. But during his Prime
Ministership his permissive yet realistic attitudes at least resulted
in the establishment of the Committee of Imperial Defence, even
if they failed to unite the Unionists over tariff reform. Moreover,
in the heyday of imperial expansion Balfour remained cool-
headed over territorial acquisitions. As early as 1880 he had
criticised Disraeli's weakness in allowing individual ministers and
officials to force him into annexing the Transvaal in 1877 and
appearing responsible for the Zulu War of 1879.[4]

By the time he became Prime Minister in 1902 Balfour had
shown little but contempt for jingos and militarists. He disapproved of any territorial expansion which did not serve clear
and precise British interests. Accordingly, his government forced
a showdown over Curzon's aggressive 'forward' policies as Viceroy towards Afghanistan and Tibet. In this way Balfour asserted
the ultimate authority of the British Cabinet in Indian policy-
making. In addition, the drift to war in South Africa racked
Balfour's conscience. He by no means always saw the *uitlanders* as a
persecuted and worthy group, although he finally supported war
as the only way of establishing British supremacy in South Africa.
But he proved consistently inept at banging the patriotic drum.

When he resigned as Prime Minister in 1905, Balfour could
claim solid achievements for his administration. The defences of
the Empire had been strengthened by the entente with France in
1904 and the renewal of the Japanese alliance in 1905. Furthermore
the Committee of Imperial Defence promised greater imperial
co-operation over defence. Curzon had been tamed, and the
Transvaal and the Orange Free State pacified after a fashion. The
electoral holocaust of 1906 has tended to obscure these triumphs,
and it is perfectly true that Balfour demonstrably failed to keep
his party united in face of Chamberlain's tariff reform campaign.
On the other hand, he had also managed to stick to his principles,
even though it became increasingly difficult to discern the nature
of these principles as the tariff controversy deepened.

The years from 1905 to 1932 amply confirmed Balfour's belief that with the Dominions the only course open to Britain was to leave them to go their own way and to co-operate with Britain when they wished to do so. Balfour was convinced that the Dominions were the sinews of the Empire, but that independence strengthened these sinews. The Imperial Conference of 1926 enabled Balfour to supervise the formal acknowledgment of this Dominion independence. Such a step caused him no qualms. He had long before discerned the strength of certain enduring inter-imperial bonds such as the monarchy, similar political institutions, and a common language, law, and traditions. Even the events leading to the tardy introduction of imperial preference in 1932 served merely to confirm Balfour's original premise that tariff reform, if associated with dearer food, equalled electoral suicide. Nor were the 1932 Ottawa agreements charters of a new age of imperial harmony. They served limited needs, and the parties involved recognised the fact.

On these issues Balfour's judgment was proved consistently sound. But these were problems involving the colonies of white settlement. Faced with the growing demands of Indian nationalists, and with the confrontation between European and non-European in Africa, Balfour's touch was less sure. Prepared in 1893 to see Cecil Rhodes as the standard-bearer of civilisation in Matabeleland, Balfour remained fundamentally unsympathetic to the real and potential aspirations of the non-European subjects of the Crown. By the end of his life he had come to accept the necessity of creating a brown Dominion out of the Indian Empire. But he did so with profound misgivings.

In South Africa Balfour denied the possibilities of equality between black and white. Nor did he believe that the abyss between the two races could be bridged by the passage of time and educational endeavour. Such pessimism ill-became the ardent advocate of the 1902 Education Act. But Balfour held gloomy views as to the potentialities of non-Europeans in general. Given this, it is not surprising that he envisaged a 'black peril' and wished to keep it at arm's length.

Despite the more liberal attitudes of some of his contemporaries on this score, it is perhaps asking for too much that Balfour should have shared their views. Born into an élite section of the highest class in one of the most civilised countries in Europe, Balfour was hardly a man of the people – even his own people. Moreover, practically speaking, for the first part of Balfour's political life there was no compelling need to see Indian problems except in the context of British interests. Similarly Balfour believed that as long as certain humanitarian standards were observed, it was more realistic in the short term to show concern for the co-operation of British and Afrikaner in South Africa, rather than insist on equality between black and white. Balfour's prophecy that the latter equality would not be achieved in the foreseeable future was entirely accurate, and for his own lifetime the British Empire remained dominated by its white citizens.

What, therefore, was the essence of Balfour's contribution to the evolution of the British Empire? Merely to discern the progress of that evolution and to adjust his ideas accordingly? But this is the contribution of the armchair observer, not of the constructive statesman. In any case, Balfour only slowly and painfully reconciled himself to the growing demands of Indian nationalism. The first flickerings of African nationalism were quite beyond his vision.

Balfour did, however, keep Britain's territorial acquisitions of the last quarter of the nineteenth century firmly in perspective. He was also unfailingly accurate in his diagnosis of the needs and identities of the Dominions. Even if the famous 'Balfour definition' of Dominion status at the 1926 Imperial Conference was not entirely his, at least it accorded with his long-standing convictions upon the subject. Above all, his sense of the practical and the realistic meant that in general his attitude towards imperial developments was permissive, not radical, and characterised by patience and detachment rather than by urgency. These were certainly the qualities of the philosopher, but they proved not inappropriate to the statesman.

PART ONE

The Defence
of the Empire

For home defence and colonial defence I believe the country
would pay anything if they saw value for their money.

BALFOUR, 1889

2 Confusion, Disaster and Reform

There is a grave necessity lying upon us at present for co-ordinating our forces for ensuring harmonious action between the Navy and the Army.

BALFOUR, 1894

It was our fault, and our very great fault, and *not* the judgement of Heaven.
We made an Army in our own image, on an island nine by seven.

KIPLING, *The Lesson*, 1899–1902

I

THE early humiliating defeats of British arms in the Boer War had revealed to a shocked public the inadequacies and contradictions of imperial defence. By the early 1870s successive governments, careful to limit expense and relying on the shield of the Royal Navy, had tried wherever possible to withdraw British troops from the self-governing colonies. Despite colonial objections, a substantial withdrawal had been effected by the end of Gladstone's first administration in 1874. Nor, despite Disraeli's rhetoric on the subject, did the subsequent Conservative government reverse the process, although it was felt expedient to maintain a garrison in the Cape to protect the Simon's Bay naval base and deal with possible native troubles.[1]

This withdrawal of British troops posed certain problems. If the Royal Navy was to defend the self-governing colonies against external aggression, should not the colonies make some financial contribution to the navy's upkeep? Again, such colonial forces as existed were hardly sufficient to face professional European armies or, indeed, serious internal difficulties – as the second Maori War, which ended in 1870, had shown in New Zealand. Such possible hazards demanded an adequate degree of imperial defence planning and also of co-operation between the British

army and the navy. By 1878, neither of these desirable conditions
had been satisfactorily achieved. Indeed, the army and the navy
were not always willing to co-operate. Moreover, the British
Cabinet, which was in the 1870s the only body possessing general
responsibility for defence policy, was ill-adapted for dealing with
such technical matters. In particular, Cabinet government had no
organ which could co-ordinate policy by means of recommendations based on expert advice and consideration.[2]

However, a Colonial Defence Committee was established in
1878 in response to the Russian war scare. But it existed for only
a year and had little influence at Cabinet level.[3] Growing fear of
Russian activities on the frontiers of India caused the Salisbury
government to revive it in 1885. Its functions were those of an
interdepartmental committee which collected and circulated the
advice and information of the various departments on matters
such as the defence of certain ports, the size and training of
colonial forces and any colonial legislation dealing with defence.
But it undertook no strategic planning and offered no advice of
its own.[4]

Hard on the heels of the re-establishment of the Colonial
Defence Committee came the first Colonial Conference of 1887,
and, in 1888, the setting-up of the Hartington Commission, to
inquire into military and naval organisation generally.[5] Despite
the Commission's recommendation that a joint naval and military
council should be created, possibly headed by the Prime Minister
and attended by the Cabinet heads of the services and their professional advisers, nothing was done to bring about this co-
ordination of policy until 1895.[6]

In that year Salisbury again took office, forming an administration with Balfour as First Lord of the Treasury and Leader of
the House of Commons. The Franco-Russian alliance of 1894,
and the retirement of the obstructive but royal Duke of Cambridge as Commander-in-Chief of the army, made it seem more
necessary and possible than before to attempt a reform of defence
organisation. Balfour, moreover, came into office with his in-
clination towards the improvement of inter-service co-operation
sharpened by correspondence with Charles Dilke, the resilient

and radical member for the Forest of Dean, and Spencer Wilkinson, both of whom were propagandists in the cause of imperial defence. Balfour himself had shown considerable interest in these problems, telling Salisbury, in 1889, that the clamour for reform by the military party in the House of Commons and by some army officers was 'not without reason', and adding that 'for home defence and colonial defence I believe the country would pay anything if they saw value for their money'.[7]

While in opposition, Balfour had made his opinions even clearer in a speech to the Commons in March 1894 when he agreed that there was 'a grave necessity lying upon us at present for co-ordinating our forces for ensuring harmonious action between the Navy and the Army, and for preparing those plans for military defence ... which every nation in the world prepares in time of peace, and which I rather suspect we have not, at all events, got in any advanced state of preparation'.[8] Reluctant to accept the creation of a Minister of Defence, whom he feared would reduce the First Lord of the Admiralty and the Minister for War to the position of Under Secretaries, Balfour suggested that 'a Committee of the Cabinet is the only method of bringing the Cabinet itself into touch with expert opinion, and through the Cabinet, giving the House practically the best advice and information they can obtain on these subjects'.[9] But he proposed that such a committee should not be merely an intermittent body called into existence to deal with some particular question, but that 'the Prime Minister, with or without his colleagues, or a Committee of the Cabinet, with or without the Prime Minister, as the case may be, should constitute themselves a body with permanent records and confidential advisers'. This, he thought, would secure continuity of administration no matter what party was in power, and would ensure that the Cabinet, who were 'the ultimate depositories of power in this matter', should have presented to them the major defence problems and the best ways of meeting them.[10]

It was therefore not surprising that in 1895 the Salisbury government set up a Defence Committee of the Cabinet. This positive step had been brought about by demands from both sides of the House of Commons, and, indeed, had even been preceded by the establishment of an advisory defence council by the moribund and divided Liberal administration of Lord Rosebery just prior to its fall.[11]

The Salisbury Defence Committee included the service ministers, the Chancellor of the Exchequer and Balfour. But it had inherent weaknesses, including a lack of real power made more acute by the absence from its meetings of the Prime Minister and such key figures as the Foreign and Colonial Secretaries and the professional military and naval leaders; nor did it have a permanent secretariat to record its deliberations. In addition, its duties and responsibilities were far from clear. Much of the blame for this belongs to Salisbury who, according to Balfour, 'never paid any attention to these things – his mind didn't work on these questions, they didn't bite on it'.[12] Nor did Salisbury encourage any precise definition of the Committee's functions, wondering whether it would not be enough to say 'that it will enable the two Defensive Departments to act together in all matters on which the action of one affects the other: and similarly to the consultation of the Defensive Departments with other Departments of the Government whenever consultation may be required'. But Salisbury thought that these 'other Departments' should only be consulted when they differed strongly with the War Office or the Admiralty. Moreover, it is clear that the Prime Minister was alarmed that 'if you make it a rule that the Committee must always be consulted whenever the Defensive Departments and the Executive Departments have to act together, you run some risk of turning it into an India Council'. It would be better, Salisbury felt, 'to avoid all pledges on detail as much as possible'.[13]

This somewhat *laissez faire* conception of the Committee's role fell short of Balfour's ideas on the subject, for, in the same month, he had advocated that 'the functions of the Committee should be to decide all questions of importance connected with Imperial Defence, which involve the co-operation of Army and Navy'. He wanted a very wide interpretation given to this definition, pointing out that 'there must be very few strategical plans of any magnitude in which the interests of both services are not to some extent . . . involved; and all such plans I should like to see passed through the Committee of Defence, and kept in duplicate by both Departments'.[14] Just how urgent was the need for such a co-ordinating body is revealed by Balfour's next sentence when he said, 'For example, the War Office have, I imagine, elaborate schemes for dealing with invasion. I do not know whether these schemes have ever been communicated to the Admiralty; but, if not, I think they ought to be, and the opinion of naval experts taken upon them'.[15]

Five days later, Balfour was informing Salisbury in tones of mild surprise, that 'there appears to have been a joint Admiralty and War Office Committee . . . in existence for some years. I have been looking through some of their reports. They are not cheerful reading.'[16] This was, in fact, the Joint Naval and Military Defence Committee formed when the Hartington Commission was completing its work in 1890. Although in that year Balfour had been deeply involved in discharging the difficult functions of Chief Secretary for Ireland, this does not, by itself, explain his ignorance of the Committee's existence, and, indeed, suggests that he did not, in 1890, concern himself so whole-heartedly with defence problems. However, the existence of the Joint Committee, together with that of the Colonial Defence Committee, meant that, by the end of 1895, there were three bodies whose functions were to co-ordinate imperial defence. But clearly these arrangements were too vague and ill-defined to allow any, or all, of the three committees to function with the necessary precision and authority.

It was, therefore, not surprising that Lord Hankey, who was Secretary to the Committee of Imperial Defence from 1912–1938, said, 'I can throw no light on the subjects dealt with by the Defence Committee of the Cabinet. I never remember seeing a single document or hearing anything about that august but ineffective body!'[17] Similarly, Balfour, when asked during the darkest days of the Boer War if there was any truth in the statement that the Defence Committee did not meet for months after its appointment, had to reply that he had not seen the statement and really did not know.[18] Certainly it was over a year after the foundation of the Committee that its chairman the Duke of

Devonshire announced that he had been asked 'to make as public a statement as can be made of the principles on which these plans [of imperial defence] are based, so that not only the public at home, but every one of our Colonial fellow-subjects may know how much it is that [the] Government are prepared to undertake in the defence of the Colonies, and the duties which, in their turn, they think ought to be undertaken by the Colonies themselves'. Devonshire went on to say that in the event of a war against France, or France and Russia, the basis of imperial defence lay in the maintenance of naval supremacy and the safeguarding of India.[19] None of this was particularly original.

With such imperfect machinery it was perhaps inevitable that little should have been achieved by the Defence Committee up to 1902, especially in view of the size of the problems that confronted it. Merely to unroll a map of the world was a sobering reminder of the immense distances to be dealt with in any consideration of imperial defence. Moreover, as Balfour pointed out, the British Empire was of so complex a character that it was impossible for the government to give the Commons a precise statement of the plans and objects of the Defence Committee – even if it had been expedient, on security grounds, to do so.[20] In fact, the Committee does seem to have dealt with a wide variety of topics such as the docks at Bermuda, Jamaica and Singapore, whether the army or the navy should control the newly-acquired base in China at Wei-hai-Wei, and to have arranged programmes for building coal depots and barracks.[21] But, as the Duke of Devonshire confessed in November 1900, the Committee 'met rarely, without any definite agenda . . . No minutes have been left, and in general there have been no definite decisions to record.[22]

The 1890s, therefore, saw no great improvement in defence planning, and indeed were marked by a lukewarm response to the proposals of the Colonial Secretary, Joseph Chamberlain, for greater imperial co-operation in trade, defence and organisation, at the Colonial Conference of 1897.[23] The self-governing colonies did not want to be organised in this way. If co-operation was sadly lacking in this respect, it was equally lacking between the army and the navy. Both services produced arguments in support

Balfour when Prime Minister, 1903

The contemplative in action – Balfour on the tennis court

Lord Salisbury (1830–1903)

of their respective claims of strategic superiority over the other –
the navy denying the possibilities of foreign invasion, the army
claiming that the navy could be dispersed by storms, or even
beaten. Such belligerence might have been better employed
against some foreign foe rather than directed at comrades-in-
arms.

2

THE full significance of this discord and confusion, however,
was not apparent to the public. Indeed, the victorious conclusion
of Kitchener's Sudan campaign in the early part of 1899 was no
preparation for the defeats and disasters which, by the end of
that year, the British army had suffered at the hands of a few
thousand Boer irregulars. The outbreak of the South African
War in October 1899 had caused a few uneasy consciences, but
little doubt as to its outcome. After all, the power and prosperity
of the British Empire was visible to all eyes, and had been conveniently, if showily, symbolised by the Diamond Jubilee of 1897.
But, despite the fact that, by the beginning of October, 67,000
British troops were either in South Africa or on their way,
Christmas 1899 saw garrisons hemmed in at Mafeking, Ladysmith and Kimberley. As for the army in the field, it had suffered
a series of reverses which culminated in three staggering defeats
at Stormberg, Magersfontein and Colenso between December
the tenth and fifteenth. This 'black week', and the apparent
indecision and ineptitude of General Buller, the Commander-in-
Chief in South Africa, seemed a poor reward for the expenditure
of £20,600,000 on the armed forces in 1899 alone.[24]

A storm of criticism descended on the government which,
despite its own shortcomings in forcing through defence reforms,
had hardly been encouraged to do so by an eager and interested
public. But by December 1899 the public *was* interested, particularly in explanations. So was the Queen, who complained to
Balfour (via Arthur Bigge, her Principal Private Secretary) that
accounts of the Defence Committee's proceedings were not being
sent to her, and that she was not being consulted about General

Buller's movements or even about the appointment of Lord
Roberts as Commander-in-Chief in place of the unfortunate
Buller.[25] Balfour told Salisbury that he had managed to soothe
her down and, indeed, that 'she was wonderfully good-humoured
and wonderfully cheerful. . . . "I will have no melancholy in
this house" is her formula – and not a bad one either in moments
of anxiety.' He feared, however, that the Queen would insist on
seeing Salisbury before she left for Osborne for Christmas, but
added that she seemed quite ready to make the hour suit the Prime
Minister's convenience.[26]

After Christmas the Queen's interest in the Defence Committee remained as intense, and inconvenient, as before. On 30
December Bigge mentioned to Balfour that the newspapers had
reported the Defence Committee meeting for two hours the day
before. 'Possibly, *even probably,* this is untrue!', Bigge added, 'But
if not, can you let the Queen know if any important business was
transacted – Her Majesty is naturally anxious to know if any
fresh developments arise during these anxious times.'[27] Within
three days Balfour had written to the Queen divulging the latest
deliberations of the Defence Committee. The Queen was, in
Bigge's words, 'apparently much pleased and interested', though,
he went on, 'you must blame me for having referred Her Majesty
to you for information. I was certain you could and would give
it quicker than anyone else.'[28]

It is clear, therefore, that at this moment of extreme crisis, the
Defence Committee had been junctioning and with some vigour.
But this did not, justifiably, avert criticism. As Bigge remarked:

No-one has ever laid down what is expected of our army – until
this is done we shall never have a satisfactory organised force. If
only someone in authority could have realised that we might be
called upon to conduct a campaign against 45,000 Boers fully
armed and equipped, and we had organised accordingly – not
forgetting India, our other colonies and Home Defence – we
might have been better prepared. However I see that you think
everything has now been supplied to the Generals but brains! In
these I imagine the Primate is arranging a special day of inter-
cession![29]

Balfour could hardly have protested that before 'black week' he was unaware of the deficiencies of generals and organisation, for as early as July 1899 a member of the Cecil family in South Africa[30] had informed him of Buller's inadequacies in strong terms: 'The general here, Buller, has refused to carry out War Office orders, and buy horses and stores for the special service officers saying "War would be an outrage" ... the more Milner takes one line the more Buller takes another ... send someone out to suppress Buller will you, because whichever way you look at it he is putting sand in the wheels.'[31] This was hardly encouraging information. Not that Balfour needed much convincing as to Buller's qualities, feeling by December 1899 that 'the case against him could be made so strong that it is hard to justify retaining him in command even of a portion of our Army. He seems quite capable of forming a good plan, but quite incapable of sticking to it ... I think this is a most melancholy story and I can only account for it by the theory that for the last ten years Buller has allowed himself to go downhill, and, for the moment at least, is not the man he once was.'[32] There were certainly rumours that Buller drank too much, and this explanation of his blunders, though not a flattering one, was perhaps more charitable than accusations of downright stupidity.

Generals, however, can be replaced. It is a more difficult and lengthy process to remedy bad planning and organisation, ample evidence of which was afforded by George Wyndham at the War Office. Writing in October 1899, Wyndham told Balfour that, since an army corps and a cavalry division were about to be sent out of the country on war strength, the War Office would present a policy of 'replacement' to the Cabinet. Replacement would involve two salient, and expensive, features: firstly, the embodiment of a certain number of militia battalions, and secondly, the issuing of contracts for mobilisation clothing to replace that being taken out. Unless this was done, a dangerous situation threatened. To begin with, the army would be left without the 'personnel and material' for adequate action, whether offensive or defensive, for a prolonged period. Also the machinery of organisation would cease to exist and, consequently, the army would be unable to train recruits or to keep its staff and regimental officers 'in the necessary exercise of their profession'. Without increasing the army establishment, there would only be eight cavalry regiments of the line left in England and Ireland, not enough for defence, or for training recruits, or for supplying the India army in the coming year. The artillery was in no happier plight, and Wyndham warned that if 'replacement' did not take place the army would be without sufficient artillery! Due to attacks in the Commons, the War Office felt itself 'on trial' over artillery, and Wyndham claimed he would have no reply to such attacks if he had to confess that 'we are left with nothing but four gun batteries. We should be incapable of Home Defence and of supplying the Indian Army with drafts next autumn'.[33]

This was a serious confession. Moreover, observers in South Africa were equally candid and revealing, and tended to blame the War Office and hence the government for a wide variety of inadequacies in preparation and execution. Balfour received from the Duke of Portland a letter from the latter's brother serving in South Africa and dated 16 December 1899. In the letter the writer wondered how the war was ever going to be finished, and claimed that 'the Boers have much longer range guns and rifles than us which is a great handicap to us and a gross mistake by the War Office'. He went on to complain that the British troops could not get near enough to shell the Boers out of their positions, and asked for a good telescope to be sent out as his field glasses were not strong enough to search out the Boers.[34] A few days later Balfour was told by Violet Cecil that the 'military folk' in Britain 'were blocking every request sent by Roberts and Kitchener; they have been refused guns [pom poms and 'galloping maxims']. We are outmatched in artillery – even field guns – the War Office is riding to give K. & R. a fall. I don't think it will succeed but many hundreds of lives and millions of money will be spent in the endeavour.' Nonetheless, it had been a fine sight to see Roberts and Kitchener take over: 'The re-organisation is to be complete as everything here was in a condition baffling description – you who know the War Office will realise the state of affairs.'[35]

Although by May 1900 Roberts and Kitchener had effectively

defeated the Boers in the field, Balfour continued to receive from
Violet Cecil admonishment and information from South Africa:
the generals' staffs were riddled with miserable intrigue; the
Intelligence Officers never knew anything! Violet Cecil continued:

I hear at home that none of you care a brass button about Army
Reform. I wish you could come to South Africa for a fortnight to
be converted. . . . I see you all making a fuss about Ladysmith – it
was a miserable performance, and the fuss is like nothing but the
fuss made by the French after the Madagascar Campaign which
we all laughed at. Oh Arthur, please don't praise the things
which are not worth it, it makes everything so disheartening.[36]

In March, St John Brodrick, then Under Secretary of State at the
War Office, had invited Alice Balfour to dine with himself,
Balfour and a Count von Steinberg who had been (so the Count
said) a military attaché with the Boers and was 'full of interesting
information as to our muddles'.[37]

Although Brodrick was able to talk airily in private of 'our
muddles', Balfour as Leader of the House of Commons was
obliged to defend the administration as best he could in public.
In private, however, he too could admit that 'the military situation
is undoubtedly the most serious . . . since the Mutiny'. Writing in
December 1899, Balfour had feared that Ladysmith would fall,
and Kimberley and Mafeking. This he felt would be 'a disaster,
not to say (from a tactical point of view) a disgrace greater than
the British arms have sustained for some generations'. He feared,
moreover, that he would have to miss his Christmas holidays![38]
A little later, Salisbury was agreeing with Balfour (and the Duke
of Wellington) that 'every gallant officer is a fool! The type remains unchanged to this day.'[39]

But three days after Balfour had written so gloomily to his
sister he was able to tell Salisbury that 'the War Office are working
away with great unanimity and energy, and with, I hope and
believe, a total absence of red tape to get a body of volunteers
who can both shoot and ride'.[40] Furthermore, during a speech
made at Manchester, on 8 December, Balfour maintained that
'looking back impartially, I say the steps we took were, in the

state of our knowledge, sufficient steps'.[41] But it was possible to
reply that the state of the government's knowledge could only
have been deplorable if judged by results. After all, the Defence
Committee of the Cabinet had been in existence since 1895; that
it had achieved so little was, at least in part, the fault of the government, amongst whose most powerful members stood Balfour
himself. Nor could it be said that the Boer War had burst, without
warning, upon a completely unprepared government.

No matter where Balfour, in private, believed the blame to lie,
in public he advanced the defence that there had been lack of
popular support for warlike preparation, and that the British
constitution made such preparations difficult. 'Our institutions,
our free institutions, have their merits and have their demerits,'
he said, 'and their demerits are intimately and inseparably bound
up with their merits. Their merit is this – no Government can act
in great affairs unless it has the opinion of the community behind
it. But the defect of that system is that, when the opinion of the
community lags behind the necessities of the case, there may be
occasions when sufficient rapidity of action is denied to the
executive Government.'[42] Salisbury too pointed out, perhaps a
little late in the day, that 'the art of war has been studied on the
continent of Europe with a thoroughness and self-devotion that
no other science has commanded, and at the end we find ourselves
surrounded by five great military powers, and yet on matters of
vital importance we pursue a policy wholly different from those
military powers'. Nor did the Prime Minister think that 'the
British Constitution as at present worked is a good fighting
machine' but 'it becomes us to think whether we must not in
some degree modify our arrangements in order to enable ourselves to meet the dangers that at any moment may arise'.[43] Both
uncle and nephew, therefore, found the constitution a hindrance
to military preparations. Nonetheless, despite Salisbury's musings
on reform, the Prime Minister made no positive attempt to adapt
the constitution to meet those vast problems of imperial defence
that he had discerned but with which he had shown himself
reluctant to deal in too precise or rigid a manner.

3

On 10 July 1902, however, Balfour became Prime Minister on Salisbury's retirement. The Boer War had been muddled through, and had not only divided British opinion deeply, even bitterly, but had revealed that Britain possessed few friends in the world and hardly any in Europe. Moreover, the growth of German naval ambitions challenged British maritime security, hitherto based on the supremacy of the Royal Navy. Diplomatic action was one way of remedying international isolation, and in this light can be seen the better relations with the United States, the Japanese alliance of 1902, and the Anglo-French entente of 1904. The entente with France was one of the most significant achievements of Balfour's administration, but the new Prime Minister also had firm opinions about the need for friendship with the United States,[44] and the Japanese alliance was seen as a way of lessening Russian pressure on India.

But the most pressing and obvious need was that of reform at home. In this sense, Balfour was both unlucky and lucky to become Prime Minister when he did: unlucky, in that the urgent process of reform would be watched by an anxious and critical public: lucky, because the Boer War had shattered complacency and put the public in a frame of mind to accept, and even call for reorganisation and reform.[45] In addition, although Balfour had been unable to breathe new life into the Defence Committee, the defence of the Empire was a subject which had long occupied his thoughts, and he brought with him to the office of Prime Minister constructive ideas and the will to push them through.

It was not, however, easy to find the formula to satisfy the varied needs of imperial defence. To begin with, the role which the self-governing colonies could be expected, or indeed were willing, to play was not clear. True, the Boer War had been the occasion for a solid, and perhaps somewhat surprising, demonstration of imperial unity, with troops from Australia, Canada, New Zealand, the Cape, Natal, and a handful from the dependent Empire, serving in South Africa – in all, 55,000 men.[46] Although a few troops from Canada and Australia had served in the Sudan campaigns, such participation seemed puny when set beside the contribution to the Boer War. The latter was all the more impressive in view of the fact that hitherto the self-governing colonies had only reluctantly contributed to the upkeep of the Royal Navy, while keeping a firm hold on their own land forces which, it was made quite clear, were not to be treated as easily available reinforcements for the British army.[47] But the Colonial Conference of 1902 was to prove the occasion for the Dominions to restate in the plainest terms their reluctance to relax any control over their land forces; there was even talk of Australia and Canada establishing their own navies in the near future. Moreover, the rejection of Chamberlain's plans for an Imperial Council and an imperial *zollverein,* or customs union, showed that the self-governing colonies were as determined as ever to preserve their internal autonomy. Any scheme for imperial defence, therefore, would have to avoid offending this ever-strengthening colonial nationalism.

The delegates from the self-governing colonies at the 1902 Conference could hardly have been reassured by the open divergences between the War Office and the Admiralty over imperial strategy. Two quite different strategic statements were placed before the Conference. The Admiralty claimed that the fleet's main function in time of war was to attack and destroy the enemy's navy, not to defend the colonies. The War Office did not assume that the navy was invincible, and suggested, indeed, that sizeable garrisons should be kept in the Empire and that the army in Britain should maintain quite a large force in readiness for use overseas.[48] Co-operation between the two services clearly left much to be desired.

Yet in November 1902, three months after the Elgin Commission – containing the critical and constructive Lord Esher – had started its investigations into the prosecution of the Boer War, the two Cabinet heads of the services presented a joint memorandum to the Prime Minister. Brodrick, the Secretary of State for War, and Lord Selborne, the First Lord of the Admiralty, urged Balfour to reorganise the Defence Committee and to make it an effective organ for the co-ordination of the work of their two departments and of imperial defence as a whole. Unless this was done they threatened to resign.

Subject to these additional pressures, Balfour found it easy to move towards a reconstitution of the Defence Committee, a measure upon which he already had firm convictions. When he became Prime Minister he had seen that 'there was no co-ordination, no co-operation between the people in charge of land and sea war, and defence'. He therefore concluded that 'it was obvious a civilian Cabinet could form no judgement, and I had the idea, which was really original. I don't say that out of conceit – I mean simply that the Defence Committee had no precedent'.[49]

Accordingly, the reorganised Defence Committee sat for the first time on 18 December 1902. The chairman was the Duke of Devonshire, whose association with the old Committee made him a suitable candidate, although it was to become Balfour's conviction that the Prime Minister should be chairman and hence visibly responsible for imperial defence. In fact, Balfour did take the chair on Devonshire's resignation less than a year later – and proved a particularly assiduous chairman. The transitional Defence Committee – or Committee of Imperial Defence as it came increasingly to be called – included at its first meeting, in addition to Devonshire and Balfour, the service ministers, and certain service representatives, among them the Commander-in-Chief, Lord Roberts, and the heads of naval and military intelligence, Prince Louis of Battenberg and Lt General Nicholson. The Joint Naval and Military Committee on Defence and the Colonial Defence Committee were both to be sub-committees of the new body under the chairmanship of Devonshire. It was thought necessary that the new Committee of Defence should meet once a fortnight – or more often if necessary – but at least once a month.[50] This was a distinct contrast to the intermittent meetings of the old Committee.

Early in 1903 Balfour made clear to the Commons the nature and possibilities of the new Committee. Contrasting it with its predecessor, he pointed out that the old Committee had, in

general, only taken up points referred to it by the Cabinet – for
example, a question between the War Office and the Chancellor
of the Exchequer which needed discussion outside those two
departments, or some problem of imperial defence which might
have, for the moment, attracted the attention of the Cabinet. In
this somewhat subordinate capacity, Balfour believed that the
Committee had done some extremely good work.[51]

But the new Committee was to be much more ambitious. Its
job was not to pick up such scraps as occasionally fell from the
Cabinet's table, but to

survey as a whole the strategical military needs of the Empire, to
deal with the complicated questions which are all essential elements in that general problem, and to revise from time to time
their own previous decisions so that the Cabinet shall always be
informed and always have at its disposal information upon these
important points. They should not be left to the crisis of the
moment, but when there is no special stress or strain the government and its advisers should devote themselves to the consideration of these broad and all important issues.[52]

For this last sentence, as for much else, the lessons of the Boer
War were clearly responsible.

Balfour believed that one of the chief drawbacks of the old
Committee had been that it was 'in the strictest and narrowest
sense of the word, a Committee of the Cabinet'. Therefore, it had
kept no record of its proceedings and had admitted no outsiders
to its meetings. Naval and military experts had, of course, been
called before the Committee but rather as witnesses to be cross-
examined than as members. Balfour meant to remedy both these
deficiencies.

The old Committee's lack of a permanent record had meant
that new administrations, considering problems of even long
standing, had often to repeat the drudgery of collecting information without having the results of previous considerations of
these topics readily available. Balfour hoped that from now on the
conclusions of the Defence Committee would be embodied not
merely in resolutions but in 'reasoned documents' to be handed on
for the benefit of future governments. 'There is one point',

Balfour told the Commons, 'on which there ought to be no discontinuity, and that is the military and naval policy of the Empire.' 'A full-blooded and detailed account' would greatly aid continuity.[53]

However, this significant break with tradition was not immediately pushed through to the logical conclusion of a permanent secretariat – which did not appear until 1904. But it did signify the disquiet which Balfour felt at the lack of record-keeping – apart from the Prime Minister's written account to the Sovereign – which was a failing of Cabinet procedure. Even Salisbury, towards the end of his Prime Ministership, and with protests falling about his ears against the leaking to the newspapers of Lord Roberts' dispatch on the disastrous battle of Spion Kop, had felt that the practice of not keeping a record of Cabinet business was a mistake.[54] Until the emergence of a full-blown permanent secretariat in 1904, therefore, the proceedings of the new Defence Committee were recorded by a Foreign Office clerk, a Mr Tyrell, who was, according to Hankey, 'a part-timer who did not pretend to know the job'.[55] As much as anything else, this half-measure illustrates the transitional, though revolutionary, nature of the Defence Committee between 1902 and 1904.

But this was not all that was new about the Defence Committee or the only thing that prompted Balfour to say that 'it differs fundamentally from anything . . . that has ever existed in the past.'[56] To begin with, there was to be a fixed, permanent nucleus of members to ensure continuity. The Cabinet members of this nucleus would include the Lord President of the Council (Devonshire), the Prime Minister, the Secretary of State for War and the First Lord of the Admiralty; non-Cabinet members would be the First Sea Lord, the Commander-in-Chief, and the Heads of Naval and Military Intelligence. The inclusion of these service leaders was an innovation that was, to say the least, a practical one.

Balfour believed that, to deal efficiently with the complex problems of imperial defence, the nucleus of the Committee should be kept small. However, he was careful to stress that this did not mean that for all time and for all purposes the Committee would consist of this core of members. If public money was to be spent, then the Chancellor of the Exchequer must attend meetings; problems of Indian defence would call for the presence of the Secretary of State for India and his military advisers. Balfour was determined that flexibility should be the keynote of the emergent Committee of Imperial Defence, and to this end he envisaged that a variety of non-Cabinet experts could be called, when needed, before the Committee. In the same way, statesmen from the self-governing colonies and Imperial proconsuls could be asked to attend meetings.

Clearly, the new Committee was to be an advisory body only, though a powerful one as its members were a blend of ministers and service leaders. Strongly opposed to a Committee exclusively composed of service experts, Balfour hoped that a mixed group would 'be full of instruction for civilians and Cabinet members, and I hope it will not be without its instructions for even soldiers and sailors'. The old system, he thought, 'in which the Navy decided its own affairs without consulting the Army, and the Army decided its own affairs without reference to the Navy ... was a very faulty system'.[57] This blending of civilians and service leaders, however, while it possessed the obvious advantages of better communication and a greater interchange of ideas, could at the same time be criticised in that the theoretical equality of membership might in practice be a myth. For example the service experts might not be able to match the ministers in persuasive eloquence and were, in a sense, their inferiors regarding future professional preferment. Equally, it could be argued that the service members of the Committee were the government's suppliants over military and naval spending. In fact, the less eloquent members of the Defence Committee did take some time to hold their own in face of Balfour's 'extraordinary powers of ready argument and quick reply'.[58] Such difficulties, however, were far from insuperable.

Balfour's transitional Committee of Imperial Defence also seemed to have settled the vexed question of Treasury control by the exclusion of the Chancellor of the Exchequer as a permanent member. This meant that the Chancellor's natural desire to limit expenditure would not act as a brake at every meeting of the Committee, although he would, of course, be called in whenever his department was particularly involved. The Chancellor's attendance, like that of every member, was at the invitation of the Prime Minister.

This, then, was the character of the new Defence Committee as it had emerged by the beginning of 1903. Balfour called it 'A great experiment on a great subject',[59] and it was certainly a decided improvement on its predecessor – having a more practical membership, and a flexibility that would encourage experiment and not scare off the wary self-governing colonies. Balfour was conscious of the tentative nature of his innovations and warned the Commons that 'no reconstruction of Departments, no attempt to deal with the Empire's problems will prevent difficulties arising in time of stress'. Nonetheless, he was confident enough in March 1903 to propose that 'the growing needs of the Empire require the establishment of the Committee of Defence on a permanent footing'.[60] It was now a question of putting these reforms into practice.

3 Laying Foundations

The value of such consultations in producing co-operation between the different parts of the Empire, is, I believe, beyond our present power of estimation.
                    BALFOUR on the Committee of Imperial Defence, 1904

I

FOLLOWING the reconstitution of the Defence Committee, the Balfour government set up the War Office (Reconstitution) Committee in November 1903. The chairman of the latter committee was Lord Esher, who had previously sat on the Elgin Commission when it began its enquiries into the unhappy early days of the Boer War.[1] Ever ready to ingratiate himself with those of influence and authority, Esher possessed equally a love of palace intrigue and a zeal for military reform. Moreover, his assiduously cultivated friendship with Edward VII enabled him to direct at least some of the royal energies towards the reforms which Esher himself held so dear.[2]

Under Esher's chairmanship the War Office (Reconstitution) Committee placed its first report in Balfour's hands in January 1904. This was prompt action. In addition, the findings of the Esher Committee in general, and its chairman's influence in particular, helped to bring about the essential modifications which completed the evolution of the new Defence Committee into the Committee of Imperial Defence.

This process was completed by the middle of 1904. But even before then it was evident that some of the potential of the new Committee had been realised. Towards the end of 1903, Frederick Borden, the Canadian Minister of Defence and Militia, had been invited by Balfour to sit with the Defence Committee as a member.

However, after a wide-ranging discussion about future military co-operation between Canada and Britain, Borden was apprehensive lest the meeting's substance should provoke hostile political reaction in Canada.[3]

Balfour, nonetheless, subsequently wrote to the King explaining Borden's attendance and suggesting, rather vaguely perhaps, that the Committee had the potential of becoming an Imperial Council. But he added that 'Unfortunately, it appears that this particular gentleman is of rather inferior quality – but we shall be careful what we say before him! And the compliment remains the same. A new precedent of great imperial significance will have been set.'[4]

Despite the condescending and disparaging remarks, an important precedent *had* been set, and Balfour was to return, at greater length, to the imperial possibilities of the Committee in a Cabinet minute of February 1904.[5] Furthermore, Borden's presence had only been made possible by the extreme flexibility of the Committee's constitution – a quality that was to prove of supreme advantage, especially in view of the reluctance of the self-governing colonies to commit themselves to any elaborate and far-reaching scheme of imperial defence.

2

But the Committee had shown other uses by the end of 1903, as the documents presented by Balfour in that year reveal. Basically, the defence of India was the major concern of Imperial strategy, excluding the need to safeguard Britain itself from invasion. In the context of Indian defence, the reliability of Afghanistan as a buffer state was a subject of considerable concern – especially in view of the Russian programme of building railways towards the Indian frontier. Moreover British policy towards the Afghans had, for much of the nineteenth century, veered violently between coercion and attempts to kill with kindness. As in the case of Ireland, this policy had failed to make Afghanistan obedient or reliable.

Balfour suggested to the Defence Committee, however, that greater co-operation would be effected between the armies in Britain and India if there was a Headquarters staff common to both forces.[6] This constructive proposal emphasised the need for more co-ordination between the two major branches of the British army in face of Russian expansion in Asia. At the same time, Balfour attempted to put into perspective Russia's role in the Far East, and to discuss this in terms of the Anglo-Japanese alliance.[7]

While showing concern for India's defence, Balfour also speculated, in a paper in November 1903, on the possibilities of the invasion of the British Isles. Basically, he saw this as a problem of reconciling army and navy views on the subject – the army believing that even the mighty British fleet offered no certain protection, the navy arguing that if it were to be beaten then all was lost, and peace should be made as soon as possible![8] This was an old quarrel. But the antagonisms involved showed very clearly how essential it was to bring the army and the navy closer together.

Before the end of 1903, however, the Defence Committee had made some progress in this task. For one thing, it had won the confidence of General Nicholson, who sat on the Committee in his capacity as the Director General of Mobilization and Military Intelligence. Nicholson made it clear that the new Committee had achieved influence at the War Office, which now accepted the principle that all important papers must be sent to the Cabinet via the Defence Committee.[9]

But what of the Royal Navy? Here the attitude of Admiral Sir John Fisher was of paramount importance. Fisher, later to be Admiral of the Fleet, exerted an enormous influence on naval planning up to the First World War. His forceful personality expressed itself in the firm handwriting and the belligerent underlining of those letters of exhortation and advice with which he sought to argue his case. In October 1903, Fisher told Balfour that an overwhelmingly powerful navy was the prime necessity for the existence of the British Empire. 'The British Empire', he said, 'floats on the British Navy.'[10]

At the same time, Fisher advised Balfour that the War Office must be reformed and 'on such lines as will ensure most intimate joint Naval and Military action.'[11] Not that Fisher had much respect for some of the generals: '(Evelyn Wood tells me he hunts four days a week!) Give old Kelly Kenny an Army Corps and then he can go shooting with the King every day without any inconvenience to the Service!'[12] Despite this flash of contempt, Fisher urged upon Balfour that naval and military requirements should be considered together. More surprisingly, he suggested that there should be *one* service, not two great departments fighting independently with the Treasury for what they could get. Perhaps there should even be a single Cabinet chief for the services – as in Austria. But Fisher also doubted the capacity of the Defence Committee to bring about this joint action by advice alone. He was particularly fearful that at Committee meetings the day would be carried by the ablest representatives, not by the most needy service.[13]

Basically, Fisher thought much more of the Royal Navy than of joint planning. But at least he was now convinced that some degree of inter-service co-operation was essential. This was all the more significant in view of the fact that Esher had chosen Fisher to serve as the naval representative to the War Office (Reconstitution) Committee. The military member was Sir George Clarke, who had previously been secretary to the Colonial Defence Committee from 1885 to 1892, as well as secretary to the Hartington Committee, and subsequently an intelligence officer, and a military and civil administrator.[14] Thus the impressive triumvirate of Esher, Clarke and Fisher not only made significant recommendations as to War Office reform, but also considered the wider problems of imperial defence and particularly the role of the new Defence Committee.

3

Esher had strong ideas as to the constitution and future of the Defence Committee. In a note of December 1903 on War Office reform, Esher stressed the evolutionary nature of the Committee which, 'originating in Imperial needs, vividly brought home to us of late years . . . has already developed capacities beyond the expectation of its founders.' Furthermore, the Committee could be strengthened by including representatives from Canada and Australasia as well as one with Indian experience. At the same time, Esher believed that the Prime Minister of the day should always be the Committee's chairman – thus throwing his authority behind its deliberations. The Prime Minister must also be able to summon at will the most competent military and naval experts to the Committee.[15] None of this differed from Balfour's ideas, and Esher warmly praised the Prime Minister's work with the Committee.

As regards War Office reform, Esher argued that the principle underlying the Defence Committee should prevail – namely, that imperial staff work and local staff work should be kept as far as possible distinct.[16] Esher also stressed the need for a Permanent Secretary to the Defence Committee with a trained strategical mind and knowledge of the problems of imperial defence. This official should ideally have a high salary. His post should be held for five years, but could then be renewed by the Prime Minister.[17]

In 1894 Balfour had advocated that any Defence Committee should have a permanent record kept of its proceedings.[18] He had then been in opposition. In 1903, and in office, he was more cautious. Faced with Esher's demand for a permanent secretariat he felt certain misgivings. In particular, he was worried about the relationship between the Defence Committee's proposed Permanent Secretary and the military and naval members. Basically, Balfour feared that the permanent secretariat would be a third body of experts which, because of its very permanence and its intimate relationship with the Committee, would be able to dominate the service experts. Also Balfour, in a flight of fancy, wondered what would happen if the British army possessed a general of the genius of Germany's Moltke. If such a man became the Permanent Secretary of the Committee how would that effect the authority of the army member? Any such developments, Balfour felt, would lessen the Committee's effectiveness – save under an extremely forceful Prime Minister.[19]

In response to these doubts, Esher amended the draft of his report in the interests of clarity. He also went to some pains to reassure Balfour that, despite the permanent secretariat, the Prime Minister's powers were to remain as free and flexible as possible. For instance, the Permanent Secretary would attend the Defence Committee meetings to keep the minutes and to perform other secretarial duties. But he was not to be a committee member and would have no right to express an opinion in council unless called upon by the Prime Minister. Moreover, the Secretary's work would consist of preparing for the Prime Minister material collected from the First Military member and the First Sea Lord. This would enable the Committee to 'lay down principles of action which would in certain eventualities co-ordinate the efforts' of the army and navy.[20]

Esher also pointed out that if Britain possessed a Moltke he would be in the field, not languishing in Whitehall as secretary to the Defence Committee. Expanding the German example, Esher reminded Balfour that whereas in Germany the Kaiser co-ordinated naval and military action, in Britain such a task could only fall to the Prime Minister. Esher insisted therefore that Balfour's fears were groundless and that his committee's recommendations would only cause the Defence Committee to be more efficient as well as adding to its permanence.[21]

Always a willing propagandist, Esher produced in March 1904 a booklet for private circulation entitled *National Strategy*. Having dealt with Balfour's qualms, Esher thus hoped to add force to his insistence on the need for a permanent secretariat to the new Defence Committee. In the booklet, Esher argued that while England had expanded her Empire she had only half-realised that imperial responsibilities involved corresponding effort. Esher claimed as a widely accepted fact that 'Imperial rule can have no other ultimate basis than adequate and organised physical force'. To temper this somewhat crude, though not unrealistic, concept, Esher was prepared to allow others to doubt whether material prosperity and moral greatness rested entirely upon imperial status. For himself, however, he returned to the necessity of organised physical force and to the vital role which the Defence Committee must play in such organisation. Calling the Committee's reconstitution 'by far the most important and far-reaching act' of Balfour's administration and 'full of hopeful possibilities', Esher felt that much remained undone. A permanent secretariat, however, could help to remedy such deficiencies.[22]

4

Subject to Esher's persuasiveness and with his recent misgivings put aside, Balfour agreed to the permanent secretariat. In August 1904 he asked the House of Commons for £2,960 a year to pay for the Secretary, two assistants and other expenses.[23] Appropriately enough the first Secretary was Sir George Clarke. Clarke had already won golden opinions from both Fisher and Esher. In October 1903, Fisher had told Arnold-Forster at the War Office that the Esher Committee, '*must* have Sir G. Clarke – *absolutely* indispensable both for the Committee stage and as permanent official'.[24] Esher was equally complimentary, telling Balfour in December 1903 that 'Clarke is excellent. All on the right lines. Very amiable – and *fat* and comfortable! A great thing'.[25] Clarke was to remain Secretary until 1907.

By the end of 1904, therefore, the fully-fledged Committee of Imperial Defence had at last emerged. It had not been easy to break down suspicion and prejudice. Morover, the future would require further definition of its functions. But, throughout 1904, nobody – not even Esher – contributed so profoundly to the clarification of the C.I.D.'s role as did Balfour. The Prime Minister's definitions were concentrated in a Cabinet paper composed in February and in a Commons debate in August. Between these two poles of activity there were other opportunities to illuminate and explain.

In his Cabinet paper of February 1904 Balfour emphasised that the C.I.D. differed in one fundamental respect from any other part of government machinery – that it was consultative, not executive. It had no administrative functions, could prescribe no policy to the Cabinet nor give orders to the army and navy. Its duty was simply to advise – although since the Prime Minister, the Secretary of State for War, the First Lord of the Admiralty, and their assistants would have agreed on the advice, their suggestions were almost certain to be accepted. But the Committee, *as such*, would have no power to enforce this acceptance.[26]

The C.I.D.'s influence, therefore, would rest chiefly in the hands of its most important member – the Prime Minister. Indeed, Balfour saw the Prime Minister as the only *ex officio* member, at least for the time being. This begged an awkward question. Namely, what if there was a Prime Minister as uninterested in the C.I.D. as Salisbury had been in the old Defence Committee? Would the C.I.D. rust away, or would one or other of the Committee members assume the leadership? Would this mean in turn that, sheltered behind the fiction of the Prime Minister's leadership, the C.I.D. would in fact be controlled by its most dominating member? Balfour does not seem to have been troubled by such doubts. Perhaps this was chiefly because he himself was to prove such a diligent chairman of the C.I.D.

Balfour considered the constitutional limitations of the C.I.D. to be a positive advantage since it was not necessary to give an advisory body statutory powers. The fact that no act of Parliament was needed to create the C.I.D. also meant that the Committee's functions were not limited by statute. Adaptability, Balfour believed, should be a characteristic of the Committee. Thus, he wanted there to be no *ex officio* members, save the Prime Minister, because this would theoretically ensure equality of status between all those called to the meetings – a vital necessity if statesmen from the self-governing colonies were to feel able to use the Committee with absolute freedom and conviction. Nothing in the Committee's construction, therefore, was to fetter the Prime Minister's discretion in the choice of members. Clearly, some would be summoned almost automatically, yet they would be there because 'summoned', not as of right. Balfour felt that a small Committee would be the most effective, and that its membership would vary with the different problems it was required to consider.[27]

In the Commons in August 1904, Balfour explained the value of continuity for the C.I.D.[28] Previously, in February, he had proposed that the King should have not only a copy of the memoranda dealing with the larger problems of imperial defence, but also copies of the minutes of each meeting. Balfour admitted that these minutes were 'usually jejune and uninteresting' (since some of the most valuable meetings were occupied with informal conversation), but at least they showed 'the number of times the Committee met, the subjects discussed, the persons who were present, and the conclusions if any.' The permanent secretariat therefore would not only keep the sovereign informed, but, more important, would keep in its archives a record of the reasoning and personal influence behind each piece of advice it offered to the Cabinet – the ultimate executive authority.[29]

But even when he asked the Commons in August for money to pay for the permanent secretariat, Balfour stressed that the C.I.D. was little more than tentative and embryonic.[30] Admittedly, he had earlier claimed that by thrashing out military problems in advance the C.I.D. had helped the problem of voting estimates by making specific proposals.[31] In August, however, he was anxious to keep expectations low about the Committee's work, reminding the Commons that the problems of imperial defence were incomparably more difficult than those facing the German General Staff – even though Britain's problems could be divided into two broad categories, home defence and the defence of India.[32]

Apart from his preoccupation with the defence of the British Isles and India, Balfour also found it attractive in 1904 to speculate as to the wider imperial implications of the C.I.D. Particularly, his thoughts turned to the possibility of making the Committee a 'truly Imperial body, in which the Colonies as well as the mother country may find an appropriate machinery for dealing with the greatest of their common interests – the interests of Imperial Defence.'[33] This was an attractive aim and had clearly been in Balfour's mind in 1903 when he had invited Borden to attend the Committee's meetings, and when he had simultaneously suggested to the King that the Committee might become an Imperial Council.[34] But the fulfilment of this aim would require caution and patience.

5

The precedents for substantial co-operation between Britain and the self-governing colonies in defence matters were not encouraging. Following the withdrawal of British troops from Canada, Australia and New Zealand in the early 1870s, the Cape garrison remained the only substantial British military commitment in the self-governing colonies. That somewhat shadowy co-ordinating body, the Colonial Defence Committee, had been born, killed off and resurrected before the year 1887 saw a significant new development in the field of imperial defence. This was the naval agreement between the Australian colonies, New Zealand and Britain whereby the former undertook to make an annual contribution to the upkeep of the Royal Navy in Australasian waters. In the first year of the agreement, £850,000 was appropriated.[35] Despite subsequent contributions and the eventual participation of the Cape and Natal in the scheme, Canada resolutely refused to make any such payment.

Australasia's apparently encouraging contribution did not stand up too well to closer analysis. Although it was possible to see in the naval contributions a glittering portent of closer imperial defence links, it is by no means certain that the colonists viewed it in that way. The colonial Prime Ministers had initially shown interest in the scheme while in London in 1887 for Queen Victoria's Golden Jubilee. It was however reason, not sentiment, which prompted their enthusiasm. The isolation of the Australasian colonies was apparent, and heightened by returning fears of 'the yellow peril' and even wild speculation as to Russian attacks.[36] If security had to be bought, then bought it must be. Canada, on the other hand, felt no need to pay up. After all, the United States would hardly allow the destruction of its northern neighbour. Furthermore, the sea lanes of the North Atlantic, bearing food to Britain, would not be lightly abandoned by the Royal Navy.

British statesmen, however, continued to hope for better things. Joseph Chamberlain in particular attacked the problem with ardour. Appointed Colonial Secretary in 1895, Chamberlain saw the main task of his office as the fostering of closer relations between Britain and the self-governing colonies. Accordingly he sought closer union in trade and defence, and even in some sort of federation. Queen Victoria's Diamond Jubilee in 1897 provided a convenient opportunity to harangue the assembled colonial Prime Ministers on the subjects dear to Chamberlain's heart. As regards imperial defence, Chamberlain told the Colonial Conference that every war fought by Britain during Victoria's reign had been inspired basically by colonial interests, or at least the interests of India or the dependent territories. He therefore asked for an interchange of military units and more subsidies for the navy.[37]

Although Sprigg, the Prime Minister of the Cape, made the encouraging offer of a cruiser to the Royal Navy, the other premiers dug in their heels. They saw their armies and even their naval contributions in terms of local defence. Moreover, Sprigg's gesture came at a time when a direct confrontation between Briton and Boer in South Africa seemed increasingly likely.[38] It was, to say the least, a timely move on his part.

Chamberlain's next formal attempt to strengthen imperial defence was made at the Colonial Conference of 1902. The surge of sentiment that had accompanied the outbreak of the Boer War had been translated into practical terms by the self-governing colonies sending volunteers to South Africa. Colonial troops poured in to fight for the mother country, and, indirectly, for themselves. The colonies' naval contributions, however, continued to arouse British misgivings, and in 1901 Hicks Beach, the Chancellor, urged the government to 'make a determined effort to induce our self-governing Colonies to take their share in the Naval Defence of the Empire, which is now practically borne by the taxpayers of the United Kingdom alone'. Hicks Beach saw the coming Colonial Conference as an opportunity for airing the matter. However, if after discussion, the colonial representatives declined 'any reasonable arrangement . . . both Canada and

Australia should be warned in the event of our being engaged in a
naval war, our Navy will have other things to do than to provide
for their defence'.[39] This was a clear threat, born of exasperation.

Furthermore, the colonial volunteers for the Boer War had
been *volunteers*. It would be dangerous to count on any similar
gesture in a future crisis. Nobody felt this more strongly than
St John Brodrick who had been Secretary of State for War during
the last two years of the South African conflict. Writing in 1903,
Brodrick claimed that the commission investigating the conduct
of the Boer War was ill-informed as to the difficulties of organising volunteer forces from the self-governing Empire. The
commission wanted matters placed on a better footing in the
event of another emergency. Brodrick explained bitterly that 'by
interviews with the Prime Ministers of the Colonies, and publicly
at the Colonial Conferences, we had pressed in every way for some
organised system on which we might count in an emergency, and
found ourselves checkmated by the determination of the Colonies
to supply troops as before on their own terms according to the
circumstances under which a war might arise'.[40]

Brodrick's harsh words reflected his and Chamberlain's failure
at the Colonial Conference of 1902 to wring further major
concessions and commitments from the colonial delegations.
Despite the optimism generated by the example of the war, the
appeals for an Imperial Reserve force and greatly increased subsidies for the navy fell on stony ground. Although Australia and
New Zealand agreed to pay slightly more to the navy, as did the
Cape and Natal, Canada still held aloof from these arrangements.[41]
The dashing of Chamberlain's high hopes emphasised the extraordinary tact and delicacy required to draw the self-governing
colonies into any wide scheme of imperial defence. The colonies
refused to be drafted. They might, however, be wooed.

6

Balfour in 1904 was determined to move cautiously. Believing
optimistically that 'the Colonies are beginning to awake to their

Imperial obligations', he at the same time argued that 'nothing more effectively checks any movement in the direction of rendering military assistance to the cause of common defence than the idea that any efforts the Colonies may make will be neutralized by the incompetence of War Office administration'. A clean sweep was therefore needed in the War Office. Furthermore, the changes must be symbolised by a fresh set of names for newly created offices.[42] The self-governing colonies would thus be made aware that significant alterations had been made. Reform must not only take place, but must be seen to take place.

But if War Office reform was one way of encouraging the self-governing colonies to participate more fully in the planning of the imperial defence, it was essential that the creation of the C.I.D. should not alarm them. This partly explains why Balfour pressed so hard to put all the members of the Committee on an equal footing, fearing that any discrimination between permanent and temporary members would place colonial delegates on a different and apparently inferior footing.[43]

Similarly, Balfour justified the Committee's lack of executive authority – which prevented it from giving 'an order to the humblest soldier in His Majesty's Army or the most powerless sloop under the control of the Admiralty' – in terms of better relations with the self-governing colonies. Recognising that 'no office in this country has any control at all' over these colonies, he nevertheless hoped that when any defence problem arose that particularly concerned them and 'even when they take a closer interest in the problems of Imperial defence as a whole, we may have the advantage of their assistance in our councils'. But Balfour continued:

I am certain that the self-governing Colonies will never allow any representative of theirs to come to the Defence Committee if [it] ... had the smallest authority to impose obligations, financial, political, military or naval, on the colonies which they represent.

Happily, because of the C.I.D.'s constitution, this could not happen.[44]

As well as being extremely permissive, Balfour's attitude was also very practical. Moreover, his Commons statement echoed his Cabinet paper of February 1904 when he had argued that 'the Colonies would certainly object to handing over to any Committee, however constituted, the right to impose on them a policy to which, for financial or other reasons, they might on consideration feel a strong objection: and I think the Colonies would be right'.[45]

Balfour's policy would thus keep unsullied, both for Britain and for the self-governing colonies, the principle of Cabinet responsibility. Indeed, the C.I.D. as Balfour saw it – a flexible, informal body restricting itself to discussion and the proffering of advice – had some elements in common with the still evolutionary Colonial Conference, to which it could also be considered complementary. There would be, in effect, a standing invitation to any self-governing colony to attend C.I.D. meetings to discuss any particular problems of defence which concerned the colony and its position in the general scheme of imperial defence. The colonial delegate would attend as a full member and would continue to attend as long as the questions in which his government had a direct interest were under discussion. There would be no drawbacks to such consultations. No jealousy or suspicion would be excited. The rights of self-government would not be interfered with. Moreover, the advice given, though it might guide, could never coerce any of the parties involved.

This was Balfour's conception of the C.I.D. Clearly there were drawbacks. The most obvious being that if the self-governing colonies boycotted it, the Committee would be, in the broader sense, so much useless machinery. On the other hand, there now existed an organ suitable for imperial defence planning. It could hardly frighten the colonies and they could use it as they chose. If this were to happen, Balfour believed that 'the value of such consultations in producing co-operation between the different parts of the Empire is ... beyond our present powers of estimation'.[46]

4 The Precedent Established

The Prime Minister deserves every credit not only for devising this scheme, but also for giving his time and energy to it after calling it into being.
                                                                HALDANE, 1904

I

UNTIL his resignation as Prime Minister in December 1905 Balfour proved a zealous chairman of the C.I.D. Not only did he consistently attend its meetings but he also submitted a considerable number of papers for its consideration. Having created the machinery he was determined to use it. Especially, Balfour concentrated his energies on home defence and the defence of India. There was little apparent concern for Australia, New Zealand and Canada. Perhaps this merely reflected the long-standing preoccupation of British statesmen with the safe-guarding of the route to India and with the defence of India itself. Moreover, the Australasian colonies were helping to maintain the Royal Navy in their own defence. It could be assumed, despite the continuing revolution in naval architecture, that this money was being well spent.

At first sight, it might seem that an invasion of Britain in the early years of the twentieth century was a possibility unworthy of consideration. But this was to forget the lack of co-ordination between the army and navy. In addition, there was the uncomfortable memory that the early demands of the Boer War had come close to leaving the army in Britain dangerously under-manned.[1] Home defence, therefore, was one of the very first concerns of the C.I.D. A report was quickly drawn up. Its purpose, Balfour reassured the House of Commons, was to provide a record for the benefit of future governments. They could use the report as a basis for further investigations. In no way was it meant to bind them.[2]

But the defence needs of Britain had to be reconciled with the wider needs of imperial defence. Furthermore, it was necessary to consider these questions in relation to the essential reform of the War Office. Towards this end, Balfour submitted a paper to the C.I.D. in June 1904. In it, he argued that imperial defence demanded of Britain 74,400 men for the Indian garrisons and 50,400 troops for the rest of the Empire. In 1904, 20,000 of the latter were needed in South Africa. Over and above this there was home defence. Balfour calculated that apart from the garrisoning of British arsenals and ports, 100,000 reinforcements should be provided for Indian service in the event of war with Russia. Also, there should be a striking force standing ready to deal with any emergency. This force would probably also form part of the Indian reinforcements.[3]

The idea of a striking force caused some controversy, and in December 1904 Balfour complained that the military members of the C.I.D. had not fully realised the significance of the proposal. Army leaders still wanted the striking force to be additional to the reinforcements for India. Balfour in turn thought that the maintenance of such a force in peace time 'for no other purpose than to capture some outlying colony, if our enemy happened to possess one, is not worth the cost which it must necessarily entail'.[4]

On the other hand, Balfour was quite clear as to what was required of the forces defending Britain itself. There should be sufficient troops to repel any invasion and also to give confidence to the public. It was also essential to maintain an excess of trained staff and regimental officers purely for home defence. Finally, Balfour wanted a supply of men 'with some small military training, even if it be only how to hold a rifle, who would supply the material for further armies if, in the course of a prolonged war, further armies were required'.[5]

This interesting proposal, though couched in vague terms and suggesting an amalgam of a home guard, a militia and a reserve force, underlined a growing debate about the possible introduction of conscription. In particular, Lord Roberts, the diminutive, forceful and teetotal hero of Kandahar and the Boer War, wanted conscription. Roberts, the most distinguished military member of the C.I.D., wanted 'universal training for all young men between 18 and 30'. This compulsory training would be for short periods spread over four years. Since 1901 Roberts had campaigned for the National Service League.[6] But he was unable to commend the schemes which he thought so 'essential to the security of the British Empire' to Balfour and the C.I.D.[7] Accordingly Roberts stumped the country in his cause. But, despite the creation of the Territorial Army in 1907, conscription was not adopted, and between 1914 and 1916 volunteers formed the British forces.

But in 1905 invasion seemed a remote possibility. Not only was the understanding with France ripening sufficiently to allow Balfour to say that an invasion by France was the last thing in the world he thought possible, but the Japanese alliance and the friendship of the United States were also healthy safeguards.[8] The reorganisation of the War Office was proceeding steadily, if somewhat erratically, and above all the continuing strength of the Royal Navy enabled Balfour to tell the House of Commons that the C.I.D., having considered the defence of Britain on the most unfavourable hypotheses possible, had concluded that a 'serious invasion of these islands is not an eventuality which we need consider'.[9]

2

The invasion of India, however, was a different matter. Despite the final establishment of British authority during the nineteenth century, India was still a tempting enough prize to encourage ambitions of conquest. Napoleon's abortive Egyptian expedition of 1798–9 and, towards the end of the nineteenth century, unambiguous Russian expansion in Asia, had made the defence of India and its approaches a matter of acute concern for successive

British governments. In these terms can be seen Disraeli's backing of 'the wrong horse' – Turkey – against Russia at the Congress of Berlin in 1878, and British determination to control Egypt and the Suez Canal and to ensure that buffer states such as Afghanistan, Persia and even Tibet were kept out of Russia's hands.

Towards the end of the 1880s, Russian expansion in Central Asia, aided and indeed in many ways made possible by the building of railway lines, was exciting interest and apprehension in Britain. In 1889, the brilliantly promising George Curzon, a future Viceroy, had argued that the whole area between the Indian frontier and the south-eastern territories of Russia must be recognised as a theatre of Imperial diplomacy and possibly of international war. The Russians, he thought, meant business.[10] Two years later, Roberts had prepared a paper analysing what was believed to be General Kuropatkin's scheme for an advance on India.[11] Subsequently, as the railway lines crept ever nearer the frontiers of India, British governments took steps to safeguard the Indian Empire.

Clearly, the control of Afghanistan was of paramount importance. So was the control of Persia. In 1892 Curzon had urged upon Balfour the vital necessity for extending British influence over southern Persia and the Persian Gulf in the event of a Russian invasion of northern Persia.[12] Throughout the 1890s, partly due to Curzon's activities, British influence was extended into those regions of Persia which would help to secure the approaches to India. In April 1904, Balfour listed the reasons why sacrifices were necessary, in the cause of imperial defence, to prevent the whole of Persia falling under Russian control. He feared that Persia could serve as a Russian base for a leisurely advance through Kandahar and Baluchistan. Also, via Persia, the Russian railway system could be linked with the railways in India. Finally, there was the danger of a Russian naval base on the Persian Gulf which could threaten the sea routes to India.[13]

These were cogent reasons for the maintenance of British influence in southern Persia and the Persian Gulf. But by December 1904 Balfour considered this influence so marked that he warned his Foreign Secretary, Lansdowne, that little would be gained by any further demonstrations of strength that 'could be interpreted as part of a scheme for turning the Persian Gulf into a British lake. We have already declared our intention of allowing no other power to do so. Is it wise to give colour to the suspicion that we mean to do it ourselves?'.[14] By 1907, however, British and Russian 'spheres of influence' had been defined in Persia, and the Gulf itself remained effectively under British naval control.

Afghanistan was a much more thorny problem. Failing to subdue the country by military intervention, British policy towards Afghanistan had rested upon attempts to keep the Amir friendly with annual gifts of arms and ammunition, and to achieve international recognition of his frontiers. But the Amir was not always sufficiently obliging. In 1885 Balfour expressed doubts as to the value of the Amir's 'friendly assurances', which appeared to him to consist of 'expressions of friendship towards England coupled with an announcement that, should he be unable to defend his frontiers he will be most happy to have our assistance; but the time and mode in which that assistance is to be rendered are to be decided by him – and that in the meantime our troops cannot enter his territory!!'[15] In view of the recent history of British-Afghan relations it was hardly surprising that the Amir wished to keep British troops out of his kingdom. In these circumstances it is difficult to see what Balfour expected from Afghanistan.

By 1902 relations did not seem much easier. Early in that year Britain was professing to arbitrate for Afghanistan and Persia over a boundary dispute involving Seistan. Despite the fact that both parties had made it plain that they wanted no further arbitration, British interests were clearly involved. Accordingly, Britain persisted in her efforts because, as Balfour pointed out, 'to recede would be a diplomatic victory for the Russians. This is a perfectly sound reason: unfortunately, it is not one we can use in public.'[16]

The Afghan problem was therefore one of extreme delicacy, and the policy of having Afghanistan as a friendly and well-armed buffer state a difficult one to pursue with certainty. Indeed,

Colonial troops at Victoria's Diamond Jubilee, 1897

Victory parade: Colonial Infantry Volunteers in London, October 1900

Made in Birmingham
Joseph Chamberlain (1836–1914) and Austen Chamberlain (1863–1937)

Sir Wilfrid Laurier,
Canadian statesman (1841–1919)

Defence reformer,
Lord Esher (1852–1930)

in 1904, Balfour told the C.I.D. that it was better to have Afghanistan as a potential but weak enemy, than as a potential and powerful ally. This was because he thought the country too unreliable. It was in any case safer to assume that, irrespective of British arms supplies, the Afghans would turn against Russian aggression if it occurred.[17] But against this comforting, though not certain, prospect. the thought of a Russian invasion was not a cheerful one, and Balfour continued to regard Afghanistan as 'the weak spot of Imperial defence'.[18]

3

Despite these misgivings, and although there were two Russian railway lines near the Afghan border by 1904, it still required a considerable stretch of the imagination to contemplate a full-scale invasion of India. Not only was there the physical difficulty of negotiating the Afghanistan passes – presumably in face of local resistance stiffened by British aid – but such ample warning would be given that the troops which might eventually emerge onto India's plains would find the Indian army suitably deployed for their arrival. Therefore, although Balfour felt concern over Afghanistan, he also spoke of past fears of Russia with some disdain – at least in public. Thus in 1904 he told the Commons that 'there was a time when the Russian invasion of India was a genuine scare, and a scare, I think, of the most foolish description, although some of the wisest of our forefathers were deeply impressed by it'.[19] By 1905 Balfour still believed that although the invasion of India might be a subject much debated by Russian officers it was not part of Russian policy.[20]

But if Russia was not likely to invade India, she was able to reap diplomatic advantages simply by her presence on the borders of Afghanistan. This meant that British policy in Asia must adjust accordingly. In a letter to Lansdowne in December 1903, Balfour analysed the problem with candour and clarity. In the Far East, he claimed, Britain was not an expansive power. She desired no more territory, and the only object of her policy was to secure

the territory she already possessed. Russia, however, was still
expanding into Asia and coveted many British possessions. But
even if Russia found India 'too big a mouthful to swallow', she
perhaps felt that by establishing her strategic superiority along the
frontiers of India the British government 'would be so much
afraid of her in Asia as to become her humble servant in Europe'.

Balfour believed, therefore, that Russia's diplomatic game in
Asia was much easier to play than Britain's. Hence Russia could
commit petty acts of bad faith which, in isolation, hardly provided
a justification for plunging the world into war. At the same time
their cumulative effect was 'a serious menace to the British
Empire'. Balfour seems to have meant 'menace' mainly in a
diplomatic sense, for he also complained of the difficulty in
erecting 'any diplomatic barrier in front of this slowly creeping
tide'. The difficulty arose because Britain had nothing she wanted
to give away and, in any case, wanted nothing in return. A diplomatic bargain was therefore highly unlikely.[21]

Nevertheless, Balfour was convinced that Russia would permanently observe certain well-defined principles – for example
that any violation of Afghan independence on their part would
lead to war.[22] Such an understanding, however, would require
the formulation of guarantees. It was perhaps more comforting,
and certainly easier, to argue that the problems of transport and
supply on the North-West frontier were so great that a surprise
Russian assault was impossible.[23] In any case, the rise of Japan as a
formidable military and naval power in the Far East eased Russian
pressure on British territory. Not only did Britain conclude an
alliance with Japan in 1902, but in the Russo-Japanese War of
1904–5 the swift and humiliating defeat of Russia reduced the
latter to a far less ambitious role in Asia. All this meant that by
1905 the Indian Empire was basically safe from external attack.

4

One of the keys to the defence of India was co-operation between
the Indian and home armies. British command of the seas guaran-

teed the route to Asia and ensured that reinforcements could be sent to India in an emergency. But how many troops should be held in readiness? In June 1904, Balfour laid great stress on the need to dispatch reinforcements efficiently.[24] However, the initial estimate of 100,000 men in June rose to 113,000 ten days later, and by December had become 158,000. Balfour's complaints about this mushroom growth were understandable.[25]

This problem was dwarfed by a greater one. Basically, this was the task of reconciling the views of the British and Indian governments on matters of defence, and on questions of policy generally. The two governments were separate but interdependent. It was possible for their interests to differ, and it was alarmingly easy for their respective rulers to quarrel. Balfour's administration, in particular, several times collided head-on with Curzon, the Viceroy since 1898. Despite his long-standing friendship with Balfour and with Brodrick, the Secretary of State for India from 1903 to 1905, Curzon's imperious and high-handed conduct of Indian policy put a severe strain on hitherto cordial personal relations.

Curzon's strong ideas on the defence of India alarmed his more cautious colleagues in London. Not only did they doubt the effectiveness of his vigorous approach to the border problems of Afghanistan and Tibet, but Balfour also found it expedient to question some of Curzon's methods. In 1903 Balfour queried, in a paper prepared for the C.I.D., the wisdom of a scheme for manipulating the waters of Seistan so as to make the country impassable and useless in face of a Russian invasion from the west. The plan was the joint brainchild of Curzon and Kitchener, the newly-arrived Commander-in-Chief of the Indian army. Unfortunately, the scheme bore marks of Kitchener's ruthlessness and Curzon's hot-headedness. Balfour told the C.I.D. that, even in wartime, men should hesitate before reducing nearly 2,000,000 human beings to starvation by a single stroke.[26] Moreover, in a personal letter to Curzon, Balfour returned to the subject, pointing out that the whole of the civilised world would condemn such action, and that there were some punishments so severe that they could never be unleashed. This, he said firmly, was one of them.[27]

Curzon's extraordinary ability to take offence was a serious disadvantage when discussing possible means of reforming Indian defences. Nevertheless, Balfour made his ideas on the subject clear through personal communications with the Viceroy, and also through the C.I.D. Above all, Balfour sought a greater degree of co-operation between the British and Indian armies. Because of the Russian threat, Balfour felt that it was more essential than ever to regard these two armies as an organic whole. He therefore told Curzon, in June 1904, that the C.I.D. was bound to consider Indian army questions although never, he was careful to add, in the absence of the Secretary of State for India. The topics for discussion ranged from a plan for making a higher proportion of the Indian army available on the frontier in the event of war with Russia, to the adequacy of transport, animals and warlike stores for mobilisation. All this was to be intimately linked with arrangements in Britain.[28]

Balfour also wanted to bring about an increased interchange of views and personnel between the British and Indian headquarters staff. Indeed, he had proposed to the C.I.D. the establishment of a headquarters staff common to both armies. This was chiefly because Balfour believed that the Committee's investigations had proved beyond doubt that Indian, not home defence, was Britain's main military problem. However, the great distance between Britain and India, and the subsequent lack of personal contact, put a severe strain on the two separate administrations and exchequers. Such a strain, Balfour claimed, was not felt by the highly centralised systems of the great European military powers.[29]

To illustrate this point, Balfour complained of the inevitable delays and inconvenience involved in any correspondence between the C.I.D. and the Viceroy and the Indian Commander-in-Chief.[30] Kitchener, for example, had allocated duties to his headquarters staff on quite different lines to those adopted in Britain. This was an obstacle to co-operation, yet it could not be removed without a considerable delay – not to speak of the clash of personalities that might be involved. Indeed in May 1905, when conflict between Kitchener and Curzon was raging fiercely, Balfour had told the Commons that he 'could not help feeling that if we had Lord Kitchener on this side of the water for a fortnight we could do more to settle all the outstanding problems, as far as they can be settled in this way, than we can do in a corresponding number of months when we have to carry on our communications by letter'.[31]

Given the bitter and highly-charged nature of Kitchener's conflict with Curzon, Balfour was perhaps being more optimistic than realistic. However, anything that helped to improve contact between the Indian and British armies would be welcome. In this context, Balfour's proposals for a joint headquarters staff had the ring of common sense. The staff officers would alternate between regimental and staff duties, and also between Britain and India. Balfour also wanted to use officers made redundant by reductions in army strength, on a staff which would make a special study of imperial, and especially Indian, defence problems.[32]

But between these plans and their fulfilment fell political expediency. Moreover by 1904, the dispute between Kitchener and Curzon over the relationship between the civil and military establishments in India threatened to quench the light of reason and destroy co-operation. It was ironical that just when the C.I.D. was beginning to find its feet and put forward sound proposals, the extent of its influence in India was curtailed by the essentially serious, but often melodramatic, confrontation between Viceroy and Commander-in-Chief. Centring on Kitchener's determination to destroy the power of the Military Member of the Viceroy's Council, which he saw as an obstacle to his own plans of reform, the quarrel rendered both participants touchy and difficult to deal with.[33]

Curzon's visit to England in the summer of 1904 showed this all too clearly. With his term of office extended in August 1903, and in view of his frequently reiterated need for rest and recuperation Curzon's leave ought to have been profitable and constructive. Instead, it revealed how sensitive he had become to any apparent interference in Indian affairs. In particular, Curzon resented an incident which occurred during a meeting of the C.I.D. on 15 June 1904, to which Balfour had invited him. A memorandum of Kitchener's on the explosive subject of Indian army reform was put before the Committee. Curzon immediately protested that the document fell outside the competence of the C.I.D. since it dealt with Indian administrative organisation, not defence. Balfour promptly withdrew the offending memorandum.[34]

While it was tactful to heed Curzon's protests, the incident also caused Balfour to define the extent to which the C.I.D. could involve itself in Indian affairs. Firstly however, Balfour told Curzon that he had not intended the memorandum to be put before the C.I.D., and that he would not think of allowing the Committee to discuss it or comment upon it. This was, to say the least, disingenuous. On whose authority had the document been introduced? Even if it had been Brodrick's doing, Balfour as chairman of the C.I.D. should have known what was going on.

But Balfour was anxious to humour Curzon. Moreover he could achieve this without sacrificing his underlying concept of the nature of the C.I.D. Thus he agreed that the Committee had no business to interfere with Indian administration. Even the stationing of a few troops on the Seistan border, for political rather than strategic reasons, fell outside the scope of the C.I.D. In fact, the Committee had no powers. It was merely an advisory body. It 'could not do a single thing, either in Great Britain or in India, except through the existing constitutional Executive Authorities.' But while it must not step outside the proper sphere, Balfour thought that within its sphere it had done, and could do, excellent work.[35]

Balfour did not go too far in his appeasement of Curzon, for he told him that he was also anxious to assure Kitchener that the C.I.D. was not to be seen as an external, still less as a hostile, critic of his actions. In view of Curzon's craving for support, the implication of these words was clear. Furthermore Balfour reminded Curzon that the Committee was advising the training, equipping and paying of 100,000 men for no other purpose than to supply reinforcements to India in time of need. In these circumstances, the Prime Minister thought his desire for closer co-operation between the two armies and administrations a reasonable one.[36] It was nevertheless evident that Balfour meant to use the C.I.D. with tact and discretion when dealing with India.

5

While it was essential to shore up the defences of India from within, another method of lessening Russian pressure lay at hand. Early in 1902, Britain signed a limited alliance with the newly emerged and powerful state of Japan. This was a tremendous step. Britain had been without formal allies since the Crimean War. Naval supremacy and mid-Victorian confidence apparently needed no allies. Even when, in the last years of the nineteenth century, this confidence had begun to wane, the doctrine of 'splendid isolation' provided a gaudy camouflage for a growing sense of insecurity. In 1898 the proposed alliance with Germany collapsed – mainly, perhaps, because the German government wanted it to.[37] The exposure of British military inadequacies in the Boer War had been accompanied by evidence of hatred and exultation throughout Europe. In the hysteria with which Britain greeted the relief of Mafeking in 1900 can be seen the reaction of a humiliated and frightened people.

The alliance with Japan was signed before the Boer War stumbled to its close. The agreement was clearly aimed at Russia. In China and Manchuria, Russian advances threatened existing British commercial interests and potential Japanese involvement. The north China Sea seemed a likely theatre of Russo-Japanese conflict. Anglo-Japanese friendship would therefore promote British interests in India, and the interests of both powers in China and Manchuria. But one drawback for Britain lay in the Franco-Russian alliance, signed in 1894. In 1902 British statesmen had no desire to be dragged into a war with France.

These considerations caused Balfour to approach the Japanese alliance with a wary step. Indeed he argued in a memorandum, composed before he became Prime Minister in 1902, that the agreement might involve Britain in fighting for her existence 'in

every part of the globe against Russia and France, because France
has joined forces with her ally over some obscure Russian-
Japanese quarrel in Korea'.[38] The final terms of the treaty,
however, provided for neutrality if one of the parties was attacked
by another power. Only if *two* powers attacked one of the signa-
tories was the other obliged to come to the rescue.

Subsequently, Balfour spoke warmly of the agreement, telling
the Commons in February 1902 that British and Japanese interests
in the Far East were identical – the maintenance of the status quo.
There could be no greater blow to the status quo than the crushing
of either Britain or Japan by hostile powers. The treaty,
Balfour claimed, would help to preserve peace and would protect
commercial interests dear to the whole world – not least to 'our
American brothers'.[39] This was certainly the end of splendid
isolation, but Balfour denied in the Commons that Britain was
merely grasping at allies and stressed that the Japanese alliance
was 'entered into for a common purpose and on terms of absolute
equality'.[40]

But by the end of 1903, mounting tension between Japan and
Russia brought home some of the implications of the alliance.
Balfour, now Prime Minister, was confident that Russia was not
capable of beating Japan on sea or land. Moreover, he told the
Cabinet that:

There could be nothing better for us than that Russia should
involve herself in the expense and trouble of a Korean adventure
with the result that at the best she would become possessed of a
useless province, which would cost more than it brought in,
which could only be retained as long as she kept a great fleet in
the Far East, and a large army thousands of miles away from her
home base, and which would be a perpetual guarantee that
whenever Russia went to war with another power, no matter
where or about what, Japan would be upon her back.[41]

Delectable though this speculation was, Balfour was opposed to
pushing Japan into a war with Russia. Rather, he believed that the
Japanese should work out their own salvation in their own way.
But if Japan should appear to be losing to Russia, then Britain
would be able to enter the conflict in the role of deliverer.[42]

Edward VII, however, needed reassurance in this time of tension, fearing that it would be disastrous for Britain to get involved in another war so soon after the South African conflict. Balfour took care to emphasise Britain's lack of immediate involvement, and stressed that now, as always, the country's interests demanded peace. But he also pointed out that should Russia be defeated, and Britain kept out of the war, Russia would not only be gravely weakened but would have created an 'implacable and unsleeping enemy in the Far East'.[43]

A day later, on 29 December, Balfour reminded the C.I.D. that Britain feared Russia as the ally of France, the invader of India, the dominating influence in Persia, and the possible disturber of European peace. This was a blood-curdling indictment, but Balfour added that in a war with Japan, Russia would lose her value to France as a potential ally against Britain. Moreover, 'her whole diplomacy from the Black Sea to the Oxus, might be weakened into something distinctly resembling sweet reasonableness'.[44]

As the Russo-Japanese War steadily approached, the C.I.D.'s usefulness and acceptance was made clear. Lansdowne, the Foreign Secretary, wanted a special meeting of the C.I.D. to discuss the situation. Balfour agreed.[45] Austen Chamberlain, the newly-appointed Chancellor of the Exchequer, thought that if the situation deteriorated further, all the members of the C.I.D. should be called to London to meet daily and follow events. He believed that this would give confidence to the public.[46]

When the Russo-Japanese War did break out in February 1904, the thorough and speedy defeat of Russia only brought benefit to Britain. The Russians also vividly demonstrated their military incompetence nearer home when their Baltic fleet opened fire on some Hull trawlers in October 1904. The discovery that Admiral Rodjesvensky had mistaken the trawlers for Japanese torpedo-boats did not excuse the fact that one trawler was destroyed and two fishermen killed. Public indignation flared, and war was rumoured. Balfour acted with restraint and the crisis subsided when Russia offered to pay compensation.[47] But the Dogger Bank incident drew Britain and Japan closer together.

Shortly before the war ended, Balfour's government signed a

new treaty with Japan in the summer of 1905. By then the
Unionist party was in disarray over tariff reform, and the Cabinet
expected defeat at the polls. One reason for Balfour's clinging to
office lay in his desire to renew and extend the Japanese treaty.
Certainly he felt qualms over the Liberals' attitude to imperial
defence. This partly explains why he ignored Austen Chamberlain's advice of an autumn dissolution, making the announcement
of the renewed treaty 'our last great work'.[48]

The new treaty bound the two allies to go to each other's aid
if either was attacked by one power, not two as before. Moreover,
Balfour saw that it was important to safeguard British and
Japanese extra-territorial interests, such as Afghanistan and
Korea.[49] Consequently the final treaty, which was due to run for
ten years, embodied guarantees of mutual assistance if the frontiers
of British and Japanese territory were threatened.

Sir George Clarke, the secretary of the C.I.D., was deeply
involved in these negotiations. He wanted to equate the strength
of the Japanese forces to be sent to India in time of war with the
size of the reinforcements to be sent from Britain, not with the
normal garrison of British troops in India. This would mean that
the Japanese contingent would be bigger.[50] Balfour approved of
this. At the same time, he was careful to assure the King that it
was not consistent with 'the security or dignity of the Empire
that the defence of any part of it should depend mainly upon a
Foreign Power, however friendly and however powerful'.[51] But
the Japanese alliance contributed enormously to the security
of the Empire, even though by 1907 the Russian government,
too, had come to an understanding with Britain. At any rate,
when the First World War broke out both Russia and Japan
fought on the British side. The British possessions in the Far East
were safe.

6

By the time Balfour's government fell on 4 December 1905, the
defences of the Empire were much stronger than before the Boer
War. The progress of War Office reform, new arrangements for

the defence of India and the British Isles, the Japanese alliance, and the efforts to get wider and more thorough discussions of imperial defence problems, were all steps in this direction. Above all, the C.I.D., established on a permanent basis with its own secretariat under the chairmanship of the Prime Minister, was both a symbol of the new determination to co-ordinate defence and a means of achieving such co-ordination.

Not that the functions and role of the C.I.D. were understood, or appreciated, as a matter of course. In July 1904, Swift Macneill, an Irish Nationalist M.P., wanted to know the precedent for Curzon's attendance at a meeting of the Committee in view of the fact that the Viceroy was 'without naval and military experience' and was not even a member of the Cabinet. In reply, Balfour emphasised the extremely valuable right of the C.I.D. to summon to its meetings anybody who could be of assistance.[52] Later in July, another questioner urged the C.I.D. to prevent officers commanding colonial forces from making public speeches about colonial defence while they were in the King's service. Balfour explained that this was a matter for the War Office not for the C.I.D.[53] A week later, Balfour was asked if the Committee had calculated the exact number of troops required to defend Britain and strengthen imperial defences. The Prime Minister replied that the problems were not capable of such a precise solution.[54]

In April 1905 Balfour was still explaining that the C.I.D.'s function was to advise the Cabinet, and it was for the Cabinet, or its head, to advise the King accordingly.[55] Asked in the same month whether the C.I.D. had worked out a complete scheme for repelling raids, since shore defences were partly under the War Office and partly under the Admiralty, Balfour was able to answer that 'submarine defences' were now solely under the Admiralty, a change that had been brought about very largely through the work of the Committee.[56]

Clarifications and justifications were all the more necessary in 1905 in view of the probability that before long a new government would be formed under Campbell-Bannerman. The Liberal leader had expressed scepticism as to the value of the C.I.D. Moreover, the Liberal party traditionally contained anti-imperialist and anti-militarist elements. There seemed a very real danger, therefore, that the Liberals would destroy the C.I.D., or at least neglect it.[57] In February 1905 Balfour felt that the Liberals were doing nothing to convince him that imperial interests would be safe in their hands.[58] This was especially worrying since he also believed that the C.I.D.'s work had shown that imperial obligations were generally underestimated.[59] However, when Campbell-Bannerman did become Prime Minister he sent Haldane, a Liberal-Imperialist, to the War Office with the cheerful comment, 'Serve him right!' Haldane insisted that the C.I.D. must be preserved.

Of Balfour's enthusiasm for the C.I.D. there can be no doubt. His long-standing interest in defence was transformed by the Boer War and the influence of Esher into a determination to improve the planning of imperial defence. Haldane did not hesitate to call Balfour the creator of the C.I.D. and to compliment him not only for devising it, but also for devoting so much of his time and energy to it.[60] In view of the fact that Balfour attended every single meeting of the C.I.D. from its reconstitution to his government's fall, this was no idle compliment. Moreover, the Committee met regularly once a fortnight.[61]

Balfour's chairmanship of the Committee and his general zest for its work favourably impressed contemporaries. In 1903 Godley, the Under Secretary for India, thought that under Balfour's chairmanship the meetings had been interesting and profitable to all who had attended them, and would become even more profitable. At first, he admitted, 'Balfour with his extraordinary powers of ready argument and quick reply' had rather overwhelmed the less eloquent members. But Godley thought that bit by bit they would learn to hold their own.[62] Lord George Hamilton, Secretary of State for India until the autumn of 1903, thought that on the C.I.D. Balfour showed both the strong and the weak side of his intellect: 'The quickness and thoroughness with which he picked up the main facts that had to be dealt with, and focussed them, was remarkable'. But Hamilton complained that once Balfour had extracted enough information to make up his mind he went on to discuss every kind of hypothesis. Some of these were 'quite impossible' and only served to distract the minds of the military members and provide much unnecessary work in the compiling of facts and figures.[63]

Balfour seems to have sometimes treated the C.I.D. as a seminar before which he could display his formidable academic talents. Clearly his love of speculation could be an administrative disadvantage. Equally it could be a stimulant for fresh thinking. But perhaps stimulation was paramount. Godley, returning to his former theme, told Curzon that Balfour had tackled the problem of the defence of the Empire with immense vigour and energy. This, he confessed, was very valuable since he had recently discerned 'a real danger that we should turn Imperialists without counting the cost, and should try to run an Empire with a Navy and nothing more'.[64] Brodrick, Hamilton's successor at the India Office, said bluntly, 'Arthur Balfour is the first Prime Minister who has given any real consideration to national defence'.[65] Also, Esher considered that 'in the hands of the present Prime Minister the Defence Committee, as those who have seen its work know, is alive and of immense value'.[66]

But the effectiveness of the Committee's work would depend largely upon the energy and persistence of the Prime Minister in seeing that advice, once accepted, was carried out by the various departments of state. Also, much would depend on the departments' willingness to accept advice. Curzon for example said that although Balfour was probably an effective chairman with less practised debaters, 'a good many of his arguments never make the slightest impression upon me because, though metaphysically beautiful, they have no connection with the facts'.[67] This was, to say the least, a debatable comment, and even ironical in view of Curzon's own tendency to sweep away whole mountains of fact in torrents of self-justification and injured pride.

However, Curzon's attitude underlined a real problem. Doubtless it was responsible for Brodrick's plea to the Viceroy on 15 October 1903, to give all possible consideration to the C.I.D.'s advice. Brodrick added that the Committee was the best conducted business body, and the most representative, yet established. The members knew 'infinitely more of their subject than the

Members of the Cabinet do on most subjects brought before them'. Furthermore, close reasoning accompanied the discussions and the participants were able to take a thorough, all-round view of defence policy. Any summary dismissal of the C.I.D.'s conclusions, Brodrick warned, would entail 'a great deal of friction'.[68]

Brodrick's close friendship with Balfour and his need to assert some sort of authority over Curzon may have coloured his remarks. However, it was certainly possible for departments and proconsuls to accept the C.I.D.'s findings and then neglect to implement them. Also, the Cabinet heads of the various departments might be reluctant to bring matters before the Committee for discussion. To overcome such obstacles would take time and energy.

Moreover, the last two years of Balfour's administration were distinctly uneasy. The problem of holding the Cabinet together was a delicate one. As public support ebbed away from the government, the C.I.D. may have suffered, for while defence fiascos can be election-losers, defence reorganisation is not necessarily an election winner. Above all, the stress which Balfour laid upon the advisory nature of the Committee meant that it was not possible to force through clear-cut results immediately.

But Balfour remained convinced of the value of the C.I.D. In May 1905 he expressed to the Commons his astonishment that previous governments had managed to get on without an equivalent body.[69] This was not merely self-congratulation. The sheer range and quality of the C.I.D.'s investigations, from the defence of India to the use of mines for home defence, to army reform and the military needs of the empire, could not fail to assist those involved in imperial defence.

More than this, Balfour's C.I.D., simply *because* of its advisory and non-executive nature could fulfil many different functions. It was capable of adaptation and organic growth. It gave assurance that the British government was determined to consider imperial defence as a whole. At the same time it could convince the self-governing colonies that any contributions of theirs to the defence of the Empire, while gratefully received, would in no way impair their independence. Thus the C.I.D. held promise for the future. Balfour was to be justified in his realistic appreciation that if the C.I.D. was used as he suggested, its value would transcend mere concern for immediate problems and point out paths of broader imperial development.

5 The Empire at War and at Peace, 1906–1930

For my part the last thing I want to see is any extension of the British Empire. I want to see its strengthening and consolidation.

BALFOUR, 1906

I hope you would not be averse from continuing your membership of the Committee of Imperial Defence which is your own child and would indeed feel an orphan without you.

BALDWIN to BALFOUR, 1929

I

BALFOUR was out of office from December 1905 until May 1915, when he was taken into Asquith's coalition government as First Lord of the Admiralty. Although Balfour was hardly the stuff of which sea-dogs are made, the appointment was not inappropriate. While in opposition he had maintained his keen interest in imperial defence, and before the Great War no branch of the services was as vital to national security as the Royal Navy.

After the German Navy Laws of 1898 and 1899 there had been growing competition between the expanding German Navy and the massive Royal Navy. However, by 1898 numbers did not count for everything. With the continuing revolution in naval design, capital ships were speedily reduced to obsolescence, and, theoretically, one brand-new, superior battleship could sink any number of out-gunned, out-torpedoed rivals. British naval supremacy could now only be guaranteed by keeping ahead of foreign technical innovation.[1] Due to the reforming energy of Lord Fisher, who became First Sea Lord in 1904, the fleets were redistributed and the Home Fleet created to meet the potential German menace in the North Sea and the Channel. Furthermore, Fisher planned to make the *Dreadnought*, a unique big-gun battleship, the linchpin of Britain's naval defences.[2] But by 1909 the acceleration of the German naval programme caused a scare in Britain that swept aside the policies of the government and their economic advisers.

Balfour was intimately concerned with these developments. In May 1906 in the Commons he called for 'a Fleet which would make us absolutely secure against any possible combination against our shores.'[3] Four months later he berated Campbell-Bannerman for misinterpreting the 'two-power standard'. He accused the Prime Minister of dismissing the hypothesis that Germany and France might combine to attack Britain. Balfour wanted a fleet strong enough to cope with any eventuality.[4]

In March 1909, the government, now led by Asquith, admitted that a recent expansion in German shipbuilding facilities meant that British naval supremacy was now minimal. The Cabinet was subjected to popular agitation for the immediate construction of eight new battleships. But the slogan 'We want eight, and we won't wait!' was repeated more discreetly in private circles. Fisher, through the agency of the ubiquitous Esher, sought to prompt Balfour's criticisms of the government. In March 1909, Esher told Balfour of the precise points on which the Admiralty wanted him to concentrate in his forthcoming speech in the Commons.[5] In April, Milner urged upon Balfour the necessity of maintaining the strength of the navy and of introducing a system of national service. Milner insisted that the Unionists were 'the party on which we can alone rely for a serious treatment of the question of Imperial Defence'.[6] Finally, in face of intensive pressure, the government agreed to build eight new capital ships, spread over the next few years, even though this was an unwelcome financial burden for an administration with plans for social reform.

When Winston Churchill became First Lord of the Admiralty in October 1911 he quite frequently consulted Balfour; for example, asking his advice on submarines and home defence in January 1912. Balfour told Churchill that he had 'long been strongly of the opinion that Submarines modify the whole question of home defence', and expressed deep interest in the new torpedoes Churchill had described.[7] Shortly after the outbreak of war in 1914, Balfour wrote cheerfully to his sister Alice: 'I am dining tonight with Winston and Fisher to talk naval "shop", and I am also meddling – for good or for evil – with military affairs. I do not know what it all comes to.'[8]

As it happened, Balfour's capacity for maintaining close contact with defence matters through the C.I.D. and private confidences led the dismissed Churchill to suggest him as his successor in 1915. Although Balfour lacked Churchill's ebullience, his profound conviction that scientific research must be fostered by the government caused him to set up a department of Invention and Research to aid the navy in its task.[9] If this was the only major innovation of his career as First Lord, it was at least typical of his ability to bring fresh ideas to defence problems.

2

Balfour was equally concerned with the land defences of the Empire. In May 1906 he told the Commons, 'For my part the last thing I want to see is any extension of the British Empire. I want to see its strengthening and consolidation.' To achieve this, Balfour wanted an overwhelmingly powerful fleet, and an army capable of rapid expansion in the event of a world war. In addition, he reaffirmed his conviction that home defence and the defence of India were crucial to imperial security: 'We have to maintain an Army adequate for home defence, which need not be on a very large scale, and an Army adequate for the defence of the north-west frontier of India.'[10]

But how, while out of office, was Balfour to impose his views on imperial defence upon the triumphant Liberal administration? There was, of course, the perpetual platform afforded by the House of Commons. Balfour made full use of it. Between May 1906 and July 1909 he made eight major speeches on defence. But speechmaking from the Opposition benches is not the surest way of affecting government policy.

On the other hand, there was the constant communication with

Esher, who had been made a permanent non-official member of the C.I.D. before Balfour's government resigned in December 1905, and was to preserve his office throughout Campbell-Bannerman's and Asquith's administrations.[11] In December 1906, Balfour assured Esher that he could not recall having given Kitchener, the Indian Commander-in-Chief, any pledge not to cut the numbers of reinforcements available for Indian service. But he added, 'I, of course, strongly disapprove of Army reductions being made before we have any working scheme of Army expansion.'[12]

Again, in May 1908, Balfour gave Esher his views on home defence. Although admitting that the forces maintained in Britain were more than adequate for defensive purposes, he showed clearly he opposed any overall reduction in reinforcements.[13] The Liberal government was under some pressure from its supporters to divert defence expenditure towards measures of social reform. Balfour believed that the defence of the Empire came first, and that the possible requirements of India were of paramount importance.

Most remarkable of all, however, was Balfour's continuing relationship with his own creation – the C.I.D. The mere existence of this body meant that imperial defence problems would be kept under consistent and expert surveillance. Despite Balfour's fears, while in office, that the Liberals would destroy the C.I.D. when they came to power, these anxieties proved groundless. The C.I.D.'s survival was due in great measure to Haldane's belief in its worth. Indeed, in July 1906, Balfour went out of his way to thank the new Secretary for War for giving full recognition to his own previous work as Chairman of the C.I.D.[14]

More than this, Balfour did not allow the Commons to forget the purpose and value of the C.I.D. In August 1906, he confessed, 'I am not sure that the character of that Committee [the C.I.D.] is even now perfectly understood by the House or by the public.' His remarks were prompted by a suggestion of Major Seely, the Liberal member for Liverpool, Abercromby, that the Leader of the Opposition should sit on the C.I.D. every three months to discuss 'questions of great Imperial strategy'. Balfour considered this to be impossible, pointing out how fundamentally he differed from the government in its desire to reduce the regular forces. There would be other basic differences. Balfour also told Seely that the C.I.D. never discussed 'single ships or single battalions' but should rather be seen as a co-ordinating body between the great departments of state.[15]

But when Asquith became Prime Minister in April 1908, he almost immediately invited Balfour to sit on a sub-committee of the C.I.D. Balfour accepted promptly, and considered plans to counter an invasion of Britain. He soon displayed his sure grasp of defence problems and treated Asquith, Grey (the Foreign Secretary), Haldane, Lloyd George (the new Chancellor) and Roberts to a detailed report that apparently left them, in Esher's words, 'dumbfounded'.[16]

Throughout 1908 Balfour remained in close contact with the C.I.D., and wrote Asquith a long letter in November insisting that the service experts 'need not think that my feelings would be hurt by their emphasizing any difference between the findings of the C.I.D. in 1908 and their findings when I was Chairman of that body. I had always recognised that there must be constant revision of every great decision arrived at.'[17] Later, in April 1909, Esher reported having met Balfour at the C.I.D., and in 1913 he was once more formally invited by Asquith to sit on a sub-committee.

All this amounted to a constitutional innovation, in which the main ingredient was Balfour's remarkable reputation as a defence expert. This is underlined by the fact that although after 1911 he was not even Leader of the Opposition it was he and not Bonar Law whom Asquith consulted in 1913. Some doubted the propriety of the precedent thus established. In May 1914, Swift Macneill, the Irish Nationalist, asked Asquith in the Commons, whether Balfour's membership of the C.I.D. was in accordance with constitutional usage. The Prime Minister denied that Balfour was a member of the C.I.D. Rather, he had been invited to take part in a special inquiry of a sub-committee 'in which his expert knowledge and judgement have proved to be of great value'.[18]

Partly as a result of Asquith's desire to consult him, Balfour had been able to tell the Commons on 29 July 1909 that 'every-thing I have been able to learn . . . as to the use which the Gov-ernment are putting the machinery of the Defence Committee, leads me to think that every hope which the original authors may have entertained as to its future utility to the country and the Empire are in the hands of the right hon. Gentleman [Asquith] being fulfilled in the highest possible measure.'[19] Although Balfour made no effort to conceal his hostility to certain aspects of Liberal defence policy, particularly the desire to cut expenditure, the confidence expressed in 1909 was in striking contrast to his fears in 1905 for the C.I.D.'s survival under the Liberals. But after all Asquith, not Campbell-Bannerman, was Prime Minister in 1909, and the Cabinet was heavy with Liberal Imperialists. In Balfour's eyes this counted for a great deal.

Moreover, the years 1906 to 1914 were characterised by the increasing conviction that Germany posed the major threat to British security. From 1906 onwards joint army staff planning replaced traditional Anglo-French rivalry. The entente with Russia in 1907, though an imperfect understanding, further rationalised European alignments. In these circumstances, inter-party con-sultation over defence was not unreasonable.

Even when Balfour was not formally participating in meetings of the C.I.D., he remained constantly in communication with Esher. Indeed, Esher was so incensed by the movement to oust Balfour from the Unionist leadership in 1911, that he told Sandars that 'he should not further interest himself in the affairs of the Unionist Party; that he would never vote for them; on the con-trary, he would work to keep them out of office.'[20]

But Esher continued to supply Balfour with documents relating to the C.I.D.'s functions. In January 1912, Balfour thanked him for a paper dealing with a Co-ordination Committee for the C.I.D. Balfour felt that 'Co-ordination is one of the funda-mental tasks of the C.I.D., and if there was one reason more press-ing than another for the institution of the body in its modern shape, it was the glaring want of Co-ordination that previously existed between the Military and Naval Departments.'[21]

It is clear, therefore, that through his public utterances and private contacts, Balfour maintained a close interest in defence matters before the Great War. But far more remarkable was his participation in the C.I.D.'s deliberations. In this way, the flexibility of the C.I.D.'s constitution was neatly demonstrated by making use of the man who had insisted on creating this flexibility. The C.I.D. had lived up to Balfour's hopes in this respect. Nor had it failed in co-ordinating the defence planning of the Empire.

3

In creating the C.I.D. Balfour had emphasised its potential as a meeting place for the Dominions and the British government. He returned to this theme in the Commons in August 1906, remarking that the self-governing colonies were assured of a place on the Committee whenever they wished. He denied Liberal allegations that the self-governing colonies had boycotted the Committee, citing Borden's attendance in 1903 and consultations with Australia in 1905. In any case, Balfour pointed out that the Dominions had no need to attend regularly since 'the interest of the great self-governing Colonies is largely naval.' Provided they felt protected by the Royal Navy there was little incentive to use the C.I.D.[22]

As regards the Dominions' land forces, Balfour was no idealist. He recognised that 'however you may model or remodel your Defence Committee, you will never induce the Colonies to give us here complete control over the military forces which they maintain and for which they pay.' Nonetheless, Balfour was confident that if an emergency arose, the Dominions would be able to co-operate with Britain through the C.I.D. with the minimum of effort.[23]

Prior to the Colonial Conference of 1907, the Commons debated, on 15 February, the desirability of the Dominions bearing a greater share of the cost of imperial defence. Balfour deplored any attempt 'to deal with the problem of Imperial defence rather in a strictly bargaining spirit than in that spirit of free interchange of services between different parts of the Empire which after all is, and ought to be, one of the greatest links between them.' More-over, he claimed that 'the cost of our Fleet would not be dimin-ished, even if we lost those Colonies which are, in my opinion, our glory and the great strength and support of our Empire.'[24]

As to charges that the Dominions were getting security for little cost, Balfour pointed out that Britain's wide-spread interests and problems could involve the different units of the Empire in a war which, as separate and isolated communities, they might otherwise have avoided. In any case, just as imperial federation was not practical politics, so any rigid system of Dominion defence commitment was equally unlikely. Balfour preferred to put his trust in voluntary colonial assistance in the event of a great war, in 'that feeling of Imperial patriotism which is no monopoly of the citizens of the Empire living in these islands, but is shared to the full by our fellow citizens in every quarter of the globe.'[25]

When the Colonial Conference met in 1907, it discussed an Australian resolution that 'it is desirable that the Colonies should be represented on the Imperial Council of Defence.' After some debate, the resolution was amended to authorise the Dominions to refer to the C.I.D., via the Colonial Secretary, for advice on local defence problems, and to send a representative to the Committee whenever they wanted to discuss a particular topic.[26] This formal-ised Balfour's desire that there should be a standing invitation for the Dominions to attend the C.I.D. But it also restricted the invit-ation to occasions when subjects of particular interest to the Dominions were discussed. Although this seemed sensible, it fell short of Balfour's wider hopes. Perhaps the Australian resolution was aimed at ensuring that the Dominions should not be com-mitted further than they desired. Perhaps it was merely an attempt to clarify the C.I.D.'s constitution. After all, this was so permis-sive as to be vague, and the original Australian resolution had even called the C.I.D. the 'Imperial Council of Defence'.

Of greater significance was Haldane's project of an Imperial General Staff, which was discussed by the Conference. This body was meant to standardise training, organisation and material for the Empire's land forces. It was also to lay down overall strategy. Clearly the C.I.D. would work closely with the Imperial General

Staff, and together the two bodies could contribute enormously to imperial military unity. This unity was all the more desirable in face of the German threat and the difficulty hitherto of achieving effective and long-term co-operation between the British army and Dominion land forces.[27]

By 1909 imperial defence co-operation was even more urgent. The German navy scare encouraged the British government to call a special Imperial Defence Conference. The delegates, including representatives of India, agreed that their peacetime preparations should follow the advice of the Imperial General Staff. At the same time, Britain accepted that the extent of the Dominions' contribution in wartime would be left to them. The Dominion delegates to the Conference also attended meetings of the C.I.D., thus establishing a precedent which was repeated in 1911 and, more momentously, in 1917.

Balfour anticipated this accord in a speech in the Commons on 29 July 1909. After reminding the Commons that the Dominions were 'rightly jealous of anything in the nature of interference by this country with forces they raise themselves and pay for themselves', he urged the government to encourage, through the agency of the C.I.D., the 'full, friendly, free and unfettered discussion of Imperial problems'.[28] Balfour's optimism was further justified by Britain's acceptance, at the 1909 Conference, of the principle of Australia and Canada establishing their own navies. The Admiralty even suggested that, to begin with, Australia should be given an annual subsidy of £250,000. Times had indeed changed, and the fact was positively recognised in both the mother country and the Dominions.[29]

The 1911 Imperial Conference confirmed these trends towards greater co-operation. For three days the delegates, led by Asquith, attended sessions of the C.I.D. which now clearly functioned as an accepted medium for discussing the wider problems of defence. At the same time, although the British government was prepared to consult the Dominions, it still maintained the right to make policy of its own accord. Asquith, however, proposed that the Dominions should be regularly represented on the C.I.D., although the details of such representation were left blurred. This at least implied that the Dominions might participate more fully in policy-forming discussions, even though the British Cabinet would take the final policy decisions.

In effect, the C.I.D., not the Imperial Conference, was now the chief forum for inter-imperial defence consultations. As Balfour had urged, the Dominion delegates were put on an equal footing with their British counterparts. Indeed the British Prime Minister was, after 1911, the chairman of both the Imperial Conference and the C.I.D. In 1912, Balfour spoke of 'the increasing support which the Dominions are giving to this country'. From this increased support must come, he felt, 'some increasing share in the responsibility for guiding the destinies of [the] Empire'. As a medium for thus sharing responsibility there was 'the very elastic constitution of the Defence Committee'.[30]

Hence, when the British Empire was plunged into war in 1914, it was undoubtedly better prepared than at any time previously. Strategy had been considered by the C.I.D. and the Imperial General Staff. Plans had been laid and were adhered to. This is not to say that the plans were always the right ones. Nonetheless, the liaison and prior consultation made possible by the permanent bodies of inter-imperial defence planning, by personal contacts between statesmen, and by the general co-ordinating role of the Dominions Department of the Colonial Office (which had been established in 1907) were considerable achievements. This liaison was particularly praiseworthy in view of the scattered and decentralised character of the Empire.

Such concord was partly a tribute to the willingness of the Dominions to set aside fears that defence planning would inevitably involve an infringement of their independent status. But it also reflected the British government's appreciation of these Dominion doubts and susceptibilities. In this respect, Balfour could take pride in the evolution of the C.I.D. Admittedly, the new arrangements did not provide the generals with more brains, or avoid the follies of the Dardanelles and Passchendaele, but they lessened disarray.

The Imperial War Conference of 1917 provided a triumphant demonstration of co-operation. The Dominions and India had already contributed heroically to the war effort. Their representatives now assembled in London where they attended C.I.D. meetings, as the delegates from the Dominions had done in 1909 and 1911. Moreover Lloyd George, who had overthrown Asquith in 1916, had created a small War Cabinet serviced by the C.I.D.'s secretariat. With the inclusion of the imperial delegates in 1917, the War Cabinet became the Imperial War Cabinet. Furthermore, until the end of 1918, some delegates remained in London as part of this Imperial War Cabinet. Indeed, one of them, Smuts, the South African Defence Minister, was even taken into the exclusive War Cabinet, which continued to run the war.[31]

But although the Dominions were so intimately connected with the conduct of the war, they also made plain their aspirations to general equality of status. Their delegates to the 1917 Imperial War Conference had stressed that they were responsible only to their own governments. Led by Smuts and by Borden, the Canadian Prime Minister, they also requested a post-war recognition of their independence. Even while Dominion and Indian armies fought loyally under British commanders, the war stimulated nationalist sentiment in the troops' homelands. After the war, the Dominions took increasingly independent paths in defence matters.[32] There was a parallel with the Boer War here. An imperial emergency bred unity, but the peace dissipated it.

4

After the end of the First World War, which had seen the Dominions and India sign the peace treaties in their own right, the C.I.D. received no new powers. Nor could the Imperial War Cabinet survive in peacetime. Occasional consultations with the C.I.D., the maintenance of the Imperial General Staff, and informal contacts, provided the basic media of defence co-operation between Britain and the Dominions. Periodic conferences continued. In 1921 the Imperial Conference revealed Dominion concern over the growth of Japanese power in the Pacific and the whole question of naval disarmament. Australia and New Zealand were particularly distrustful of Japan, and although the British Prime Minister, Lloyd George, toyed with the idea of a naval competition with the United States, Canada could hardly contemplate such rivalry. In the end, Britain agreed to terminate her nineteen-year-old alliance with Japan. The whole problem of naval and Far Eastern affairs was thrashed out at a conference in Washington from November 1921 to February 1922.[33]

Balfour, then Lord President of the Council in Lloyd George's coalition government, led the British delegation. Since he had been involved in the making of the Japanese alliance in 1902 and in its renewal and extension in 1905, Balfour was a singularly appropriate choice for a mission which was bound either to end the Anglo-Japanese treaty, or to transform it into a more general agreement. Although Balfour felt strong personal regret at the prospect of ending the treaty, other factors prevailed.

Above all, a war between the United States and Japan in the Pacific would have presented Britain and the Dominions with a hideous dilemma. As early as 1910 Balfour had given Esher his opinions on the implications of such a conflict. Balfour thought it would be 'quite impossible, treaty or no treaty, for this country to join Japan in a war waged ... against the United States in order to obtain emigration privileges into Anglo-Saxon North America. Nor can I imagine any treaty binding us to such a course.' Balfour doubted whether, in these circumstances, the Empire could be kept together.[34]

These doubts were even more valid in 1921. Admittedly, in the event of an American-Japanese war Britain would have only been obliged to remain neutral. But Australia and New Zealand, and especially Canada, with some 15,000 not altogether integrated Japanese immigrants on her western coast, would have found their position extremely difficult. Apart from this there was ample cause to anticipate an extension of Japanese influence in China, where central government had collapsed. In particular the Versailles peace treaty had ceded to Japan the territory and privileges previously enjoyed by Germany in the Shantung peninsula. By the time the Washington Conference opened, however, China had not accepted this parcelling-out of her territory.[35]

Almost immediately, the Conference produced an agreement to limit naval armaments. The United States proposed the scrapping of battleships under construction, a ten-year pause in building more, and a ratio of 5:5:3 for Britain, the United States and Japan respectively. Balfour accepted this offer in principle, although further negotiation failed to secure the total banning of submarines. Nonetheless, four powers (Britain, the United States, Japan and France) signed a naval disarmament treaty in January 1922, which limited the construction of battleships in the way the Americans had originally proposed.[36] Britain had to scrap nearly 600,000 tons of battleships under construction or at the planning stage. Even though there was no agreement to limit lighter warships, the curb on battleship competition was a healthy achievement for post-war diplomacy.

Balfour also negotiated the ending of the Anglo-Japanese alliance, and its transformation into a four power treaty which included the United States and France. The four powers agreed to respect each others' Pacific possessions, and not to fortify strategic islands. In addition, the Sino-Japanese quarrel was patched up in February 1922 when the two countries signed an agreement which restored the Shantung peninsula to China. Balfour, who with Hughes, the American Secretary of State, had been instrumental in supervising these negotiations, also announced that Britain intended to hand back her lease on the naval base of Wei-hai-wei. The Washington Conference was completed when a nine power treaty was signed for maintaining Chinese territorial integrity and the open door for trade.[37]

All in all, the Washington Conference was a striking example of international good will. Although Bolshevik Russia and a defeated Germany were not part of the treaty-making, the agreements arrived at were brave attempts to guarantee world peace. For Balfour, the conference had been a triumph. The Dominions had been reassured and American friendship retained. Borden, the former Prime Minister of Canada, paid Balfour a handsome tribute in 1929, when he told Professor Stewart of Dartmouth College, Hanover, New Hampshire, that at the Washington Conference: 'The American Delegates were a very powerful aggregation. On the other hand, the immense prestige, wide experience and pre-eminent ability of Lord Balfour who headed the British Empire Delegation gave him a commanding influence.'[38] The British government valued Balfour's contribution no less, and he returned from Washington to be greeted at Waterloo Station by the Prime Minister and Cabinet. The bestowal of the Garter was followed, in May 1922, by an earldom.

But despite the favourable portents of the Washington naval agreements, Australia and New Zealand continued to feel disquiet at the growth of Japanese power in the Pacific. One way of alleviating these anxieties was to build a great British naval base at Singapore. The project had been discussed by the C.I.D., and had been approved at the Imperial Conference of 1921. During the Washington negotiations, Balfour had been made aware of the concern of the Australasian and Indian delegates that this plan should be implemented.[39]

But the first Labour government of 1924 suspended work at Singapore for reasons of economy. Balfour accordingly made an urgent appeal in the Lords in March 1924 for the establishment of this second base, apart from Britain, to give security to Australia and New Zealand whose 'whole scheme of political thought depends upon the idea that they are not bound to us by legal and constitutional ties, but that we are prepared . . . and I hope always shall be prepared – to throw every ounce of strength we possess to protect them in case of need.'[40]

Balfour believed firmly that 'the British Empire is . . . among other things, an arrangement for mutual protection, and it is unlimited in its character.' Therefore, although he subscribed to the objects of the League of Nations, and indeed headed the British delegation at the first meeting of the Assembly in November 1920, he put more trust in informal imperial ties. On 24 July 1924 he told the House of Lords:

There you have actually existing within the League not a treaty of mutual defence but a unity which gives mutual defence. Every member of this great Commonwealth of free communities knows that if it is attacked, every other member of the British Empire, without question, without delay, without raising any problems, national or international, will spend its last shilling in its defence. No mutual arrangement, no subsidiary league or treaty under the League of Nations can equal that in strength.[41]

This was a somewhat optimistic assessment of the mutual loyalties of a Commonwealth which included, in 1924, the newly independent and battle-scarred Irish Free State, and a South African government headed by the avowedly anti-British Hertzog. But perhaps imperial patriotism was strongest in the Antipodes, and could be stiffened by the establishment of the Singapore base. Balfour continued to argue the case for such a base throughout 1925. Ironically, despite the millions of pounds poured into the construction of the base at Singapore, it capitulated to the Japanese in 1942 after only a brief resistance. The surrender of this allegedly impregnable bastion for Australasia, involved the imprisonment of thousands of Australian and New Zealand troops.

But this disaster was not to be foreseen in the 1920s. Nor was Balfour unrealistic to applaud attempts to guarantee international peace, while insisting that the defences of the Empire must be maintained. Thus he praised the Treaty of Locarno in 1925 as 'one of the greatest steps ever taken to lift the community of nations out of the slough of difficulties . . . and to open for ourselves and for our posterity a happier era', while pressing for the strengthening of the navy.[42] In the same way he expressed high hopes in the League of Nations, yet considered Commonwealth loyalties to be more reliable safeguards.

Above all, Balfour remained convinced of the value of the C.I.D. as a body of infinite adaptability. It had also established an important precedent for inter-imperial co-operation. In March 1925, Balfour told Baldwin of a scheme, modelled on the C.I.D., which MacDonald's government had considered 'for organising and advising on many problems – economic, hygienic and scientific – which affect the different fractions of the Empire.'[43]

Moreover, in June 1926 Balfour made it clear that he opposed the creation of a single Minister of Defence on the grounds that:

The Committee of Imperial Defence does that work which no Minister of Defence could do . . . It is capable, as no other institution can be, of covering the whole ground by its Committees, dealing with questions the most disparate and the most complicated, and belonging to the most different spheres of activity. . . . Co-ordination is being given us, may more and more be given us, by the Committee of Imperial Defence.[44]

Balfour's connection with, and commitment to, the C.I.D. lasted until the end of his life. In this time he had seen the Committee grow from infancy until, in the late 1920s, it boasted fifty-one Subcommittees – thirty-eight Military and thirteen Civil.[45] When he at last retired from active politics in 1929, he was within one year of his death. Even so, Baldwin wrote to him on 25 May 1929 saying 'I hope you would not be averse from continuing your membership of the Committee of Imperial Defence which is your own child and would indeed feel an orphan without you.'[46] Given the past differences between Balfour and Baldwin, this tribute was a generous one and completely apt.

PART TWO

The Chamberlains and Tariff Reform

The peace of shocked Foundations flew
  Before his ribald questionings.
He broke the Oracles in two,
  And bared the paltry wires and strings.
He headed desert wanderings;
  He led his soul, his cause, his clan
A little from the ruck of Things.
  Once on a time there was a Man.
                    KIPLING, 1904
Things and the Man (In Memoriam, Joseph Chamberlain)

It is not by any means only the Fiscal Question upon which I differ from them (the Chamberlains). It is their whole way of looking at politics. It appears to me to be utterly sordid and materialistic, not yet corrupt but on the high road to corruption.
                    ROBERT CECIL to BALFOUR, 1906

6 Balfour and Chamberlain

The difference between Joe and me is the difference between youth and age:
I am age.

BALFOUR

I

ALTHOUGH Balfour and Chamberlain were the two giants of
Lord Salisbury's administration from 1895 to 1902, the differences
between them were singularly marked. Not only was Balfour the
Prime Minister's nephew and hence a scion of the house of Cecil,
he was also his political heir. Beneath a languid exterior Balfour
concealed a fine intelligence and a taste for philosophical speculation. Delighting in conversation, he relished any topic. But he
scorned demagoguery, tending to leave his audiences unmoved.
Equally, events of great moment seemed incapable of ruffling his
constant poise. Hardly a man of business, Balfour's last days were
clouded by the financial troubles of his once healthy inheritance.
He had ascended the Conservative hierarchy effortlessly. For him
there was no greasy pole, only an assured preferment.

Chamberlain entered the Unionist administration in 1895 with
boundless energy and a chequered political past. A Non-confor-
mist, he had made a fortune from the Birmingham screw-manu-
facturing firm of Chamberlain and Nettlefold. Thence he became
the radical, reforming mayor of Birmingham, sweeping aside the
worst abuses of industrialisation. Birmingham repaid him with a
loyalty which even the most violent of political contortions could
not shake. When he entered the House of Commons as a Radical
in 1876 Chamberlain took with him the reputation of a republican
and democrat. Passionately devoted to politics, he possessed

equally a businessman's shrewdness and an idealism which he sought to bolster with facts and figures as well as with appeals to the emotions. Above all, Chamberlain had style and dynamism, and with his eyeglass and his habitual orchid was an instantly recognisable figure. He could inspire love or hatred, but never indifference.

Yet this was the man who became Balfour's colleague in 1895. Having served in the Liberal government of 1880–5 as President of the Board of Trade, Chamberlain deserted Gladstone in 1886 over the issue of Home Rule for Ireland. Within nine years, the fiery radical who in 1883 had attacked Salisbury for constituting 'himself the spokesman of a class – a class to which he himself belongs, who toil not neither do they spin', had joined an administration headed by that same Salisbury.[1] Even in 1885 Balfour had called Chamberlain 'the most vindictive of men'.[2] But after the election of 1892 which removed the Conservatives from office, Balfour could not conceal his admiration for the way in which Chamberlain had maintained control of his Birmingham fief: 'You *do* know how to manage things in Birmingham. I never saw such smashing results.'[3]

Although some of his former colleagues assailed Chamberlain as a traitor and turncoat, he had as early as 1886 told Balfour, 'My Radicalism at all events desires to see established a strong government and an Imperial government.' Balfour thought that in Chamberlain the Conservatives would find, 'so long as he agrees with us, a very different ally from the lukewarm and slippery Whig, whom it is so difficult to differ from, and so impossible to act with.'[4] Chamberlain saw no contradiction in his advocacy of radical reform at home and imperial expansion overseas. Rather, the intelligent and businesslike ordering of the Empire's resources seemed to him the key to social change and material improvement in Britain. Repelled by socialist doctrines of nationalisation and welfare, Chamberlain preferred the old Radical virtues of thrift and self-help.

Without doubt, this explains Chamberlain's insistence on taking the Colonial Office in 1895 when the victorious Conservatives handed out spoils to their Radical and Liberal Unionist allies. He felt that the Birtish held the key to advancement in their own hands, but barely recognised the fact. If he could further closer unity between Britain and her colonies he would have made a tremendous contribution to sustaining his country in its world role. Chamberlain's choice of the Colonial Office surprised both Salisbury and Balfour. In view of Chamberlain's remarkable ability to deliver the votes of Birmingham and his talent for electoral organisation generally, he could have taken any major office save the Foreign Secretaryship, which Salisbury added to his responsibilities as Prime Minister. Indeed, Salisbury and Balfour offered Chamberlain both the Home Office and the Chancellorship of the Exchequer. But Chamberlain was resolute.[5]

Chamberlain's tenure of the Colonial Office from 1895 to 1903 made it the power-house of the Unionist administration. His irresistible and forceful personality caused 'a total transformation; the sleeping city awakened by a touch.'[6] Chamberlain's urgent assault on imperial problems, incorporated not only attempts to bring about greater co-operation between Britain and the self-governing colonies in the fields of defence, trade and organisation, but also the bid for supremacy in South Africa and the determination to divert investment and commercial initiative to neglected corners of the Empire.

He did not always carry the support of his colleagues with him. Balfour was hardly an ardent advocate of all of Chamberlain's enterprises. Indeed his passive and patient approach to the controversial imperial causes supported by Chamberlain was in marked contrast to the Colonial Secretary's sense of urgency. Perhaps Chamberlain had less time in which to achieve his ambitions than Balfour. In 1895 when he took only the second major office of his career Chamberlain was in his sixtieth year. In the same year Balfour was only 47 and had 34 years of active politics in front of him, whereas Chamberlain was to be crippled by a stroke in 1906. In these circumstances, it was fortunate for Chamberlain that he possessed such driving energy.

Balfour and Chamberlain were, of course, aware of their differences in temperament, and Chamberlain once said, 'Arthur hates difficulties: I love 'em.' Balfour put it more elegantly when he remarked. 'The difference between Joe and me is the difference between youth and age: I am age.'[7] More important than this was the question of whether the Unionist party could contain and satisfy 'Radical Joe', or whether he would burst the party open and leave it wrecked, as the Liberals had been wrecked by the events of 1886.

Certainly Chamberlain's methods were not Balfour's. In February 1898 the Colonial Secretary found Balfour disinclined to take strong action against the increase of foreign, especially Russian, influence in China. Britain's trade with China was tremendously important, and Chamberlain argued that, 'If matters remain as they are, our prestige will be gone and our trade will follow. I would not give a year's life to the Government under such conditions.'[8] Six months later, Chamberlain complained that Balfour 'was letting the Chinese off very easily after their treatment of us in the Pekin–Hankow contract ... I thought you meant to mark your displeasure.'[9]

Chamberlain was equally impetuous during the negotiations in the early part of 1898 for an Anglo-German alliance. Chamberlain put high hopes in such an alliance, even though his activities in Africa were not calculated to endear him to the Germans. Indeed, in April 1898 Balfour told Salisbury of a dinner-time discussion 'out of the nebulous friendliness of which I gather very little, except that the Germans did not at all like Joe's methods of procedure in Africa.'[10]

Salisbury even wondered whether Chamberlain wanted a war with France in order 'to push' the alliance with Germany.[11] Balfour, for his part, thought Chamberlain 'very impulsive', and described how the Colonial Secretary 'went very far in the expression of his own personal leaning towards a German alliance.'[12] Ironically, four months later, Chamberlain's impulsiveness came near to ending the delicate Anglo-German negotiations over the Portuguese African colonies. Anxious to seal off the Transvaal's access to the sea, and concerned lest Britain should surrender too much to Germany and so destroy the hypothetical extension of an imperial *zollverein* to Mozambique, Chamberlain's intransigence was far removed from his enthusiasms of April 1898. But in

August, Balfour had to resolve Chamberlain's doubts before he could conclude the agreement with Germany.[13]

With the approach of the Boer War, Balfour's cool appraisal of the *uitlander* problem had provided an antidote to Chamberlain's more bellicose arguments. Moreover in December 1899, with the war under way, the Colonial Secretary had once more shown concern over Portuguese East Africa. Balfour thought it sensible to offer to lease the Portuguese colonies for the duration of the war. But Chamberlain urged that if the Portuguese refused to lease, 'let them immediately declare war on the two Republics. We must of course be prepared to support them against attack and I like the idea of sending Indian troops for this purpose. I do not think it would be open to the same objections as bringing them into the Colonies.'[14] This ambitious scheme came to nothing.

2

Although Balfour and Chamberlain may have differed over methods, there were broad areas of policy where they were in accord. Both wanted greater co-operation between Britain and the self-governing colonies, even if they saw different ways of achieving this. Furthermore, both believed in the allegedly unique virtues of the Anglo-Saxon race. But here again, the emphasis was different. Chamberlain boasted, 'I have been called the apostle of the Anglo-Saxon race, and I am proud of the title . . . I think the Anglo-Saxon race is as fine as any on earth.'[15] This unambiguous race patriotism was not without its dangers, and Chamberlain could, on rare occasions, slip into anti-semitism.

Balfour, on the other hand, contented himself more with amused speculation on the Anglo-Saxon gift for 'muddling through' than with clarion calls for racial unity. Anti-semitism did not in the smallest degree enter his political philosophy. Indeed, he was an outstanding supporter of Zionism, and when in May 1930 he lay dying, his last visitor was his friend Chaim Weizmann whose cause Balfour had taken up long before and with such effect.[16] If the famous Balfour Declaration of 1917 and the mourning of Jewry in 1930 absolve Balfour of anti-semitism, Chamberlain can claim no such dispensation. Furthermore, his tariff reform campaign after his resignation of September 1903 was marked, in its later stages, by a distinct anti-foreigner emphasis.[17]

Less controversially, both men conceived Anglo-Saxon co-operation to include Anglo-American amity. As a private, though no doubt uncalculated, gesture of confidence in this ideal, Chamberlain took an American as his third bride in 1888. More to the point was his outspoken support of the United States during the war with Spain in 1898. From America an admirer congratulated Chamberlain on having 'revolutionised the political creeds of all American politicians, whose one watchword has so long been "our historical foe" – now "our one natural friend and ally". '[18]

Similarly, Balfour claimed to be the 'most earnest advocate of a harmonious co-operation between the two great Anglo-Saxon States.'[19] In 1905 he told Choate, the American ambassador in London, of his feeling 'that the two great co-heirs of Anglo-Saxon freedom and civilisation have a common mission.'[20] Though far removed from the more extravagant dreams of Cecil Rhodes, both Balfour and Chamberlain subscribed to the benefits of Anglo-Saxon co-operation.

In more practical terms, the Boer War brought Balfour and Chamberlain closer together. The Colonial Secretary was seen as the architect of war, and the fury of pro-Boers and Irish Nationalists was vented upon him. Chamberlain gave as good as he got. Nonetheless, Balfour consistently put his dextrous mind and his caustic parliamentary invective at his colleague's disposal. Chamberlain never forgot the support thus afforded.

Doubtless Balfour's path to the premiership was made some-what easier by the cordial relationship he had established with Chamberlain by the close of the Boer War. July 1902 seemed an appropriate time for Salisbury to retire. The Prime Minister's powers were in noticeable decline. He confessed to finding it increasingly difficult to stay awake during Cabinet meetings, and during one celebrated day at Sandringham in 1901, he not only picked up a photograph of the King, remarking pensively, 'Poor

Buller, what a mess he made of it', but also asked the King the identity of a clerical guest, to be told, 'Only the Bishop of London, whom you presented to me three months ago.'[21]

Despite the approach of senility, it had seemed appropriate for Salisbury to see the Boer War through. By 31 May the war was over. Well before this date, however, there had been speculation over the succession. None doubted that Balfour was the crown prince. His Cecil blood and the tribalism of the Conservative hierarchy ordained it. Moreover, since 1885 few had equalled his proximity to the sources of political power. But doubts remained. Was Balfour rugged enough to cope with the great problems facing Britain? Problems ranging from the need to reorganise imperial defence and end isolation, to the urgent necessity of combating the ever-strengthening challenge of German and American industry and commerce. Furthermore, in Britain the newly en-franchised masses were demanding overdue social reform. In an increasingly democratic age, how much of a democrat was Balfour?

While Balfour's reponse to these challenges was as yet largely unknown, Chamberlain's position was perfectly clear. Not only was he dedicated to social reform, but he had long since discerned the extent of Britain's commercial and industrial difficulties. What is more, he believed that in greater imperial unity he had discovered the remedy to revitalise a failing economy and ensure Britain a foremost place in the challenging twentieth century. Nor was he short of admirers, and in March 1902 *The African Review* described him as 'the man marked out by his qualities to lead the nation.'[22]

Of course, Chamberlain stood no chance of succeeding Salisbury. He had already helped wreck the Liberal party. His new allies were equally vulnerable. Moreover, many of the Conservatives and Whigs who now dominated the Unionist party were suspicious of his radical past and uneasy at his democratic style. The qualities that fitted him most for leadership in the new age, were the very ones to ensure that he would not become Unionist Prime Minister.

Chamberlain knew this. Moreover, he had made it plain that he would not challenge Balfour's right to succeed. He had told Sandars, Balfour's private secretary, that he was not a candidate, adding that 'he had always been most deeply touched by A.J.B.'s splendid and unselfish loyalty towards himself, and that every member of his family shared his feeling.'[23] On 11 July, the day Salisbury resigned, Chamberlain wrote reminding him of a conversation he had with Salisbury's heir, Lord Cranborne. 'I wished you to know', Chamberlain insisted, 'that if at any time you contemplated retirement my supposed ambition would not prevent me from giving to Arthur any support that it might be in my power to render.'[24]

Ironically, even if Chamberlain had planned a palace revolution to destroy Balfour's claims in the few days preceding Salisbury's resignation, he would have been unable to execute any such designs. On 7 July, the Colonial Secretary's head was badly cut in a cab accident and he was confined to bed. On 11 July he was still indisposed. Even so, Balfour thought it tactful to call on Chamberlain before accepting the King's invitation to form a government. Despite being asleep and under doctor's orders not to be disturbed, Chamberlain was woken up, and assured Balfour of his support.[25] But this ritualistic precaution did not guarantee future tranquillity, for in little more than a year, Chamberlain's tariff reform proposals had smashed Balfour's Cabinet and threatened the Unionists with electoral extinction.

3

The first rumblings of the tariff reform controversy had been heard in 1902 before Balfour became Prime Minister. Although the value of British exports had begun to rise again between 1899 and 1902, for nearly thirty years previously there had been alarming fluctuations. Moreover, by the end of the nineteenth century the once acknowledged industrial supremacy of Britain had been sorely tested. Not only had the United States and Germany taken enormous strides in industrial expansion, but they had proved eager to avail themselves of new techniques, often the products of intensive scientific research. By 1900, Germany's steel production had outstripped Britain's.[26]

Foreign salesmen were wresting traditional markets from

Britain, and even in the industrial Midlands German buttons and screws competed with their Birmingham equivalents. Furthermore, by 1900, Germany, France, the United States, Italy, Austria-Hungary and Russia had erected substantial tariff walls behind which their expanding industries flourished. Yet Britain clung to her free trade principles. The progress of mid-Victorian England had seemed to spring from the abandonment of protection in the 1840s. Britain had subsequently bought food for her increasing population and raw materials for her booming industries at the lowest price she could get. Correspondingly she had sold her manufactured goods for the best possible price to whoever would buy them. Free trade seemed to bring commercial success, and even the periods of economic stagnation in the last third of the century had not shaken the Liberals or the great majority of Conservatives from their faith. Nor had bouts of unemployment destroyed the working man's belief that free trade ensured cheap food. Long memories reached back to the 'hungry forties', to protection and want.

By 1902, however, Joseph Chamberlain had come to believe that some measure of tariff reform was essential. In the broader view, he hoped that by the establishment of a system of imperial preference the self-governing colonies would be encouraged to take a step nearer that imperial *zollverein* which Chamberlain had proposed unsuccessfully at the Colonial Conference of 1897. Nearer home was his conviction that his long-cherished scheme of old age pensions would be indefinitely deferred unless some means was found of raising extra revenue.

The heavy expense of the Boer War threatened the introduction of old age pensions, even more than the disapproval of Salisbury and Hicks Beach, the Chancellor, for such a radical measure. Unwilling to countenance a substantial increase in income tax, Chamberlain had proposed as early as 1894–5 that an import duty on wheat would defray the necessary expense of a pensions scheme.[27] On 14 April 1902, Hicks Beach announced in his budget speech that he planned to revive the registration duty of 3d cwt on imported corn and 5d cwt on imported meal and flour.[28]

What did this mean? Hicks Beach was a convinced free trader who believed in Gladstonian principles of economic husbandry.

He made it perfectly clear that the new duty was for the sole purpose of raising revenue to pay for the Boer War debts. But in Canada, Prime Minister Wilfrid Laurier claimed optimistically that 'a step had ... been taken that would make it possible to obtain preference for Canadian goods.'[29] In other words, perhaps Canadian wheat would be allowed to enter Britain without being subject to the new duty. This would be a belated reward for the raising of Canadian tariffs against foreign manufacturers in 1897 and 1900, which had the effect of giving Britain a preference of $33\frac{1}{3}$ per cent by 1900. Canada had still taxed British goods, but less heavily than those of the foreigner. In view of the firm protectionism of the self-governing colonies, the Canadian gesture was not without promise and had even moved Kipling to write commemorative verse.

On 16 May 1902, Chamberlain encouraged speculation on this score by announcing:

If by adherence to economic pedantry, to old shibboleths, we are to lose opportunities of closer union which are offered us by our colonies ... if we do not take every chance in our power to keep British trade in British hands, I am certain that we shall deserve the disasters which will infallibly come upon us.[30]

In this context 'economic pedantry' could only mean free trade. Moreover, shortly afterwards in July 1902 the Colonial Conference met in London. Chamberlain was bound to take this opportunity to reiterate his arguments for imperial preference – and this time the corn tax provided something to surrender as part of a bargain. Naturally this had been anticipated by the Cabinet, and on 30 June Gerald Balfour, President of the Board of Trade and Balfour's younger brother, had presented an elaborate document entitled 'Memorandum on Preferential Trade Arrangements with the Colonies'. The document had warily reiterated the familiar arguments against an imperial *zollverein*, notably that imperial trade only accounted for one third of the British total. How would Britain find compensation for the losses in foreign trade which would certainly accompany a policy of protection? But, more controversially, the memorandum suggested that Britain 'for the sake of the Imperial idea ... might ... concede reciprocity on existing duties or upon duties in the future imposed for revenue purposes.'[31]

Thus fortified, Chamberlain approached the Colonial Conference in July. Discussion revealed that serious difficulties remained in the way of achieving an imperial *zollverein*. Rather than lowering their duties on British goods, the best the self-governing colonies seemed able to offer were the advantages from still higher tariffs against the foreigner. However, with the corn tax in mind, the Canadian delegation showed interest in a limited reciprocal agreement – an exchange of gifts.

Mildly encouraged by the colonial response which tended to confirm his previously formed opinions, Chamberlain proposed at a Cabinet meeting of 21 October that the corn duty should be remitted in the case of the self-governing colonies.[32]

This was hardly heresy, and Balfour immediately told the King, 'There is a very great deal to be said in favour of this proposal. ... But it raises very big questions indeed – colonial and fiscal – and the Government which embarks upon it provokes a big fight. On the whole Mr Balfour leans towards it; but it behoves us to walk warily.'[33]

But although Balfour was no die-hard free trader, he had not seen fit, on Hicks Beach's resignation in July 1902, to send a more open-minded successor to the Treasury. C. T. Ritchie, the new Chancellor, was a staunch free trader who disagreed with the Cabinet's proposal, in November, to make a remission on the corn tax in favour of the colonies, on the grounds that he could not commit the Treasury to such a policy so long before the budget. While Ritchie sought for delay, Chamberlain was sure that the Chancellor would introduce the recommended preference at a later date. Believing that Ritchie had been overruled, Chamberlain left for his trip to South Africa 'with an easy conscience'.[34]

4

Chamberlain was in South Africa from November 1902 until March 1903. One of his biographers has stated that Chamberlain made this trip 'virtually the condition of his remaining in the Cabinet'.[35] This is debatable. At any rate, Balfour positively encouraged Chamberlain's plans, telling him on 4 October 1902 that he was 'sure it would do a great deal of good to the Colony; and you certainly deserve something in the nature of a rest and a change of scene.'[36] Moreover, since Balfour was still playing himself in as Prime Minister, the absence of the most dynamic and volatile member of the Cabinet was not without its immediate advantages.

Chamberlain returned from his Roman triumph inspired, but listless and irritable.[37] Worse still, he discovered that a fortnight before his return Ritchie had shown his true colours and told Balfour that he could not be responsible for a budget which introduced a measure of imperial preference. As a further blow, the Chancellor demanded the abandonment of the corn tax and threatened resignation unless he had his way.[38] Rather than lose Ritchie a few days before the budget, Balfour gave way, but only after two Cabinet meetings had discussed the matter. Accordingly, the budget of 23 April 1903 swept away the corn tax. Ritchie and free trade orthodoxy seemed triumphant.

Chamberlain had reason to feel betrayed. Ritchie had been in a minority of two when the Cabinet had agreed in November 1902 to introduce a preference on corn. Now he had employed the crudest methods to avoid implementing this decision. Admittedly the Cabinet had not been precise about details, but the spirit had been clear. Balfour, towards the end of his life, confessed that:

Joe was ill-used by the Cabinet. We had discussed the principle of taxing food-stuffs before he left the country, and he certainly had a right to suppose that the bulk of the Cabinet were in favour of a shilling duty on corn, or some analogous small tax. That was my impression, and I was perfectly horrified at what happened.[39]

Nonetheless, Balfour had managed to preserve the appearance of Cabinet unity. Ritchie had not resigned, nor had Chamberlain. However, Balfour was convinced that Ritchie was completely under the control of the Treasury officials Mowatt and E. Hamilton. The Chancellor could not be expected to budge, even though the majority of his colleagues, including Balfour, were anxious to consider the desirability of fiscal reform. Nor had it been expedient to accept Ritchie's resignation, although Gerald Balfour had urged this course. Further time had been bought by the Cabinet's decision, when considering Ritchie's ultimatum over the budget, to use the summer of 1903 to investigate fiscal reform thoroughly.[40]

But this was to assume that Chamberlain would not speak out on a theme he considered so vital to the future prosperity of the Empire. Having been worsted by the second-rate Ritchie, and convinced that time was short, such forbearance on his part was unlikely. In his fears for Britain's economic survival, Chamberlain was not merely a prophet of doom. Nor, despite Birmingham being hard-hit by German competition, was he simply a selfish local politician with his eye on the Midlands' vote. The Boer War would not be the last great cause to empty the Treasury. The heightening tension of naval competition would call for enormous and continuous expenditure.

Without a reappraisal of free trade dogmas Chamberlain felt that the British economy could not fully deal with these problems, and could certainly not sustain the social reforms which he considered essential. Moreover, his South African trip may have enlarged his vision of an Empire that, 'If we chose . . . might be self-sustaining; it is so wide, its products are so various; its climates so different that there is absolutely nothing which is necessary to our existence, hardly anything which is desirable as a luxury which cannot be produced within the boundaries of the Empire itself.'[41]

Within a month of Ritchie's budget with its reaffirmation of free trade orthodoxy, Chamberlain had launched his counter-attack.

7 Cabinet Crisis, Party Discord

Now I am, and always have been a free-trader.

BALFOUR, 1903

You encouraged my father to go out as 'a pioneer'; you gave your blessing to his efforts for closer union with the colonies.

AUSTEN CHAMBERLAIN to BALFOUR, 1904

I

ON 15 May 1903 Chamberlain delivered a controversial speech, choosing as his platform Birmingham town hall. Unwilling to accept Ritchie's recent triumph as a permanent set-back, the Colonial Secretary now called for a new definition of free trade. He deplored the fate of the corn tax and, while denying that he was a protectionist, he argued that the British people faced an entirely new economic situation. The choice before them was whether 'it is better to cultivate the trade with your own people or to let that go in order that you may keep the trade of those who ... are your competitors.'[1]

The impact of this speech was tremendous. Leo Amery, who had served with Milner in South Africa, and was to become one of Chamberlain's most ardent supporters, called the speech 'a challenge to free thought as direct and provocative as the theses which Luther nailed to the church door at Wittenberg.'[2] But the Liberals were also delighted. Their divided party could at least rally in the sacred cause of free trade. Asquith, indeed, thought the speech 'wonderful news ... it is only a question of time when we shall sweep this country.'[3]

Chamberlain provided the Liberals with fresh ammunition in two Commons debates on 22 and 28 May. On the first occasion,

Lloyd George taunted him with abandoning old age pensions, and he replied that funds might be available after 'a review of that fiscal system which I have indicated as necessary and desirable at an early day.'[4] This was merely a reaffirmation of the government's intention to investigate the fiscal system that summer. However, the implications of this statement were clear. Food taxes could conjure up the cry of 'dear bread', and could swing the masses away from the party that introduced them. Dearer food would bring destruction at the polls. Unionist opinion was already disturbed, and Balfour went out of his way to reassure the young free trader Winston Churchill on 26 May 1903:

I have never understood that Chamberlain advocated protection, though, no doubt, he is ready – and indeed anxious – for a duty on food stuffs, which may incidentally be protective . . . but whose main object is to provide an instrument for fiscal union with the Colonies – a very different thing.[5]

On 28 May, Balfour and Chamberlain spoke in the Commons. Replying to Opposition fears that a fiscal revolution and food taxes were imminent, Balfour called for open minds, defended Chamberlain for 'ventilating the question', and reiterated the Cabinet's decision to carry out an investigation into the subject. But Chamberlain went much further. He made no concessions to either his colleagues or his opponents. Rather, he emphasised the opportunity to draw closer to the self-governing colonies. As for dearer food, Chamberlain recognised that the working class would have to bear most of the cost of imperial preference, but he dangled before them the bait of social reform.[6]

Clearly, Chamberlain was not content to wait for a leisurely, and perhaps inconclusive, government investigation. Contemplating an early election, he was determined to strike as soon as possible. The electorate, not the Cabinet, should decide. His provocative attitude ruffled Balfour's tranquillity. The Prime Minister was determined not to hustle his party into internecine debate. Indeed, the day before Chamberlain's outburst, a Cabinet meeting on 27 May had resulted, Balfour told the King, in 'a long and inconclusive discussion' on imperial preference. Although he thought

THE ZOLLVEREIN CAKE-WALK

Old Joe a-kicking up behind and before,

there was much to be said for the scheme, Balfour still felt that it was 'most imprudent to attempt to "rush it", either in the Cabinet or in the Country.'[7]

In August 1903, Balfour was to recall bitterly Chamberlain's two speeches of 22 and 28 May. Writing to the Duke of Devonshire, a free trader whose unimpeachable political and social respectability made him an ornament of the Unionist administration, Balfour said:

Neither of these speeches was the least necessary. The first was a distinct violation of an arrangement come to with me, while the second was a quite gratuitous challenge both to his colleagues and the world after what I had myself said in the course of the same debate at an earlier hour. It is these two utterances which have caused most of the soreness and suspicion which have been so unhappily aroused in connection with this subject, and for neither of them was there, in my opinion, justification or excuse.[8]

During the summer of 1903, tension mounted. Not only were the Liberals girding themselves for combat, but it was evident that the Unionists were drifting into civil war. Balfour was naturally anxious to keep the Cabinet together, and hoped that ministers would keep an open mind over tariff reform. But this was wishful thinking. A head-on collision could hardly be avoided between Chamberlain and the irreconcilable free traders, Ritchie, Hamilton and Balfour of Burleigh. Moreover, there was Devonshire, whose comforting presence Balfour wished to retain.

In the country, Unionist free traders and tariff reformers were staking out their positions. On 1 July fifty-four Unionist M.P.'s inaugurated the Free Food League. In practice, this organisation was somewhat weak and lacking in funds, but it at least put pressure on Balfour. On 16 July he wrote to his cousin Lord Hugh Cecil, one of the leaders of the Free Food League, telling him that 'the serious mistake into which I think you have fallen is that of supposing that the Unionist Party were put into office for the purpose of preserving, in every particular, a version of Free Trade doctrine which . . . I, at all events, have never accepted.'[9]

But if Balfour settled for agnosticism, the Tariff Reform League was decidely evangelistic. The League held its first

WHEEL AND WOE

Balfour attempts to steer a middle course

meeting on 21 July, three weeks after the foundation of its rival, the Free Food League. Nothing could have been more striking than the contrasting organisation of the two Leagues. The Free Fooders were an adamant but weakly body. The Tariff Reform League, however, marshalled beneath its banners captains of industry, aristocratic Tory landlords, the bulk of the Unionist M.P.s, the *Daily Express*, and survivors of the protectionist National Free Trade League. It made a determined bid to proselytise trade union leaders and the workers.[10] Moreover, it had the inspiration of Chamberlain, and after his resignation from the Cabinet in September, his full-time leadership.

Balfour could not remain inactive while the free trade and tariff reform stalwarts fought for control of the party. In a memorandum entitled *Economic Notes on Insular Free Trade* which he put before the Cabinet on 1 August 1903, Balfour hoped to paper over the widening cracks in his ministry. While displaying his basic independence of both groups of campaigners, Balfour plumped for the comparatively uncontroversial policy of retaliation. Retaliation involved taking discriminatory fiscal measures to protect the self-governing colonies from the coercive commercial activities of foreign countries.[11]

At the same time as he espoused retaliation, Balfour advocated that all should keep an open mind on the subject of tariff reform. But if unsettled convictions appealed to Balfour, they were no universal panacea. Nonetheless, the Prime Minister made a brave attempt to list the points on which there was general Cabinet agreement. These included retaliation, and the feeling that 'if a tax is otherwise sufficiently desirable, the mere fact that it carries with it some flavour of Protection is by no means a conclusive reason against it.'[12]

Balfour also believed that there was 'unanimity in the Cabinet as to the desirability of knitting our somewhat loosely connected Empire more closely together, not merely in matters political but in matters commercial also.' This pious generality was reinforced by the specific argument that if a disappointed Canada withdrew her preference, this might lead 'to an ultimate fiscal alliance with the U.S.A., which would certainly mean dependence on her powerful neighbour, and might possibly mean something even more unstaisfactory.' If nothing was done, Balfour felt that 'these contingencies are not only probable; they are almost inevitable.'[13]

Balfour had made a bid for the middle ground. Acutely aware of the echoes of the old Corn Law controversy and cries of 'dear bread', he denied that any food tax was contemplated simply for protective purposes. If a food tax was incidentally used for a preferential tariff, it 'should be so framed so as to avoid any material increase in the budget of working men, whether artisans or agricultural labourers.' Balfour summed up his position thus:

Now I am, and always have been a free-trader, though I do not share the loudly-expressed opinions of many who proclaim themselves members of the same company. Being a free-trader I should greatly regret to see a reversion to the policy of Protection, which I think wrong fiscally, and very inconvenient politically; inconvenient I mean because it subjects the Government of the day to pressure from every interest which conceives itself to be threatened even by the most legitimate competition.[14]

Unfortunately, Balfour's balancing act could not satisfy the Chamberlainites or reassure the free traders. The less perceptive were merely confused by the *Economic Notes*. 'One of my colleagues,' Balfour wrote to Lady Elcho on 9 August, 'who is *not* going to leave me, frankly admits that he can make neither head nor tail of it!!' Clearly Balfour was thinking in terms of resignations, for he continued:

At one time I thought I should keep Devonshire. . . . Now however I think I shall lose him, and with him, of course, all the waverers. As I understand D's position he does not disagree with *me*: but thinks that Joe will push us all into a further and less tenable position. Why not wait and see?[15]

There was not much longer to wait. The fiscal inquiry of the summer could not be continued indefinitely. A Cabinet meeting of 13 August failed to agree on a fiscal policy, and a final decision was postponed until the next meeting on 14 September. Balfour found the prospects gloomy, telling the King on 14 August that 'Mr Balfour does not feel justified in entertaining any confident hope that he will retain the co-operation of all his colleagues for the scheme he himself favours. . . . But if (as he does not doubt) Mr Chamberlain shows a readiness to accept Mr Balfour's scheme and to modify some of the plans which he has from time to time put forward rather hastily, Mr Balfour is of the opinion that the majority of the Cabinet will support him.'[16] Balfour was evidently prepared to lose the free trade ministers if he could persuade Chamberlain to modify his position. Although the latter event was unlikely, the Prime Minister actually went out of his way to ensure the resignation of the free traders.

2

Balfour had already provoked the free trade ministers by putting two documents before the Cabinet on 13 August. In addition to his *Economic Notes*, which were a hazy compound of reassurance and mild fiscal radicalism, there was a Treasury memorandum which discussed the advantages of preferential tariffs and food taxes without necessarily advocating them. Ritchie, Lord George Hamilton, Balfour of Burleigh and Devonshire were alarmed by this second document.[17] They spent the intervening period before the vital Cabinet meeting of 14 September in consultation and the preparation of their own defence.

On 9 September Chamberlain also took action. He wrote a letter of resignation to Balfour explaining that ever since his speech of 15 May, he had been intent on raising 'a question of the greatest national and Imperial importance'. Deploring the subsequent show of faction in the Unionist party, Chamberlain felt that, while remaining absolutely loyal to Balfour's government, he could best promote his heart-felt cause from outside the Cabinet.[18]

Balfour made no immediate response. An hour before the Cabinet meeting of 14 September he managed to meet Chamberlain, and gathered that the Colonial Secretary would certainly go if all hope of preferential duties vanished. Balfour still felt that a food tax was not practical politics.[19] In the Cabinet meeting Chamberlain threatened to resign. Since his colleagues were used

'MUM'S THE WORD'

Going to the Cabinet Council (14 September 1903)

to such demonstrations from the Colonial Secretary, they were comparatively unmoved. Some took him to be serious, some did not. Balfour did not dispel the confusion. Rather, he made no mention of Chamberlain's letter of resignation, thus keeping his colleagues in ignorance.

Next, Balfour turned on Ritchie and Balfour of Burleigh and virtually drummed them out of the Cabinet for the unrepentent free trade memoranda they had submitted. On 15 September, Hamilton resigned also. Three days later, Balfour announced the resignations not only of Ritchie and Hamilton, but also of Chamberlain. Balfour of Burleigh's resignation was made known later. The free trade ministers subsequently expressed indignation that they had not been informed of Chamberlain's letter of resignation.[20] Clearly, their position had been completely undermined by Balfour's silence. In a word, he was glad to get rid of them, even though he still hoped to keep the Duke of Devonshire. But the Duke was torn with doubt and indecision. He resigned, then withdrew his resignation when he knew that Chamberlain had gone, only to resign finally at the beginning of October after Balfour had stated his fiscal policy in a speech at Sheffield on 1 October. Balfour resented the Duke's final desertion, especially after he had gone to some lengths to retain him. But at least the adamant free traders had been cut out of the Cabinet.

More mystery surrounds Chamberlain's departure. Both Balfour and Chamberlain doubted the realism of the other's plans for fiscal reform. But if Balfour aimed for moderation and at least the semblance of Cabinet unity, Chamberlain's titanic energies threatened to burst such restrictions. Balfour's interests were best served by giving Chamberlain his blessing for the tariff reform crusade. If the electorate were converted, Balfour would benefit. If Chamberlain failed, at least he would have failed outside the Cabinet.

The circumstances of Chamberlain's departure indicated a bargain with Balfour. Esher even called it an intrigue. Certainly Balfour was anxious that Chamberlain should be seen to remain close to the government. No more obvious token of such amity was possible than the promotion of Austen Chamberlain in the place of Ritchie, the fallen Chancellor. At the Treasury a tariff reformer and a Chamberlain replaced a free trader and an anti-Chamberlainite. Austen Chamberlain would keep communications open between his campaigning father and the Prime Minister. Indeed, Austen even went so far as to persuade a doubtful Arnold-Forster that he would not be acquiescing in the abandonment of Joseph Chamberlain's fiscal policies if he remained in the Cabinet.[21]

Austen's enthusiasm was to evaporate within the next year in face of Balfour's refusal to abandon his chosen middle ground in the tariff controversy. In August 1904 Austen wrote to Balfour reproachfully, 'You encouraged my father to go out as "a pioneer"; you gave your blessing to his efforts for closer union with the colonies.'[22] This evidence of collusion is reinforced by a letter written by Mrs Chamberlain to Alice Balfour on 11 October 1903:

It costs my husband a strong pang to sever his official connections with him [Balfour], but he, and we all are happy in the thought that though they are no longer colleagues they are not separated in sympathy and friendship, & we hope that it will prove that under present circumstances the help that he can give from outside may be more efficacious than from [inside?]. After the splendid reception in Glasgow after the Sheffield meeting I think we have every reason to believe that will be the case.[23]

Mrs Chamberlain evidently considered Balfour's Sheffield speech and her husband's Glasgow speech to be the opening salvos of a joint campaign. However, the shots were not necessarily aimed at the same targets. Chamberlain's Glasgow speech was decidedly protectionist. Balfour's speech on 1 October at Sheffield was more ambiguous. Admittedly, he regretted the introduction of protection into the self-governing colonies, and argued that the British Empire in order to compete with other great empires 'must bind in bonds of reality, bonds substantial as well as sentimental, these great communities which own with us a common Sovereign.'[24] This was not far removed from Chamberlain's call at Glasgow for 'the maintenance and increase of the national strength and prosperity of the United Kingdom', and 'the consolidation of the British race'.[25]

However, Chamberlain insisted that food taxes were necessary.

Balfour did not think that public opinion was ready for such measures, although he condemned exaggerated and illogical reaction to any mention of food taxation. Moreover Balfour had no wish to tamper with the fiscal autonomy of the self-governing colonies. Practically, he advocated the policy of retaliation while displaying enough radicalism to be able to answer in the affirmative the rhetorical question, 'Do you desire to reverse the fiscal tradition, to alter fundamentally the fiscal tradition which has prevailed during the last two generations?'[26]

The Sheffield speech was hardly a crystal clear exposition of Balfour's policy, although it illustrated accurately his dilemma. But protectionists would demand more surrender to their cause, while the free traders would continue to feel misgivings. Conscious of the various interpretations which could be put upon his statements, Balfour helpfully produced a guide for ministerial speech-making entitled *Speeches on Fiscal Policy*. This memorandum was placed before the Cabinet on 13 October. It was a curious document, and contained several 'pious opinions, which might legitimately be entertained by Members of the Administration.' Among the 'pious opinions' were the necessity of fiscal reform, the liberty to threaten and enforce retaliation, and the political impracticability of food taxes. At the same time, Balfour confessed that there 'may be some of my colleagues (I do not know whether there are) to whom Protection, in the true sense of the word, commends itself.'[27]

Whether this clarified the position for the Cabinet is doubtful. In the constituencies, Balfour's real policy seemed equally obscure. His cousin Robert Cecil, a leading free trader, wrote on 5 November to Sandars, Balfour's secretary, to express his mystification:

The P.M. has stated ... that he is a free trader & advocates Retaliation as a means towards freer trade. This does not appear to be Chamberlain's understanding of Retaliation at all. He preaches economic doctrine indistinguishable from Protection. He also advocates Preference to the Colonies by arguments some of which are very startling ... and you will know that J. Chamberlain in more than one speech has stated that in the 'Retaliation' part of the policy he & Mr Balfour are of one mind.[28]

By the beginning of 1904 more dangerous signs emerged. Brodrick warned Balfour that, from his letters, Chamberlain seemed 'to be going further every day'.[29] Moreover, in the Spring Chamberlain captured control of the powerful Liberal Unionist Association from the free traders. Ominously, by-election results showed a uniform trend against the government.[30]

The Unionist party was in disarray. Chamberlain's campaign, especially if it began to fail, was likely to drift further towards outright protection. As for Balfour's espousal of retaliation, it was a half-hearted measure, which would deceive neither free traders nor tariff reformers. Campbell-Bannerman had some trenchant, though not discontented, thoughts on his opponent's difficulties in November, 1903:

But J. C. appears to have missed the mark owing to his over-statement of his case; vacillating argument; inaccuracy.

The contemptible person is the 1st L. of Treasury – never was anything more immoral, dishonest and unconstitutional, than the rigging up of retaliation as a formal policy while proclaiming adhesion to Joe's.[31]

In the Commons in March 1904, Balfour took part in a remarkable scene with Asquith and the dismissed Lord George Hamilton. Hamilton insisted that Balfour had placed two documents on fiscal reform before the fateful Cabinet meetings in August and September 1903. Balfour denied that the document which had so disturbed the free trader had been put before the Cabinet on 14 September. A little before this, he had not admitted that there had been two fiscal statements at either meeting. Asquith persisted:

> If one was produced in August, there it was. At any rate it was not withdrawn.
>
> *Balfour:* But it was not there.
> *Asquith:* Well, but it was there in August.
> *Balfour:* Yes.

Amid Opposition laughter, Balfour went on to claim that his fiscal policies were 'as precise as language could make them'.[32]

In March and May further attempts were made in the Commons to extract some firm or incriminating statement from Balfour.

George Hamilton grew apocalyptic on the menace of the flame lit by Chamberlain, which neither he nor Balfour could now quench. He described the Unionists as rent from top to bottom, and prophesied that at the election 'the heaviest defeat on record awaits the Unionist Party.' In reply, Balfour could only flourish his 'Sheffield programme', and apologise for his obscurity in defining his fiscal doctrines.[33]

3

The summer recess of Parliament brought Balfour little respite. Austen Chamberlain had grown restive at the very real differences that had been revealed between his father and Balfour. Believing that the Unionists could not possibly win the next election, Austen wanted to bridge the yawning gap between Balfour and Chamberlain and plan in terms of winning the election after next. He also proposed that Balfour should announce that if returned to power he would summon a conference of colonial and Indian delegates to discuss imperial trade. This, if successful, would serve to resolve Balfour's own doubts and would command sufficient support in Parliament.[34]

To add point to this request for constructive action, Austen wrote:

You encouraged my father to go out as 'a pioneer'; you gave your blessing to his efforts for closer union with the colonies; you assured us who remained that we too thus served the interests of Imperial union & we were thus induced to leave him for the time almost single handed in his herculean task. He undertook this work believing in our sympathy, believing that when he had proved that the obstacles were not insuperable, you and your Govt. would be prepared to make some advance.[35]

This contained more than a hint of special pleading. If the tariff reform was succeeding, Chamberlain did not need bridges. Sandars, Balfour's secretary, thought that 'Joe has failed. . . . Austen's letter shows that he knows he has, and he wants to save what he can at some price. Why should we damage ourselves by paying that price?' Sandars also denied that Balfour had encouraged Chamberlain to go pioneering: 'Joe was anxious to get out of office. Evidence of this is overwhelming. Having decided to retire all you could do was to wish him success.'[36]

Nonetheless, Balfour had to reply to this challenge. He delayed an answer for a fortnight, and then wrote only two days before Austen left for an Italian holiday. Although he stuck firmly to his Sheffield programme, Balfour agreed that it would be sensible to summon a Colonial Conference to discuss the whole question. But he proposed that the government should then seek to commend any satisfactory proposals to the party and the country. Moreover, he insisted on a 'free' Conference:

The Imperial and Colonial question thus dealt with to be explicitly disassociated from protection (*true* protection) with which indeed it has no connection, logical or sentimental: – protection to remain what it has long been, a doctrine largely held in the party but with no place in its official creed.[37]

Lest this should fail to revive the dying hopes of the Chamberlains, Balfour strove to find common ground. Although he believed that his 'plan', based on the imprecise Sheffield speech, was the best for encouraging imperial unity, he admitted that it differed 'perhaps from some suggestions which he [Joseph Chamberlain] has thrown out from time to time in the course of his Imperial propaganda':

But unless I am much mistaken these suggestions are not of the essence of his policy, but are in the nature of (as the schoolmen would have said) more or less 'separable accidents'. What he has fought for, what he has done more than any man to promote, is *Union* – fiscal union, military union, naval union, Union in short, of every kind which is compatible with the self-government of the free Colonies.[38]

Austen Chamberlain was not deceived, telling Balfour on 12 September 1904, 'Our differences are ... greater than I had thought or you had supposed.' Believing that colonial preference was 'the greatest object to which we in our time can devote ourselves', Austen condemned Balfour's policy as wrong. Nor did he see how, if Balfour persisted, they could come into line for the next election. He accused Balfour of spurning a compromise which would have been acceptable to Joseph Chamberlain. As for the prospective Colonial Conference, Austen issued a ringing call for vigour and determination. The 'timid' colonial statesmen must be inspired: 'If *we* show doubt & hesitation we are lost & with us goes the last chance of the permanent union of that Greater Britain of which we are still the centre and the heart.'[39]

This apostolic fervour brought a cold response from Balfour. He believed that 'our differences (if they are to be called differences) are neither as great or as irreconcileable as you suppose. Time will show it.'[40] But his next public pronouncement at Edinburgh on 3 October was basically a reiteration of the 'Sheffield programme'. Even the one innovation, the double election plan, did not commend itself to the Chamberlains. Indeed, Austen had already resisted Balfour's advocacy of the scheme in their exchanges of September. The double election meant that the Unionists would go to the polls without any precise fiscal proposals, but pledged to summon a full and free Colonial Conference if they were returned to power. If this Conference was able to agree on a satisfactory formula for tariff reform, the proposals would then be submitted to the test of a second election before any action was taken.

Balfour's double election scheme at least possessed the merit of optimism. By October 1904 few would have staked a penny on a Unionist victory in the first, let alone the second, election. But the proposal also illustrated the ingenuity of Balfour's speculative mind. When he chose, he could express himself with extraordinary clarity. On other occasions, he could spin a cocoon of paraphrase, qualification and ambiguity around the most fundamental issue, and remove it from the level of plain speaking to the often confusing heights of metaphysics. The double election scheme was yet another protective tissue. Under its shelter, Balfour could resist specific concessions to the Chamberlains.

The Chamberlains made the best of the Edinburgh speech. Robert Cecil was worried by their apparent enthusiasm, and told Balfour on 7 December 1904 that the tariff reformers were 'going about all over the country saying A.J.B.'s policy is but the first step to J.C.'s, that in substance they are the same, and that his declaration against Protection only meant that duties should not be imposed "for the purpose of" Protection.' Robert Cecil wanted a clear rejection of these interpretations.[41]

But Balfour was not prepared to make clear statements on tariff reform. By November 1904, Joseph Chamberlain had perceived that the Prime Minister was trying 'to "wriggle" about the meaning of the Edinburgh speech.'[42] Moreover, although Balfour still sought to cast a magic veil of ambiguity over the controversy, there were real and fundamental differences between himself and Chamberlain. The last year of the Unionist administration was to reveal these differences unmistakably.

8 Disunity and Annihilation

For you to be defeated and for Joe to get in would be, in my view, the greatest electoral disaster that could occur to us.

ROBERT CECIL to BALFOUR, January 1906

I

DESPITE Chamberlain's differences with Balfour, the Tariff Reform League campaigned with undiminished vigour throughout 1905. Determined to allay the fears of working men, the tariff reformers had hit upon the slogan 'Tariff Reform Means Work for All'. An enormous flood of leaflets and pamphlets were produced. Doorstep canvassers argued the League's case from house to house, while, more conveniently, Chamberlain's recorded voice was heard in hundreds of small halls and meeting houses. Tariff reform songs enlivened the music halls, and the public was regaled with poetical exhortation:

> When wealth and mirth refill the earth,
> Let each man tell his neighbour,
> All this we owe to Chamberlain!
> Hurrah! Hurrah! Hurrah![1]

This was grass-roots, democratic campaigning in the American fashion. Indeed, Chamberlain's voice had been put on record in imitation of the successful use Grover Cleveland had made of the gramophone in the United States. But though this democratic style might suit radical Joe, it would have ill become Unionist aristocrats like Balfour, Lansdowne, Curzon or the Cecil brothers. Both Balfour and Robert Cecil professed alarm at Chamberlain's methods, Balfour even accusing him 'of bribing each class of the

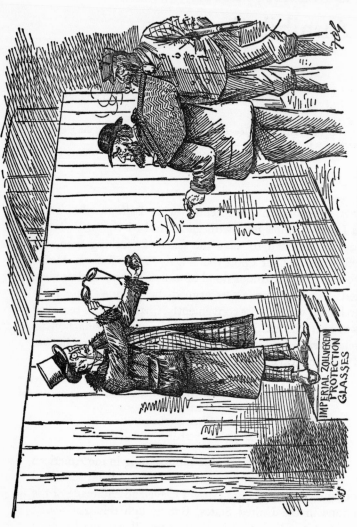

SPECTACULAR DECEPTION

JOE: Now then, gents, you may think this loaf is a little 'un, but you just look at it through these patent Imperial Protection double magnifying spectacles.

THE WORKING MAN: That's all very well, mister, but we want to *eat* the loaf, not to look at it.

community in turn'.[2] Robert Cecil wrote scathingly of the Chamberlains after the electoral disaster of 1906, 'It is not by any means only the Fiscal Question upon which I differ from them. It is their whole way of looking at politics. It appears to me to be utterly sordid and materialistic, not yet corrupt but on the high road to corruption.'[3]

Worse still, Chamberlain's Tariff Reform League threatened the Unionist organisation at constituency level. By the end of 1904 Chamberlain had not only captured control of the Liberal Unionist Association, but his Tariff Reform League branches in the constituencies rivalled the Conservative National Union. He had even suggested, though without success, that a representative of the Tariff Reform League should be placed in the Central Office.[4] These challenges reinforced Balfour's misgivings over the direction of Chamberlain's campaign.

The Prime Minister was also sceptical as to how far the self-governing colonies were prepared to make gaps in their tariff walls for Britain's benefit.[5] Ever since Germany had withdrawn her most-favoured-nation treatment from Canada in 1897, trade had continued to increase between the two countries. Between 1897 and 1902 annual German exports to Canada increased in value from $6,493,368 to $10,919,994, while Canadian exports to Germany rose from $764,589 to $1,298,654.[6] Chamberlain, however, was convinced of Canadian enthusiasm for imperial preference, and told Balfour that at the Colonial Conference of 1902 the Canadian delegates 'had already begun to discuss with the Board of Trade the possibility of reconsidering and altering in our favour their existing tariff.'[7] But despite distinct Canadian interest, it is at least arguable that the Canadian delegates saw a trade agreement with Britain mainly as an encouragement for other countries to offer them reciprocal tariffs.

Australian attitudes were no less business-like. Northcote, the Governor-General, made this plain to Balfour, telling him in August 1904 that:

The most that can be said of Australian sentiment is that they would rather sell to the Mother country than to a foreigner, if they can get as much for their article. Sentiment will come in again if we are landed in another war; but not in matters of business. Of course if we are prepared to give Australia a pull over foreign countries in matters commercial they will respond, and, if we give them a shilling, they will, or may, give us 10 pence.[8]

Although Deakin was 'a fanatical Chamberlainite', Northcote told Balfour three months later that Australian 'public sentiment is in favour of building up the Tariff wall higher against the foreigners, rather than lowering it against the Englishman. This can be of little use to us. . . . The difficulty of making these people think Imperially or of aught but securing a maximum of pay for a minimum of work is incredible.'[9]

As for New Zealand, a member of the business community there told Monk Bretton, Chamberlain's secretary, that 'It is difficult to say whether there is a general desire on the part of the inhabitants of New Zealand for a closer relationship with the U.K. . . . I think . . . that people as a whole do not take very much interest in the question but the commercial community are distinctly in favour of closer relations and reciprocal tariffs.'[10]

If reactions from the self-governing colonies were mixed, the Indian government protested in an unequivocal dispatch of October 1903 against any scheme for preferential tariffs. But, in any case, Chamberlain had apparently excluded India from his tariff proposals.[11] Curzon indeed called him 'colony mad', and Balfour was at pains to reassure the Commons in June 1903 that 'it will be impossible to exclude India, and it never has been excluded, from any consideration of the fiscal policy of this country and its effects.'[12]

But Chamberlain was concerned predominantly with the white colonies and even with specific groups within those communities. On 1 January 1905 Balfour showed his disapproval of this policy in a letter to Northcote in Australia:

What you tell me of the cross currents of public opinion in Australia on the Tariff Question in no way surprises me. It is hard enough to induce people to take a broad and unselfish view of Imperial Questions even in the Mother Country. It is, I suppose, in consequence of this particular difficulty that Joe has run a policy which his enemies describe as 'protection', and which certainly is in the nature of an appeal to particular interests, in double harness with his Imperial propaganda. Personally, I think it is a mistake; and so far as I am concerned I play for the big ideal in its simplicity, and nothing else. It may fail, but even in its failure I think, if properly managed, the movement will carry within it seeds of good that may develop later. We shall see.[13]

2

In February 1905, Joseph Chamberlain expressed alarm that he and Balfour were drifting apart. He wrote requesting a man-to-man meeting over a quiet dinner. The meeting, on 17 February, provided Chamberlain with the opportunity to attack Balfour's double election plan. Basically, he doubted the possibility of a successful second general election so soon after the first. Balfour defended his scheme, and wrote to Chamberlain the next day to press the point home. In his letter of 18 February, the Prime Minister explained that without a second election a completely free Colonial Conference would be out of the question, and he repeated his doubts as to how far the self-governing colonies were prepared to sacrifice their commercial interests for Britain.[14]

Refusing to be pinned down by Joseph Chamberlain, Balfour displayed equal agility in the Commons. After John Morley had challenged him to express his fiscal views on half a sheet of note-paper, Balfour complied, and told the Commons that although he was sometimes accused of indulging in metaphysics, his brief statement could be understood by any man with an impartial mind.[15]

On 22 March, the ex-Chancellor Hicks Beach put down some free trade resolutions in the Commons. Balfour argued that 'it would be unfortunate ... mainly so far as the Colonies are concerned, that we should set an example, which the Colonies might be only too ready to follow, of embodying our special views in a formal Resolution, and thereby hamper those who are to take part in that free conference which I believe to be the only way of finding a final solution to this question.'[16] Determined not to be bound by a formal vote, which would only illustrate the tariff reformers' strength on the Unionist benches, Balfour led his supporters out of the House of Commons.

To these trials was added the invective of the convinced free trader Winston Churchill, who had crossed the floor of the House in 1904, and in March 1905 asked Balfour whether he considered 'his retention of office consistent with his public duty or his personal honour.'[17] On 22 May, both Balfour and Lyttelton, the Colonial Secretary, when attempting to speak on tariff reform, were interrupted with shouts of 'Divide', 'Go to the Old Bailey', and 'Send for the police'.[18]

In May 1905 Balfour's relationship with the Chamberlains reached a new crisis. Confident that two-thirds of the Unionist M.P.s either fully supported imperial preference, or would do so if it became the government's official policy, Joseph Chamberlain and his ally Herbert Maxwell met Balfour on 16 May. To their surprise Balfour agreed to put imperial preference at the forefront of the party's programme. Further discussion revealed that nothing in Balfour's previous fiscal pronouncements need prevent the impending Colonial Conference of 1906 being treated as the 'free' conference, to be followed by the general election. This would dispense with the double election programme which Chamberlain found so unacceptable. On this basis it seemed possible to reunite the party – excepting the most stubborn free traders. Chamberlain even offered to return to the government as a minister without portfolio and to support tariff reform from within the administration.[19]

But the Unionist free-trade M.P.s, despite their numerical weakness, would not stand for this. They threatened to vote with the Opposition in a motion of censure put down for 30 May. This would turn Balfour out of office if enough tariff reformers also abstained. Balfour still wanted to remain in office, mainly to renew the Japanese alliance and complete his reordering of the Empire's defences. He surrendered to the free traders. On 26 May, a despairing Austen Chamberlain told his father of 'a most serious hitch – I fear an absolute breakdown – in the suggested arrangements about fiscal policy. I have not been able to have any talk with Balfour.'[20]

A few hours later, the Chamberlains met Balfour, Lansdowne and Lyttelton at 10 Downing Street. Here they were told that Balfour did not intend to remain in office until the autumn of 1906, an essential feature of the recent agreement. Although the disappointed Chamberlain could have brought down the government in the approaching debate, this was the last thing he wanted. He still sought for a compromise. After meeting Austen Chamberlain on 27 May, Lyttelton told Balfour that 'Joe *wd*. be satisfied if you stated in the H. of Commons on Tuesday at the same time at which you gave the assurance as to a dissolution preceding the automatic conference that fiscal reform including Colonial Preference *wd*. be the first item of your next Election programme.' At the same time, Lyttelton had emphasised that such a declaration might involve more Cabinet resignations.[21]

Austen Chamberlain added a personal appeal by urging Balfour, in his forthcoming speech in the Commons, to 'put Tariff reform, including colonial preference, in the front of your programme whenever you go to the country.' Both the Chamberlains would accept this as a way out of the immediate crisis.[22] Balfour accepted this course, even though he realised it was a concession. Accordingly, he wrote on 27 May a tortuous letter to Lyttelton, which represented more a retreat in good order than a call to arms:

If by 'Colonial Preference' is meant (as I suppose it is) closer commercial union with the Colonies (as per 'half sheet of notepaper'), and if by 'first item in my programme' be meant (as I suppose it is) that I regard it as the most important part (though the most difficult) of fiscal reform, and fiscal reform itself as the most important part of the Unionist policy, why should I not give the assurances asked for? – and why should any colleagues resign? . . . 'First item' must not of course be understood as meaning necessarily *first carried out*, because 'preference' requires a conference, while retaliation does not. But on this I suppose all agree.[23]

If this was a pledge, it was a highly involved one. It was Lyttelton's task to communicate it to Austen Chamberlain. In the event Balfour's scholasticism infected him also, and he felt obliged to define his terms, emphasising that every time he spoke of 'colonial preference' the reader should understand 'that the definition of Col. Pref. in the first para. governed the whole letter.' Lyttelton added to the confusion by changing Balfour's statement that colonial preference was not to be 'necessarily *first carried out*' to 'not necessarily carried out' – a very different promise.[24]

Camouflaged by this verbal smoke screen, Balfour continued to hold office. Through the summer and autumn of 1905 he tried to play down the tariff controversy, contenting himself with public statements which were, in substance, evasive. Refusing to denounce the tariff reformers, he insisted on keeping the free fooders at bay also. There were other pressing matters to deal with. Curzon's dispute with Kitchener was reaching its crescendo, and the Opposition were revelling in the Chinese labour outcry. The Japanese alliance had to be seen through in July, and in August and September the holiday season made a general election impossible.

Having failed to make Balfour their captive, the Chamberlains would have welcomed an early election. Austen pressed Balfour in August for an autumn dissolution, making the renewed and extended Japanese alliance 'our last great work'.[25] In November Balfour revealed to Joseph Chamberlain that he was contemplating resignation in the January or February of 1906. Ill-pleased with these prevarications, Chamberlain ignored Balfour's plea for unity at the party conference on 15 November, and a week later in Bristol called for an aggressive campaign for tariff reform.[26]

In real terms, of course, campaigning had been in progress since Chamberlain's famous speech in Birmingham on 15 May 1903. But in the autumn of 1905 it rose to new heights, revealing in clear perspective the divisions between Balfourians, Chamberlainites and free traders. Nor was the Cabinet spared acrimony as when Lord Londonderry, President of the Education Board, indulged in blatant free trade speechmaking from public platforms, offending Austen Chamberlain. Balfour went out of his way to pacify his Chancellor in a letter of 3 November 1905:

We are surely the most extraordinary Cabinet that this country has ever seen! Every other Cabinet that I have ever heard of carried on unending internecine conflict within closed doors, but put a decent face on it in public. Within *our* Cabinet room there reigns eternal calm, and it is only on the platform that these regrettable incidents occur.[27]

Balfour himself was soon to suffer public rebuff at Joseph Chamberlain's hands at the party conference, and through Chamberlain's Bristol speech. Perhaps these auguries were sufficient to make up his mind about the dissolution. At any rate, Balfour resigned on 4 December 1905. Campbell-Bannerman took office and immediately asked for a dissolution. The election campaign now began officially.

3

Balfour had few illusions about the result to be expected. As early as March 1903 he had told Curzon that he did not necessarily expect to be in office in 1905. By the autumn of 1904, colleagues like Austen Chamberlain and Selborne were merely hoping to win the election after next. Moreover, on hearing the news of Balfour's resignation, Northcote had written from Australia in valedictory style assuring him of the nation's gratitude 'for the cool head and firm hand that guided the nation's destinies', but adding, 'Of course the Unionists are in for a bad licking. Ever since 1903 I have felt that to be inevitable.'[28]

In these gloomy circumstances, the main concern of the Cecils and the Unionist aristocratic hierarchy was to keep the party out of Chamberlain's clutches. An attempt was even made to discover the views of the dead Lord Salisbury on the divisive topic of tariff reform. Family enquiries revealed that there had been no basic opposition to such plans, only a desire to avert a Unionist split.[29] More practically, Balfour, speaking in Leeds, reaffirmed his policy of retaliation within the free trade system.

In the early part of January 1906 Balfour was campaigning hard in his constituency of East Manchester, where on 8 January he wrote a cautionary and thoughtful letter to his cousin Robert Cecil:

I hold that the haste and temper of the Free Fooders in the early stages of the controversy have been one of the greatest difficulties I have had to contend with in preventing the Party going bald-headed for Protection. They constantly rejected my advice: they refused . . . to follow my lead: and, so far as the House of Commons was concerned, they have proved themselves more impracticable than even the extreme Tariff Reformers. And if they have been less mischievous in the country, it is, so far as I can see, because they lack the organization, and not because they lack the will . . . I am having a very tough fight here, and am absolutely overwhelmed by the multiple claims of fighting my own constituency, helping other people fight theirs, and carrying out a general correspondence with our supporters. Our difficulties here are Chinese Labour and the Independent Labour Party.[30]

Robert Cecil was alarmed at the prospect of Balfour's defeat, telling him that 'For you to be defeated and for Joe to get in would be, in my view, the greatest electoral disaster that could occur to us.'[31]

In the event, Robert Cecil's worst fears were realised. Polling began on 12 January. Among the first results to be announced was Balfour's defeat in East Manchester by some 2,000 votes. This was only the beginning of an avalanche of Unionist losses which included the seats of Gerald Balfour, Lyttelton and Brodrick – all Cabinet ministers. Ironically, Chamberlain's Birmingham citadel held firm, returning seven tariff reformers, some with increased majorities. Clearly tariff reform had done Chamberlain little damage.

Elsewhere, the Unionist split over imperial preference merely accentuated electoral disenchantment with a party that had been in power since 1895 and had done little in the way of social reform. Nor was it easy to forget the vivid humiliations of the Boer War. At any rate, although the Unionist vote rose from 1,676,020 in 1900 to 2,463,606 in 1906, the combined Liberal and Labour vote soared from 1,520,285 in 1900 to a total of 3,111,929 in 1906.[32] The mass vote had swung against the Unionists and annihilated them. In the Commons the Liberals had an overall majority of 84, and with the Irish Nationalist and Labour vote, a majority of 356. The Unionists were reduced to a scant 157 seats.

Typically, Balfour expressed profound and quizzical interest in the heavy Labour vote. He told Northcote that 'the really interesting development is the organised Labour Party, a subject on which you in Australia will have a great deal to teach us.'[33] To Knollys, the King's secretary, he wrote on 17 January:

We have here to do with something much more important than the swing of the pendulum or all the squabbles about Free Trade and Fiscal Reform. We are face to face (no doubt in a milder form) with the Socialistic difficulties which loom so large on the Continent. Unless I am greatly mistaken, the Election of 1906 inaugurates a new era.[34]

Of more immediate importance than philosophical speculation, however, was the future of the Unionist party. Of the 157 Unionist M.P.s, 102 were Chamberlainites. Until Balfour could find a safe seat, who else could lead them but Chamberlain? In addition, it was clear that Chamberlain could demand some concession to his tariff reform views in return for continuing to support Balfour. The old guard of the Unionist leadership were now within a hair's breadth of that democratisation of the party that Chamberlain's methods had long since threatened. The Cecil family were alarmed. The die-hard Lansdowne was belligerent, telling Balfour on 20 January, 'It is not necessary that we should recant our opinions as to retaliation or Colonial preference.'[35]

Immediately on hearing of Balfour's defeat in Manchester, Joseph, Austen and Mrs Chamberlain offered their commiserations. Mrs Chamberlain told Alice Balfour that they could not believe their ears at the news, and emphasised 'how deeply we regret it – & how truly we sympathise with him and with you. . . . It is a blow to us all. . . . Please tell Mr Balfour that I can think of nothing else today.'[36] But more ominously, the Unionist press demanded a scapegoat, and an alarmed Alfred Lyttelton warned Balfour, via Sandars, that 'Joe means business – *His policy* or *yours* with *his lead* or *yours*'.[37]

Early in February, even before he had been returned as the

member for the City of London, Balfour met Joseph and Austen Chamberlain privately to try to thrash out their differences. Chamberlain had demanded a party meeting on 15 February. If this became the occasion for a confrontation between Balfour and Chamberlain, the latter certainly possessed a strong hand. At the same time, it was by no means certain that the party as a whole were prepared to overthrow Balfour. Nonetheless, the prospect was an unpleasant one, and his meeting with the Chamberlains in the first days of February did nothing to alter it. Betty Balfour, Gerald's wife, gave a revealing account of this meeting to Alice Balfour on 4 February, telling her that it 'apparently . . . produced no good result:

Joe sticks to an immediate calling of a party meeting to decide at once between the two policies and says if A.J. [Balfour] refuses this he will call a meeting of his own followers. He says whatever the result he will not lead the Conservative Party – but if a majority are with Arthur, he will split off with his own section! G. [Gerald Balfour] still thinks the great majority of the party will refuse to leave Arthur for Joe. . . . He says of Joe – it is the action of a madman – he has become a monomaniac and is ready to sacrifice everything to his policy of Tariff Reform; and the machinery by which he could have carried it – namely the Conservative Party – he is actually going to shatter. A.J. told him [Gerald] that he, Joe, Austen and Mrs. Joe sat on discussing the matter at the dinner table and that Joe and even Austen were 'nasty' – and that he, A.J., kept his temper 'like an angel' & that Mrs. Joe at the end was almost in tears! . . . I think if Joe is able to be so unreasonable the time has come when it will be better for him to break with Arthur – even if temporarily it is disastrous to the party.[38]

Even allowing for the legitimate exercise of family loyalty, Betty Balfour's account shows that the Chamberlains were putting enormous pressure on Balfour and that his room for manoeuvre was minimal.

Balfour was under no illusions on this score. A few days after his meeting with the Chamberlains he stayed, appropriately, with his cousins at Hatfield. There Lord Hugh Cecil found him exhausted and 'anti-Joe' and did not believe that 'he will move in Joe's direction at all.'[39] But anti-Chamberlainite sentiments were no remedy for Balfour's poor tactical position. Moreover, tariff reform was not an issue over which he was prepared to sacrifice everything. His academic mind rejected dogma, and he was able to see the flaws in all the fiscal schools of thought. In this sense, the lead he gave was to stand almost motionless.

But if Balfour now had to surrender something more to Chamberlain over tariff reform, perhaps he could at least keep the party machinery in his own hands and resist a Chamberlainite take-over. This is what happened. On the 14 February a truce was arranged between the two men. In return for a promise of support, Balfour produced yet another verbal concession. In these 'Valentine letters' Balfour wrote:

I hold that Fiscal Reform is, and must remain, the first constructive work of the Unionist Party. That the Objects of such reforms are to secure more equal terms of competition for British trade, and closer commercial union with the Colonies.[40]

More significantly, Balfour spoke of 'the establishment of a general tariff on manufactured goods, not imposed for the purpose of raising prices or giving artificial protection against legitimate competition, and the imposition of a small duty on foreign corn' as being 'not in principle objectionable'. For his part, Chamberlain replied, 'I entirely agree with your description of the objects which we both have in view, and gladly accept the policy which you indicate as the wise and desirable one for the Unionist Party to adopt.'[41]

For the tariff reformers it seemed that Balfour had at last accepted their programme in principle. At the party meeting on 15 February there was a unanimous vote of confidence in Balfour's leadership. But in their enthusiasm the tariff reformers had over-looked two vital factors. To begin with, the party leadership was still in Balfour's keeping and was to remain so until he was replaced by the protectionist Bonar Law in 1911. Also, Balfour was adept at verbal juggling. There was no reason to suppose that he would not exercise this skill as Leader of the Opposition as effectively as when he had been Prime Minister. How much was his concession of 14 February worth?

In practice, Balfour tried to avoid precise commitments. He was opposed to concentrating energy and attention exclusively on any issue, and pleaded 'do not let us become a party of one idea, for if we do become a party of one idea, we shall fail to carry even that idea to a successful issue.'[42] But typically, in 1907, he told Austen Chamberlain that 'so far as fiscal reform is concerned, the Party are so deeply committed to it that it is quite inconceivable that they should ever take office without making it their main business to carry it through.'[43] As it happened, the Unionists were out of office until 1922, although they participated in the Asquith and Lloyd George coalitions between 1915 and 1922. In this sense they were incapable of implementing tariff reforms at all.

One other calamity befell the tariff reform movement after the Liberal landslide of 1906. In July of that year Joseph Chamberlain celebrated his seventieth birthday. After indulging in the festivities with his habitual freedom, he suffered a severe stroke from which he never fully recovered before his death in 1914. Although attempts were made to disguise the extent of Chamberlain's incapacity, his political activities were now confined to urging on his followers from his sickbed.

For Balfour this was an outright blessing. He even went so far as to get a medical opinion on Chamberlain's chances of recovery through the examination of a published photograph. In this way he learnt that Chamberlain's affliction was permanent.[44] The demoniac energies of radical Joe had been circumscribed by sickness, and it was against men of lesser stature that Balfour had now to deploy his Fabian tactics.

9 Dangerous Policies: the Unionists and Tariff Reform, 1906–1932

We are face to face with those who wish for . . . socialism in political matters, who wish unduly to extend, as I think, the functions of the State, and who are going to get themselves and the whole community into difficulty by their action.

BALFOUR, 1907

Those are the issues you will be called upon to decide . . . Free institutions and Free Trade . . . on the other hand Privilege and Protection.

LLOYD GEORGE, 1908

I

BALFOUR remained Leader of the Unionist party for nearly six years after the electoral catastrophe of January 1906. These years were marked by great domestic convulsions, centring on the House of Lords' obstruction of Liberal legislation, Lloyd George's 'people's budget' of 1909, and the violent controversy surrounding the Parliament Act of 1911. Attention was also focussed on the Home Rule question, and the apparently uncontrollable spread of socialism. As party leader Balfour was inevitably deeply involved with all these developments. At the same time, it was expedient to attempt to resolve the tariff reform controversy within the Unionist ranks.

Until the 1906 election, Balfour's labyrinthine defences had left him free of outright commitment to Chamberlainites or free fooders. If the Valentine letters of February 1906 had apparently signified a movement towards Chamberlain's position, they had at least been part of a bargain that left the party machine in Balfour's hands. Moreover, the serious stroke suffered by Chamberlain meant that his place in the Liberal Unionist Council and Tariff Reform League was taken by Austen Chamberlain. Although resolute in the defence of his father's policy, Austen hardly possessed the same commanding personality. There was some truth in F. E. Smith's remark that 'Austen always played the game and always lost it.'[1]

By the beginning of 1907, Balfour was assured that Joseph Chamberlain could never return to active political life. But this by no means ended Chamberlain's influence, which could be exerted through his son, through extremely able followers like Leo Amery and Bonar Law, and through the still mighty apparatus of the Tariff Reform League. Indeed, the League's funds grew steadily, its propaganda continued unabated, converts entered its ranks. The bulk of the Unionist press spurned Balfourian sophistry for straightforward tariff reform, and looked to the inspiration of editors such as J. L. Garvin and Leo Maxse.

In January 1907, Sandars warned Balfour that the party wanted a statement on tariff reform that would refer sympathetically to closer union with the colonies and acknowledge that social reform could only be paid for by finding new sources of revenue. Sandars urged that such a speech could be made appropriately when Balfour attended the meeting of the National Union on 15 February.[2]

Balfour was also under pressure from Professor Hewins, one of Chamberlain's most distinguished supporters, and the ex-Director of the London School of Economics. Hewins told Balfour in a letter of 11 February that tariff reform should be seen as 'the substitution in our economic policy of Imperial interests for the interest of the consumer.' He advocated, therefore, freer reciprocal trade within the Empire. At the same time, Hewins dismissed the possibility of an imperial *zollverein*, or of an imperial council. He also considered that food taxes were an integral part of imperial preference, and he argued, temptingly, that tariff reform could provide enough revenue for the growing needs of the state without the government having to resort to heavier direct taxation.[3]

Several of these authoritative arguments were reproduced faithfully by Balfour nine days later in the House of Commons. Admittedly, much of Hewins's thinking accorded with Balfour's own, especially as to the impossibility of halting the growing national awareness of the Dominions. Nonetheless, Hewins's influence was clearly marked in Balfour's speech of 20 February 1907. On the lethal subject of food taxes, Balfour made no precise statement, but he insisted that Britain must abandon hope of either an imperial council or an imperial *zollverein*. In addition, he called for 'some form of commercial preference with the Empire'. Only by acknowledging that the Dominions themselves had proposed a system of imperial preference could Britain make the best use of the chance offered her. Balfour condemned the Liberals for not keeping an open mind on this question in view of the fact that the 1907 Colonial Conference was only a few months away. But he did not underestimate the difficulties of achieving imperial unity, calling it 'the greatest problem which any Empire has had to face', and asking 'how an Empire which consists of these separate self-governing Colonies is both to grow in strength, in numbers, and at the same time in unity.'[4]

The substance of these remarks, however, could have been found in Balfour's earlier, somewhat convoluted, utterances on tariff reform. What was new in the speech of 20 February was a reference to the menace of socialism and the dangers of increased taxation. Balfour claimed that:

We are face to face with those who wish for ... socialism in political matters, who wish unduly to extend, as I think, the functions of the State, and who are going to get themselves and the whole community into difficulty by their action.

Also, Balfour thought that, with the increasing demands made on the exchequer, the present basis of taxation could not be maintained. But he made it clear that the extra revenue could, and should, be found through the introduction of imperial preference rather than through increasing the standard rate of income tax, which stood at one shilling in the pound.[5] These doctrinal innovations in Balfour's tariff reform statements had all been prompted by Hewins.

The Colonial Conference of 1907 came nowhere near to achieving imperial preference. Alfred Deakin of Australia pressed hard for preference, and was supported by four of his fellow Prime Ministers. But Laurier of Canada, and Botha of the Transvaal held back. In any case, the Liberal government was bound to set its face against tariff reform, and even if tempted to flirt with the idea, would have been sobered by recalling the Unionist holocaust of 1906.

Balfour was at least able to turn the outcome of the Colonial Conference to some advantage. For one thing, he proceeded to berate the Liberals in the Commons for slamming 'the door . . . in the face of those who come to us with a policy on which they are all agreed.'[6] For another, Balfour could partially placate tariff reform opinion within his party by declaring at the Albert Hall on 3 May that the Dominions' enthusiasm for imperial preference had inspired him also. Moreover, at the annual meeting of the National Union of Conservative Associations in the Autumn of 1907 he once more attacked the government for throwing away the chance of tariff reform at the Colonial Conference.[7]

But Balfour's espousal of imperial preference somehow lacked conviction. Certainly he was unable to give his party an inspiring lead. Demonstrably lacking Joseph Chamberlain's dynamism, his periodic enthusiasms for the Chamberlainite creed seemed mere strategems designed to keep the party together in opposition. Not that such manoeuvres were valueless. The wilder spirits of the Tariff Reform League (Garvin and Maxse) longed to destroy the free food Unionists. They chafed against the leadership of the League itself – notably that of Austen Chamberlain.[8] If Austen lacked radicalism in their eyes, Balfour seemed doubly cautious. There was no reason why, if they remained unsatisfied, the extreme tariff reformers should not set up their own candidates against official Unionist nominees in by-elections – even in general elections.

As it happened, the Unionist party was saved from such self-destructive impulses by the necessity to unite in face of a double threat. On the one hand, there was cause for disquiet at the steady growth of socialism among working men. On the other, the Liberal government, frustrated by the obstruction to reform afforded by the House of Lords, and anxious to finance their plans for social improvement while maintaining the supremacy of the Royal Navy, decided to provoke a massive conflict with their enemies. In the shadow of this confrontation, the tariff reform controversy was to appear insignificant.

2

In 1907 Philip Snowden published a pamphlet entitled *The Socialist Budget*. In it he called for a differential rate between taxation on earned and unearned income, for the graduation of income tax rates, and for the introduction of a super-tax on incomes of over £5,000 a year. Snowden also advocated the repeal of food taxes, a duty on uninhabited houses, and a land tax.[9] In speeches in the Commons, Snowden amplified the socialist programme. It was evident that this centred on meeting the cost of social reform and government spending by greatly increasing income tax and reducing indirect taxation.

As early as 1903, Snowden had attacked Chamberlain's tariff reform proposals in a tract called *The Chamberlain Bubble*. He dismissed the idea that the Empire could be self-sustaining, and argued that extra revenue must come from sources other than those afforded by tariff reform. Principally, Snowden believed that the nationalisation of the railways and the mines would save millions of pounds a year, and that 'national taxation must be taken off the poor and the industrious of every class' and levied on those who could best afford it.[10]

Snowden, expounding his policies with care and restraint, was far removed from a blood-stained revolutionary. A British Labour movement that was unmistakably dedicated to reform through democratic means threw out a powerful challenge to Liberal, tariff reformer and Unionist free trader alike.

By October 1907, Austen Chamberlain was sufficiently alarmed to tell Balfour that 'Labour-Socialism is making enormous strides among working men.' This progress he attributed to the united voice and positive policies of socialism. The Unionists demonstrably lacked such qualities, and Balfour was doing little to remedy these defects. Austen Chamberlain believed that Balfour should announce his support for a general tariff and for social reform. This would have a double advantage. Tariff reform promised to find extra revenue without resorting to a policy of soaking the rich. Social reform, notably old age pensions and perhaps a housing policy, would draw the teeth of the Liberal tiger and the Socialist paper tiger. Particularly, Austen wanted Balfour to declare his support for a contributory scheme of old age pensions on the German model – one third from the workman, one third from the employer and one third from the state. Such a measure would provide an alternative to the universal contributory scheme favoured by Asquith, the Chancellor.[11]

Partly to allay these anxieties, and partly to re-assert his leadership, Balfour made a brave attempt at the assembly of the National Union in November 1907 to declare for a Chamberlainite programme of reform. He went far in his support for imperial preference. and assured the tariff reformers that time was on their side. A resolution calling for an attack on the free trade elements in the party was not even formally discussed. Indeed, any such move would have led to violent objections from the delegates from Lancashire and Yorkshire, where in 1906 the electorate had swung violently to free trade candidates, virtually annihilating the Unionist representation.[12]

Party unity was Balfour's aim, and he had reason to feel that this cause had been furthered at the National Union assembly. He had even been able to pay an appropriate tribute to the stricken Joseph Chamberlain, whose absence from the proceedings had aroused an emotional response from many delegates, although Balfour might possibly have rejoiced at Chamberlain's empty chair. Not that Balfour's position as leader was completely safe. At about this time he wrote to a friend:

As regards the attacks on myself, I quite understand your point of view that they might do harm to the Party, and therefore ought, if possible, be put an end to. But you will admit, I think, that I can do nothing to put an end to them. I am certainly not going to go about the country explaining that I am 'honest and industrious', like a second coachman out of place! If people cannot find it out for themselves, they must, as far as I can see, remain in ignorance.[13]

This nonchalant attitude towards his reputation as Unionist leader was soon to cost Balfour dear. When Asquith became Prime Minister in April 1908, he appointed Lloyd George as Chancellor. In this new role, Lloyd George employed all his gifts of inspiration, guile and demagoguery to launch a ferocious attack on the Unionists in general and on the reactionary bulwark of the House of Lords in particular.

1908 was a year full of portent. Prices fell steadily, and an economic depression set in. No matter how many measures of social security were prominent in the Liberal party's programme, this could not outweigh the working man's concern at short-time and an uncertain economic future. Tariff reformers believed that the moment of national conversion to their faith had arrived. There were good reasons for their optimism. A succession of by-elections went against the government, several for outright tariff reformers.[14]

Balfour was not slow to see the implications of this trend. In March, his secretary Sandars told Alice Balfour that tariff reform was making rapid strides in the country and that the party was daily more enthusiastic on the subject, although 'the Cecilian cousinhood do their best to make every difficulty they can . . . . At present your brother is doing all he can to restrain the more ardent Tariff Reformers from driving them [the free fooders] out of their constituencies.'[15] The crippling divisions in the Unionist ranks were clearly unresolved, and the tariff reformers, rejoicing in their recent success, were once more pressing for the elimination of their opponents.

The by-elections trend obviously threatened the Liberals also. Although the Old Age Pensions Act was carried through Parliament in 1908, other measures such as the 1906 Education Bill and the radical, but hardly liberal, Licensing Bill had been destroyed the the House of Lords. By the end of 1908, therefore, Asquith and Lloyd George had decided to make the budget of 1909 the antidote to tariff reform and a challenge to the House of Lords.[16] At one stroke, they planned to revitalise their party, scatter their enemies, and steal the increasingly attractive clothes of the socialists.

The 'people's budget' of April 1909 implemented Snowden's proposals for altering the ratio of direct and indirect taxation. It increased income tax, supertax, and death duties. But it also levied substantial amounts on tobacco, liquor and stamp duties, and motor taxes. These measures, although displeasing for many Unionists, were not extraordinary, and, indeed, hardly a source of joy for all the Liberal supporters either. But Lloyd George also proposed to impose new taxes on land, and to link them with a Land Valuation Bill. This was a direct blow at the land-owning classes, who saw that the way was now open for a long-term assault on their property. Equally, radicals and socialists welcomed the innovations.

For Balfour, the budget held out both infinite promise and the threat of disaster. By a headlong assault on the budget, he could rally behind his leadership tariff reformers and free traders alike. But the massive radical majority in the Commons was impervious to such tactics. Once the budget was put before the Lords, however, the Unionist peers could destroy it at will. Here was the crux. Not since 1869 had the Lords rejected a finance bill sent up from the Commons. To do so in 1909 would be tantamount to suicide, for the Liberals and their allies would seize upon the chance thus afforded to further limit the constitutional rights of the Upper House. In these circumstances, should Balfour encourage the peers to fight, or ensure that they survived to block other government measures?

For over six months the choice did not have to be made, for the Finance Bill was making its painful progress through the Commons, constantly attacked by the Unionists. Balfour began to trim his sails to the tariff reform wind. Even before the introduction of the budget he had told the Commons on 19 February, 'I was an advocate of Colonial Preference, and would have liked to see a 2s. duty on imported corn, before the fiscal controversy arose at all in this country.'[17] This was a surprisingly plain statement, and had little in common with previous Balfourian prevarication on the subject.

More than anything else, the bellicose speeches of Lloyd George and Winston Churchill were pushing Balfour into the arms of the tariff reformers. The attacks of these Liberal firebrands on the privileges of the House of Lords and the landed classes, had the effect (like hanging), of concentrating Balfour's mind wonderfully. On 21 December 1908, at Liverpool, Lloyd George claimed that 'when a Liberal Government comes in you have these old Tories dug out of the cellars of the House of Lords ... stuff bottled in the Dark Ages.' He denounced the House of Lords as 'a tool of the Tory chief Agent', and told his audience 'those are the issues you will be called upon to decide, and you cannot tell how soon. . . . Free institutions and Free Trade . . . on the other hand Privilege and Protection.'[18]

Lloyd George was here preparing the ground for the coming confrontation over the budget. In this skirmishing he was ably abetted by Winston Churchill who, on 13 January 1909, repeated the Chancellor's battle-cry that the issue was one 'of aristocratic rule against representative government . . . between reversion to Protection and the maintenance of Free Trade.'[19] The apostasy of the aristocratic Churchill was heightened by the zeal of his crusade, and goes far to explain the lingering and bitter hatred that was felt for him in some Conservative circles.

If Liberal leaders were staking out their positions in advance, so were the Confederates – the hard core of the tariff reform movement. Indeed, in the middle of January 1909 the *Morning Post* published the names of eleven Unionist free trade M.P.s against whom the Confederates vowed to set up tariff reform candidates at the first possible opportunity. The big guns of the Unionist press were by now ranged behind the tariff reformers, with Garvin's *Observer* playing a formidable part, supported by Maxse's *National Review*. In May, after the budget, Joseph Chamberlain's now muffled tones made themselves heard, urging resolute action. Garvin reported his old chief as saying 'This budget tries to knock the House of Lords out of the Constitution. – Hope the Lords will knock *it* out! – Fear they won't; fear they will prove rather cowardly lot.'[20]

Although Chamberlain, from his wheelchair, longed for a battle to the death, Balfour exercised more prudence during the first half of 1909. But Lloyd George's Limehouse speech of 30

July, which seemed a declaration of class war, encouraged Balfour to see the budget mainly in terms of the insidious introduction of socialist finance. In these circumstances, Balfour decided to go the whole hog for tariff reform.

Balfour agreed to speak on 22 September at Bingley Hall in Birmingham, an appropriate platform for a recantation. Prompted by Garvin's insistence that the budget's land clauses meant land nationalisation, that certain features of the Development Bill would lead to the nationalisation of the railways, and that the liquor clauses would lead to the nationalisation of public houses, Balfour denounced this supposedly covert socialism. The choice before the nation, he said, was a simple one: to become immersed in 'the bottomless confusion of socialist legislation'; or to advance with 'the hopeful movement of tariff reform'.[21] Joseph Chamberlain had good cause for the satisfaction he expressed at Balfour's performance.

Balfour's new-found militancy could only lead to the Lords' rejection of the budget. On 30 November 1909, the peers defeated the Finance Bill by 350 votes to 75. It was clear that a general election would follow hard behind.

3

Parliament was prorogued on 3 December 1909. The election was to be fought in January. Balfour could at least lead a united party to the polls, for even the free trade Unionists would rally against the allegedly socialistic budget and in defence of the House of Lords. Moreover, the Unionist press, joined now by the previously recalcitrant *Spectator,* redoubled their efforts to unmask the 'evil conspiracy' behind the budget, and to present Balfour to the public as a dynamic, popular leader.

Unfortunately for the Unionists, the ordinary voter felt more kinship for Lloyd George and his radical colleagues than for the aristocratic, though galvanised, Balfour. In any case, it is doubtful whether many of the electorate comprehended the niceties of the fiscal debate. As for the House of Lords, elaborate Unionist justifications of its delaying powers would not convince those who saw the Commons–Lords conflict as a struggle between democracy and privilege.

The election results of January 1910 failed to bring down the Liberal government. Although 275 Liberal M.P.s were returned, as against 273 Unionists, the 40 Labour M.P.s could be relied upon to help the government through the constitutional crisis. In addition, the 82 Irish Nationalists, led by Redmond, would support the Liberals – at a price. It was evident that the price would be Home Rule, but this was, after all, Liberal and Labour policy, and Redmond was already being hailed as the 'Irish Botha'.

When the new Parliament met, the government re-introduced the 1909 budget, which was passed by both Houses. But the government then proposed measures to prevent the Lords from vetoing money bills, and to restrict their delaying powers over other legislation to a period of two years. Having gained a popular mandate for the budget, Asquith now felt obliged to go to the country again over the reform of the Lords. Although Asquith would have preferred an election in the summer of 1910, the death of Edward VII rendered this unacceptable. Between June and October 1910, the Liberal and Unionist leaders sought to find some convenient means of settling the conflict between the two Houses. The government rejected the idea of a referendum on the proposed reforms, and the Unionists objected to the possible wholesale creation of Liberal peers to carry the House of Lords for the government. This constitutional conference, therefore, came to nothing.

Faced with a second general election in 1910, how was Balfour to play the tariff reform issue? In April 1910 he told Alfred Milner that the tax on colonial corn should be abandoned altogether, since such proposals had helped many of the successful Unionist candidates in the January election to fight the 'dear loaf' slogan. Balfour lent weight to this argument by saying, 'It seems Joe has always been in favour of the free importation of colonial wheat, and committed himself to this policy in his earlier statements.'[22]

But Balfour, under Garvin's influence, was shortly to advocate that the mention of food taxes should play no part in the forthcoming election campaign.

Unfortunately, the Chamberlains regarded any such proposal as heresy. In November, Austen Chamberlain dismissed the idea with disdain. Rather than revive the schism between them, Balfour surrendered. But Garvin persisted in his desire to limit the advantages the Liberals could reap by exploiting popular disquiet over tariff reform. He wanted a straight fight between simple creeds; imperial and industrial consolidation through tariff reform versus socialist utopianism. To remove the blemishes from tariff reform, he now suggested that Balfour should promise the electorate that when tariff reform was first introduced, it should be submitted to a referendum.[23]

The Chamberlains vigorously opposed any such dilution of their faith. But in a speech at the Albert Hall at the end of November 1910, Balfour pledged himself to the tariff referendum. Despite their disappointment, the Chamberlains continued to support Balfour, although Maxse and his followers found such loyalty unpalatable.

As it happened, these doctrinal compromises brought little joy at the polls. The election results of December 1910 produced a dead heat between the Liberals and the Unionists, with 272 seats each. Labour had 42 and the Irish 84. There was in reality no change from January, and the climax of the constitutional deadlock was now near at hand. In the event, Balfour's own overthrow was also close.

4

At three general elections between January 1906 and December 1910 the party that had been associated with tariff reform had lost. 1911 was no more propitious. In January the details became known of a reciprocity agreement between Canada and the United States.[24] This dealt a savage blow at dreams of imperial preference. Although it by no means prevented the introduction of reciprocal imperial preference, the morale of the extreme tariff reformers suffered a severe setback, even though they strove to disguise the fact.

Balfour did not hide his disappointment at Canada's action. On 6 February 1911, he told the Commons that he had 'preached annually . . . that the British Empire has reached a point of development now at which this country is simply the first among equals so far as the great self-governing parts of our Empire are concerned.' Nonetheless, Balfour felt that 'there has been a departure begun by the two Governments of Canada and the United States which must have the most far-reaching, and . . . the most disastrous consequences upon the future of the Empire.'[25]

Three days later, Balfour felt moved to attack the Liberals for their lack of enthusiasm for tariff reform at the Colonial Conference of 1907. Presumably the 1911 Conference would face the same difficulty. The Liberals would 'not treat the Colonies better than they treat foreign nations, and that is the broad difference between us.'[26] Certainly the 1911 Conference saw no abandonment of free trade by the government. The Dominions recorded their continuing interest in imperial preference, but evoked little response. A Liberal government and tariff reform were not compatible.

1911 was not marked by any fundamental harmony in the Unionist party either. In July, the government let Balfour and his colleagues know that in the previous November the new King, George V, had given Asquith a pledge to create enough peers to pass the Parliament Bill. There was now no way of preventing the Liberal reform of the House of Lords. Balfour, sensibly, was for surrender. But the die-hards of his party, led by militant tariff reformers and enraged aristocrats, despised such tactics. Although the Parliament Bill was passed by the Lords on 10 August, helped by the votes of 37 Unionist peers and by many abstentions, a bitterly hostile campaign was mounted against Balfour's leadership.

Leo Maxse's unsophisticated yet effective slogan of 'Balfour Must Go', found a more discreet, though hardly less venomous, response in the highest Unionist circles. The humiliations of the Liberal victories of 1909–11 roused tariff reformers and free traders alike to call for Balfour's overthrow. The Halsbury Club was founded in October 1911 to achieve this very end. The tariff reformers could now wreak their vengeance upon the man who had seemed to support them, but never whole-heartedly. Still convinced that imperial preference was the bulwark against socialism, the tariff reformers now easily swept aristocratic free traders into their camp.

By the end of October, Balfour had decided to retire. He was weary of party strife, and told Sandars, 'It is no gratification to me to be their leader.'[27] On 7 November he informed the King of his intention, excusing himself on the grounds of health. At first sight, the battle for the leadership seemed to be between Austen Chamberlain and the Tory traditionalist Walter Long. Deadlock between them resulted in both standing down for Andrew Bonar Law. Law was a Glasgow ironmaster, and a Canadian by birth. He had a hard-hitting platform style but a somewhat grey character. However, he was an out and out tariff reformer and had long since won his spurs in that tumultuous band. He had little in common with Balfour, and Short, Balfour's personal secretary, wrote on 13 November 1911, 'Bonar Law's methods are open to much criticism. In this struggle he has been run by Max Aitken, the little Canadian adventurer who sits for Ashton-under-Lyne, introduced into that seat by him. . . . The real Bonar appears to be a man of boundless ambition, untempered by any nice feeling.'[28]

5

Law remained leader of the Unionist party for twelve years, dying in 1923 only a few months after becoming Prime Minister. The Great War and the Home Rule issue had meanwhile conspired to push tariff reform behind the scenes. In any case, it was not until October 1922 that the Unionists again took power in their own right, free from the encumbrance of coalition allies.

It is true that the war had eroded free trade principles, with protective duties placed on certain 'luxuries' in 1915 and not removed at the coming of peace. In 1921, moreover, several key industries were protected against hostile foreign action. But when Law, the protectionist Prime Minister, fought the election of November 1922, he specifically repudiated protection, and won.[29] However, in 1923, an Imperial Economic Committee was formed as an ancillary to the Imperial Conference, and the delegates undertook to recommend substantial measures of imperial preference to their respective Parliaments.

But disaster overtook the British offer. Faced with deteriorating economic conditions, Baldwin, Law's successor, decided to plump for the old panacea of tariff reform. Chamberlain's doctrines were revamped and another attempt made to woo the country. The electorate remained unconverted. The election of December 1923 cost the Conservatives ninety seats and brought in the first, but minority, Labour government. Protection had once more crippled the Conservatives, and Baldwin hastened to repudiate it. Zealous protectionists had to make do with the Empire Marketing Board of 1926, and exhortations to the Dominions to 'buy British'.[30]

As Balfour had always believed, outright protection spelled electoral suicide. But the Wall Street crash of 1929 and the Great Depression promised to rescue Chamberlain's dream of imperial free trade. The Ottawa Conference of 1932 produced twelve reciprocal trade agreements between different parts of the Empire. But this was a token measure only. The Dominions still effectively protected their industries. Britain still steered clear of food taxes.

To the last, self-interest triumphed over imperial patriotism. Only the shrinking world markets had caused the British to turn their eyes towards the markets of the Empire. Although inter-imperial trade increased, Britain's trade elsewhere soon picked up, but not enough to prevent the continual decrease of overseas trade as a proportion of Britain's national production.[31] Even the Ottawa agreements had been hard-headed bargains with little room for sentiment. In the midst of a great commercial crisis, the Dominions and Britain had thought of themselves first. Balfour had been dead for two years when the Ottawa Conference met, but its character would not have surprised him.

PART THREE

South Africa

His favourite method of dealing with the South African sore is by the free application of irritants.
B ALFOUR on Joseph Chamberlain, 1897

Personally, I look forward with great confidence and hope to the future of South Africa.
B ALFOUR to Louis Botha, 1909

The pioneer behind his desk:
Cecil Rhodes (1853–1902)

The inheritor: Sir Leander Starr
Jameson (1853–1917), ex-Prime
Minister of the Cape, celebrates
his election as chairman of the
British South Africa Company,
1913.

*Louis Botha (1862–1919)
as a pillar of the Empire*

*Colonel Younghusband (1863–1942)
of the Tibetan expedition 1903–*

Slim Jan and Honest Stan: Smuts and Baldwin at the 1923 Imperial Conference

10 The South African War: Prelude

Were I a Boer, brought up in Boer traditions, nothing but necessity would induce me to adopt a constitution which would turn my country into an English Republic, or a system of education which would reduce my language to the 'patois' of a small and helpless minority.

BALFOUR, 1899

I

THE discovery of gold on the Rand in 1886 concentrated attention upon the future development of South Africa to a degree hitherto unknown. To the strategical advantages of the ports and coaling stations of the Cape and Natal was now added the lure of real and potential mineral wealth, not only in the Transvaal but even across the Limpopo river. But southern Africa was divided between British and Afrikaner interests. Britain had retained the Cape after the Napoleonic wars. Disliking British control, which they equated with egalitarianism between black and white, and fearing anglicisation, the more militant Afrikaners trekked north from the Cape from 1836 onwards. They were spurred on their way by distrust of British frontier policy, and also, in some cases, by economic hardship.[1] But the ox wagons seemed pursued by the British authorities. The *voortrekkers* blazed a trail into Natal and across the Orange river: the British government annexed Natal and then the Orange Free State. Only on the other side of the Vaal river did the migrants shake off British control. However, the Conventions of Sand River in 1852 and Bloemfontein in 1854 granted autonomy to the Transvaal and the Orange Free State, while providing some safeguards for the Africans. There were now two Afrikaner republics in the north, while in the Cape,

F

self-governing after 1853, and Natal, a separate colony by 1856,
British influence predominated.

From the 1850s until 1876, southern Africa gave Whitehall no
cause for grave anxiety. There were certainly clashes between
Boer and Bantu, and proposals for federation came to nothing,
but basically security was undisturbed. This security was exactly
what the British government wanted, and it had been in order to
keep some check on Afrikaner dealings with the African tribes
that it had pursued the trekkers with claims of British overlordship. After all, the Cape's real value for Britain lay in its strategic
position on the sea route to India and the east. But while control
of the coast was essential, the hinterland could not be allowed to
fall into anarchy and turmoil.

In 1876 turmoil threatened. The Transvaal faced war with
the well-drilled Zulu impis of Cetewayo. Despite their rifles and
their bibles, the Transvaalers had an empty treasury. Britain
could ill afford a conflict that would menace the peace of southern
Africa. Under pressure from Lord Carnarvon, the Colonial
Secretary, and with the Transvaal government half-willing,
Disraeli annexed the Transvaal in 1877. The Zulu menace faded
momentarily, only to be revived by Bartle Frere's unambiguous
ultimatum in 1879. The resulting Zulu War damaged British
prestige and reinforced growing discontent in the Transvaal. In
1881, after negotiations spurred on by the sharp defeat of the
British army at Majuba Hill, Gladstone's government restored the
Transvaal's independence while maintaining vague claims to
suzerainty.

Balfour and Salisbury had little respect for Disraeli's Transvaal
policy or the events leading to the Zulu War, and were convinced
that on both occasions the Prime Minister had surrendered to
Colonial Office and royal pressure.[2] However, by 1881, Gladstone
seemed to have washed his hands of the Transvaal. But the
discovery of gold in 1886 demanded a reorientation of British
policy in southern Africa. The Transvaal grew rich, and rather
than becoming increasingly dominated by the Cape threatened in
turn to overshadow all of South Africa. Foreigners, mainly British,
controlled the expanding industry. These *uitlanders* posed a serious

problem, however. To what extent should they be granted civil rights in the Transvaal – the stronghold of militant Afrikaner-dom? Just when British supremacy seemed in jeopardy in southern Africa the *uitlanders* threw a life-line to the British government. As long as British subjects were denied civil rights, London could claim an interest in the Transvaal beyond the shadowy limits of suzerainty. Nor was this all. Embarrassing though his activities sometimes were, the emergence of Cecil Rhodes as the champion of the British cause in southern Africa at least gave Kruger of the Transvaal a worthy rival. The stage was set for a struggle for supremacy in southern Africa. It only remained to choose the weapons.

2

Rhodes himself was one such weapon, although hardly a secret one, as Salisbury and Chamberlain were to lament.[3] But if Rhodes found it difficult to keep a secret, he was able to throw the wealth of his great companies, De Beers Consolidated Mines and Con-solidated Goldfields Limited, behind his plans to spread the influence of the English-speaking race. Furthermore, he became Prime Minister of the Cape in 1890, even though he was de-pendent on the support of Jan Hofmeyr and the Afrikaner moder-ates to keep him in office. Beyond the borders of the Cape, Rhodes' ambitions were gratified by the charter granted by the Salisbury government in 1889 and enabling him to open up the lands across the Limpopo river. The forces of the British South Africa Company, as they pushed aside the Matabele and Mashona, hoped that they were founding a British colony big enough and rich enough to counterbalance the Transvaal to the south.

Not that the treatment meted out to the Matabele pleased every onlooker. In the Commons in 1893, hostile questions were asked. Balfour revealed, in reply, how thankful the government had been to leave the whole business to 'one large single and responsible association' which did not cost the taxpayer a penny. Moreover, he argued that the nation was 'exceptionally fortunate ... in the man who has been the guiding spirit of this great organization.'

Balfour felt that Rhodes was 'extending the blessings of civilization.'[4]

Approval was not so forthcoming for Rhodes' involvement
in the disastrous Jameson Raid of 1895–6. The *uitlanders*, armed
by Rhodes' agents and inspired by the military intervention of
forces led by Dr Jameson, Rhodes' close friend and lieutenant,
were supposed to rise in rebellion and force Kruger to grant them
a say in the republic's future. Since it was estimated that the male
uitlanders outnumbered the Afrikaner males, any vote might well
have swung the Transvaal towards Britain. Robinson, the British
High Commissioner in South Africa, stood ready to intervene.[5]

But the plan disintegrated. The *uitlander* rebellion went off at
half-cock. Perhaps they were more interested in making money
than in helping Rhodes change the course of history. Jameson
and his band were rounded up and ignominiously bundled back to
the British authorities. Rhodes resigned as Prime Minister of the
Cape, his alliance with Hofmeyr ruined. Moderation in the
Transvaal was damaged and Kruger's popularity restored. What
was the British government's attitude to the Raid? From a safe
distance, Balfour said that he would 'probably have joined
Jameson had he lived there, . . . that Jameson's character was the
only attractive feature in the matter, tho' he ought to be hung all
the same.'[6] But that was in private. In a public speech in Manchester on 15 January 1896, Balfour while not 'attempting to
excuse the inexcusable' hammered home the *uitlander* problem and
Britain's claim to suzerainty. Difficulties, he said, were bound to
arise 'with a State whose inhabitants are so arbitrarily divided
between those who pay and those who govern. We must hope
that the Boers, who have behaved with generosity, will see this in
their interests as well as ours.' But Balfour saw that the cause of
the controversy was the underlying dispute over British suzerainty. He claimed that Britain's right to control the external
relations of the Transvaal were 'not denied by any foreign Power,
and we intend to maintain them.'[7]

While Balfour tried to make the best of a bad job, suspicion
centred on the new Colonial Secretary, Joseph Chamberlain. Had
there been collusion between Rhodes and Chamberlain? Cham-

berlain had certainly known something was in the wind.[8] Perhaps he was deeply involved.[9] While he would have welcomed a sweeping success for Rhodes and Jameson, he knew that failure would face Britain with new difficulties, even though a triumphant Kruger might make concessions to the *uitlanders*.[10]

Chamberlain's immediate problem was the inquiry that followed the Jameson Raid. He expected 'no good . . . only a raking of the mud' from any inquiry. 'But how can we resist it without raising a suspicion that there is something behind it?'[11] In a printed document which he sent to Balfour, Chamberlain declared ambiguously that he 'did not believe that there is much to be discovered; and if the worst that is alleged was proved, I do not think it would make much difference in the course which ought to be pursued. . . .' To temper this defiant note, Chamberlain advocated that the forces of the British South Africa Company should be controlled by officers appointed by the Crown. But he added, 'having thus drawn their teeth, I believe that the Company will remain the best body to develop the resources of the country; and my opinion on this point would not be altered whatever may turn out to have been their complicity in recent events.'[12]

Chamberlain would have preferred the inquiry to have been handled by a Joint Committee of both Houses of Parliament with 'the widest possible references'. In fact a Commons Committee was set up. Chamberlain told Balfour that it would not 'do any harm'.[13] The Committee of Inquiry cleared Chamberlain of complicity, and treated an unrepentant Rhodes with restraint.[14] Probably this was to be expected. Neither the Unionists nor many Liberals wanted to dig too deep, feeling that enough harm had been done already. Rhodes was discredited and many Afrikaners in the Cape alienated. The Orange Free State had drawn nearer to the Transvaal, where a greatly strengthened Kruger hastened the arms build-up. Chamberlain was suspect. Germany had made plain her support for the Transvaal. All in all, British policy had suffered a prodigious reverse. Yet the *uitlander* problem still provided the British government with a moral obligation, an excuse for action. Perhaps South Africa would not be Afrikaner-dominated after all.

3

By April 1897 Chamberlain was on the offensive. He asked that the British garrison in South Africa should be increased by 3,000 or 4,000 men. Balfour remarked of Chamberlain:

His favourite method of dealing with the South African sore is by the free application of irritants; and although it does not easily commend itself to me, this method may possibly be the best. In any case however I cannot think it wise to allow him to goad on the Boers by his speeches, and to refuse him the means of repelling Boer attack, when as a responsible minister, he earnestly and persistently presses for them.[15]

Balfour himself believed that the Afrikaners would only take the offensive if they were convinced that the British government was going to attack them first. But he pointed out that if the telegrams between Rhodes and his agent Harris were laid before the Committee of Inquiry, as now seemed inevitable, the Afrikaners would be encouraged to fear the worst. If this were to happen, Balfour thought it was 'a nice point whether the sending out of 3,000 or 4,000 men will prove it to be a sedation or a stimulant.'[16] But the Harris-Rhodes telegrams, which were thought to incriminate Chamberlain, were not produced. Chamberlain claimed that the full contents of these telegrams would be misunderstood abroad. At any rate, the Committee of Inquiry was content with the Colonial Secretary's quotations, from memory, from the telegrams.[17] In view of Chamberlain's reticence and Balfour's anxieties, Harris had probably been led to believe that Chamberlain was fully in sympathy with Rhodes' plan for the Raid, even if he had not wanted to know too much about it.

But although early in 1897 Chamberlain was rubbing salt into the wound caused by the Jameson Raid, this was hardly enough to regain the diplomatic initiative in southern Africa. However, the appointment in April 1897 of Alfred Milner as the new High Commissioner was meant to redress the balance. Milner took to South Africa outstanding qualities of mind and character. A first-class administrator and an undoubted race patriot, he could also be inflexible and perhaps rather cold. But he provided Chamberlain with a splendid partner. Although initially cautious, Milner's attitude hardened after Kruger's triumphant re-election as President of the Transvaal in February 1898. Seven months later, the defeat of Rhodes' Progressive Party in the Cape confirmed his suspicion that moderation could not be expected from the Afrikaners. Milner now believed that there must be a showdown with the Transvaal.[18]

While Milner set to work in South Africa, Britain detached Germany from her support for the Transvaal. The occasion was the Anglo-German agreement of 1898 which dealt with the Portuguese African colonies. In the wider context, Chamberlain was urgently advocating an alliance with Germany. This came to nothing, possibly, according to Balfour, because of German dislike for the changes of government implicit in British democracy[19]. But the narrower agreement remained. It was a diplomatic triumph for Britain, and also for Balfour, who took over the Foreign Office in Salisbury's absence in August 1898. The original problem arose when the bankrupt Portuguese government offered Britain her African colonies as security for a loan. This was an attractive proposal for Britain, since the Transvaal's only access to the sea through non-British territory was the railway line to Delagoa Bay. Although Britain already had the right of pre-emption on Delagoa Bay, a further agreement was to be welcomed.

Germany also had interests in the Portuguese colonies. She was prepared, however, to make a bargain with Britain. Indeed, Hatzfeldt, the German ambassador, let Balfour know that an Anglo-German arrangement 'would be a public advertisement to the Transvaal Government that they had nothing more to hope for from Germany, or indeed from any European power, by which our task in South Africa would be greatly lightened.'[20] With this bait dangling before him, Balfour made haste to reassure Chamberlain, who feared that too many concessions would be made to Germany. Having persuaded Chamberlain that negotiations with Germany should not be broken off, and that, in the event of trouble with the Transvaal, Britain could make a temporary arrangement over Delagoa Bay and the railway, Balfour brought the discussions to a successful conclusion on 30 August 1898.[21]

The Anglo-German convention confirmed the British claim to Portuguese East Africa, if these territories were ever to be given up. Germany was to have similar rights in Angola, while a secret clause in the agreement excluded any third power from gaining Portuguese African territory.[22] The Transvaal now stood isolated. In September 1898 Balfour stated that Germany had resigned 'all concern in Transvaal matters'. The optimistic Hatzfeldt claimed that a new era of Anglo-German co-operation was beginning. Balfour offered 'no estimate on the value of this prophecy'. Indeed, he doubted whether Germany 'would ever have actively supported the Transvaal.' But now that the Transvaal was denied all hope of European assistance he felt that the republic would perhaps prove more amenable.[23]

However, relations between the Transvaal and Britain continued to deteriorate. Early in 1899, with Germany bought off, and the tense situation created by the Anglo-French confrontation at Fashoda relaxing, Chamberlain and Milner stepped up the pace in South Africa. Either fundamental concessions must be squeezed out of Kruger or, failing this, the British public must be convinced that all possible avenues of negotiation had been fully explored. At the end of May 1899, the Bloemfontein Conference opened. It was a face-to-face meeting between Milner and Kruger to discuss the *uitlander* franchise and related problems. The British government hoped that it would state its case effectively at Bloemfontein. Even before this there had been dramatic events. 21,000 *uitlanders* had petitioned the Queen, and Milner had publicly, although histrionically, compared them to helots. Moreover in May Chamberlain had issued a dispatch reaffirming British suzerainty over the Transvaal.[24]

In May, before the dispatch was sent, Balfour attempted to analyse the situation in a rational and fair-minded manner. In a paper prepared for the Cabinet, he denied that the difficulties in the Transvaal sprang from recollections of Majuba Hill or the Jameson Raid. Rather, he discerned a situation quite unparalleled in history, and posing novel problems. 'No case', he claimed, 'has

ever occurred in which the majority of a community are alien in
blood, different in language, superior in cultivation and wealth, to
a minority which constitutes the original national stock to whom
the country politically belongs.' Balfour also looked at *uitlander*
demands from the other side. Although the enfranchisement of
the *uitlanders* might seem to be an electoral reform, 'the Boers
might describe it as a transfer of nationality – and can anyone say
they are wrong?' Similarly, the teaching of English in the schools
would mean to the Transvaalers that 'the national language will in
no short time be eliminated and an alien language put in its place.'
Doubtless, Balfour argued, the Transvaal could not remain for
very long a Boer republic but, 'were I a Boer . . . nothing but
necessity would induce me to adopt a constitution which would
turn my country into an English Republic, or a system of education which would reduce my language to the "patois" of a
small and helpless minority.'[25]

But what was 'necessity'? Balfour realised that the British
government could ask for concessions, but that 'international law
would [not] justify us in doing more than asking for them.' He
admitted the seriousness of *uitlander* grievances, including restrictions on the franchise, excessive taxation, exclusion from
juries, restrictions on public meetings, attacks on the independence of the press and the law courts, the 'proscription of English', harsh laws on the immigration and expulsion of aliens,
inadequate municipal institutions, and governmental corruption.
This was a formidable list, but Balfour wondered whether 'the
redress of any of a like character has ever been forced upon one
nation by the other at the point of a bayonet.' Only the exceptional circumstances of the Transvaal, Balfour felt, justified the
British government in contemplating the use of force. Even so,
he only wanted force to back up demands for 'reparations for
outrages against individuals in the Transvaal'.[26]

Why did Balfour argue the Boer case? For one thing, he still
felt that the Raid had left Britain morally in debt to the Transvaal.
This debt must be paid off before strong measures could be considered appropriate. Of course, Milner and Chamberlain were
doing their best to propagate the *uitlander* cause, and this would

help. Also, in discussing the Colonial Secretary's proposed draft dispatch of 29 April 1899, Balfour wanted the Cabinet to consider the 'side which Sir A. Milner has somewhat ignored, and which will undoubtedly be very forcibly brought to our notice both here and at the Cape should Mr. Chamberlain's dispatch be the prelude to more vigorous action.'[27]

In a word, Balfour wanted the British case to be perfectly watertight. This meant influencing Chamberlain. The two men had already disagreed in Cabinet over the value of the Colonial Secretary's proposed dispatch. On 5 May 1899, Balfour wrote to Chamberlain to pursue the point:

I do not want to press my views respecting the Transvaal Policy further than I have done in Cabinet, partly because I feel that there is no use in being critical unless I am constructive also, and partly because my objections (such as they are) to sending the Despatch are not so much due to the Despatch itself as to my fears lest it should not lead neatly and securely up to our next move.'[28]

Balfour's objections balanced uneasily between the argument that 'if the Transvaal were to be dealt with on ordinary principles, there does not seem to me to be anything like a *casus belli* established', and the fear that if Chamberlain's dispatch was ignored it would damage Britain's standing. The assumption that the *uitlanders* were in a majority in the Transvaal seemed to Balfour possibly to justify 'exceptional measures', but the Cabinet would have to resolve this point with more care than they had shown hitherto; it could not be dismissed as pure metaphysics. Practically, Balfour suggested to Chamberlain that some measure of municipal reform to secure liberty, property, the right to jury service and a fair deal for schools teaching English, might 'be fairly *insisted* upon.' He recognised, however, that this seemed to interfere with the Transvaal's internal affairs, something which Chamberlain's dispatch wished to play down. This otherwise curious statement of Balfour's emphasises how anxious some members of the government were in May 1899 to seek a settlement with the co-operation of Kruger. For himself, Balfour displayed no patriotic enthusiasm for the *uitlanders* if they could not be satisfied with his proposals for municipal reform. Indeed, he considered them to be 'rather unreasonable'.[29]

4

Balfour was not alone in the Cabinet in wishing to keep the *uitlander* problem in perspective. Salisbury and Hicks Beach, the Chancellor, by no means saw eye to eye with Chamberlain and Milner.[30] But the failure of the Bloemfontein Conference on 5 June 1899 began a new phase in British policy. By 7 June, Chamberlain and Milner were already discussing the form of an ultimatum to the Transvaal, and also, on 20 June, the question of reinforcements for South Africa.[31] But the diplomatic game continued unabated. On 18 July it became known that Kruger had granted the *uitlanders* a seven years retrospective franchise and five new seats.[32] Did this mean the end to the crisis? Clearly, Kruger was not thirsting for a war which he could hardly win, and in which foreign allies would be denied him. His only policy was to play for time. Whether in fact his concessions were genuine was another matter.

Milner was alarmed lest the Cabinet should snatch at Kruger's offer. Writing on 26 July, from South Africa, Violet Cecil told Balfour that Milner had not been 'rushing the thing', but that:

He is afraid of an agreement being come to without any sufficient guarantee. He is afraid of the Cabinet wobblers because if they let this crisis fizzle out it will be years before we regain our ground during which time heavy punishment will fall on the Outlanders as having caused the whole thing. He is in favour in some ways of arbitration and in saying all this he talks neither like a jingo nor a theoretical radical but like a man of sense. 'It's no use worrying the Boers – it's not talk we want but united action and preparation', and again 'they rely on our division'.[33]

Milner, therefore, was committed to strong action, and fearful of compromise and division. Balfour was one of the Cabinet 'wobblers' in July, though he was to wobble less as the crisis deepened. But all was not well at the Cape either. Buller, the

Commander-in-Chief, and Milner were at loggerheads.[34] Moreover, there were two other dangers in the Cape. The first, that the
numerous Cape Dutch would find British policy too aggressive;
the second, that Rhodes and his followers would feel that it was
not aggressive enough. Violet Cecil, indeed, urged Balfour that
'if the Colony under Rhodes wishes to separate itself from England ... we shall let them do it – morally speaking they are not
worth fighting for, tho' I suppose we want the Cape as a coaling
station.'[35]

As it happened, Chamberlain and Milner carried all before them
during the vital months of August and September. British public
opinion was prepared for war, and the leaders of the Liberal party
did not deny British claims to suzerainty over the Transvaal.
There were certainly outspoken opponents of war as Britain
hovered on the brink of hostilities, but they were out of tune with
the prevailing mood. Rhodes was nearer the mark when he cabled,
'Only way to deal with Kruger is by ultimatum with time limit.'[36]

But threats were useless without the appropriate force. Although on 4 October, 67,000 troops were either in South Africa
or on the high seas, there were serious misgivings on the British
side. Not only had doubts been expressed over Buller's qualities,
but it was by no means certain that Britain's military preparations
were adequate. Lansdowne, from the War Office, told Salisbury
on 4 October that 'we are going to fight an enemy more formidable than any whom we have encountered for many years past'.[37]
From South Africa, Milner had already warned Chamberlain
that serious reverses could be expected at Mafeking on the
Bechuanaland border if the Boers attacked. Chamberlain, in turn,
blamed the War Office for earlier vetoing his proposals for a
substantial troop build-up.[38] Moreover, the War Office itself,
judging from Wyndham's urgent letter to Balfour of 7 October,
was in danger of having the army run short of essential men and
supplies unless a policy of replacement was quickly adopted.[39]
These were not happy omens.

There had, of course, been good reasons why troops had
not been poured into South Africa earlier. Kruger would rightly
have interpreted it as tantamount to a declaration of war. Also,

there had been the desire to keep President Steyn of the Orange Free State out of the Transvaal's camp for as long as possible. Although economically the Orange Free State was an extension of the Cape, the political sympathies of the vast majority of its citizens were elsewhere. Balfour told Chamberlain on 2 October that he felt that Britain's relations with the Orange Free State might 'prove to be our "Achilles Heel".' Vital as it was to have free access through the Free State to attack the Transvaal, Balfour did not want Britain to appear to be 'deliberately picking a quarrel' with President Steyn since this would encourage Britain's critics in the belief 'that we cannot tolerate the independence within our sphere of free republics.' He therefore proposed that Britain should not negotiate with the Free State, but treat the militant resolution passed in its Volksraad 'as an official declaration of hostility'.[40] In fact, both the Transvaal and the Orange Free State presented an ultimatum to Britain on 9 October which called for the immediate withdrawal of British troops from the Transvaal's frontiers and the recall of all British reinforcements dispatched since June. Conveniently, the Afrikaners had themselves taken the final step.

Balfour's attitude had hardened sufficiently by the beginning of October for him to display calculating ruthlessness over the fate of the Orange Free State. In May he had argued the Transvaaler's case. Perhaps this was mainly an academic exercise. Even by August he had told his intimate friend Lady Elcho that although he thought war would be avoided, he questioned whether this would be 'in the long run for the good of mankind.'[41] Frequently, Balfour displayed an ambiguity that only in the last resort stiffened into a resolute defence of government policy. When Parliament reassembled, he denounced the Transvaalers on 19 October, for 'conceiving liberty for themselves and no liberty for anyone else', while asking whether it was unnatural that the Boers should fight, 'not for anything that can be described as their rights, but for a system from which they gain such infinite profit?'[42]

More realistic, and more honest, was Balfour's letter to James Bryce written on 2 October before the opening shots of the war required more conformist sentiments:

As not uncommonly happens in difficult circumstances, we – the Government and people of this country – have got to find, not the course which is best, but the course which is least bad. I am afraid that this will involve a military expedition – I am still sanguine enough to hope not a *war*.

The outcome of the present crisis can hardly, I fear, make the feeling between the English and Dutch-speaking population much worse than it is. My hope for the future lies in the expectation that when our supremacy, and, as a consequence of our supremacy, equal rights are really established through South Africa, race jealousies may die down as they have . . . under similar conditions in Canada.

Everyone must regard the present state of things with deep regret, and few of us, I should think, are sufficiently self-satisfied to be absolutely confident that the particular course we may happen to recommend is beyond all question the right one – yet in this case I feel little doubt.[43]

5

Once the discovery of gold had changed the Transvaal from an agricultural backwater into a thriving, expanding community, the British government was drawn into a battle for supremacy in southern Africa. Although the Simonstown naval base would almost certainly have been safe even in an Afrikaner-dominated republic, this was no longer the issue after 1886. Thus when Balfour spoke optimistically of the lessening of hostility between British and Afrikaner, his optimism was underpinned by the assumption that this would occur only after the establishment of British supremacy.

The *uitlander* problem was for the British government a heaven-sent opportunity to tilt the balance in South Africa away from the Afrikaners. Convenient though it would have been to achieve this peacefully, Kruger and the Transvaalers were in no hurry to surrender their independence. Chamberlain and Milner, however, saw that unless they took the offensive the opportunity would be lost, perhaps for ever. Nor would it serve their purposes to have a gradually enfranchised *uitlander* population contained within

Kruger's republic and perhaps turning its back on British loyalties. Ultimately, the attainment of British supremacy in South Africa rested on the use of force. When Balfour became convinced of this he swallowed his qualms and supported the war. But the war itself was to give rise to uneasy consciences.

11 A Fight for Supremacy

He's an absent minded beggar, and his weaknesses are great –
But we and Paul must take him as we find him –
He is out on active service, wiping something off a slate –
And he's left a lot of little things behind him!
Duke's son – cook's son – son of a hundred kings –
(Fifty thousand horse and foot going to Table Bay!).

KIPLING, 1899

I

PERHAPS the chief characteristic of the Boer War was the power of endurance displayed by the participants. The conflict lasted for over two and a half years, despite the fact that the British Empire sent 448,000 men to conquer a largely amateur army of 40,000 Afrikaners. But the men of the Transvaal and the Orange Free State could not have held out so long if the British army had not displayed incompetence and indecisiveness on the grand scale. This was an advantage which the Boers had not expected. This, in addition to their modern weapons bought with the Transvaal's gold, and their unorthodox and effective tactics in the field, goes far to explain the war's protraction. If the Boers were sternly tested in the war, the British had to endure early defeat, humiliation, the barbs of international hatred, and the frustration of not being able to finish off Boer resistance.

The first weeks of the war confirmed Milner's worst fears. Boer forces invaded Natal and the Cape. They besieged Kimberley, Mafeking and Ladysmith and pushed on towards the Naamurport and Stormberg junctions in an attempt to control vital railway lines. Although the main body of British reinforcements had not landed by the beginning of November, these Boer successes took some explaining. Balfour confessed to his sister Alice his surprise that at Ladysmith 'so large a garrison ... amply supplied as I believe they are with ammunition and food can be in any danger. ... On the whole ... I am dissatisfied.'[1]

But there were some things to be thankful for. Natal was, of course, solid in the British cause. Even in the Cape, there was no wholesale Afrikaner rebellion. In the areas penetrated by Boer commandos, several thousand of the Cape Dutch rallied to the republics' standards. But elsewhere, Anglo-Afrikaner rivalry found expression in press debates, mutual insults and social ostracism, and in what Milner considered to be the over-sympathetic attitude of the Cape government to rebels and republicans.[2] Moreover, despite evidence of virulent anti-British feeling in Europe, there was no intervention on behalf of the Boers. Late in November, with the main British army disembarked, Balfour reported to Salisbury the Kaiser's pleasure that the Anglo-German agreement of 1898 had settled 'the relations of the two countries in South Africa "for all time".' The Kaiser was also 'full of the warmest admiration for the way in which the mobilisation and transport had been effected', and said, 'it was a feat unique in the history of the world.' The Kaiser's admiration did not, however, extend to British tactics in the field, for he remarked, 'whenever war occurs in any part of the world we in Germany sit down and make a plan.'[3]

In South Africa, Buller was able to make plans but unable to execute them. In December the British army was defeated three times in the disasters of 'black week'. Buller himself was repulsed at Colenso while trying to relieve Ladysmith. He then stood devoid of purpose. Balfour, after consulting Lansdowne, the Secretary for War, ordered Buller either to relieve Ladysmith or lay down his command. The Defence Committee then proposed that Lord Roberts should replace Buller as Commander-in-Chief in South Africa.

Roberts was widely popular, but sixty-seven years of age. Balfour overcame Salisbury's objections to Roberts' age by agreeing that he should have as his second-in-command Kitchener, of whom Balfour later remarked 'we knew nothing but good in those days.'⁴ Roberts expressed the greatest satisfaction at having Kitchener to work with, and dismissed doubts as to his own physical vigour with the words, 'for years I have led a most active and abstemious life, waiting for this day.'⁵ By May 1900, Roberts and Kitchener had turned the tide in South Africa.

The early humiliations in South Africa caused widespread anxiety and distress in Britain. The Queen maintained a vigorous interest in events. For her ministers this had its drawbacks. Balfour had to deal with royal complaints that she had not been consulted over Roberts' appointment or informed of the proceedings of the Defence Committee. According to Ponsonby, the Queen's private secretary, Balfour was always 'a great success with Victoria, although to me he never seemed to treat her seriously.'⁶ At any rate, he was able to tell Salisbury on 19 December that he had calmed the Queen down. Balfour had also made it plain that he could not accept on constitutional grounds a further complaint from Victoria that she should have been consulted before the dispatch of the telegram ordering Buller to relieve Ladysmith.⁷

As well as facing an irate Queen, Balfour was the first minister to speak to the public after the misfortunes of 'black week'. On 8 and 9 January he made three speeches in Manchester, where he represented the constituency of East Manchester. These speeches aroused widespread criticism, not so much from the audiences, who were prepared to cheer anything, but from the press and the public at large. Balfour was not a mob orator who could effortlessly bang the patriotic drum. Nor would he throw military or political scapegoats to the public. Rather he preferred to defend the government's policy in sophisticated and, to the untutored ear, obscure terms.

At the same time, Balfour put his finger firmly on the dilemmas facing the government's policy-making in South Africa. He emphasised how the Jameson Raid had tied the government's hands in dealing with the Transvaal's subsequent arms build-up. This meant that Britain 'entered upon this war insufficiently prepared on the spot to deal with the military situation we had to face.' But the government had done all that 'it thought necessary to meet defensively the eventuality of war, if, as was improbable, but possible, war should be the ultimate issue of negotiations.'[8] This was less than convincing. Chamberlain and Milner had discussed reinforcements on 20 June, and Chamberlain had subsequently been overruled by the War Office in his demand for more troops.[9] As for defence, the first months of the war had been fought outside Afrikaner territory and to the detriment of substantial British forces. Although the suspicions left by the Jameson Raid had made it imperative not to alarm the Boer republics unduly, war had been very much in the minds of Chamberlain and Milner from the failure of the Bloemfontein Conference onwards.

Balfour next advanced a criticism of the constitution to defend the British defeats. He claimed that the government could not have gone to the Commons for immense supplementary supplies in mid-August without encountering substantial opposition. He also believed that without the public behind it, any government was denied sufficient rapidity of action when dealing with any crisis beyond a certain magnitude. This was hardly an argument to inspire an anxious public, no matter how keenly Balfour believed it.

He did however admit that the military capacity of the Boers had been underrated, and that 'the unhappy entanglement of Ladysmith was beyond any calculation that we formed', but felt that the Boer invasion should not 'frighten even the most timid.' Balfour denied that the Boer artillery was superior, and claimed that the generals had been given a completely free hand. Moreover, he denied 'the need, as far as my colleagues and I are concerned, of any apology whatever.'[10]

This was strong stuff, but somewhat contradictory. Balfour's speech the next day was no clearer. It was true that the war 'had been a disappointment', but it was *not* true that there had been 'strange and exceptional reverses'. Balfour was on safer ground when he spoke of the ennobling sacrifices of war, and of the 'enthusiastic patriotism which is from day to day knitting closer every branch of the English-speaking race.' In view of the solid support of the self-governing colonies for Britain, there was some justification for this remark. More high-flown was Balfour's claim that when the victory, and equality between Boer and British, had been achieved in South Africa, the British would have fulfilled their 'destiny as a great nation'.[11]

Next day, 11 January, *The Times* commented severely, 'Mr. Balfour we are sorry to see, continued to speak yesterday in the jaunty and almost frivolous tone he has thought it fit to assume in discussing the great crisis in which we stand . . . . Mr. Balfour seems to look upon himself and his colleagues as neither more nor less responsible for our reverses in South Africa than "the man in the street". . . . There have been, he admits, a few hitches, deficiencies and regrettable incidents in the campaign and our Army system is not necessarily perfect!'[12] Balfour had not caught the public mood, although there was perhaps some credit in this. Nor did he satisfy his colleague Lord George Hamilton who complained, when Parliament reassembled on 1 February, that Balfour 'again failed to strike a patriotic chord.'[13]

Balfour resented the flood of criticism. Privately he told his brother-in-law, the philosopher Henry Sidgwick, that he had been unwilling to admit his conviction that 'the mistakes which have occurred are entirely due to the advice of experts respecting matters on which experts alone have the right to form an authoritative opinion.'[14] On 24 January Balfour returned to the subject denying that his speeches had been flippant, and stressing how he had been through a time of anxiety 'far greater than anything of which I have had experience even in the worst periods of our Irish troubles.' He insisted, rather, that the whole key of his speech had been the statement that the government had underrated the military strength of the Boers. He continued frankly:

I not only think blunders have been committed, but I think they have been of the most serious kind, imperilling the whole progress of the war. But I do not think those blunders are due to War Office mal-administration, and, until I see reason to think so, nothing will induce me to say so. The chief blunders have been made, in my private opinion, by our Generals in the field; but I do not of course think it desirable to make any such statement in public . . . I have said in these speeches not all that I thought, but nothing that I did not think. I cannot give my full opinions without blaming gallant men whom I do not wish to blame; but I entirely decline to make a scapegoat of people who I do *not* think deserve any such fate. Far rather would I leave public life for ever.[15]

But as the war progressed, fresh evidence of professional incompetence and maladministration accumulated. Accordingly, Balfour became determined to re-organise the apparatus for defence planning, notably the Defence Committee of the Cabinet. And even though he refrained from criticising military ineptitude during the war, he did not forget, for example, Sir George White's performance at Ladysmith. In 1905, the King proposed that the newly established Order of Merit should be given to Sir George. Balfour replied caustically that he had 'little to say of this excellent officer except that nobody has ever supposed that he is a man of great abilities, military or otherwise [and] though the O.M. would add to his reputation, I do not think he would add to the reputation of the O.M.'[16] The King, with his somewhat unsophisticated admiration for men of action, had already protested to Balfour in November 1904 that Sir George had been removed from his post in too abrupt a manner.[17] All this, while not quite a vendetta, at least shows that Balfour could weigh military reputations accurately.

Generals were not the only cause of embarrassment for the government. In April 1900 the Queen was much disturbed by rumours that Rhodes had wished to surrender when besieged at Kimberley. The rumour was particularly ironical in view of Rhodes' previous role as the war-lord of Anglo-Saxon expansion. The government did not expect tact from Rhodes. As Chamberlain had complained to Salisbury in January 1899, 'I do not trust Rhodes at all. He is unable to keep a secret.'[18] But nor did it expect him to show cowardice. Balfour asked Chamberlain the truth of the recent rumours, and was told 'that Rhodes did threaten to surrender or something equivalent, but that this was only temper – a kind of bluff – to get . . . what he wanted.' Rhodes had evidently wanted the relieving general, Kekewitch, to rescue him with more alacrity. Growing impatient, he and the Mayor of Kimberley had sent an ultimatum threatening surrender, to

Roberts, over Kekewitch's head. On being rescued, Rhodes had criticised Kekewitch who had promptly told the government everything. Balfour and Chamberlain worked to stifle these re-criminations and to reassure the Queen.[19]

But at least Kimberley *had* been relieved. In February 1900, Roberts accepted the surrender of Cronje and his army after the battle of Paardeberg. It was now only a question of time before the siege of Ladysmith and Mafeking was lifted. In May, Violet Cecil told Balfour from South Africa, 'now at least we are be-ginning to see the end . . . Kitchener has carried this campaign through on his back, he and the love everyone has for "Bobs".'[20] But the war would not end. The Boer generals in the field, Botha, Smuts, de la Rey and de Wet fought on. Two Afrikaner emissaries of peace who approached them were shot.[21] The huge British army was strung out over hundreds of miles of veld trying to round up the Boer remnants. In desperation, the army burnt down Boer farms, hoping by a scorched-earth policy to starve the commandos into submission. By the end of 1900, Roberts handed over to Kitchener and returned to honour and glory in England. But the war still had a year and a half to run.

2

In order to strengthen its hand, the government fought the 'Khaki' election in October 1900. The apparent victory in South Africa could be relied upon to return the Unionists to power, even though the early failures had disenchanted many of the electorate. But the election aroused bitter feelings. Basically, the country was asked to judge Chamberlain and the government's South African policy. Although Unionists could not fail to respond to what amounted to a patriotic appeal, the Liberal party's attitude was ambiguous. By October 1900, the Liberals were split into three factions over the war. The Liberal Imperialists Asquith, Grey, Haldane and Rosebery supported the war though reserving the right to criticise the methods employed. The Liberal leader Campbell-Bannerman wanted above all to minimise the split within his party, but had said in June 1899 that nothing in the South African situation could justify war.[22] Moreover he was later to condemn the 'methods of barbarism' employed by the British army, and to press for a liberal settlement. On the left wing of the party were the pro-Boers led by Harcourt, Morley, John Burns and the up-and-coming David Lloyd George. These men were unqualified in their condemnation of the war, even though in Lloyd George's case it endangered life and limb when he spoke in Chamberlain's stronghold of Birmingham. In the Commons, the Irish Nationalists unhesitatingly supported the Boers, with whom they could identify themselves as an oppressed nation.

Chamberlain was heavily attacked during the campaign. When it was over, he thanked Balfour for 'the kind things you said in my defence.' Chamberlain complained of attacks of a private character which all the Liberal leaders, save Grey, had failed to repudiate, 'allowing the insinuations to be distributed by the Radical Association at 5/- per thousand.'[23] Salisbury, too, congratulated Balfour on his opportune campaigning, 'for the political world was running the danger of being divided into pro-Boer and pro-Joe; which I think is not an exhaustive statement of the sentiments of Her Majesty's subjects.'[24]

The 'Khaki' election returned the Unionists with a slightly enlarged majority. While this could be interpreted as a mandate for pushing the war through to the bitter end, it did not escape notice that for every eight votes cast for the government seven were cast against it. In the new House of Commons, Chamberlain faced renewed attacks. He denied ever using the slogan 'A seat lost to the Government is a seat sold to the Boers', claiming instead that he had merely passed on by telegram a statement from the Mayor of Kimberley which ran, 'A seat lost to the Government is a seat *gained* by the Boers'. Due to the negligence of the Post Office official, Chamberlain insisted, the vital word *gained* had been altered to *sold*. This was a thin explanation, but Balfour dismissed the accusation against Chamberlain as an absurd story.[25]

Four days later on 10 December, Balfour again came to the

rescue of the beleaguered Colonial Secretary. Chamberlain had been accused of profiteering from the war by failing to sever his connections with several companies holding government contracts. Balfour poured scorn on the accusers, asking who would satisfy them as fit to hold office, 'Wanted, a man to serve Her Majesty, with no money, no relations, and inspiring no general confidence.'[26] Perhaps the vigour of the assault on Chamberlain was an attempt by the Liberals to hide their divisions, and Balfour was not slow to point out that the electorate had preferred a united party to one hopelessly split by faction.[27]

3

The Liberals, however, continued to provide the government with vigorous opposition in the House of Commons. Controversy centred on the conduct of the war and the prospects for peace. Farm-burning was meant to destroy the commandos' resistance. Perhaps it was also the hand of vengeance. Between June and November 1900 over 600 farms were burnt in the Orange Free State alone.[28] Since the Boer soldiers wore no uniforms they could be, in Balfour's words, peaceful agriculturists or effective combatants as they chose. Although Kitchener had let it be known when he assumed Roberts's command that he was not in favour of burning farms, Balfour told the Commons in 1902 that there were 'by the laws of all civilized warfare ... circumstances which render it expedient, right and even necessary.'[29] As a step towards reconciliation, however, a sum of £500,000 had been placed on the estimate in August 1901 to compensate the victims of farm-burning. Asquith doubted its adequacy.[30]

Farm-burning created another problem. The British authorities were faced with hordes of homeless and hungry refugees. These they placed in camps, where early deficiencies in diet and sanitation caused the deaths of many. About 20,000 inmates had died by the time the war ended in June 1902, most of them women and children. A public outcry in England caused an improvement in conditions in the concentration camps, and after the war Chamberlain claimed that the mortality rate in the last six months of fighting had been lower than in peacetime.[31] But the scandal lent point to accusations of barbarism, and Lloyd George even spoke of a policy of extermination.[32]

Apart from beating the Boers into submission, what inducements could the government offer in the cause of peace-making? Balfour called the Boers 'brave men ... fighting for independence', and assured them in August 1901 that the government was not 'animated in the smallest degree by a vindictive spirit against those who are ranged against us in the field.'[33] However, he continued to demand that their independence should be surrendered, and added for good measure, 'we do mean to subjugate the Boers ... we do mean to conquer them. We do mean to annex them, we do mean to incorporate them within the Empire.'[34]

But Balfour also spoke in terms of bringing to South Africa freedom and equality, 'the blessings associated with British colonial rule in all parts of the globe', and was undeterred by the forceful statement of Tim Healy, an Irish Nationalist member, that 'it would be better for the Boers to be dead than to be English.'[35] Balfour did not, of course, mean freedom and equality to be extended to the non-European inhabitants of South Africa. The government had shown considerable awareness of Afrikaner susceptibilities on this score, and although the army had used some coloured and African assistance, there had been no question of arming them wholesale and turning them on the Boers. Subsequently, British overtures for peace made no demands for the enfranchisement of non-Europeans in the Transvaal or the Orange Free State. Nor had Indian troops been sent to South Africa, although they had simultaneously played a major part in destroying the Boxer rebellion in China.

All of this amounted to an exercise in tact. But what future awaited the Transvaal and the Orange Free State if they surrendered? In June 1900, Roberts had demanded unconditional surrender from the Transvaal. It was natural, therefore, that the Boer commandos should try to resist as long as possible and hope for a change of government in London. Campbell-Bannerman certainly seemed to offer an easier future to the republic than the Unionist government. Indeed, Balfour expressed horror at Campbell-Bannerman's advocacy of the speedy establishment of full representative institutions, as in the Cape or Australia, after a Boer surrender.[36] But although Balfour dismissed such 'absolute insanity' in February 1901, he simultaneously told the Commons that the Boer leaders 'know perfectly well that if they were to lay down their arms they could do so ... with the certainty that their property and persons would be respected ... that equal rights would be granted to the inhabitants of the two colonies, and ... that when it became possible, autonomy, free institutions, would also be granted.'[37]

The Boers were entitled to know exactly what this offer meant. In the same month, February 1901, Kitchener had presented draft peace proposals which also promised a degree of responsible government 'as soon as possible'.[38] But the Boers still refused to surrender their independence. They could hardly have been encouraged to do so by a Balfourian discourse in the Commons which denied that the government's policy of unconditional surrender meant the unconditional surrender 'of the individual, but unconditional abandonment of the idea of an independent Government of the Transvaal or Orange Free State.'[39] Harried by the relentless Kitchener, with their country occupied and the smoke rising from burning homesteads, the commandos were hardly likely to respond to such metaphysics.

In January 1900, Balfour had already put forward his private plan for dealing with the Boer republics. In a Cabinet paper, he argued that Johannesburg should be removed from 'the stagnant, backward and disloyal portions of the Transvaal, which for an indefinite period must be given up to the farmer of Dutch descent.' More important, Balfour wanted a constitution that would deny the Afrikaners the opportunity to flout British rule, but would 'give them quickly and completely – the essential elements of internal self-government.' He proposed that the conquered republics should each have a Governor-General with enough troops to crush rebellion, and a constitution on the lines of the Orange Free State before the war – but without the right to raise their own troops. If the system was abused, the Governor-General could suspend the constitution and revert to crown colony rule. Any armed threats by the Afrikaners, or attempts 'to establish inequalities of status between whites of different nationalities, or to exercise gross tyranny over the natives', would enable the British government to suspend the constitution without effort.[40]

Naturally, the Governor-General must be ensured the means of coercion. Balfour did not believe that it was sufficient to give Natal, outstandingly loyal during the war, control over part of the railway line linking the Transvaal with Delagoa Bay. More useful would be Britain's right to ban any arms imports which threatened security in South Africa. Also, Balfour agreed with a proposal of Chamberlain's that the government should have some control over troops recruited in South Africa. But he argued that this would hardly be possible unless the British government agreed to pay part of the necessary expenses. This idea he felt was well worth considering, and could be equally beneficial to Britain and to South Africa.[41]

Although it was essential to consider these safeguards, there was some contradiction between Balfour's private proposals and his public assertion that, 'The intention that the English colonial system in South Africa shall be what it is everywhere else, a free system, has never been disguised.'[42]

But apart from the Transvaal and the Orange Free State, the Cape presented problems of its own. Balfour had little sympathy for Afrikaner rebels in the Cape, and in July 1900 wondered whether a more severe deterrent than five years' disenfranchisement was needed.[43] At the peace, in fact, a proclamation disenfranchised all Afrikaner rebels for life. Furthermore, the operation of martial law, and the temporary suspension of the Cape Parliament provoked criticism in the Commons in January 1902. Balfour hoped that the number of executions under martial law would soon be made available. As for the suspension of the Cape constitution, he argued that military necessity and the need to protect the supply routes to the armies in the field demanded it, adding for good measure that it had only been carried out by Milner on the advice of the Cape government.[44] This controversy was to be renewed later.

4

The war in South Africa demanded government inquiry. In October 1900, Chamberlain suggested a strong commission of inquiry to Balfour.[45] Balfour was equally convinced that 'after what had passed, an enquiry is inevitable. Nor, if an enquiry be started into any part of the conduct of the war, do I think it possible to limit its scope so as to exclude from review the conduct of the military commanders responsible for the earlier phases, at least, of the campaign.'[46] In February 1901 Balfour promised the Commons that an inquiry would begin as soon as the war was substantially over and the necessary witnesses available. The government, he claimed, wanted to conceal nothing.[47] Admitting that 'undoubtedly, great mistakes as regards military anticipations have been made', Balfour made a vigorous attempt to whitewash the administration in terms of 'the performance as a whole'. The War Office's 'power to provide great bodies of troops, and to supply them with every necessary – nay, with every luxury – has been remarkably demonstrated, and is a performance which has been unequalled so far in the history of the Empire.'[48] Privately, Balfour was less sanguine over the possible revelations of an inquiry, although the exposure of military deficiences was to afford him incalculable benefit in his determination to reshape the structure of imperial defence.

But this was to come after the war. At last, at the end of May 1902, terms were agreed between the still defiant Boer leaders and the British authorities. The peace of Vereeniging was followed by the surrender of over 21,000 commandos – far more than either Kitchener or Milner had believed to be active. On 2 June, Balfour announced the peace terms to a crowded House of Commons. The terms included a grant of £3,000,000 to restore families to their homes and supply them with the necessities of life. Loans, interest free for two years, were also made available. The Boer troops, if they surrendered and recognised British sovereignty, were to be allowed to take up their civilian lives again free from legal prosecution. The question of enfranchising non-Europeans was shelved until self-government returned to the Transvaal and the Orange River Colony. As for the two annexed colonies, military government was to give way as soon as possible to 'Civil Government, and, as soon as circumstances permit, representative institutions, leading up to self-government will be introduced.' Having read out the terms, Balfour said no more, and it was left to Campbell-Bannerman to claim that the peace would 'cause the most profound and universal satisfaction, not only at home but within the whole bounds of the Empire.'[49]

Boer losses had been daunting. 20,000 dead in the concentration camps, 3,800 killed in the fighting and 31,600 taken prisoner. Both the family and the land were badly scarred. The Transvaal and the Orange River Colony were dragged into the Empire, but they carried with them a stronger, and perhaps more subtle, Afrikaner nationalism. The British hardly expected amity from the Afrikaaners, but they hoped for co-operation. After all, the treaty of Vereeniging had deferred the bitter problem of native enfranchisement. In effect, this meant that the non-Europeans as a whole had been sold for the sake of a white man's peace. Having swept this conundrum aside, and with their supremacy at least temporarily asserted, the British authorities now faced the enormous task of reconstruction.

12 Reconstruction

Men are not born equal. They cannot be made equal by education extending over generation after generation within the ordinary historical limit.

BALFOUR, 1904

I

IN the early months of peace it was not only the defeated Boers who had wounds to lick. Scandal and recrimination still surrounded the government. Balfour became Prime Minister in July 1902, one month before the Elgin Commission began its investigations into the preparations and conduct of the war. The government could hardly look forward to the production of the report with relish. Balfour indeed had told his uncle Salisbury in January 1901, 'there *is* some possibility that one of the results of the Commission of Inquiry may be to provoke very unedifying recriminations between the soldiers, and, possibly, between the soldiers and the Civil Government.'[1]

Even before the war had ended M.P.s had tried to expose matters the government would have been pleased to forget. In August 1901 Dillon, the member for East Mayo, asked Balfour whether a grant was planned for the unfortunate Buller.[2] More serious was the revelation in April 1902 that two Australian officers had been court-martialled and shot for murdering Boers. This incident had ugly overtones, and Balfour refused to make public the proceedings of the courts martial.[3]

The findings of the Elgin Commission, however, could not be suppressed. In 1903 it reported grave faults in military organisation and exposed the ineffectiveness of the Cabinet Defence Committee. Balfour accordingly set up the War Office (Reconstitution) Committee in November 1903. This in itself he found no easy task, complaining to the King of the delays caused by searching for a military member who was not identified with any particular military clique or with the War Office.[4] Not only were the soldiers sensitive to these inquiries; Brodrick, who had been at the War Office during the conflict, also complained bitterly, after the Elgin Commission's report, of its lack of information and its misconceptions.[5]

But Balfour found the Elgin Commission and the War Office (Reconstitution) Committee useful weapons in forcing through fundamental defence reforms. In this sense their findings were not wholly displeasing for him. But there was scant comfort to be drawn from the report of the Butler Committee in the last months of the Unionist administration. The Committee revealed that after the peace, enormous quantities of military supplies that the army no longer needed were sold off in South Africa. Unfortunately many supplies had been sold at a heavy loss, and some had disappeared altogether. Even worse, it was quite clear that certain British officers had defrauded the government and pocketed the proceeds. Balfour confessed in the Commons that 'some of the transactions . . . seem to me quite incapable of explanation.' The Liberals claimed that the government had been robbed of something like £7,000,000.[6]

However, by June 1905 Balfour was able to admit past defence deficiencies more freely. This was chiefly because he had set up the Committee of Imperial Defence and encouraged War Office reform. It was now possible for him to claim that there was a new organisation, 'which I hope and believe, in the unfortunate event of a great war again, will be able to deal satisfactorily with these matters.' When Lloyd George insisted that the supplies had vanished *after* the Boer War not during it, Balfour admitted that 'the machinery in operation was the ancient and traditional machinery, which was imperfect. It was inadequate. It has been changed.'[7]

Not that the Boer War afforded unbroken gloom. Balfour saw particular significance in the voluntary contributions of the self-governing colonies to the war effort. 'For the first time,' he said,

'we have had an Army entirely composed of British subjects
... this indicates a very great revolution in the military position
of this country ... never before when we have sent a really considerable force beyond the seas have we been without allies or mercenaries other than of English nationality and English blood.'
Why had there been this enthusiasm? Balfour thought it sprang
from the conviction 'that some great, common, Imperial need
requires of every member of the Empire an equal sacrifice.' But he
preferred, he said, to measure the contribution of the self-governing
colonies in terms of sentiment rather than of men and supplies.[8]

Balfour was not alone in believing that a new chapter in the
history of imperial co-operation had begun. To those who, like
Joseph Chamberlain, sought eagerly to bring about greater
imperial unity, the Boer War seemed rich in promise. But they had
confused demonstrations of loyalty and sentiment with a more
profound declaration. The self-governing colonies had rallied to
an imperial idea symbolised more accurately by Queen Victoria
than by schemes of political federation. Balfour was right to place
emphasis on the sentiment involved. But even this was not a
sufficient explanation. The colonies relied on a strong Britain for
their ultimate defence. Equally, they could ill afford to see the
privileges and rights involved in British citizenship denied by the
Transvaal Boers. In this sense, the *uitlanders'* cause was their own.

Nor had the mustering of the volunteers been without complica-
tions. In Canada, Prime Minister Laurier's offer of Canadian
contingents had caused a Cabinet split.[9] Moreover, in February
1902 Lansdowne, the Secretary for War, was at pains to deny
Rosebery's allegation that, at the start of the war, the government
had snubbed the self-governing colonies by discouraging them
from sending mounted troops. Lansdowne claimed that eventually
4,700 mounted troops had been accepted.[10] As for Balfour's
boast that the army in South Africa was overwhelmingly composed
of British stock, the government had deliberately refrained from
using Indian troops and had accepted African and coloured
assistance with reluctance. It had been a white man's quarrel and
a white man's fight. Nonetheless, it is easy to see why the colonial
war effort had generated optimism in government circles.

Viceregal visit: Lord and Lady Curzon at the palace of the Maharaja of Peishkar

A parade of ex-proconsuls:
Curzon (left) and Milner,
1918

Imperial Conference, 1926
Left to right: *Mackenzie King* (*Canada*), *Baldwin, Bruce* (*Australia*), *Balfour,*
Hertzog (*South Africa*)

The new model Hertzog with the new model Wolseley Viper, London, 1930

2

Perhaps the millennium had arrived for South Africa too. The Boer republics were subdued and British supremacy asserted. Industrialists and investors anticipated a golden future. Now that the flood gates had been forced open, there seemed unlimited opportunities for capitalists and immigrants alike. Perhaps a United States of South Africa would emerge in the dark continent, rivalling the prosperity and energy of the great Union in the New World.

But in June 1902 reconciliation was the first priority. Not merely between the English and Afrikaner-speaking communities, but within Afrikanerdom itself. For the war had sifted Afrikaners into those who had fought for independence, those who had taken no active part, and those who had supported the British in one way or another. The war had provided the Afrikaners with a common experience but different ways of interpreting it. It was the task of the new leaders, Botha, Smuts and Hertzog, to find some formula to maintain the identity of their nation. Perhaps the best way was Botha's – a nationalism contained within, and essential to, a Greater South African nation.

Crucial to the future of the Afrikaners was the attitude of the victors. Balfour had declared himself 'for as large and liberal an amnesty as it is possible to give as part of a final settlement ... temporary disenfranchisement may be necessary. But on the broad policy of a large and liberal amnesty I am as clear and convinced as on any subject of politics at the present time.' This was practical, and far removed from a bloody assize. In any case, there were more pressing matters. The vast British army had to be sent home. Moreover, there were 32,000 Boers in prison camps, and another 110,000 in the concentration camps. It was winter, and food and grazing were scarce. The vanquished would not find survival easy.

The proclamation of crown colony rule in the Transvaal and the Orange River Colony as soon as war ended, gave Milner wide powers and the opportunity to push ahead with a programme of anglicisation. But ironically he ran into unexpected trouble with

G

the *uitlanders*, for whom crown colony government meant little more self-determination than Krugerism had done. The Cape Parliament, too, was restive. Although Rhodes had died early in 1902, his followers in the Progressive party wanted a suspension of the constitution and a redistribution of seats to reduce the representation of the Cape Dutch, many of whom had been blatantly disloyal during the war. Milner, too, wanted the Cape constitution suspended, believing that this would enable him to impose federation on South Africa without observing constitutional niceties. It would also side-step blocking tactics by the Cape Dutch.[11]

The struggle over the Cape constitution was protracted. In September 1902, Balfour told Chamberlain that the Cape Parliament seemed 'likely to give us even *more* trouble than our own.'[12] Chamberlain agreed that 'the so-called Progressives' were working for Parliament's downfall. However, the Colonial Secretary opposed Milner's arguments for suspension, believing that such a move would run counter to Britain's democratic traditions and prove offensive to the self-governing colonies. Milner was distinctly less of a democrat than Chamberlain. At any rate, Chamberlain's influence helped preserve the Cape constitution, even though he told Balfour that he was trying 'to keep out of the conflict as much as possible leaving responsibility where it belongs – to the government of an autonomous Colony.'[13]

In August 1902, three Boer generals, Botha, de la Rey and de Wet, came to London to ask the government to modify the terms of Vereeniging. Balfour thought their demands 'so impudent that I feel tempted to think they wish to pick a quarrel.'[14] Chamberlain dealt with the generals, who were given an enthusiastic popular reception in London, with a blend of firmness and cajolement. At least, he was able to tell Balfour on 9 September that 'the demands of the Boer generals had fizzled out.' Moreover, he had sounded out Botha 'as to the possibility of his joining the Government. I have not yet received his reply but his general tone was quite friendly.'[15] Although Botha refused the offer of a seat on the Transvaal's Legislative Council, Chamberlain found, when he arrived in South Africa in December 1902 to see the situation at first hand, that the Boer leaders were now reconciled to making the best of the treaty of Vereeniging. The tensions in the Cape Parliament had also subsided.

The possibility of an Afrikaner rebellion, however, could not be ruled out. Although by March 1903 the British forces in South Africa had been cut down to 30,000 men, and were further reduced to 18,600 by October 1904, Milner strongly opposed further reductions. Lord Roberts took his part, believing that Afrikaner elements were stirring up unrest, and calling for the establishment of a reserve force to deal with emergencies in South Africa.[16] In January 1905, the concern of Milner and Roberts prompted the King to urge Balfour that any idea of further reducing the garrison should be immediately abandoned.[17]

These fears were reinforced by Lord Selborne, Milner's successor in South Africa. Writing in May 1905 to Alfred Lyttelton, the new Colonial Secretary, Selborne expressed alarm at German troop concentrations in the neighbouring colony of South West Africa. Denying that he was an alarmist or a teutonphobe, Selborne claimed that there were 16,000 German regulars in South West Africa plus 3,000 to 4,000 armed Boers recruited in the Transvaal. It was rumoured that a further 14,000 troops were en route from Germany. Selborne felt that Germany wanted to exert diplomatic pressure through the threat of a Boer uprising, 'and rise they would, be under no delusions on that score.'[18]

Selborne's fears were not realised. At the same time, it was clearly expedient to reconcile the Boers as quickly and fully as possible to the new crown colony status of the Transvaal and the Orange River Colony. If Milner could not federate South Africa from above, it was essential to determine the immediate constitutional future of the two annexed republics. In the Commons in August 1904, Balfour refused to reveal whether the government would act by statute or order-in-council when it introduced representative institutions. In any case, he denied that the Commons had the right to demand a prior discussion of the government's policy.[19]

On 31 March 1905, the Transvaal was given its new constitution by an order-in-council. Basically Milner's brain-child, the constitution established an elected Legislative Council of up to thirty-five members. It completely ignored the claims of non-Europeans, and submitted to the Afrikaner insistence that anyone who was not white was a 'native' and could not be enfranchised. Not that the British members of the Transvaal's Labour and Progressive parties were any more enthusiastic for racial equality than *Het Volk*, the Afrikaners' party.

Balfour's ministry had given the Transvaal representative government, but not by statute. Perhaps letters patent were speedier. Perhaps a divided Unionist party was thus spared an all-out and lengthy assault by the now united Liberals. But the Opposition were still able to wring from Balfour a defence of his government's policy. The Liberals wanted the ex-republics to be given full responsible government. Balfour insisted that the introduction of representative institutions was 'a necessary and inevitable stage on the road to full responsible government. It has been so in all, or at all events, in the great majority, of our Colonies, and what is sound policy for colonies almost entirely composed of colonists of English blood is certainly not less necessary in a colony in which racial divisions undoubtedly now exist.' Balfour's argument that representative government was 'a very long stage' on the road to self-government did not satisfy Campbell-Bannerman and his followers.[20] But the Unionists would go no further.

The introduction of the Transvaal's constitution was meant to coincide with Milner's departure from South Africa. The great proconsul left much work uncompleted. Although the war had been won, and a customs union for the whole of South Africa established by March 1903, federation had not been achieved. Nor had Milner's plans of anglicisation made much headway – the first Prime Minister of the independent Transvaal was to be an Afrikaner, not an Englishman. All this fell somewhat short of Chamberlain's hope, expressed during Milner's conqueror's welcome in London in the Spring of 1901, that the High Commissioner would be able 'to crown the work which he has undertaken, laying broad and deep the foundations of a united South Africa, as free, as prosperous and as loyal as the sister federations of Canada and Australia.'[21]

By October 1904 Milner was determined to resign. Even in the winter of 1902, Chamberlain had written from South Africa that Milner could not contemplate staying on indefinitely, for personal and political reasons:

He is sensitive, lonely, and misses very much the intellectual environment to which he has been accustomed. Yet he admits the importance of the work, the great opportunity of making an undying reputation as one of our Empire builders, and recognises that his resignation at this moment would be almost an act of cowardice. His influence is extraordinary, and his successor will at any time have a hard task to gain in equal measure the confidence of the people.[22]

Who could fill the enormous gap left by Milner? The critical importance of the choice led Milner to tell Balfour in October 1904, 'you may think I fly very high. But the thing really is very critical. A good man here for the next 3 or 4 years might mean the final pacification of S.A. – its removal from the first rank of Imperial problems. On the other hand, with a weak hand at the helm you may find S.A. a fearful drag for another quarter of a century.' Milner then emphasised the crushing responsibilities of his office:

I hope the time is coming when at least two of the great outside posts, i.e. India and South Africa, will come to be regarded as interchangeable with high office at home. That would be of appreciable assistance in drawing closer the ties which unite different parts of the Empire – the great problem always confronting us which seems so fearfully difficult to solve in a practical way.[23]

Milner suggested to Balfour that Lyttelton should go from the Colonial Office to South Africa. Balfour opposed this. Not that he thought that Lyttelton would be taking a step down if he became High Commissioner, but that he considered it 'practically certain' that the Unionists would 'be defeated, perhaps severely' at the next election. At this critical juncture he did not want to appoint a new Colonial Secretary barely a year after Joseph Chamberlain's resignation in October 1903.[24]

By the end of 1904 no replacement for Milner had been found.

Milner, however, felt that 'we have turned the corner here – economically. There is no mistake about it. . . . Politically things are much as they always have been, & will be for the next 10 years, or more.'[25] The gigantic task of reconstruction, involving the new constitution, Boer uneasiness and the problems of foreign labour would require, in Alfred Lyttelton's words, 'a first rate man, if possible of proved strength and capacity & I think that our own high reputation as Imperialists rather than party men in the matter of appointments is involved in finding such a man.'[26]

Eventually the government lighted on 'Willie' Selborne, Balfour's cousin by marriage, but hardly a man of the first rank. However, Selborne was 'able, approachable and a keen farmer'.[27] Perhaps in this sense he had more in common with the Boers, than with the Rand capitalists and the white goldminers. Balfour told Milner in February 1905 that Selborne would be a great loss to the government, adding that Milner's own departure made 'it impossible . . . not to lament the great loss which South Africa and the Empire will sustain by your withdrawal from the stage where you have won "name and fame".' Balfour believed the government's prospects to be 'necessarily uncertain', and felt anxiety for imperial interests if the prospective Liberal victory took place.[28]

In the Commons in March 1905 Balfour denied accusations that Milner's resignation had been engineered so that the government could, almost at its last gasp, appoint a successor. Rather, he had begged Milner to stay, but the High Commissioner had found it 'absolutely impossible, for reasons of health, to continue to bear the continuous and unremitting strain which he has borne for eight years.' Balfour also repudiated suggestions that Selborne was not fitted for his new post because he had been Under Secretary at the Colonial Office during the still controversial Jameson Raid. Nor did Balfour think that imperial proconsuls should be drawn from the ranks of administrators rather than of politicians. Milner, of course, was a glittering example of the administrator as proconsul. But Balfour was not lost for contrary examples: Lord Durham's 'administration of Canada [was] the beginning of a better state of things.' As for India, 'everybody knows that . . . the most brilliant examples of great administrative capacity have been drawn from among the ranks of the politicians'.[29]

Turning to the offensive, Balfour insisted that because of the delicate hand required to operate the government of the Transvaal, what was needed was a 'man whose life has been spent in dealing with popular forces, in popular assemblies, and in that kind of management . . . which can be acquired, and acquired alone, within the walls of a representative assembly.'[30] This glowing tribute to the democratic Lord Selborne finds a striking contradiction in the sentiments of his wife, writing a year later from South Africa:

Meanwhile we are getting ready for our parliament, and are going to play at making this a white man's country for some time yet. We are even trying to start a Labour Party, but that I think must be a failure. We are not going to be democratic here, but we are going to pretend we are, as it looks nice and Colonial. Really we are going to keep everyone in their proper place by every means in our power.[31]

Lady Selborne was not, mercifully, High Commissioner. Nor need her words be given more significance than tea-party gossip. But the vast political and commercial problems facing South Africa could not be brushed aside in a facile or arrogant manner.

3

When Balfour spoke of racial equality in South Africa he excluded non-Europeans from his speculations. None but the purblind, however, could ignore the fundamental problems posed by the presence in South Africa of three distinct groups of non-Europeans – the coloureds (of mixed race), the Africans, and the Indians, brought over mainly as indentured labourers. In the Cape there was no bar to enfranchisement on the grounds of race, although there was a property qualification and a literacy test. In Natal there was a higher, more prohibitive property franchise. In the Transvaal and the Orange Free State there had been an all-white vote before the war, and the peace of Vereeniging did nothing to alter this.

The growth of the mining industry in the Transvaal had made the organisation of unskilled African labour an economic necessity. Before 1886 European policy towards the native people throughout South Africa had been broadly based on the desire that they should not impede the extension of white occupation and control. Methods had varied. The Afrikaners wasted little sentiment on the Bantu and felt no need to contemplate racial equality. The British authorities had above all tried to restrict conflict between Boer and Bantu and to inhibit aggression on the frontiers. This severely practical ambition had been tempered by the humanitarian influence exerted by missionary societies and philanthropists.

When it became apparent that a British victory over the Boers was only a matter of time, the Commons debated problems implicit in the racial composition of South Africa. In July 1901, Balfour acknowledged the ever-present 'native difficulty', but added that the Africans had proved themselves 'loyal . . . to British rule, in mere self-defence and for mere purposes of self-protection.'[32] Certainly the Africans had no cause to side with the Afrikaners, whose vengeance had fallen heavily upon those non-Europeans who had actively supported the British against them. Asquith spoke for many when he told the Commons in August 1901, 'that apart from the injustice of the Uitlanders, the great blot and stain on the Boer Government . . . was its treatment of the native races.'[33]

Not only the Afrikaners stood condemned. British mine-owners had hardly proved the most considerate employers of African labour. 96,000 Africans had worked in the mines in 1899, but had been subject to the strict control of the pass laws, which Asquith found 'impossible to defend', and to the abuses of the liquor laws which stimulated an illicit trade in unwholesome liquor. In August 1901, Balfour declared the government's intention of reforming the labour laws and administering them with purity and equity. As for the sale of liquor, the government was already insisting that only 'kaffir beer' should be sold, not stronger brews.[34] Equally no assistance would be given to mine-owners or

South African governments to force African labour down the mines.[35]

This accorded with Balfour's affirmation that the government meant 'to apply to the native population all those humanitarian principles which, I think, are dear to every party and every section of opinion in this country.' However, the white population was to be governed by 'equal laws', and the non-whites by 'humanitarian principles'.[36] Unfortunately, humanitarianism can vanish. There was more security in equal laws.

But Balfour did not believe that whites and blacks could work or live together on equal terms in South Africa. Basically, he denied that the two races could be brought to equality. He told the Commons in March 1904 that 'the theories of the eighteenth and early nineteenth centuries, that all men were born equal, have been refuted in this, and many other instances, by the advance of science. Men are not born equal. They cannot be made equal by education extending over generation after generation within the ordinary historical limit.'[37]

This argument was distinctly at odds with Balfour's advocacy of the 1902 Education Bill, which he was instrumental in piloting through Parliament. Then he had claimed with conviction, 'there are at stake issues greater than the fortunes of any political party; there is at stake the education of your children for a generation, . . . if we . . . hesitate . . . we shall receive the contempt of the parents and children living and to be born, and that contempt we shall most fully earn.'[38]

White children, then, were not immutable. As for black children, Balfour preferred to emphasise the 'unbridgeable abyss' between the two races. Moreover, it was 'folly to suppose that your petty educational regulations . . . can obliterate distinctions deep-seated under the laws of nature.'[39] The enthusiasm of the educational reformer had vanished when faced with the future of the inhabitants of South Africa.

If Balfour dismissed the possibilities of equality, what remained? Although he 'entirely sympathised' with the immigration restrictions practised by Australia and New Zealand, there were already eight Africans to every European in South Africa. They were unlikely to die out as the aborigines in Australia had done – a convenient phenomenon of which Balfour confessed, 'even if I am charged with inhumanity, I cannot find it it my heart to regret it.' But the Africans were there to stay. Balfour put some hope in emigration, believing that 'one of the great objects which this House should have in view is the augmentation, if possible a great augmentation, in the amount of the white population in South Africa, as compared with the population of any other race.'[40]

However the flood of white emigration to South Africa never materialised. Balfour was right to imagine a future confrontation between 'this enormous black population' and 'a great community of whites of all classes, who, nevertheless, are . . . an aristocracy over a proletariat class.'[41] The whites were there to stay, too, and the vast majority could be relied upon to unite against African aspirations to equality. The Rand goldmines were hardly a fruitful breeding ground for racial harmony when, in 1903, skilled European workers struck against both the employment of unskilled Europeans and the introduction of Italian labour.[42]

Lord Roberts was not exaggerating when he wrote from Johannesburg, in October 1904, that throughout South Africa there was a very strong feeling that the 'native' must be kept under and never placed on an equality with the European. Recoiling from the prospect of an African rising, Roberts described an 'Ethiopian movement' that went about preaching 'Africa for the Africans'. Nothing, Roberts insisted, should be done to help the Africans realise the power that combination would give them.[43]

Roberts's soldierly fears for security were matched by Lady Selborne's patrician condescension when she told Alice Balfour in August 1906:

I have a certain leaning towards negrophilism. Of course I don't go too far, & have no wish to give them a vote, but I do rather like them and simply adore seeing a war dance . . . this will be a country with a white aristocracy. There will probably be a coloured and Indian middle class. There will be a few blacks of equal intellectual capacity to the whites who will give a great deal of trouble by demanding equal rights with whites.[44]

The expression of such opinions makes it clear why the Africans could not expect enfranchisement in the Transvaal or the Orange River Colony. The British government had taken an enormous stride towards Anglo-Afrikaner co-operation at Vereeniging when it had postponed the question of the native vote. The Afrikaners were hardly likely to revive the subject, and English-speaking South Africans could only do so if they were prepared to shatter whatever amity existed between the whites. Nonetheless, the problem would have to be dealt with somehow, and Balfour was only realistic when he said, 'I do not envy those who have got to deal with that situation of the future.'[45]

4

But in 1903 the British government was more concerned with industrial stagnation on the Rand than with votes for Africans. In 1899 gold production had been worth £15,452,000; in 1902 £7,297,000. In 1899 the mines had employed 96,000 Africans; in 1903 only 63,000.[46] And this despite the fact that by the middle of 1903 nearly 300 mining companies had been floated. Although Milner had forced mine owners to improve working conditions, and had appointed a medical committee in order to reduce the high death-rate, the mines were an estimated 129,000 men short in 1903. Nor did attempts to drum up African labour from much further afield succeed.

Faced with this contradiction of the prophecies of South Africa's boom future, the Transvaal Legislative Council proposed the importation of Chinese coolie labour. Milner saw this measure as essential to his own work of restoring prosperity and stability to South Africa. In the autumn of 1903 he came to London to argue his case. The Unionist government, and particularly Chamberlain, had shown little enthusiasm hitherto on this score.[47] But by the end of September 1903 Chamberlain had been succeeded at the Colonial Office by Lyttelton who, far from being able to dominate Milner, felt himself the subordinate of the great proconsul. The government agreed to sanction Chinese labour, and on 10 February the Chinese Labour Ordinance was passed by the Transvaal Council.

The indentured labourers were to reside in compounds, which they could only leave with a permit. Even then, they could go no further than the vicinity of the camp. They were to work for ten hours a day, six days a week. A minimum wage of two shillings a day was subsequently fixed. The Chinese had no property rights, and were denied access to law courts; instead, the compounds had their own legal code. By the end of 1904, 23,000 coolies had arrived and 20,000 more were on their way. The effect on the gold industry was unmistakable. Between 1903 and 1906, gold production doubled.[48]

The British political scene was affected no less dramatically. Radicals and Liberals attacked the government with unabated fury. Working men were convinced that Chinese labour diminished their own value. Humanitarians were appalled at the conditions in the compounds. Those who hated Milner and the Rand capitalists saw further justification for their hatred. Chamberlain had been right when he foresaw trouble.

As Prime Minister, Balfour defended the government's policy. In this task he compounded an odd mixture of arguments. In May 1904 he claimed that, as regards Asiatic labour, the government intended to treat the Transvaal as a self-governing colony and, as a responsible government, the Legislative Council had asked for the Chinese.[49] Balfour pointed to previous instances of the use of indentured labour, citing British Guiana, Trinidad and Australia. He refuted allegations of introducing slavery. Rather, he insisted that to exclude the Chinese from the Transvaal would be to deny them the opportunity of earning fifteen times their normal wage.[50]

Balfour chose to represent the issue as one vital to the future of South Africa. Denying that he was pleading for the Rand capitalists, Balfour broadened his appeal:

I plead for the great white population, agricultural or mining, who depend, and so far as I can see will depend for an unlimited time, on labour other than white labour; I plead for the artisans, I plead for the shopkeepers, I plead for the great body of the population of European blood whose fate in the colony depends on your decision.[51]

After informing Campbell-Bannerman that if he had been Prime Minister he would have taken the same course, Balfour told the Liberal leader to stop making 'vague and irrelevant speeches about slavery'. As a further diversion, Balfour argued, not unrealistically, that the problem of how Britain was to use hers 'illimitable technical power' in relation to her Empire was 'one of the most difficult and one of the most important problems with which this Assembly has got to deal.' Balfour saw the future of the Transvaal's gold industry in these terms.[52]

But the Liberal party, already drawing closer together in face of Chamberlain's tariff reform campaign, had found in the cry of 'Chinese slavery' a slogan of widespread appeal. By June 1904, Balfour wrote to Northcote, the Governor-General of Australia, that 'in the country our chief difficulty is the misrepresentation over Chinese labour . . . which is opposed on the preposterous ground that it is slavery, but is really unpopular because it is erroneously supposed to substitute yellow for white labour.'[53]

This was less than fair to those whose genuine anxieties were substantially confirmed when, in April 1905, the coolies on the New Randfontein mine struck against abuses which included the illegal deduction of wages, the dishonouring of promises of higher pay, and bullying treatment – even flogging. Balfour had previously doubted the Opposition's sincerity, and had accused them of immoral exhibitions of platform indignation.[54] But the Liberals were understandably overjoyed at the heaven-sent opportunity to exploit the government's embarrassment. Their criticisms even prompted Balfour to wonder whether the Opposition would oppose the appointment of either Selborne or Lyttelton as Milner's successor, on the grounds of their identification with 'the Yellow Labour policy'.[55]

It had been Milner himself who had added immeasurably to the government's troubles by sanctioning the use of flogging by the mine overseers. As the outcry in Britain mounted, Balfour looked ahead to the dissolution of Parliament and saw, in September 1905, that:

The worst rock ahead from a purely electioneering point of view is due to the quite inexplicable illegality of which Milner seems to have been guilty in permitting, before he left, overseers in the mines to inflict corporal punishment. I am anxiously awaiting to see what excuse if any he can produce for this amazing blunder which seems to violate every canon of international morality, of law, and of policy.[56]

Lyttelton at the Colonial Office and Selborne, when he reached South Africa, were quick to end the flogging. For his part, Milner calmly accepted fully responsibility, although he was later to admit that he had made a mistake.[57] But although Milner had to endure the execrations of radical newspapers and rejection by his former admirers in the Liberal party, it was Balfour who had to face an imminent election. In October, with the dissolution less than two months away, Balfour told Lyttelton that he thought it unwise to publish Milner's letter explaining the decision to allow flogging. Complaining bitterly at Milner's carelessness, Balfour said, 'It is a bad business, and, in my opinion we have great and just reason to complain over what has occurred in connection with Coolie Labour. But, there is no use crying over spilt milk!'[58]

When Campbell-Bannerman became Prime Minister on Balfour's resignation in December 1905, he almost immediately requested a dissolution of Parliament. Naturally, one of the burning issues during the ensuing election campaign was Chinese labour. On 21 December, Campbell-Bannerman told an election meeting in the Albert Hall that orders had been given 'to stop forthwith the recruitment and embarkation of coolies from China.' But at a Cabinet meeting on 3 January 1906, the Prime Minister allowed himself to be persuaded that 14,000 import licences for coolies issued in November 1905 could be taken up.[59] Even contracts dealing in human beings were deemed sacrosanct. Moreover, Campbell-Bannerman's long-standing pledge to give the Transvaal self-government at the earliest opportunity meant that the fate of the coolies would be left in potentially unsympathetic hands. In fact, in June 1907 the Transvaal government decided to send the coolies home.

The 'Chinese slavery' issue lost the Unionists thousands of votes in the election of January 1906. The Liberal party made the most of the opportunity to rally their traditional Noncomformist,

Radical, and working man's vote against the party which seemed to serve the interests of the Rand capitalist and ignore human rights. But perhaps the voters were merely strengthened in their resolve to destroy the Unionists at the polls. Clearly, many trade unionists and workers swung their vote from the Liberals and the Unionists to the embryonic Labour party in 1906. Maybe they were voting against competition from 'yellow labour' as much as for humanitarian principles.

In this respect, the conflict over Chinese labour was not decisive in determining the Unionist defeat. By 1906 the electorate had ample reasons for turning to the Liberals or to Labour. The tariff reform controversy had split the Unionists and awakened fears of dearer food. The battle over the 1902 Education Bill had aroused sectarian passions. Also, the Boer War had revealed gross inadequacies in military organisation. Balfour's party paid the price of this disenchantment. Yet the rejected Prime Minister had used the clamour for reform caused by the Boer War to good purpose. War Office reform and the Committee of Imperial Defence had risen from the ashes of military incompetence. Out of an imperial crisis that bitterly divided opinion in Britain, machinery for the better co-ordination of imperial defence was created. If this was a paradox, it was, for Balfour at least, a pleasing and convenient one.

13 The Union of South Africa

I think the admirable manner in which the leading statesmen ... in South Africa, men who have been in the sharpest conflict in times not long gone by, have combined in a common interest to carry out a great national and Imperial object, is worthy of all admiration, and is producing, and is likely to produce, most admirable fruit.

BALFOUR, 1909

I

CAMPBELL-BANNERMAN's government announced on 19 February 1906, in the speech from the throne, that self-government was to be given forthwith to the Transvaal and the Orange River Colony. Admittedly, while in opposition, the Liberals had argued so consistently for such action that they could hardly have shifted position when in office. But there was in any case no desire in the party to change course. Nor is there any reason to believe Smuts's claim that his meeting with Campbell-Bannerman in 1906 caused an overnight conversion to the policy of self-government.[1] The Liberal leader's position had long been perfectly clear, and rested on the fundamental belief that future British-Afrikaner amity would result from a generous constitutional settlement.

Balfour, while Prime Minister, had frequently spoken of the need for harmony between the Europeans in South Africa. But Campbell-Bannerman was prepared to take action to achieve this end, just as he had halted the fresh importation of Chinese coolies shortly after he had formed his administration. However, neither the grant of independence to the ex-Boer republics, nor the ending of Chinese labour appeared wholly satisfactory or praiseworthy to Balfour.

The 'Chinese slavery' outcry had been raised by the Liberals to hound Balfour's government to its death. From the Opposition benches, Balfour doubtless took some pleasure, in March 1906, in accusing the new government of contradictory policies towards the Transvaal. Although Campbell-Bannerman planned to grant self-government to the Transvaal and the Orange River Colony, he had already forbidden the issuing of any fresh licences for importing Chinese coolies, and had given leave for any coolies to return home if they wished.[2] Moreover, the government had revealed their intention of fixing a date, before the Transvaal had attained self-government, for ending the notorious Chinese Labour Ordinance. But after independence, the Transvaal was to decide the fate of the remaining Chinese, even though Britain reserved the right to alter any future Labour Ordinance.[3]

Balfour, on 14 March 1906, called the government's policy towards the Transvaal a hybrid one:

On the one hand, you say that you are making the Colony self-governing; and at the very same moment ... you also inform them that, as regards the industry on which their whole prosperity depends, they are not to be masters in their own house. ... They are to be ... the slaves of the Colonial Office as far as the forms of any future Ordinance is concerned. This Colony which you profess to endow with all the privileges you have given to Canada and Australia, with regard to its nearest and dearest interests, is to be put under the heel of Downing Street.[4]

This was a somewhat inspired interpretation of the Liberal government's generous proposals for a settlement in the Transvaal. Admittedly, the problem of labour for the Rand mines was vitally important and not given to easy solutions. On 14 March, Winston Churchill, the newly-appointed Under-Secretary of State for the Colonies, had remarked, inelegantly, that 'the mines on the Witwatersrand Reef are worked with the cheapest and worst labour in the world – clumsy Kaffirs and sullen Chinese who leave before they have time to become skilful workmen.'[5] But then, Churchill, the recent convert to Liberalism, had yet to discover the English poor, let alone appreciate the difficulties of non-European labour on the Rand.

Balfour remained unrepentant over the introduction of the Chinese. On 21 March 1906 he told the Commons that he 'honestly came to the conclusion that the introduction of Chinese labour was in the interests of South Africa and the Transvaal, and was absolutely necessary.' He denied that the Rand magnates had in any way influenced the government's decision. At the same time, he acknowledged that Liberal objections to coolie labour did 'represent a very genuine, real, and deep-rooted conviction in large classes in the community.'[6] This was, at least, in contrast to Balfour's previous accusations of hypocrisy and political sharp practice.

As to the future of South Africa, Balfour agreed that the picture which appealed to him most was of a community much augmented by British immigration, and consisting not only of a white middle class but also depending chiefly upon white labour. But how practical was the realisation of this society? Balfour believed that the first essential for South Africa was to ensure that the gold industry continued to function. To achieve this, unskilled non-European labour was needed, and he questioned whether government policy would guarantee this in ample supply.[7] These were reasonable doubts, for although the gold mining industry recovered steadily after the dislocations of the Boer War, it did so through the labour of unskilled non-Europeans rather than that of whites.

Both Balfour and Milner continued to bear the stigma of the Chinese labour controversy. On 21 March 1906, in the Commons, Balfour attacked a Liberal motion which condemned the flogging of Chinese coolies allowed by Milner when High Commissioner. Although the motion did not, after amendment, mention Milner by name, the implication was obvious. Balfour deplored this condemnation of Milner, and begged the House: 'do not let it be said that one indefensible blunder and one alone, not carrying with it great consequences, soon remedied, not in any way connected with the great lines of policy which it was his business to deal with – that that incident . . . alone, is to be selected and have the honour of mention in journals of the House.' Milner, insisted Balfour, was one of 'the rare fruits of the great political education which

this country ... has been able to give to her sons in such measure.'[8]
These pleas were ignored. The radical temper of the Commons
carried the motion by a majority of 220.

A year later, in March 1907, the Chinese labour issue was still
very much alive. On 11 March, however, Balfour was afforded the
welcome opportunity of turning the tables on the government by
condemning them for allowing indentured labour in the condominium of the New Hebrides, ruled jointly with France. He said:

If indentured labour is provided by a Unionist Government,
if the people who benefit are owners of goldfields, and the people
indentured are Chinese – this is slavery (Cheers); yes, but if indentured labour is arranged by a Radical Government, if the
indentured labourers are not Chinese, but people far less capable
of protecting their own interests and if those who benefit by the
indentured labour are people less important than the great
industry on which the whole of the prosperity of the Transvaal
depends, then that indentured form of labour is not slavery – it is
social reform.[9]

More satisfying still from Balfour's point of view was the
Liberals' eventual abandonment of the coolies to the mercies of
the independent government of the Transvaal. On 23 March 1908,
he was able to remind the Commons that they had been assured
by the government that the Chinese labour arrangements would
end when the Transvaal was granted independence. This had not
happened, and Balfour accused the government of persistently
deceiving the Commons.[10] In fact, Campbell-Bannerman's
administration had little option but to leave the Transvaal to deal
with the coolies once it became a self-governing colony. In any
case, although in January 1907 there were 54,000 Chinese on the
Rand, in December the number had slumped to 12,000, whereas
the number of African workers had risen from 94,000 to 150,000
and even the number of Europeans involved had increased from
17,000 to 18,600.[11] There was no need, in these circumstances, to
continue to employ Chinese labour which was to some extent a
deterrent to further European immigration. By March 1910 the
last of the Chinese had left South Africa.

2

The Chinese labour debate had dragged on for four years, and had proved capable of generating heated antagonisms. Yet it was, in effect, supplementary to the controversy surrounding the grant of self-government to the Transvaal and the Orange River Colony. In April 1906 the West Ridgeway Commission was sent to South Africa to pave the way to independence. The situation in the Transvaal occupied most of its attention. Basically, the Commission wanted to construct a constitution that would allow British and Afrikaner moderates to hold the balance between the extremist British Progressive party and *Het Volk*. In this aim it was positively assisted by the desire of the leaders of *Het Volk*, Botha and Smuts, that the first ministry of the independent Transvaal should not be composed of Afrikaners, since they believed this would only have the effect of exacerbating already grave difficulties. In any case, *Het Volk* wanted to reserve their position. Afrikaner unity was as yet paper-thin. It might be irretrievably damaging to the party to accept office, only to be shackled by a watchful Colonial Office in London.

Under the Commission's supervision, good sense seemed to triumph in the Transvaal. White manhood suffrage was agreed to, and after some haggling, inspired mainly by the not particularly progressive Progressive party, the seats for the Legislative Assembly were allotted on the basis of 33 to the Rand, 6 to Pretoria and 30 to the rest of the Transvaal. *Het Volk* had thus agreed to a partition which seemed to guarantee a majority of British representatives, drawn from the Progressive and Labour parties, and from the Responsible Government Association which was, however, allied with *Het Volk*.[12]

The Commission resolved two further problems. To begin with, it advocated that the second chamber of the Transvaal's legislature should at first be nominated, and hence effectively dominated by British and moderate interests. Also, it deferred the question of the non-European franchise to the supposed wisdom and goodwill of the new legislature. Deeply conscious of the united front presented by Afrikaners and British on this issue, the Commission decided to avoid a confrontation over the political advancement of non-Europeans.[13] As at Vereeniging, the real losers were the Africans, Indians and coloureds. Colonial Office assurances that non-Europeans in the Transvaal would be fairly treated after independence were practically worthless.

Having performed its balancing act in the Transvaal, and finding little need for such feats in the Afrikaner-dominated Orange River Colony, the Commission presented its report on the Transvaal at the end of July 1906. It was clear that self-government for the Orange River Colony would also follow quickly.

Balfour expressed grave misgivings over the Commission's proposals. He told the Commons on 31 July 1906 that South Africa's greatest problem was the future relationship between whites and blacks. Still convinced that 'the white and black races . . . are born with different capacities which education cannot and will not change', he deplored the extension of manhood suffrage to the Transvaal because this might indicate 'that there is some right connecting the possession of manhood with the possession of suffrage.'[14]

Recoiling from this assumption, Balfour proceeded to paint a gloomy picture of the problems involved. Supposing non-Europeans were allowed to participate in the Transvaal's legislative system, how was this to be reconciled with the theory of white manhood suffrage? If the non-European majority 'were judiciously organised, in their hands alone would rest the whole interest of civilisation, culture and religion – in the hands of a race which is by birth less intellectually and morally capable of dealing with these problems than the white race.' To this plain, if illiberal, argument Balfour added another. The Cape's franchise was based on a property and literacy qualification. Since this was not to be the case in the Transvaal, Balfour insisted that 'you could never associate the Transvaal with the Cape in any future scheme of federation unless either the Cape or the Transvaal changed its franchise.'[15]

Equally disturbing for Balfour was the grant of immediate self-government to the Transvaal. He claimed it was not a question of *whether* independence should be given, but *when* this should happen – three years after a bitter war was too soon. The Afrikaners were a homogenous population with, as yet, no inborn loyalty to the British throne and people. Why might they not begin preparing quietly, and even constitutionally, for a new war? What security was there against this danger? Finally, Balfour adamantly refused to accept responsibility 'with the Government for what I regard as the most reckless experiment ever tried in the development of a great colonial policy.'[16]

This was an unashamed rehearsal of familiar conservative arguments and somewhat out of joint with Balfour's previous insistence that Afrikaners and British must be encouraged to live in partnership. Moreover, if Balfour feared for the fabric of white civilisation in South Africa in face of the non-Europeans, a generous settlement in the Transvaal and the Orange River Colony would help to strengthen the white laager. But in July 1906, Balfour seemed to want not only the permanent paramountcy of white over black, but the indefinite supremacy of Britisher over Boer.

As it happened, the Transvaal's elections to the new assembly in February 1907 denied the British their supremacy. The Afrikaner vote went solidly to *Het Volk*, while the British vote was split between the Progressive, Labour and Responsible parties. Accordingly, *Het Volk* won 37 seats, the Progressives 21, the rest 11. The rural districts polled more heavily than the Rand, 72·5 per cent as against 65·1 per cent.[17] Afrikaner unity had triumphed over British disarray.

On 4 March 1907, a reluctant Lord Selborne had Botha sworn in as Prime Minister of the Transvaal. Those who despaired of British supremacy could draw some small comfort from the remaining safeguard of the nominated upper chamber. In fact, the main guarantor of tranquillity was Botha himself. He assured the British that their interests were safe with him, and that the Afrikaners would not forget the trust shown in them by the grant of independence. Above all, Botha was remarkably well-suited to his complex task of conciliation and retrenchment. Lord Selborne described him to Edward VII as, 'A born leader of men, with plenty of moral courage, a man of natural dignity of manner and reserve, who does not wear his heart on his sleeve.'[18]

Botha was tenacious, patient and tactful. His personality never rivalled that of Smuts either in imaginative range or in deviousness. In shifting times, he supplied reliability and good sense rather than brilliance. This was what the Transvaal needed. British fears were allayed. Gold shares remained steady. Moreover Botha's alliance with the English-speaking Responsible party was a symbol of reconciliation, and an omen for Anglo-Afrikaner co-operation on a larger political stage.

Shortly after his triumph, Botha represented the Transvaal at the 1907 Colonial Conference, where his voice was added to Laurier's of Canada in opposing the establishment of a permanent joint commission as a link of Empire. The newest self-governing colony allied naturally with the oldest in resisting such centralising tendencies.[19] In the event, this was to prove a healthy augury for an Empire which was soon to recognise the equal status of its self-governing members.

Balfour had not lost his scepticism over South Africa's future when he met Botha in London during the Colonial Conference of 1907. An exchange between them has been recorded and is, indeed, not unlikely:

Balfour: Well, Botha, you have done it; you have got your constitution. What will come of it?

Botha: I believe that in five years I shall return to this country to ask for the confederation of South Africa.

Balfour: No! This thing is impossible, incredible!

Botha: We shall see.[20]

As it happened, the union of South Africa was only three years away.

3

At first sight, it is remarkable that the Boer War and Milner's subsequent bid to guarantee British supremacy should have been followed so soon by union in South Africa. Federation schemes had foundered hitherto on Anglo-Afrikaner distrust. The war was not calculated to increase friendship, nor did Milnerism reassure those Afrikaners who feared for their language and national identity. But the convulsions of war had their positive effect. For one thing, the old-fashioned and inward-looking Krugerite leadership of the Transvaal was superseded by Afrikaner leaders with broader vision – men like Botha and Smuts. Even in the predominantly Afrikaner Orange River Colony the continuing influence of Steyn and even the emergence of Hertzog were not unfavourable omens.[21] Moreover the positive steps towards reconciliation taken by the Campbell-Bannerman government provided an appropriate atmosphere in which to work for further co-operation.

Not that co-operation came easily. Harsh memories of the war, of burnt farms and the concentration camps, lingered on, feeding militant Afrikaner nationalism. Nor were English-speaking extremists anxious to admit to equality the Afrikaner people and the Afrikaner tongue. When Balfour voiced fears of an Afrikaner resurgence he did not speak merely for himself. Six months after the Transvaal's election of February 1907, Milner urgently warned Balfour that Botha's government in its appointment of officials was carrying out 'a wholesale substitution of Boers for British'.[22]

But in South Africa itself moderation prevailed. By February 1908 the administrations of three of the four self-governing colonies in South Africa were led by men in favour of union: Botha and Smuts in the Transvaal, Steyn and Fischer of the *Orangia Unie* party in the Free State, and Merriman in the Cape.[23] Only in solidly British Natal was there a decided coolness towards the idea of union, although federation found more favour.

On 3 May 1908 representatives of the four self-governing colonies met in Pretoria. Ostensibly the conference was called to discuss the renewal of the South African customs union. But Smuts looked beyond this limited objective. On the second day of the conference he proposed that a National South African Convention should meet to produce a draft constitution which would unite the four colonies under the British crown. Optimistically, Smuts wanted provision made for the subsequent addition of Rhodesia. The conference agreed unanimously to his proposal.[24]

Grave difficulties remained, however. Was union or federation the appropriate formula? How possible was it to guarantee a strong central government and also achieve flexibility? Would there be parity between the English and the Afrikaner languages? Above all, how could the liberal non-racial franchise of the Cape be reconciled with the all-white vote in the Transvaal and the Orange Free State? Balfour had already laid his finger on this point in July 1906, when he had criticised the introduction of European manhood suffrage into the Transvaal.

Remarkably, these problems were resolved at the meetings of the National Convention between October 1908 and February 1909. By 3 February the draft constitution was unanimously approved. A unitary state was agreed to, with legislature, executive and judiciary tactfully bestowed between Cape Town, Pretoria and Bloemfontein. Overwhelmingly concerned with the co-operation of British and Afrikaners, the Convention agreed to equal language rights and universal European male suffrage. The non-Europeans fared less well. With compromise in the air, the Cape delegates agreed to their exclusion from the national Parliament, even though the coloured and African franchise in the Cape was to be entrenched in the constitution. Perhaps Merriman and Schreiner from the liberal Cape believed that toleration would spread to the north. Perhaps Afrikaners in the Transvaal and the Orange Free State were confident that the Cape would be converted eventually to the acceptance of racial inequality. At any rate, the delegates spent relatively little time discussing the problem. The achievement of union was the immediate goal; long-term difficulties would have to be worked out after this consummation.

Balfour's reaction to these events was in marked contrast to his Cassandra-like hostility to the grant of independence to the Transvaal. Writing to Sir Percy Fitzpatrick, a leader of the Progressive party, while the National Convention was still hammering out the draft constitution, Balfour said, 'I am glad you take no despairing view of South Africa's future. I do not believe in pessimists.'[25] Clearly, the determined attempts to further reconciliation in South Africa had forced Balfour to cast aside his gloomy prophecies. There was no more talk of clandestine preparations for an Afrikaner rebellion. By 1908, Balfour evidently considered the Afrikaner leaders to be politically housetrained. Equally, British supremacists were displaying a more becoming temper.

When the National Convention ended in February 1909, Balfour spoke in the Commons of 'the happy events which have recently taken place in South Africa.' He added:

I think the admirable manner in which the leading statesmen – Dutch and English – in South Africa, men who have been in the sharpest conflict in times not long gone by, have combined in a common interest to carry out a great national and Imperial object, is worthy of all admiration, and is producing, and is likely to produce, most admirable fruit.[26]

By September 1909 the Union of South Africa Act had passed through Parliament and received the royal assent. The Bill's passage had been a relatively smooth one, with the fiercest squalls arising from members' misgivings over the rights and future treatment of non-Europeans. The Unionists supported the Bill, and the dissentient voices came from the Labour party and from some radical Liberals.

Balfour stood firmly behind the Bill. On 16 August 1909, during its second reading, he emphasised that now 'the real race problem' was not the relationship between Afrikaans-speaking and English-speaking South Africans, but 'the problem of the European against the overwhelming majority of men of a wholly different potentiality of culture. Darkness hangs over that problem. I do not look forward to it with any assurance.'[27]

With his doubts as to Afrikaner good intentions now set aside, Balfour revealed a single-minded, and not altogether charitable, determination to ensure white supremacy in South Africa. He believed that 'we in this House, however violently we may have differed about the war itself, all agreed with the idea of having in South Africa one European race dominating.'[28] Balfour's justifications for his attitude were plain, and by no means original. In some respects, his speech in the Commons on 16 August 1909 was a repetition of an earlier speech of 21 March 1904. Certainly his denial of European-African equality was as vehement:

All men are, from some points of view, equal; but to suppose that the races of Africa are in any sense the equals of men of European descent, so far as government, as society, as the higher interests of civilisation are concerned is really, I think, an absurdity which every man who seriously looks at this most difficult problem must put out of his mind if he is to solve the problem at all.[29]

But Balfour's solution to the problem remained obscure. Acknowledging the extraordinary complexity of race relations in the West Indies and the United States, as well as South Africa, he continued to believe that non-Europeans could not be given equal rights 'without threatening the whole fabric of your civilisation'. What therefore remained? Balfour spoke of the ideals of justice, equity, kindness and forbearance. However, he then proceeded to criticise the Cape constitution, which at least made some provision for implementing these ideals on a multi-racial basis. Balfour was sure that 'you cannot lay down – that the Cape solution is the solution for all time.' He also rejected the idea of the British Parliament maintaining any rigid control over the South African Parliament in respect of the rights of non-Europeans. This would be an insupportable interference with the principles of self-government.[30]

In essence, Balfour's solution was the passive one of hoping for the best:

I am convinced ... that the only possible way, the only glimmer of hope of dealing successfully with the real race problem in South Africa is not to attempt to meddle with it ourselves, but, having made this Union Parliament, to trust the men of a like way of thinking as ourselves to rise to the occasion which will most undoubtedly come forward.[31]

Given Balfour's resolute convictions on the subject of African potentialities, this advice fell little short of advocating a complete surrender to permanent white minority rule. There is, in fact, little reason to doubt that this is what Balfour wanted. Asquith, indeed, following him in the debate on 16 August 1909, chided him amiably, telling the Commons that, 'It is a matter upon which I should be loath to dogmatise, but I am not sure that I take so strong a view as the Leader of the Opposition of what I may call the inherent and indelible differences which exist between races.'[32]

But Botha, who was spending several months in Britain, was moved to write a grateful letter to Balfour on 23 August 1909 thanking him 'for the manner in which you and your party have supported the Bill in the Houses of Parliament.' Botha had no doubt as to the implication of Balfour's speech in the Commons on 16 August, for he wrote:

I have read your speech with great interest & beg to assure you that South Africa will appreciate the attitude which you and your party adopted in Parliament. . . . I feel confident that Great Britain will never regret the day when she granted South Africa its constitution.[33]

Balfour replied on 3 September:

My Dear General Botha . . .
I was at one time a little anxious lest the Labour Party, and a certain section of the Radicals, would put the Government in some difficulty over the South Africa Bill. I am glad to say all went well. Personally, I look forward with great confidence and hope to the future of South Africa. No doubt the problems connected with the Native population are likely to be embarrassing not merely to this, but to subsequent generations. . . . But . . . no difficulty should prove insurmountable.[34]

4

On 31 May 1910 the Union of South Africa was formally established. The first Governor-General, Lord Gladstone (son of the former Prime Minister), proclaimed union and invited Botha to form a government. Botha was preferred to Merriman of the

Cape, who was always capable of arousing violent animosities. The Cabinet was an inevitable compromise between provinces and personalities. Four ministers came from the Cape, three from the Transvaal, two each from the Orange Free State and Natal. Similarly, Botha's moderation could be set against the more dogmatic tendencies of Hertzog, whose Free State Education Act of 1908 had insisted on instruction in both languages in the senior grades and had consequently antagonised many English-speaking South Africans.[35]

The election results of September 1910 were ambiguous. Although Botha's South African National party, the result of a merger between *Het Volk* and the Responsibles, won 67 seats in the legislature, Botha and two other ministers lost their seats owing, in great measure, to hostile reaction to Hertzog's education policy. This was not only embarrassing, but a reminder of enduring disunities. Moreover, the electorate had voted fundamentally on nationalist lines. The Unionists, an alliance of the Progressive parties of the Cape, the Transvaal and Natal, gained 39 seats. Elsewhere the British vote was divided between the dedicated patriots of Natal who returned 11 Independents, and the Labour party which returned 4 members.[36] The Senate reflected the political complexion of the provinces as well as containing eight nominated members, four of whom were to concern themselves with the interests of non-Europeans.

The new Union did not altogether justify Balfour's optimism. Led by Botha, for whom a safe seat had been found, the government grappled with the enormous problems of education, defence, industrial relations and the civil rights of Indians, coloureds and Africans. In 1912 Botha dropped the dangerously inflexible Hertzog from the Cabinet, but only created a rallying point for convinced Afrikaner nationalists. The outbreak of the Great War in 1914 revealed strong neutralist tendencies among some Afrikaners and the will to rebel among others. Pro-German sentiment, and the desire to snatch at an independence guaranteed by Berlin, led to a rebellion in the early months of the war. Although Botha and the Afrikaner loyalists crushed the revolt, the defection of Generals de la Rey, de Wet, Beyers and Maritz showed clearly that the old resentments lay just beneath the surface.

At the end of the war, Hertzog's Nationalist party joined with Labour in opposing the government. As a reaction, and to counterbalance the secessionist tendencies of the Nationalists, the South Africa party fused with the Unionists in 1921. But the Nationalist–Labour alliance was strengthened by the great strike on the Rand in 1922. This bloody episode cost South Africa more lives than did the whole of the South West Africa campaign of 1915.[37] Subsequently, the election of 1924 made Hertzog Prime Minister. For the first time since 1910 South Africa was led by a man outspokenly sceptical of the imperial connection.

This boded ill for Balfour's optimistic hopes for a united imperial family. In the event, Hertzog's nationalist fire was dampened down. Balfour can take some of the credit for this. Hertzog led the South African delegation to the momentous 1926 Imperial Conference, which was to define and clarify the status of the Dominions. Balfour was chairman of the vital Inter-Imperial Relations Committee. Hertzog was so satisfied with the subsequent definition of Dominion status, and incidentally so beguiled in private by Balfour's tact, sympathy and erudition, that he returned to South Africa and publicly recanted:

He said emphatically that he no longer feared the Empire. He had been a life-long opponent of Imperialism and had feared the Empire. That was because the Empire had been represented as a sort of super-State, but this conception had been scotched at the Imperial Conference. There was no question any longer of domination or superiority over the Dominions. . . . That made all the difference to his thoughts of the Empire.[38]

If Hertzog had been mollified, he was in good company. Botha and Smuts before him had gone much further in their desire to co-operate with Britain. Despite his mistaken opposition to the Transvaal's independence, Balfour could only have drawn satisfaction from the subsequent roles of Botha and Smuts. In the Great War, apart from smashing the Afrikaner rebellion of 1914, Botha donned British uniform and personally led the conquest of

German South-West Africa. Smuts did even better. Not only did he command the forces which overran Tanganyika, but in 1917 he was taken into Lloyd George's powerful and exclusive War Cabinet. This was a token of reconciliation so powerful as to be overwhelming. Certainly Smuts was dazzled by it, and even laid claim in 1918 to lead the American armies against the Germans.[39] Mercifully perhaps, this came to nothing. But in 1919 when Botha died, Smuts was his undisputed successor as Prime Minister. London could feel relieved that the reign of honest Louis would be followed by that of 'slim Jannie'.

But not even the astute Smuts was capable of solving the basic problem of the relationship between blacks and whites in South Africa. Indeed, the already rudimentary rights of non-Europeans were to be consistently eroded; this was the price of further reconciliation between European parties and communities.[40] Balfour's blind belief that goodwill would eventually resolve fundamental racial antagonisms was, in this respect, woefully inaccurate. On the other hand, as non-European grievances multiplied, British-Afrikaner friendship strengthened, and it was in this amity that Balfour placed all his hopes for the future progress and prosperity of South Africa.

PART FOUR

The Indian and Colonial Empires

As long as we rule India we are the greatest power in the world.
                                        CURZON, 1901

Then 'ere's *to* you, Fuzzy-Wuzzy, an' the missis and the kid;
Our orders was to break you, an' of course we went an' did.
We sloshed you with Martinis, an' it wasn't 'ardly fair;
But for all the odds again' you, Fuzzy-Wuz, you broke the square.
        KIPLING, on the Sudan Expeditionary Force, 1896–9

H

14 The Keys of the Citadel

We shall never continue to hold this country except by convincing the mass of the people that our rule is juster, purer, more beneficent than either any other . . . rule could be, or than would be the rule of their own men.

CURZON, 1901

I

WHEN Balfour first became an M.P. in 1874 the great dependency of India was the most valuable Imperial possession. British interest in India, first stimulated by the spice trade, was fostered throughout the eighteenth century by the increasing commercial activity of the East India Company. This widening circle of trade rapidly involved the Company in administration where mere influence failed. The conquests of the Company's troops brought great tracts of land under British rule. In Parliament the nabobs, rich on India's trade, exerted their influence and excited jealousy. Rumours of corruption among the Company's administrators resulted in the spectacular and lengthy impeachment of Warren Hastings from 1788 to 1795.

But even before Hastings faced his accusers, the trade of the East India Company was declining steadily. Moreover Pitt's India Act of 1784 asserted greater governmental control over the Company and was meant to inaugurate an era of reform and purification.[1] The administrative functions of the Company grew in weight and complexity. Beginning as a means, administration became almost the end itself. By 1857, the Company's power rested on three armies manned mainly by Indian mercenaries and guarding the three bastions of British rule – Bengal, Bombay and Madras. Not only this. British administrators sought to make their rule more efficient and to improve the fabric of Indian life.

Accordingly, they built roads, improved irrigation and communications, extended justice, and even dabbled in schemes of education. Yet at the same time, their abhorrence of the practice of suttee could be interpreted as an attack on the Hindu religion, just as their reforms in general seemed to threaten the ancient structure of Indian society and culture. Nor was the Company slow to assume the privileges of paramountcy. Those Indian rulers that displeased it were set aside.

The great revolt of the army of Bengal in 1857 was a compound of mutiny and rebellion. Perhaps above all it was an attempt to restore the past.[2] Whatever its motives, its suppression began far-reaching reforms. The India Act of 1858 destroyed the rule of the East India Company, whose authority had been outgrown by its responsibilities. The Governor-General was given the additional title of Viceroy. Reorganisation spread to the army, to administration, to justice. On the other hand, the mutiny diminished trust between rulers and ruled. While the mid-Victorian age saw the wholesale granting of responsible government to the white colonies, in India it seemed as if the Raj was there to stay. Increasingly, a sense of administrative duty towards the Indians replaced speculation about Indian self-rule. Moreover, by the 1880s 'India . . . had become of the first importance to the economy. The British had invested some £270 millions there, not much less than one fifth of their entire investment overseas. India had become a valuable exporter and importer, taking about 19 per cent of British exports.'[3] In addition, the Indian army, free from the control of the British exchequer, was a readily available source of manpower.

Far from wishing to abandon India, British governments looked to its protection with a zeal hardly exceeded by the need to safeguard Britain itself. Balfour had only been an M.P. for two years when the Royal Titles Act of 1876 bestowed upon Queen Victoria the title of Empress of India. This was Disraeli's doing, and had far more shadow than substance. Nonetheless, it had a convenient symbolism and perhaps helped to bind the already loyal Indian princes still more closely to the Raj. But it was the character of British administration in India that Parliament tended to debate.

The Commons did not lavish their time on discussing why, and for how long, the British were ruling India. Those members who felt disquiet could draw comfort from Gladstone's hope in 1883 that the Commons would go on with the 'noble and upright and blessed work of gradually increasing the Indian franchise.'[4] But this reference to the limited success of Ripon, the Viceroy, in attempting to introduce some measure of local self-government still left the underlying problem virtually untouched.[5] Nor did the all-out attacks of Irish Nationalist and radical members alter basic assumptions about the future of India.

2

For the first part of his political career Balfour paid little attention to Indian affairs. Initially this seems curious in view of the fact that his maiden speech, on 10 August 1876, had dealt with Indian silver currency. However, Balfour later admitted that his nervousness led him to choose a topic which could be guaranteed to empty the House. 'I desired', he said, 'security not success.'[6] In 1893 Balfour showed interest in the Commons' resolution calling for simultaneous Civil Service examinations in Britain and India. This proposal, made in Gladstone's last ministry, was meant to ensure that Indians who wished to enter the Indian Civil Service could sit the examination in India and so avoid the expense and inconvenience of travelling to Britain. Without simultaneous examinations the mechanics of the system discriminated against Indians and made mock of the idea of equality of opportunity for both races. Balfour regarded the proposed reform coolly, asking Gladstone whether 'the Government mean to imply that, in some shape or other, the Government of India are obliged to carry out this Resolution?' Balfour hoped that in sending the resolution 'the Government will not lay down any principle.'[7]

After this intervention, Balfour seems to have made no contribution to Commons debates on India until July 1900. Curzon, Viceroy since 1898, had begun his sweeping and controversial reforms, and it was with Curzon rather than with India that Balfour was to become entangled. But in 1900 India was in the grip of severe famine. Millions had perished or were threatened. The government of India was almost helpless to prevent the calamity. In the debate on the Indian budget, Maclean, the member for Cardiff, criticised the Maharaja of Gwalior for offering to finance the building of a military hospital in China during the Boxer rebellion. This money, it was suggested, should be given to alleviate the sufferings of the Maharaja's countrymen. Moreover, Indian interests were hardly served by a gift towards the maintenance of European commercial domination in China. Balfour was quick to defend the Maharaja as 'one of the most energetic, public-spirited and patriotic Princes reigning under our suzerainty in India.' Furthermore, he had already given 'generous assistance' to his famine-stricken subjects.[8]

This was more than a routine defence of an Indian ruler whose interests were clearly served by close co-operation with the Raj. Indeed, Balfour began a discourse on India's position within the Empire. He showed that he opposed the voting of financial aid to India, claiming that 'Any charitable donation made by the House at the expense of the British taxpayer would be made to India without India requiring it, and in advance of any necessity.' Balfour denied that he meant that British interests were so alien from Indian interests 'that we regard India as a possession from which we derive indirect profit and direct glory, but to which we feel ourselves so little responsible that we are not willing to come to their assistance'. In that case it could be said that 'the British Empire was indeed unworthy of our great Indian possession.' But, Balfour insisted, the government did not mean this. 'All we say is that sound principle requires that the financial responsibility of the different parts of the Empire should be kept separate, and it is only when the financial resources of the Empire absolutely fail that it is legitimate to call upon the rest of the Empire for assistance.'[9]

It was true that the Indian government was not impoverished in 1900. In addition, Balfour's dislike of government charity was echoed by Curzon. The Viceroy wanted the Indian government to 'spend its last rupee in the saving of human life.' At the same time Curzon attacked prodigal philanthropy, believing that 'any government which, by indiscriminate alms-giving weakened the fibre and demoralised the self-reliance of the population would be guilty of a public crime.'[10] Given the state of the Indian peasantry, it was to say the least condescending of Curzon to lecture on 'self-reliance' from the midst of viceregal pomp.

Equally, Balfour believed that 'the most fruitful parent of social troubles is financial irregularity and extravagance.' He did not want 'to infuse into the veins of the Indian financial system a principle of corruption from which it would never recover.'[11] Turning from this spectre of Indian sloth stimulated by British bounty, Balfour applied his arguments to the Empire as a whole. The British Empire, he claimed, was 'run on a system never tried in the world before. . . . It is all paid for, as an Empire, by these islands.' This was an exaggeration, and Maclean interjected 'India pays its own way.' Balfour agreed that 'India pays her fair share', and went on to admit that 'the balance of payment between these islands and India is equitable.'[12]

Nonetheless, Balfour insisted that since the Empire as a whole was run by Britain, it would be unreasonable to expect the British taxpayer to bear the cost of every imperial calamity. As imperial responsibilities grew, and expenditure too, any additional burden would bear heavily on British wealth, enterprise and patriotism. The whole future of the Empire, Balfour thought, was involved in this problem. He wanted the Commons to affirm 'that the financial responsibility for the various portions of the Empire rests primarily upon those portions of the Empire.' This principle, though no doubt reassuring for the British taxpayer, also meant that the economically backward territories of the Empire, particularly the tropical dependencies, could not hope for lavish and consistent financial aid from the British government. Thus, if private investment was not forthcoming, the state would not advance the necessary funds.

While Balfour's reasoning was perfectly clear, it hardly accorded with Joseph Chamberlain's desire to promote the commercial development of the tropical dependencies. Also Balfour seemed completely unmoved by estimates 'that from 18,000,000 to 20,000,000 will perish in this death now spreading over the whole peninsula.' Referring to this horrifying estimate, Samuel Smith, the member for Flintshire, and long a friend of India, said, 'If this is not a case of extreme necessity I do not know what is.' 'It is not financial necessity', was Balfour's reply.[13]

3

Between 1900 and 1905 Balfour became deeply involved with Indian affairs. In view of his previous lack of interest this may seem remarkable. However, the fact that Salisbury's powers were declining between 1900 and 1902 meant that Balfour gradually shouldered more responsibility. Also, from 1902 to 1905, Balfour was himself Prime Minister and intimately concerned with the government of India. Above all, for Balfour, India between 1900 and 1905 could be seen almost wholly in terms of Curzon. Balfour and Curzon had long been friends. Both had entered the political scene without difficulty. Both seemed destined to provide the Unionist party with brilliant leadership. Both had formidable powers of intellect. Both had belonged to the 'Souls', a *fin de siècle* group of distinguished young men and women who met for the pleasure of each other's company and conversation, and included, apart from Balfour and Curzon, Margot Tennant (later Asquith), Alfred Lyttelton, St John Brodrick, George Wyndham and, from time to time, the young H. G. Wells.

Despite their similarities, the differences between Balfour and Curzon were marked. Curzon was vain, convinced of his own excellence. Balfour was more diffident. Whereas Curzon sooner or later offended colleagues with his impatience and contempt, Balfour was consistently and indiscriminately polite. Curzon wore himself out with grinding toil. Balfour spent most of the morning in bed. Curzon sought to master detail. Balfour was capable of completely forgetting vital facts and figures, substituting counties for provinces, and squadrons for regiments.[14] If both men had a cold side to their natures, Curzon's could dissolve into heated self-justification. Balfour, on the other hand, rarely felt pity for himself and it was almost impossible to make him lose his bland self-control. Above all, Curzon tackled reforms with disconcerting energy. Balfour sometimes lacked the stamina of a first-rate administrator.

Basically, Curzon despised Balfour's speculative and, as it seemed to him, shallow mind. After Balfour's speech on the Indian budget in July 1900, Curzon wrote a scornful letter to Lord George Hamilton, the Secretary of State for India:

It was eminently characteristic of the cultured ignorance of Arthur Balfour to talk of Sindhia as 'the Sindhia' throughout his speech. How the House of Commons would laugh if someone were . . . to speak of *the* Bannerman or *the* Chaplin. Again, in speaking of our position in India, he used the word 'suzereignty'. This is an expression which . . . has legal and technical justification, but it is one which I never myself by any chance employ. I always speak of 'the sovereignty of the Queen'; or, where that expression does not appear suitable, of 'the paramount authority' and 'the Supreme power'. Suzereignty is a term of vague extent and doubtful application, which has caused us a great deal of trouble in the past (witness the Transvaal) and which I always myself religiously avoid.[15]

Before he became Viceroy, Curzon had corresponded fairly frequently with Balfour. In March 1901, however, he wrote from Nepal apologising for not communicating with Balfour for the last two and a quarter years. This lapse, Curzon protested, was due to his knowledge that Balfour disliked correspondence and his doubts therefore as to whether he would get a reply to any letter. This explanation from so formidable a letter-writer as Curzon was a little unconvincing. Perhaps he simply wished to talk about his viceregal problems.[16] Also, Curzon subsequently felt that Salisbury had never acknowledged India's contribution to the crushing of the Boxer rebellion and her assistance during the Boer War. Probably he hoped that the Prime Minister's nephew and political heir would make amends.[17]

Curzon recalled, in March 1901, that Balfour had said that he (Curzon) would either kill himself in India or make a great name. Curzon felt that he was not so far doing the former, 'and even if I never do the latter I can still I think leave a useful mark.' The

Viceroy then wondered 'whether 100 years hence we shall still be ruling India. There is strong growing up a sort of national feeling. As such it can never be reconciled with an alien government. The forces and tendencies at work are on the whole fissiparous not unifying; and I believe that a succession of two weak or rash viceroys would bring the whole machine toppling down.'[18]

Nationalist sentiment *was* stirring in India. In 1901 it was still comparatively mild, but the Indian National Congress, created in 1885, was a medium for expressing resentment and criticism. Not that Congress in 1901 was demanding self-government. Rather, it gave voice to grievances over the number of Indians employed in the higher grades of the Civil Service, asked for the liberalisation of the legislative councils, for a reduction in military expenditure, or that in legal cases involving Indians and British, the latter should not be shown favouritism.[19]

Curzon was particularly anxious that British soldiers and civilians should not escape punishment if they committed outrages against Indians. His lack of colour prejudice was not based upon any deep sympathy for Indians, whom he regarded as inferiors, but upon his low opinion of the vast majority of mankind. Fundamentally as ignorant of the condition of the lower orders of society in Britain as he was of the Indian masses, he saw no reason why both should not be given good administration. Consequently, the Viceroy insisted on punishing soldiers of the Royal West Kent Regiment who had raped a Burmese woman in April 1899, and in October 1900 he limited the issuing of shooting passes which had hitherto led to the allegedly accidental deaths of a number of Indians at the hands of British soldiers turned sportsmen. In April 1902, Curzon followed this up by condemning and securing the punishment of the Ninth Lancers, from commanding officer to the humblest trooper, after two soldiers had beaten to death an Indian cook.[20]

Curzon's resolute action made him unpopular with large sections of the army and administration, even though it brought him staunch support from the Indian press. It illustrated his conviction that 'we shall never continue to hold this country except by convincing the mass of the people that our rule is juster, purer, more beneficent than either any other . . . rule could be, or than would be the rule of their own men.'[21] Curzon did not waste time on prospects of Indian self-government. Indeed, he believed that the real strength of his position lay in 'the extraordinary inferiority, in character, honesty and capacity of the (Indians). It is often said why not make some prominent native a member of the Executive Council? The answer is that in the whole continent there is not an Indian fit for the post. You can see therefore how difficult it is to keep the natives loyal and contented at the same time as one absolutely refuses to hand over to them the keys of the citadel.'[22]

Determined to keep the keys of the citadel for himself, Curzon complained to Balfour that although India was little thought of in Britain, 'it is out and away the biggest thing the English are doing anywhere in the world. As long as we rule India we are the greatest power in the world.' Moreover, Curzon prophesied that if Britain lost India she would immediately become a third-rate power.[23] Clearly the need to defend India and its approaches had prompted previous British governments to assert their control over strategically important territories from Cyprus, to Egypt, Aden and East Africa. The loss of India would make the retention of these territories less vital for Britain. But was Britain a great power *because* she ruled India, or did she rule India *because* she was a great power? Such speculation did not concern Curzon. He wanted to purify and improve the British Raj and thus to extend its authority well into the future.

4

In March 1901, Curzon felt that he had 'defeated all the forces . . . arrayed against reform or movement of any kind.' This was an over-optimistic claim. But at the same time it indicated the mood of Curzon's viceroyalty. He was determined to investigate every corner of Indian administration and to root out inefficiency and incompetence. To this end, he set out to enforce governmental authority effectively and to combat corruption. The fight against famine concerned him deeply, despite his hostility to undue liberality, and by March 1903 the government of India had been given a new famine policy. The organisation of the railway system was improved. Agricultural research was encouraged, and better credit facilities made available for farmers. A commission investigated the possible extension of irrigation. In addition, Curzon established a department of archaeology to preserve India's ancient monuments. He also sought to improve Indian education at both university and school level. Judged solely by the scope and intensity of his reforms, Curzon had cause for the complacency in which he frequently indulged. However, although he could overawe his colleagues in India, the British government proved less amenable.

Curzon believed that India, by which he frequently meant himself, was misunderstood and underrated at home. Consequently he proved extra sensitive to supposed slights. The coronation of Edward VII on 9 August 1902 provoked such a reaction. Curzon objected to the Indian government having to pay the expenses of the Indian representatives at the coronation in London. He made the point that the self-governing colonies were to be spared this expense, and he asked Balfour to extend the same privilege to India as a 'simple act of generosity and consideration'. To bolster his argument Curzon stressed India's contribution to the imperial cause over the previous three years: 'She saved Natal for you. She fought your battles in China. She accommodated 9,000 of your Boer prisoners. She has preserved through a crisis of imperial gravity an atmosphere of unprecedented loyalty and tranquillity.'[24] Faced with this formidable and not inaccurate catalogue of Indian achievement, Balfour agreed to Curzon's request. The Viceroy sent him a letter of congratulation.[25]

More controversial, however, were the arrangements for the Delhi durbar which was to be held in January 1903 and was to be ancillary to the King's coronation at Westminster. In November 1902, Curzon told Balfour of his plans for making the durbar a landmark in the history of British India. To this end, the Viceroy wanted the King's speech at the durbar to be something more than

'a few platitudes' which would only make the occasion 'a disastrous failure'. Anxious to appeal to the hearts of Indians, Curzon
believed that this could best be done through their pockets.
Accordingly, he asked permission to announce a specific remission
of taxation for the Indian people. Unless this was done, Curzon
felt that his cherished cause of binding the Indian people to the
throne would be ruined.[26]

Curzon felt strongly enough on this issue to telegraph his
wishes to the King. On 24 November Sir Francis Knollys, King
Edward's private secretary, passed the Viceroy's telegram on to
Balfour who was thus able to see that Curzon had told the King
that Hamilton, the Secretary of State for India, was opposed to
the sort of announcement the Viceroy wanted.[27] Three days later
Knollys let Balfour know that the 'King approves of the Viceroy
making a general statement in the terms he proposes, but not a
specific one – this is what the Cabinet I think has practically
approved of.'[28]   In face of this opposition to his durbar proposals,
Curzon gave way and on 10 December sent Balfour the text of the
durbar speech which only promised, in general terms, relief to the
Indian people.[29]

Curzon had only surrendered after his appeal to the monarch
behind his colleagues' backs had failed. He argued that this was
justified because the King's position was affected by the durbar
proposals. Balfour disagreed, and criticised Curzon for 'carrying
on an independent correspondence with [the King] on a point of
high policy without the knowledge or assent of your colleagues.'
Nor did the Prime Minister believe that Hamilton, for more than
a year, had allowed Curzon to expect the government's agreement
to specific tax concessions. To prove his point, he quoted from
the appropriate correspondence.[30]

But Balfour was careful to sugar the pill. If Curzon needed
rebuking he also needed compliments. Balfour accordingly spoke
warmly of 'our admiration for your great services as an Indian
administrator'. However, he continued, 'you seem to think that
you are injured whenever you do not get exactly your own way!
But which of us gets exactly his own way? Certainly not the Prime
Minister: certainly not any of his Cabinet colleagues.' Moreover,

Balfour doubted 'whether any of your predecessors have ever received so large a measure of confidence from either the S. of S. [*sic*] or the Home Government. I am ready to add that probably none had deserved that confidence more.' While Balfour did not rule out future differences of opinion, he assured Curzon that 'nothing will for a moment diminish either the warmth of my friendship or the enthusiasm of my admiration.'[31]

The next three years were to drain a great deal of the warmth out of the friendship and also cloud the admiration. But Curzon's immediate response was to thank Balfour for portraying him as 'a self-willed imperious colleague'. This had drawn from him 'more than a smile'. Whether the smile was one of recognition or disbelief Curzon did not make clear, although he next insisted that he got on extremely well with his colleagues in the Indian Executive Council. This innocent declaration was quickly followed by a somewhat fulsome compliment congratulating Balfour 'upon the brilliant Parliamentary statesmanship – unequalled I believe during the past half century – which has enabled you to place your Education Bill upon the Statute Book.'[32]

Despite the mutual congratulations, this skirmish was only a foretaste of deeper conflict. Even so, the dust of battle was slow to settle. In December Curzon refused the Knight Grand Cross of the Order of the Bath, making the King wonder whether the Viceroy was still upset over the Delhi durbar.[33] In addition, Curzon let the press know about the dispute over tax announcements. This prompted Knollys to write to Balfour's secretary, Sandars, in January 1903, deploring that Curzon had 'gone to the Press Camp. It was not very dignified, certainly not necessary, and it looks as if he wished to be "written up", which perhaps he does.'[34]

Some of the tension that increasingly characterised Curzon's dealings with the home government was doubtless due to the intensity with which he attacked his administrative duties. Consistently, Curzon worked for the whole day and far into the night. No detail was too small to merit his attention. To the strain of this self-imposed toil was added the recurring pain of an old spinal injury. Some of the Viceroy's peremptory behaviour can be explained in these terms.

In January 1903, Curzon sounded out Balfour on the subject of leave for high-ranking Indian officials. Balfour had little sympathy with the idea, although he realised that the intricacies of Indian and Far Eastern affairs could only benefit from consultation between the British government and the Viceroy or the Indian Commander-in-Chief.[35] Undeterred, Curzon asked for a leave of six months and, in effect, for the subsequent extension of his viceregal term of office. Writing in February 1903 Curzon put his case to Balfour:

You will acquit me, I know, of vanity or egotism in anything that I am about to say. It is commonplace that I have undertaken a work of reform in India in almost every branch of the administration such as has not been attempted at any period during the past half century, and that might well require 10 or 15 or 20 years to complete rather than 5. Some of these reforms I have already carried through to a successful issue. I think, too, that there may be some advantage for the sake of military reform in the continued co-operation of Kitchener and myself.[36]

In March, Balfour replied to this optimistic and self-congratulatory letter. Although he admitted that an extension of Curzon's term of office was a good idea, Balfour wondered whether, by 1905, his government would still be in power in view of the long and costly Boer War. At the same time, he told Curzon that the King had suggested a shorter leave of between six weeks and two months. To soften this blow, Balfour speculated as to India's fate if Curzon was away for too long. He suggested that either India would get on too well without the Viceroy, or the administration would collapse.[37]

Curzon was neither pleased with these proposals nor diverted by the lighthearted teasing. In April he wrote to the King deploring the prospect of a long term in India without a break of at least three or four months.[38] A month later, Balfour informed Knollys that Curzon now wanted to be in England from the end of May to the start of September. Balfour admitted 'being much disappointed at the tone and temper of [Curzon's] letters.'[39] The tone had been set by Curzon's vehement denials that it had been his 'plan' or 'suggestion' to extend his viceroyalty. Rather, Curzon insisted, he had merely offered to stay on in the public interest if the government so wished. The distinction here between an 'offer' and a 'suggestion' was, to say the least, a narrow one. Moreover, Curzon was equally firm about his leave. Claiming that two months was inadequate, the Viceroy was quick to point out that Milner, the High Commissioner for South Africa, had been in England three times during roughly the same period as his (Curzon's) Indian service.[40]

Balfour could not let this pass unanswered. In June, Curzon was reminded that it *had* been his own idea to extend his term of office. But Balfour was careful to add that he still thought this a very good idea. With the approach of the tariff reform crisis, Balfour told Curzon that his letter '(if things go awry) . . . may be the last I shall address to you as Prime Minister.' But, 'at all events you have the satisfaction of knowing that your Indian administration has added great lustre to a government which will be thought, in time to come, to have done much for the country.'[41]

A few days later, Balfour informed Curzon that the objections to the lengthening of his term of office had been overcome. In the same breath he protested over the Viceroy's 'epistolary style'.[42] Curzon, in reply, regretted that he had caused offence, but plainly considered that Balfour had treated the idea of his 'sacrifice' of an extended term grudgingly.[43] Despite, or perhaps because of, the vigour with which Curzon had conducted his campaign he had got his own way. Not only was his viceroyalty extended, but he was also granted six months leave. While Curzon's Indian reforms lent strength to a government which Balfour clearly thought near collapse in June 1903, it was still a substantial risk to extend his term of office.

Curzon left India for his leave on 30 April 1904. On his arrival in Britain he was made Warden of the Cinque Ports. Although still racked with pain, he attended many functions in his honour and made a good number of speeches. He was also able to renew personal contact with colleagues like Balfour and Brodrick, Hamilton's successor as Secretary for India, and to discuss problems ranging from Kitchener's proposed army reforms to policy towards Afghanistan and Tibet. Even so, Curzon's boundless energy caused him to fret over uncompleted work. In order to occupy the Viceroy's leisure, Balfour made an interesting proposal in May. Referring to a recent observation of Curzon's which he said accorded with his own thoughts, Balfour wrote:

You said that when you had an opportunity you would like to bring in a Bill for the alteration of the Government of India Act of '58. I am convinced that the changes, internal and external, of the Indian Empire during the last two generations render it at least probable that some change in that Act is eminently desirable. As your holiday seems to be in danger of being spoilt through want of work, why not crystallize your views and draft the heads of such a Bill as you would like? It would commit neither you nor me, and I am sure it would be most useful for us to talk the matter over. Possibly we might have time to pass a measure next year.[44]

This was a mysterious invitation. Curzon seems to have ignored it. At least, he put forward no draft bill. Balfour's government passed no India Act. Indeed the mounting dissension within the Unionist party over tariff reform would not have made 1905 a propitious year for such a fundamental reform. Probably Balfour wanted to provide Curzon with a token of esteem. The implied compliment might go far to render the Viceroy's leave constructive and his relations with his colleagues cordial. Unfortunately, this was not to be the case. Indeed, when Lord Ampthill, Curzon's deputy in India, wrote to the King in December 1904 saying how glad he would be of the Viceroy's return, the sentiment might well have been echoed by several members of the Cabinet.[45]

15 Guarding the Frontiers

To allow a Viceroy to run his own foreign policy . . . irrespective of the foreign policy of the Home Government, would be to copy the blunder which has brought Russia to disaster and humiliation – the blunder, namely, of having one Foreign Minister in the Far East and another at home, not necessarily acting in accord.

BALFOUR, 1905

I

CURZON was in England from May to November 1904. Although he was frequently fêted during these months he faced discomfiture as well. The circulation of Kitchener's memorandum on Indian army reform at a C.I.D. meeting in June, and Curzon's protests, emphasised the growing antagonism between Viceroy and Commander-in-Chief. Moreover, Curzon had no high opinion of Brodrick, the Secretary of State for India. Relations between the two men deteriorated steadily. This was particularly unfortunate in view of the crucially important role Brodrick could play in ameliorating the Curzon-Kitchener dispute and the differences of opinion between the Viceroy and the Cabinet over Indian frontier policy.

The defence of India's frontiers had long occupied Curzon's energies. In December 1900 the Cabinet had sanctioned the formation of the North West Frontier Province situated between Kashmir and Baluchistan on the Afghan border. Curzon was showered with praise for his initiative.[1] However, he did not allow matters to rest there. Convinced that Russia was menacing Persia, Tibet and Afghanistan, Curzon was determined to take appropriate counter-measures.

Balfour believed that Afghanistan was too unreliable to be a firm ally and must rather be considered a potential, but weak, enemy. This contradicted Curzon's insistence that a formal and more exacting treaty should be concluded with the Amir, Habibulla. Particularly, Curzon wanted the Indian army to have the right to enter Afghanistan in the event of a Russian invasion. But the Amir was insistently opposed to this, and determined to retain the maximum freedom of action. Despite lengthy negotiations at Kabul, despite his presence in England, Curzon had failed to win his case by the time he returned to India. Shortly after his return, the British government signed an agreement with the Amir in March 1905 which merely continued the previous rather vague arrangements for guaranteeing Afghan independence.[2]

Curzon was incensed. He considered that the Amir had been allowed to dictate his own terms. He accused the Cabinet of an 'Afghan surrender', adding that it was due to 'the terrors of a moribund Government, with fear of Russia on the brain.'[3] Typically, this viceregal outburst ignored the unfortunate blow dealt to Disraeli's government, in the election of 1880, by the disastrous invasion of Afghanistan initiated by the Viceroy, Lord Lytton. Moreover, undue pressure on the Amir might push him into the arms of Russia. Although the Cabinet had played safe, there were good reasons for doing so.

2

Curzon's Tibetan policy was hardly more successful. Tibet lay under shadowy Chinese overlordship, and Curzon believed that Russian influence there was growing steadily. He determined, therefore, to send a mission to Tibet to assert British interests. In October 1903 the matter was discussed by members of the Cabinet. The dangers were clear enough. Although the proposed mission was ostensibly of a commercial nature, it would be tempting for Curzon to use it to extract military and political concessions from the Tibetans. Nor did he consider it strictly necessary to get Cabinet permission for his enterprise beyond a general authorisation to proceed. The Viceroy believed that if the mission was successful all would be forgiven him.

Balfour was wary of the whole affair. On 28 October 1903, he told Brodrick:

I am not very happy about the movement in Tibet. The cost will fall of course wholly upon the Indian Government, so that this element ... does not immediately concern us. ... But I strongly deprecate permanent entanglements in Tibet, partly because I think we have as much on our hands as we can look after, partly because if we 'Manchurianize' what is technically a part of the Chinese Empire, we may greatly weaken our diplomacy in the Far East.[4]

There was certainly a danger that a lengthy British involvement in Tibet might lead to an embarrassing double confrontation with Russia – on the heights of the Himalayas and also, in the event of a Russo-Japanese War, in the Far East or Afghanistan. But with Curzon clamouring for an advance, these doubts had to be stifled. Balfour did so with misgiving, complaining that:

The perennial difficulty of governing the Empire lies in the fact that the rulers in its outlying portions have great local knowledge, but no responsibility and little thought for the general situation; and we at home are naturally reluctant to over-rule people on the spot who say, and often with truth, that their policy is the only one which will save bloodshed and money in the long run. ... I suppose we must assent to George Curzon's suggestions; but surely we might wait for Cabinet sanction? If military considerations render this expedient, I authorize you to approve – but I do so reluctantly.[5]

The next day Brodrick telegraphed Curzon telling him that the Cabinet had 'showed a strong and unanimous feeling against any permanent entanglement in Tibet.' He also believed that the India Council in London 'would probably join vehemently with the Cabinet in deprecating further advance.'[6] But by December 1903 the Tibetan expedition was on the move, led by Colonel Younghusband, an explorer and mystic. Progress was slow however. Furthermore, in March 1904 the expedition clashed with Tibetan forces, several hundred of whom were mown down with Maxim guns. In May, a second Tibetan attack was repulsed, again with heavy losses.[7]

These bloody incidents made nonsense of the government's insistence that the mission was only meant to iron out a few outstanding trade problems. Mounting indignation was expressed in Parliament and the press. While Curzon insisted that the two battles illustrated the impossibility of dealing with the Tibetans by normal diplomatic means, this did not reassure liberal consciences. Hardly more reassuring was Balfour's defence of the expedition in the Commons. Basing his arguments on Tibetan infringements of frontier agreements, Balfour professed indignation at Opposition criticism. The latter regarded 'the pulling down of boundary pillars as a small matter, and the occupation of fragments of pasture land as a thing that can be passed over, and they have demonstrated that nothing has occurred between Tibet and India which is worth the cost and risk involved in this Mission. That land of political arithmetic is rotten from the beginning. . . . Is it suggested that we were indefinitely to allow the Tibetan Government and its subjects to violate the solemn treaties entered into by them?'[8]

Balfour's position was beset with contradictions. Although his government had reluctantly agreed to the mission, it had been made clear to Younghusband in November 1903 that there was no question of installing a British Agent in Tibet or occupying territory. Yet, urged on by Curzon, the expedition seemed to have a will of its own. The government of India was leading the British government by the nose. What is more, it was leading it into the sort of entanglement it most wished to avoid. In the Commons, Balfour dug deep into his reserves of argument, sometimes scraping the bottom of the barrel in his endeavours. Without the mission, he said, there could be no negotiations at all with the Tibetans. Moreover, 'Tibetan methods, unlike Western methods, put an impenetrable wall between those responsible for the Tibetan Government and the Indian Government.'[8] While it was true that Tibetan representatives had proved difficult to contact, Balfour's analysis of the situation completely ignored the physically imposing barrier of the Himalayas – themselves hardly a help in communications.

Failing to make clear what the government wanted from Tibet,

Balfour was at least certain what he did not want. 'I should greatly deplore it if [Tibet] should fall under our influence,' he said. 'I do not want anything to do with the Tibetans in a political sense. Let the Tibetans manage their own affairs . . . I desire nothing better.' Balfour did not want a British Agent in Tibet. But he felt that Tibet should not exclude British influence while allowing other nations to exert theirs. Who were these other nations? Balfour did not say. But he accepted 'absolutely' Russian claims that they wished to play no part in Tibet.[9] This was a flat contradiction of Curzon's insistence that the Russians were seeking to control Tibet. Indeed, the British government had very recently given the Russian Government assurances that no occupation of Tibet was contemplated. Perhaps the two rivals could agree to leave Tibet free from foreign domination.

Debarred from saying this in plain terms, Balfour was reduced to expressing the wish that 'our treaty engagements are not made the laughing stock of the Oriental world.' Optimistically, he claimed that the mission 'will result, without further bloodshed, in putting the relations between India and its northern neighbour on a permanently satisfactory basis, while it will prove for all time to the Tibetan Government that they cannot treat us with the contempt with which they have treated us in the last thirty years.'[10] This was an attempt to have the best of both worlds.

In August 1904, Younghusband reached Lhasa. There he concluded an agreement with the Tibetan government, which was signed on 4 September. Although the convention did not mention the establishment of a British Agent, it did provide for the occupation of the strategically important Chumbi valley against the payment, in seventy-five instalments, of an annual indemnity. Also, trade relations were regulated. While the trade agreement was welcomed, despite Balfour's scepticism as to its value, Brodrick insisted that Younghusband had disregarded two telegrams (of 6 and 16 July) instructing him to impose only a three year indemnity on the Tibetans. Accordingly, the Cabinet now demanded that the indemnity be reduced by two thirds and made payable over three years.[11] The agreement with Russia, quite apart from a dislike of long-term involvement, helped to bring this about.

Had Younghusband ignored his instructions, or had he not received them? He claimed that the Tibetans requested a seventy-five year indemnity, and that having agreed to this he felt bound to disregard the subsequent arrival of official instructions ordering a three year period of repayment.[12] But for once the man on the spot did not win. Younghusband returned to England, according to Ampthill, Curzon's deputy, 'greatly distressed at having misapprehended and exceeded his instructions.' But Ampthill hoped that since Younghusband had so improved Tibetan relations his final mistake would be condoned.[13] The King admired Younghusband's determination and made him a Knight Commander of the Order of the Indian Empire, although Brodrick vetoed two higher awards. If royal sympathy rewarded Younghusband, Curzon received no such token. Rather he stood humiliated and exposed. Probably it was what he deserved. He had, while in England, supported an adventure which embarrassed his colleagues in the British Cabinet. Moreover, he had instigated the adventure in the first place.

Balfour was under no illusions. He told Knollys, the King's secretary, that Younghusband, 'by disobeying orders', had placed his country 'in a very false position'. He repeated that he wanted interference in Tibet kept to a minimum. Balfour also felt that a seventy-five year occupation of the Chumbi valley would merely resemble the Russian policy of allowing a frontier officer to make territorial gains which officially ran counter to government policy. In the broader perspective, Balfour considered China, in October 1904, as 'perhaps the most sensitive spot in international diplomacy'.[14] A year later Balfour again emphasised that 'Tibet is under the suzereignty of China, and China is the storm-centre of international politics.'[15]

Since the Russo-Japanese War had been raging since February 1904, there were good reasons for circumspect diplomacy involving China. Britain's desire not to be drawn into the war on Japan's side also explains the government's cautious handling of Russian interests in Tibet. Such considerations afforded Curzon little comfort. But his disagreements with the Cabinet over frontier policy did not ruin his Indian career. This was the result of a more titanic conflict.

3

On 17 October 1902, Kitchener, the hero of Omdurman, the conqueror of the Boers, left England to take up his appointment as Commander-in-Chief of the Indian army. Kitchener had a sense of duty and an obsession with detail that rivalled Curzon's own. At the same time, he was capable of neglecting important files and ignoring routine in an infuriating way. To a soldierly directness, Kitchener added a passion for floral display, porcelain, and lavish living. While he could be callous and autocratic, he could on rare occasions allow sentiment to overwhelm him. On meeting Kitchener after his triumphant return from the Sudan, Balfour had doubted how far he 'could adapt himself to wholly different and perhaps larger problems than those with which he has been dealing.'[16] The command of the Indian army was one such problem. Moreover, a clash between men as wilful and self-righteous as Curzon and Kitchener seemed probable.

Curzon had set his heart on getting Kitchener appointed. When the Viceroy asked Balfour in 1903 to extend his term of office, he had written optimistically that 'there may be some advantage for the sake of military reform, in the continued co-operation of Kitchener and myself. Many amiable people have been speculating how soon we should fall out. I am afraid they will be woefully disappointed. I am not going to get a man of his unrivalled knowledge and authority without providing an ample field for both, and, with my support, he will be able to accomplish a great deal in a very short time.'[17]

Perhaps Curzon believed that Kitchener's presence would add lustre to his viceregal achievements. Brodrick, the Secretary of State for India, was uneasy. He had attempted to prevent Kitchener going to India before Curzon had left. This had not proved possible. Furthermore, the extension of Curzon's viceregal term meant that the two men would now be in lengthy contact with each other. Brodrick, who claimed he knew both men better than anyone in the Cabinet, would 'have wagered half my fortune that there would be a clash between them.'[18]

In Egypt, on his way out to India, Kitchener told Lord Cromer, the British Agent and Consul-General and the effective ruler of Egypt, that he intended to abolish the Military Member of the Viceroy's Council.[19] To one of Kitchener's imperious temper, the system of dual control over the Indian army, whereby the Commander-in-Chief shared overall responsibility for military matters with the Military Member, could only be anathema. Not only did the Military Member, Major-General Elles, supervise army expenditure and supply, but he was also Kitchener's junior in rank. Kitchener did not, therefore, have autocratic control over his army. This was all the more frustrating since, after surveying Indian defences and noting the Russian menace on the frontiers, Kitchener was determined to reform the Indian army.

Although he soon forced through a fundamental reorganisation of the army, Kitchener did not immediately get his own way over the Military Member. By the time Curzon arrived in England in May 1904 for his leave, Kitchener's demands that dual control should be abolished had caused a rift between the two men. Nor did the Viceroy's reputation as the scourge of army misconduct make relations easier. Balfour optimistically believed that Curzon's presence in England would solve any number of Indian problems. In particular, he believed that the military controversy could be settled.[20]

Despite the unfortunate incident of the circulation of Kitchener's memorandum on army reform at the C.I.D. meeting of 15 June attended by Curzon, Balfour tried to effect a compromise in November, 1904. He told Curzon of Kitchener's view that the effective defence of India was impossible without military reorganisation. Balfour felt that Kitchener would resign if nothing was done, and that in this event public opinion in Britain would favour the military hero rather than the reforming Viceroy. Declaring himself against drift, Balfour said, 'we must make up our minds to modify, or at all events, thoroughly re-examine, the present relations between the C-in-C and the Military Member of the Council.'[21]

But the drift continued. Curzon's leave ended with no solution in sight. According to Brodrick, the Viceroy 'left for India a physical wreck. He broke down at Victoria when leaving, and had another breakdown in Bombay.'[22] Hardly refreshed by his leave in England, Curzon perhaps drew comfort on his return from a letter from Balfour of 1 January 1905. The Viceroy had complained about the interference by the India Council in London. Balfour told him that 'as at present advised, all my sympathies are with you. I do not believe in these systems of elaborate checks and counter-checks.'[23]

These soothing words carried an implied threat for Curzon. If Balfour did not believe in checks and counter-checks surely he would not agree that the Military Member was an essential counter-poise to the power of the Commander-in-Chief in India. This was the heart of Curzon's case. At the same time, Balfour was not altogether pleased with Kitchener. In December 1904, referring to plans to send reinforcements to India in wartime, Balfour complained that, 'Owing to the extreme difficulty of carrying on a discussion with Lord Kitchener which shall be both fruitful and rapid, we are still without any reasoned account of the method in which these enormous reinforcements are to be used, or even how they are to be lodged in India, or fed in Afghanistan.'[24]

In India the situation deteriorated further. At a meeting of the Viceroy's Council on 10 March 1905, Curzon and Elles, the Military Member, submitted papers on the explosive subject of dual control. Kitchener maintained a defensive silence.[25] Shortly afterwards Curzon wrote melodramatically to Balfour, emphasising the seriousness of the matter. He and his colleagues on the Council were convinced, 'that if His Majesty's Government propose to subject the existing system and to impose upon us Kitchener's plan of military autocracy, they will be doing what would not merely not be accepted in England, but what will be the source of great and lasting harm in India.' Surprisingly, Curzon still insisted that he got on well with the Commander-in-Chief, but added forcibly, 'Kitchener came out to India in order to destroy the Military Department (of which he then knew nothing) and to set himself up as a Military Dictator in its place.'[26]

This emotive appeal bore Curzon no fruit. The government simply could not allow the quarrel over dual control to drag on indefinitely. Anglo-Russian relations, made more delicate by the Dogger Bank incident and the Russo-Japanese War, demanded a united British front in India. The government, advised by a special Cabinet Committee, therefore decided to give Kitchener what he wanted in substance. The Military Member's duties were confined to supply, and the Commander-in-Chief now had a free hand to deal with military matters. This decision, which had the full support of the Cabinet and, with two exceptions, of the India Council in London, was sent to Curzon in a dispatch of 31 May 1905.[27]

The dispatch was a thunderbolt to Curzon. He had already hinted darkly at 'the inability of myself, and, as I thought not unlikely, of my Colleagues to accept over-ruling at the hands of the Home Government' on a matter which we regarded as vital'.[28] Probably he believed that Balfour's government, for which he had no high regard, would surrender at the last minute. Certainly the Unionist administration, their party fragmented over the tariff reform controversy, seemed to be tottering to its fall in the summer of 1905. But Balfour did not give in to Curzon. Rather, he represented the fateful dispatch as a compromise measure, and hoped that it would 'prove to be of great administrative importance.'[29]

Curzon was not so dispassionate. He refused to write any further letters to his former friend Brodrick, simply firing off 'excited telegrams at intervals'. Although prostrate with his old spinal trouble he forbade any press correspondent to mention it. At the same time, he struggled to enlist the support of the press. There were leakages of secret telegrams, and (according to Brodrick) one important press agency allowed the Viceroy to edit its messages in return for money from public funds. Curzon even went so far as to address his Council in rash and extravagant terms.[30] One speech prompted Balfour to tell the King that it was 'deplorable in taste and temper; and that no such public exhibition of disloyalty to the Home Government has ever yet been made by an Indian Viceroy. Mr Balfour looks forward to the development of the incident with the gravest anxiety.'[31]

Predictably, Curzon appealed both to monarch and Prime Minister. He told Edward VII that the government's action was 'universally and unanimously condemned by public opinion here. . . . The instruments of your Majesty's rule in India cannot be openly humiliated without weakening the foundation of the rule itself.'[32] This ominous statement was repeated in a letter to Balfour two weeks later, with the added insistence that 'Every blow that you inflict upon the prestige of the Indian Government is a blow to British Government'.[33] Curzon claimed that the decision over dual control had 'created a unanimity of dissent in this country which I imagine to be without parallel. It applies to all classes, European and Native; it is not confined to the civil population but is shared by the military. The public has been shocked at the spectacle of the Home Government showing such complete indifference to the unanimous and earnest opinions of the Indian Government on a matter directly affecting our own constitution.'[34]

To strengthen his case, Curzon denied that the long-suffering members of his Council were also his 'slaves and puppets'. Ironically, this was true in the summer of 1905, when some Council members at last made plain their criticism of the Viceroy's stand over dual control. Hitherto, the Council members had been overwhelmed by the Viceroy's drive, initiative, and pathological aversion to criticism. But Curzon chose to dwell on the unanimity of his support. To this persuasive, but questionable, argument Curzon added another. 'The Viceroy of India', he said, 'is not an agent whom you send out to execute your orders or to act as the instrument of a policy conceived at home. He is, outside of England, the first public servant of the Crown. He is head of the greatest subordinate government in the world.'[35]

Lest these strictures should fail to move the government, Curzon also threatened resignation. In July the King was told that the Viceroy had 'informed the Prime Minister several months ago that he must resign if the safeguards of our Indian constitution were . . . undermined or destroyed.'[36] Curzon also asked Balfour why, if he was so dissatisfied with him, was he not recalled and the reasons made public? Protesting that he was 'quite willing to retire from high office or even from political life', the Viceroy dramatically placed his future in Balfour's hands.[37]

These histrionics were brought to a close early in August. Following the failure of his attempt to appoint Sir Edmund Barrow, notoriously opposed to Kitchener, as the new Military Member of the Council, Curzon telegraphed his resignation to Balfour on 5 August. Balfour's beleaguered administration could ill afford this further blow to its prestige. But neither could it afford Curzon's intransigence and hostility. Not only was Curzon's relationship with Brodrick in ruins, but if the Viceroy stayed, Kitchener might well go. Of the two men, the loss of Kitchener would be the most disastrous in the public eye. Nonetheless, Balfour made a half-hearted appeal to Curzon; claiming that the government 'with every desire to meet your wishes . . . are unable to understand your position and earnestly desire you to reconsider it.'[38]

But the Cabinet had already anticipated Curzon's departure and, after failing to secure the services of Milner, recently returned from his arduous work in South Africa, appointed Lord Minto as the next Viceroy.[39] Nor were voices lacking to urge Balfour to accept Curzon's resignation. Balfour's cousin, the new Lord Salisbury, was afraid that, thwarted in his Afghan and Tibetan plans, Curzon would try to bring about a failure of the alternative policies. How could such a man be left in power? The last thing that the Cabinet wanted was a war in Afghanistan.[40] The King, too, now thought that Curzon should resign, since it was 'evident that he will now never get on with the Home Govt.'.[41]

On 21 August Balfour formally accepted Curzon's resignation. Two days later he wrote a private letter to Curzon, deploring the way in which the vast distance between Britain and India distorted disputes. At the same time, Balfour reminded Curzon of his accusations that Brodrick 'desired secretly to drive you to resign' and that 'the Afghan surrender' was due to 'the terrors of a moribund Government with fear of Russia on the brain.' He added, 'I only saw your letters from which I have made these extracts today. I shall make a point of forgetting them to-morrow. . . . Of one thing only shall I be mindful – that for nearly seven years, in sickness and in health, you have devoted with untiring energy your splendid abilities to the service of India and of the Empire – And this is enough.'⁴²

4

Despite Balfour's generous letter to Curzon, relations between the two men had been severely strained. But although Balfour had been exasperated by Curzon's conduct, it was the latter who had descended to vituperation. In August 1900 Curzon had written slightingly of Balfour's 'cultured ignorance'. He had followed this up by listing Balfour's alleged deficiencies in a letter of April 1903 written to Godley, the Under Secretary of State for India. Curzon claimed that a good many of Balfour's arguments 'never make the slightest impression on me because, though metaphysically beautiful, they have no connection with the facts. . . . I remember his long telegram about the King and taxation in India – utterly academic. Of a similar character was his plea that if we sent a mission to Lhasa we should raise the question of the integrity of China.' Curzon regard Balfour's arguments 'as mere soap bubbles, just as iridescent and equally unsubstantial.'⁴³ This strikingly unfair generalisation showed to the full Curzon's incapacity for objective self-analysis. Perhaps Balfour's arguments were metaphysically beautiful, but at least they never rivalled Curzon's emotional and almost unbalanced diatribes. Moreover, Balfour aroused Curzon's contempt firstly because he sought to alter the Viceroy's wilder schemes, and secondly because he was generally supported by the British Cabinet.

Curzon's resignation did not end Balfour's problems. On 1 September, the King pressed Balfour to grant Curzon an earldom, hoping that 'considering the Viceroy of India's character, such an offer made immediately might soothe his feelings.'⁴⁴ Three days later Knollys, the King's secretary, returned to the subject. Arguing that the Indians regarded the Viceroy as a sort of demigod and the Commander-in-Chief as far inferior, Knollys wondered whether viceregal prestige would suffer through the apparent triumph of Kitchener. To lessen this danger he again suggested an appropriate honour for Curzon.[45] On 6 September, Knollys, after congratulating Balfour on his conciliatory letter to Curzon, repeated his request.

Balfour was unmoved by this persistent pressure from the palace. The bestowal of an honour at that stage could have been variously interpreted. It could mean that the Cabinet now admitted a mistake, or that they wanted to gag Curzon with an earldom. Balfour explained his position in a Cabinet minute of 6 September entitled 'A Peerage for Lord Curzon'. Believing that it was not a question of *whether* Curzon should receive an honour but *when*, Balfour indicted the Viceroy for 'fighting inch by inch against the effective execution of a policy which he has never pretended to approve, but which he declared himself ready to accept.' This struggle had set Viceroy against Commander-in-Chief, had embittered old friendships, and, via the Indian press, had made the Indian public aware of secret documents. Balfour regretted having extended Curzon's term of office.[46]

In this context, Balfour believed that an honour for Curzon 'would encourage the dangerous conviction that India is not, in any direct or vital sense, subject to the control of Parliament and of the Cabinet, and that the Viceroy, if only he possesses sufficient resolution and capacity, may fearlessly pursue a policy of his own, sure that success and failure, co-operation and obstruction, will, at the termination of his office, be equally rewarded.'[47] Such an assertion of viceregal power had previously caused Balfour to remark that Curzon's claims 'would raise India to the position of an independent and not always friendly power.'[48]

Balfour developed this theme:

It must be recollected that the foreign policy of India is now an inseparable and integral part of the foreign policy of the Empire to a degree which was not the case in times gone by. Thibet is under the suzereignty of China, and China is the storm-centre of international politics. Afghanistan touches Russia and Persia and is the weak spot of Imperial defence. To allow a Viceroy to run his own foreign policy in those regions, irrespective of the foreign policy of the Home Government, would be to copy the blunder which has brought Russia to disaster and humiliation – the blunder, namely, of having one Foreign Minister in the Far East and another at home, not necessarily acting in accord. I believe that Lord Curzon would be the last to deny that this general theory is sound; but he has found it a hard theory to carry fully into practice. He entertained strong opinions, founded on great study; he probably held in no very high esteem either the abilities of the Indian Council or the oriental knowledge of the Cabinet; and even when obliged to give way, his reluctance sometimes showed itself in a manner not conducive to the smooth working of that very complicated machine, the Government of India.'[49]

Having analysed Curzon's unsatisfactory relationship with the home government, Balfour did not stint his praise of the Viceroy's achievements. The partition of Bengal in 1905 had unleashed a flood of Indian criticism and hostility. Indeed, Curzon's reforming zeal was bound to cause antagonism among many sections of both the administration and the people. Balfour chose to see Curzon's unpopularity 'as evidence of his political virtues rather than of any supposed political shortcomings.' In India any reformer, unless very diplomatic or exceptionally lucky, was bound to have bouts of unpopularity. Curzon was a masterful character who courted unpopularity. Believing that 'Lord Curzon will be ranked by the impartial historian as among the greatest of the British Rulers of India', Balfour nonetheless felt disquiet at the prospect of Curzon's return.[50] For his own part, he proposed to wash no dirty linen in public, rather to remember the many debts the Empire owed the Viceroy.[51]

Curzon returned to England in December 1905, having publicly shaken hands with a reluctant Kitchener and greeted Lord Minto, the new Viceroy, wearing shooting clothes and slippers. With such trivial shows did a great reforming Viceroy bid farewell to India. On his return, Curzon may have drawn some pleasure from the discovery that Balfour's government had resigned. At least, he refrained from public criticism of the fallen administration. This was probably due to an earnest appeal by Edward VII issued on 15 September. At any rate, Curzon maintained a steady silence which was as remarkable as it was untypical.

For Balfour the whole affair had been one of unalloyed misery. Convinced that Curzon was wrong in his dispute with Kitchener, he later admitted that the extension of the Viceroy's term of office was the greatest mistake of his political life.[52] Although Balfour's friendship with Curzon was eventually repaired, it had been badly damaged. At the same time, the home government had at least asserted its primacy in the face of Curzon's dangerous frontier policy and his demands for a freer hand. Perhaps the final irony was that the whole purpose of Curzon's energetic reforms had been to so improve the British Raj that India would remain part of the Empire indefinitely. But these reforms either left untouched or even aggravated new Indian demands and needs. Efficient administration, which Curzon sought to embellish and sustain, could no longer provide an acceptable alternative to growing national awareness. In this sense, Curzon left the foundations of British rule in India weaker than he found them.

16 Independence for India

If you leave India to herself it is as absolutely certain as anything can be that she will relapse into what is the natural organisation of society in that part of the world, which is absolute government.

BALFOUR, 1924

I

IN November 1900 Curzon told Hamilton, the Secretary of State for India, 'that the Congress is tottering to its fall, and one of my greatest ambitions while in India is to assist it to a peaceful demise.'[1] But five years later, when Curzon resigned as Viceroy, India was faced with an unprecedented radical nationalism which, growing within the twenty-year-old Congress movement, threatened to burst it at the seams. Curzon's partition of Bengal and his refusal to heed subsequent Indian protests had fed this revolutionary spirit. There were, of course, deeper discontents. Despite the reforms of Ripon and Curzon and the latter's zealous assault on corruption, India seemed little further advanced along the road to self-rule. The Civil Service and the commissioned ranks of the Indian army were still dominated by the British. The government of India remained the goverment of Britain-in-India.

Although it seemed impossible that Britain could hold India indefinitely against the will of her people, it was difficult firstly to ascertain what the will of the people represented, and secondly to envisage the nature of India's independence. Gokhale and the Congress moderates were, by 1905, asking for status equivalent to that of the self-governing colonies. But radicals like Aurobindo Ghose and Tilak were demanding less passivity and an autonomy not necessarily within the confines of the Empire.[2] External events strengthened these aspirations. The Japanese defeat of Russia between 1904–5 made nonsense of theories of European superiority. Moreover, the United States introduction of representative institutions into the Philippines, and the Liberal government's grant of self-government to the conquered Boer republics, were galling examples of generosity for Indian nationalists who had played the restrained Congress game for twenty years.

Although the advent of the Campbell-Bannerman government meant the end of almost twenty years of Unionist rule, India felt no immediate benefits. The new Secretary of State, John Morley, made no concession over the partition of Bengal and looked askance at requests for an extension of parliamentary institutions in India.[3] Indeed, there was apparently little to distinguish Morley's attitude from Balfour's. On 17 May 1906, both men spoke at a luncheon to celebrate the return of the Prince and Princess of Wales from a four and a half month's visit to India. As King George V, the Prince of Wales was to take a genuine and steadfast interest in his Indian Empire, as in his other dominions. On 17 May he spoke in traditional terms of the need to dispel misunderstanding between Britain and India, and the need to foster sympathy and brotherhood and 'a closer union of hearts'.[4]

Balfour extended this theme, emphasising the ties of loyalty but doubting the usefulness of parliamentary institutions in India:

If a great Empire is to be kept together, sentiment and loyalty must enter into the emotions by which its component parts are animated, and I am assured in my own mind that when you are dealing with, possibly any population, certainly when you are dealing with a great Oriental population, it is vain to hope that sentiment will crystallize round abstract institutions of which they have no immediate or personal experience. It will not crystallize round Parliaments or Governments or councils. It will find its true goal . . . in the personal affection and the personal loyalty to an individual . . . who they understand . . . a great Sovereign and a great Emperor.[5]

Morley echoed Balfour's words, and added that sympathy, 'justice and clemency are the corner stones of our strength' in India. The Secretary of State also subscribed to the belief that a 'diversity of faith and race draws a veil down between the intercourse of any Western and any Asiatic.' This was little more than a comparatively sophisticated paraphrase of 'East is East and West is West and never the twain shall meet.' However, Morley allowed himself one piece of sober speculation:

The Government of India . . . is complex and very ambitious, and it may be that, not in our time perhaps, but before any very, very long time, the great fabric which was erected by the Act of 1858 . . . may have to be revised. But that certainly is not for my day.'[6]

This was hardly a radical statement, and reflected Morley's cautious Liberalism rather than any burning desire for change. But in India a campaign of agitation had begun. Led by Aurobindo Ghose, the rebels within the Congress movement demanded an end to British autocracy. These 'Nationalists' advocated passive resistance and a boycott of British goods and British administration. Gokhale and the moderates argued that progress towards Indian independence within the Empire must necessarily be painfully slow and marked more by failures than by striking successes. This divergence of aims came to a head at the meeting of Congress at Surat in December 1907. Although bitterly divided, Congress was not destroyed. But the moderates tried, in April 1908, to frame a constitution for Congress that bound its members to the object of achieving Dominion status for India by constitutional means.[7] The Nationalists stood aloof and unreconciled.

Mainly to draw the Nationalists' fire and to bolster the moderates, Morley and the basically conservative and authoritarian Viceroy, Minto, decided to introduce limited reforms. By 1908, Morley had come to believe that only such reforms would save the Raj. Although Minto did not go as far as this, it seemed expedient to make concessions which would, at the very least, avoid any obstruction of the administrative machinery by militant extremists. The principle of gracefully conceding political advance was enshrined in British liberalism, and not unpalatable even to conservatives. By extending this principle to India, it might prove possible to rally the Congress loyalists.

2

The Morley–Minto reforms of 1909 admitted two Indians to the Secretary of State's council in London, and one Indian each to the executive councils of the Viceroy and the provincial Governors. In addition, the legislative councils were to be liberalised: more Indians were to be elected to them, and the councils were allowed to discuss budgets more fully, and to criticise legislation with more chance of achieving amendments. These measures aroused a storm of opposition from the British administration in India, from the British press and the Unionist party, and drew hostile reactions from Edward VII and the Prince of Wales.[8]

Fortunately for Morley the appointment of Indians to the Viceroy's, the Secretary of State's and the provincial Governor's councils did not need a statute. But the reform of the legislative councils was embodied in the India Councils Act. In April 1909 the Bill was given its second reading and was fought tooth and nail by the Unionists. Balfour voiced his party's objections in two speeches of 1 and 26 April. Basically, Balfour refused to accept the principle on which the Bill was based. He agreed that representative institutions were 'the highest development as yet discovered by the human race in dealing with national affairs', but he attacked the once 'fashionable' doctrine 'that no Government could be good Government unless it was based upon the rights of man and that the rights of man carried with them the right of representation . . . yet I think that view of the world has vanished . . . even from democratic debating societies in provincial towns.'[9]

Balfour repeated with approval Morley's opinion that 'not only is India not fit for representative Government, but, unless I am misrepresenting him, it is difficult to conceive how it can ever be fit for representative government until the whole structure of Indian society . . . undergoes radical and fundamental modifications.' Balfour therefore declined to believe that the India Councils Bill was a step towards representative government, although he feared that it would give India the disadvantage of popular government without any of the advantages. The main disadvantage in Balfour's eyes was the extra burden that would be placed on the administration by the right of Indian majorities on the councils to criticise and obstruct legislation. To add substance to this doubt, Balfour imagined the British administration forced to defend itself 'against some ingenious native lawyer whose delight and pleasure, and perhaps whose road to fame, and it may be to income, consists of embarrassing the Administration in respect of which he is absolutely independent.'[10]

As a more positive argument, Balfour recited the virtues of British rule:

British administration, good or bad, lacking or not lacking sympathy with native feelings in all directions, is at all events an honest administration sincerely desirous of protecting the poor and the masses of the community by stopping corruption and oppression, which are too common in all countries, and which are the special and poisonous growth of Oriental despotism. Such a Government you do not want to control by these unofficial majorities, because to control them in that way prevents them carrying out their duties impartially.[11]

Balfour was not opposed to Indians sitting on the legislative councils, but he did object to their being in a majority. However, when the India Councils Bill became law, it could hardly be said that the reign of democracy had begun. Although the numbers of Indians on the provincial legislative councils were doubled, their majority was only made possible by the votes of nominated members. Moreover, the electorate was severely limited, the elections for the most part indirect, and there was special weighting in favour of landowners and Muslims. These reforms had strong conservative overtones.

This was what Morley and Minto wanted. Neither contemplated self-government for India and, like Curzon before them, both sought to improve and adapt the Raj and thus to prolong its life. Significantly, a year after his opposition to the India Councils Bill, Balfour felt able to cast a more benevolent eye on the reforms. In February 1910, he told the Commons of his pleasure that 'the new development in the machinery of the Government of India has been brought into operation under conditions which seem a hopeful augury for the future.' Explaining that it had been his duty to criticise the India Councils Bill in 1909, Balfour felt that the time for criticism had now passed.[12]

Clearly, Balfour was still convinced that the Morley–Minto reforms were palliative rather than fundamentally radical in character. He did not see them as a major step towards parliamentary self-government, and in this he was at one with the great majority of his countrymen. However, Indian nationalists thought otherwise. Above all, they demanded that British policy towards India should be made plain. Stop-gap reforms and hazy assumptions of good intent were no longer acceptable. Both moderates and extremists demanded a new definition of British aims in India.[13]

Events in 1911–12 shed some light on British intentions. On 12 December 1911, a dispatch was published from the Viceroy (Hardinge) and the Indian government, to the Secretary of State Lord Crewe (who had succeeded Morley in 1910). The dispatch excited immediate attention on the grounds that it seemed to advocate the eventual establishment of federal home rule in India – with the provincial governments responsible for domestic affairs, although under the surveillance of the central government, which would also deal with 'matters of Imperial concern'.[14] When Parliament reassembled in February 1912, two ex-Viceroys, Curzon and Lansdowne, attacked the dispatch, which was being joyfully acclaimed by Indian nationalists. Although Lord Crewe was quick to minimise the implications of the dispatch, the Under-Secretary for India, Edwin Montagu, stated on 28 February 1912 that a goal had been set, however distant, and that Indians could now discern British plans.[15]

Unfortunately, Montagu's optimistic claim that drift and prevarication were ended was somewhat blunted by Crewe's insistence that real self-government should not be conferred on an alien people. This not only served to tantalise Indian nationalists, but failed to appreciate that in education, and in political tastes and methods, many leading Indians had a great deal in common with their rulers. But in the event, the next great surge towards Indian independence was not far distant.

3

In great measure, the Montagu–Chelmsford reforms were won on
the battlefields of Flanders and Mesopotamia. India responded to
the Great War with a display of magnificent loyalty. Indian troops
fought side by side with British and Dominion forces in Europe,
the Near East and East Africa. Indeed, the Indian army provided
essential manpower for an Empire which was woefully short of
trained men until the massive volunteer forces conjured up by
Kitchener could be sent to the front. More than this, Indian
nationalists closed ranks in support of the King-Emperor and
Britain's cause. Doubtless they hoped that their loyalty would be
rewarded with constitutional reform. But this was an entirely
reasonable hope. In any case, in the early days of the war, the deep
gratitude felt in Britain for India's contribution created a climate
which encouraged such aspirations. India was playing an immense
part in the Empire's war effort, and could expect appropriate
recognition and repayment.

Recognition came in 1917. In that year India was admitted to
the Imperial War Conference and guaranteed attendance at future
Conferences. Although India's role in the war demanded such
rewards, the Canadian and Australian governments had shown no
great enthusiasm for the proposal when it was first made towards
the end of 1916. Perhaps they feared a debasement of the
Imperial Conference as a meeting place for self-governing
countries. At any rate, three delegates from India, Sir James
Meston, Sir Satyendra Sinha and the Maharaja of Bikaner came to
London in 1917. The two Indians in particular created a very
favourable impression, and all three delegates argued India's
case for self-government within the Empire.[16]

India's admission to the Imperial Conference, and the example
of the destruction of Tsardom in 1917, rendered it doubly
expedient for the British government to make a statement of their
plans for Indian advancement. The appointment of the liberal and
sympathetic Edwin Montagu as Secretary for India in July 1917
increased the pressures for such a pronouncement. However,

Montagu's original proposal that both the British and Indian governments should announce that they had 'in view the gradual development of free institutions in India with a view to ultimate self-government within the Empire', met with opposition in the Cabinet.[17] Curzon disapproved, and so did Balfour, then Foreign Secretary.

Balfour admitted in a Cabinet paper of 7 August 1917 both the strength of Montagu's case (which was substantially that of his predecessor Austen Chamberlain) and the misgivings it aroused in him. In Balfour's opinion, the whole difficulty centred on the phrase 'self-government':

This according to the highest authorities, both in India and at home, is the 'word of power'. If we promise Self-Government at however remote a period, Indian public opinion will, it seems, be satisfied. If we promise anything else, however desirable, and however easy of attainment, we shall promise in vain. Moderate reformers and extremists will combine against us, and the Government of India will become difficult or impossible.[18]

Nonetheless, Balfour marshalled a regiment of objections to the principle of self-government. Taking this to mean parliamentary government on a democratic basis, he claimed that 'everybody admits that for India, as it is, this form of Government is totally unsuitable.' As for the future, Balfour employed arguments which he had previously applied to South Africa; notably, that education could not remedy racial deficiencies, 'for education cannot fundamentally alter the material on which it works, and it is the essential character and variety of that material which in India is the bar to political advance along the rather narrow and specialised lines which have been found to yield good results in England and America.' For Balfour, 'East is East and West is West. Even in the West, Parliamentary institutions have rarely been a great success, except among English-speaking peoples. In the East, not only have they never been seriously tried, but they have never been desired, except by intellectuals who have come under Western influences.'[19]

Balfour asked whether India as a whole possessed 'the characteristics which would give Parliamentary Government a chance?

To me it seems that it does not. People often talk as if democracy produced equality. The truth is that democracy is only successful where equality – fundamental racial equality – approximately exists already.' Acknowledging that India had no racial divisions equivalent to those of South Africa or the deep south of the United States, Balfour still believed that 'the differences are quite sufficient to make real Parliamentary institutions unworkable in the future, as they are admittedly unworkable in the present.'[20]

This cautionary diagnosis led to a further dark prophecy:

The demand for [Parliamentary institutions] comes from Eastern intellectuals inspired by Western models. This does not make the demand less formidable, but it does make the fulfilment of it much less likely to succeed. Parliamentary institutions in English-speaking countries are of natural and spontaneous growth. In India they would be utterly alien and artificial. Graft them upon the ancient and unchanging social system of the East, and you will produce a hybrid which will certainly be worthless and probably dangerous.[21]

Balfour, therefore, believed that 'if we promise Self-Government we shall be promising something which, in the sense already defined, we neither can nor ought to give. A system under which India will more and more be governed by Indians, we may well hope to develop. If it be thought that such a form of Government may properly be described as Self-Government (as perhaps it may) we might defend in this way the inclusion of the magic word in our statement of policy.' But Balfour feared that Indian nationalists would fail to interpret self-government in this limited way.[22]

Faced with this and similar objections from members of the Cabinet, Montagu amended his declaration to exclude a specific promise of self-government. Consequently, the formula approved by the Cabinet referred to the policy of 'the increasing association of Indians in every branch of the administration, and the gradual development of self-governing institutions, with a view to the progressive realisation of responsible government in India as an integral part of the British Empire.'[23] The declaration of August 1917 thus contained a promise of Dominion status. Indian nationalists were enthusiastic, and indeed it was possible to discern a major turning-point in British policy towards India and hence, by implication, towards other dependent territories. However, the timing of this process was at the discretion of the British government. It was to be self-government by instalment.

The Government of India Act of 1919 embodied the reforms recommended by the Montagu–Chelmsford report. The Viceroy's Executive Council was now to be composed of four Europeans and three Indians. It retained wide powers of supervision over the provinces, although surrendering much control over local finance. The central legislature was divided into two houses – a Council of State and an Assembly. In both houses elected members were in a majority, but the franchise was high and reflected, perhaps too nicely, communal differences. In any case, the Viceroy could if need arose legislate with the support of only one house or, subject to approval from London, by himself.

In the provinces and Burma, one chamber legislatures were established with considerable elected majorities. Furthermore, certain executive posts were handed over to Indian ministers – education, public health, local government and economic development. These ministers had to be members of the provincial legislatures and responsible to them. But significantly the administration of law and order, the press, finance, land revenue, famine relief and irrigation were kept in British hands.[24] Only the lesser keys of the citadel had been surrendered.

Still, the path to responsible government within the Empire seemed clearly marked out. But 1919 brought tragic disillusionment to Indian nationalists. In April of that year, General Dyer ordered troops at Amritsar to fire on demonstrators, killing over four hundred and wounding more than a thousand. British restraint seemed to have been replaced by hot-headedness. Worse, the Hunter Committee of Inquiry appeared to many Indians to whitewash Dyer and his colleagues. In addition, the Rowlatt Act of 1919 authorised the government of India to retain the summary powers it had acquired during the Great War.[25]

These events suggested that an uglier mood lurked behind the sweet reasonableness of the Montagu–Chelmsford reforms. The character of the Raj apparently had something in common with

that of Dr Jekyll. Nor did the unfriendly temper of much of the
European community reassure those Indians who hoped to proceed
to independence to the strains of the national anthem. Among those
alienated by 1920 was the loyalist Gandhi, whose previous desire
to co-operate was transformed into non-co-operation and
rebellion.[26] Convinced of the value of the British constitution,
Gandhi sought to obstruct it in India. Warm in his respect for
British qualities, he also wished to goad the British conscience.
Congress, too, swung away from moderation and pursued a harder
line.

In January 1924, the first Labour government took office, and
Indian hopes for a more liberal policy were raised. Voices
demanded the revision of the 1919 Act, and full responsible
government for India. On 27 February Balfour spoke in the Lords.
He defended the 1919 Act, but deplored Indian nationalist
agitation and denied that the gradual introduction of constitutional government in India was 'a perfectly natural operation'.
He dismissed as 'one of the most profound delusions that ever
possessed mankind' the impression that 'we are acting simply as a
drag upon a natural movement towards representative institutions
which, but for us, would run a safe, a happy and a useful course.'[27]

Balfour did not believe that non-co-operation in India was
hastening the achievement of Dominion status, and continued:

Free institutions . . . are among the most difficult institutions in
the world to manage properly. Free government is very difficult
government. The easy government is the government of an
absolute autocracy. The notion appears to be that if you leave
India alone India will at one great stride – taking the example from
Great Britain, from the great British Dominions, from the United
States of America . . . join their ranks as a natural equal. This is
entirely to ignore the teaching of history.[28]

Balfour refused to use the words inferior or superior in reference
to British and Indian civilisation, and indeed acknowledged that
India 'has a civilisation compared with which ours is contemptible
in point of date. . . . But we are different.' In Balfour's eyes a
fundamental difference lay in the attitude of Indian nationalists to
the constitution:

They have shown all the qualities of contrivance, and ingenuity of Parliamentary obstruction, and all the smaller arts which hang about the practice of free institutions, but what they have not shown is that fundamental desire to make the Government of their country work, without which free institutions are not only perfectly useless but may be absolutely dangerous.[29]

Balfour believed that in India Britain had 'been able to combine something that is good in the system of free institutions with all that can be found of good in absolute government.' But what was to replace this compelling mixture? Balfour was certain of one thing only:

If you leave India to herself it is as absolutely certain as anything can be that she will relapse into what is the natural organisation of society in that part of the world, which is absolute government. There may be a transition of free institutions, possibly – certainly. But it would probably be found unworkable, intolerable in practice, unintelligible to vast masses of the population, and no prophecy can be so certain than that the destruction of British rule means the resumption of all that is least good in the gradual growth of Indian society.[30]

In the event, the Labour administration of 1924 did little to justify Balfour's fears. Although deeply sympathetic towards Indian aspirations, Ramsay MacDonald's minority government was in no position to carry radical reforms, and was anxious to appear responsible before a critical and suspicious electorate. In India itself, Gandhi's non-co-operation movement failed to clog the machinery of administration. On the other hand the increasingly influential Jawaharlal Nehru began to deny the relevance of Dominion status and to call for complete independence and no truck with British imperialism.[31] Subsequently, Gandhi's attempt to control his more militant followers was greatly assisted by the report of the Inter-Imperial Relations Committee at the 1926 Imperial Conference. Under the chairmanship of Balfour this Committee defined Dominion status in such acceptable terms that even the previously hostile Hertzog of South Africa was convinced of the genuine equality existing between Britain and the Dominions. Indian moderates could now claim that Dominion status was equivalent to the independence demanded by Indian extremists.

Further, contradictory tokens of British intent followed. In 1927 a Statutory Commission headed by Sir John Simon was appointed to investigate the application of the Montagu–Chelmsford reforms. The Commission was perhaps better than nothing, but its exclusively British composition seemed a calculated insult to Indian susceptibilities. However, in 1929, before the Simon Commission presented its report, the Viceroy Lord Irwin (later Lord Halifax), attempted to mollify Indian doubts. The Irwin declaration unambiguously promised India Dominion status – no mean commitment in 1929.

Although the initiative had come from Irwin, the second Labour government could take some pleasure from the declaration. On the other hand, Dominion status had been repeatedly dangled before India since 1917. But even Conservatives now professed themselves reconciled to the eventual establishment of a brown Dominion. In the Commons, on 7 November, Baldwin acknowledged that when India achieved full responsible self-government within the Empire she must be on a completely equal footing with the Dominions.[32] This was, however, not the same thing as advocating immediate independence. Baldwin's mixture of reasonableness and circumspection prompted Balfour, now seriously ill and confined to his rooms, to write one of his last letters touching public affairs:

My Dear Baldwin,
   I am very unnecessarily troubling you with a letter intended to express the feelings which I cannot keep to myself of intense admiration for your great utterances in the House of Commons yesterday. You treated the greatest of political themes in a way . . . which will for all time give you an unchallenged position among the orators of the English-speaking race. . . . It is a delight to me to think that on a subject which has so greatly occupied the thoughts of my declining years, it has fallen to you, as leader of the Party, to give utterance in fitting language to great thoughts on the greatest of all subjects.
                    Yours ever,
                         Balfour.[33]

This letter implied no death-bed conversion. Indian independence was still far from being attained. Indeed, the report of the Simon Commission in 1930 made no mention of Dominion status.[34] Balfour was safe in applauding Baldwin's speech. Nonetheless he had moved, unwillingly, with the times. For one who found it easy to conjure up a 'black' peril,[35] and who remained unalterably convinced of the natural and and irreconcilable gulf between the coloured and white races, this was, at least, an achievement of some sort.

17 The Competition for Colonies and Trade Routes

The danger of a good deal of this expansiveness ... is that it withdraws the energies and enterprises of our countrymen from markets which they used to control ... in the vain pursuit of what is little more than a will-o'-the-wisp ... of a market which does not exist.

CAMPBELL-BANNERMAN, 1899

I

IT is commonplace to suppose that the successful revolt of the American colonies marked the end of the 'First British Empire'. But this is only a half-truth. In 1783 there was still a substantial Empire left. The West Indies, for so long the joy of investors and mercantalists, remained. So too, did the Canadian colonies where neither French nor British settlers were drawn into the vortex of revolution. In Madras, Bombay, Bengal and beyond, the British East India Company were staking out new claims and accepting new responsibilities. Moreover, when James Cook met his death in Hawaii in 1779 he had already put Australia and New Zealand on the map, although it was to be left to later generations to give substance to the outline.

The long, bitter struggle with France was brought to a victorious conclusion in 1815. If the triumph was mainly due to naval supremacy, it also made essential the maintenance of that supremacy. Not only were Canada and India saved, but there were spoils too. To protect the routes to India and the Far East, the Cape and Ceylon came under British rule. There were also pickings in the West Indies even though, 'King sugar' held less sway than hitherto. Hence Trinidad, Demerara, Essequibo, St Lucia and Tobago were kept at the peace making, as were Heligoland, Malta and the Ionian islands further afield.[1]

After this crop of colonial possessions, British statesmen did not seek for more. Yet the need to protect trade routes and to foster trade itself exerted strong pressures. But if free trade could be sustained without military intervention, let alone administration, so much the better. The growth in Anglo-American trade after the revolt of the thirteen colonies seemed to prove that trade did not necessarily follow the flag. Perhaps it was better, therefore, not to hoist any more flags. In any case pride could be taken in the destruction of the slave trade after 1807 and in the abolition of slavery throughout the Empire in 1833 – even though the emancipation of the West Indies labour force coincided with, and perhaps even accelerated, the decline of the sugar industry.

Mid-Victorian statesmen were no more acquisitive than their predecessors. Having stamped out slavery in West Africa by the 1860s, little remained there except 'three tiny, poverty-stricken colonies (Gambia, Sierra Leone and the Gold Coast); a few useful but difficult fields of private enterprise, notably on the Niger; hundreds of anti-slave trade treaties with minor chiefs, and paramount influence along a vast stretch of coast.' In 1865, a Select Committee of the House of Commons recommended eventual withdrawal from all the West African settlements save, possibly, Sierra Leone.[2] East Africa told a similar story: coastal influence to destroy the slave trade, and an understanding with the Sultan of Zanzibar to further that end and prevent Zanzibar falling to hostile powers who had an eye on the Indian Empire.

Tropical Africa held out little promise to investors and businessmen. Even further south, Britain was concerned mainly with protecting the Simon's Bay naval base and trying to limit Boer expansion at the expense of the Bantu. British governments above all wanted southern Africa to be peaceful and free of trouble. The opening of the Suez Canal in 1869 lessened the value of the Cape route to the east while it also concentrated British attention more steadily on Egypt.

In Asia, India saw the consolidation of British rule in the 1860s following the mutiny of 1857. The dictates of trade and defence had extended British influence in Singapore, Malacca and Penang while, more eccentrically, Rajah Brooke ruled in Sarawak. The opening of China's trade, symbolised by the cession of Hong Kong in 1842, repeated the African pattern: coastal influence and a reluctance to delve deeper inland. Indeed, in the 1860s British exports and investment went first to the United States and South America, and only secondly to India and Australasia.[3] But the flag did *not* fly over New York and Buenos Aires. The economic facts were plain.

2

Yet when Balfour entered Parliament in 1874, Britain stood on the threshold of great territorial expansion. By 1902 British control had been effectively asserted over Egypt and the Sudan, in the Gold Coast and along the Niger river, in Kenya, Uganda and Somaliland. Even the Transvaal and the Orange Free State had fallen, while further north Cecil Rhodes's South Africa Company had crossed the Limpopo and subdued the Matabele and Mashona. Nor was Africa the only field for such activities: Burma had been incorporated fully into the Indian Empire; British interests in the Malayan peninsular had been rationalised; and, reluctantly surrendering to sustained Australasian pressure, Fiji, South-East New Guinea, the Gilbert and Ellice islands, Tonga, some of the Solomon islands, and (jointly with the French) the New Hebrides, were brought under British rule or protection.

Why did this expansion take place? It is not enough to seek the explanation in Disraeli's florid speeches on the subject of empire, nor to ascribe undue potency to considerations of 'prestige', 'duty' and 'honour'. Humanitarian voices *were* raised, and business interests *were* urged, but even these supply only part of the answer. Perhaps above all, the British extended their Empire to preserve what they already possessed and to strengthen the sea routes which bore their commerce to India, Australasia and the Far East. At no point was there expansion for expansion's sake.

An examination of Balfour's letters and speeches shows in a clear light his reactions to the territorial acquisitions of late-Victorian England. Aristocratic, philosophical, unemotional,

Balfour recoiled from displays of vulgar jingoism and patriotic excess. He had scant respect for the military mind and deplored the use of force. Nor did he necessarily welcome territorial expansion. In 1898 he told the Commons, with some pride, 'we did more for the preservation of Siam, for the maintenance of its independence, by the arrangement which Lord Salisbury entered into with France on that subject than the late Government [the Liberal administration of 1892–5] or any preceding Government have ever done'.[4] It was of course possible to argue that Britain had preserved Siamese independence to keep French influence away from British possessions. But Balfour was at least consistent when he claimed, in the same speech, 'neither this country, nor any other country, I believe, desires the partition of China'.[5] Again he told Lansdowne in 1903 that, 'In the Far East we are not an expansive power. We want no territory that we have not already got, and our subject is to make that secure.'[6]

In 1880 Balfour had written disapprovingly of Bartle Frere's ultimatum to the Zulus in 1879, believing that if the Governor of the Cape had been recalled as soon as his action was known in England, the government would have avoided the responsibility and odium of the resulting Zulu War. Despite Cabinet opposition to Frere, Disraeli took no immediate steps to recall him.[7] Balfour had also shown himself in 1899 distinctly cool to forcing a redress of *uitlander* grievances in the Transvaal 'at the point of a bayonet'.[8] Nor had he welcomed the proposal to send a military expedition to Kano in Northern Nigeria in 1902. He told Austen Chamberlain that, 'I think we have been rather ill-used in the matter of information by Lugard, and I am very sorry to think that we seem likely to have another little war upon our hands. But it can't be helped.'[9]

However, there were British interests which Balfour recognised clearly. Although he wanted to preserve Siamese independence, he did not want an Anglo-Siamese agreement to prevent the practically autonomous provinces to the north of Britain's Malayan possession 'falling, in natural course, into our hands'.[10] British commercial interests in north China, faced with German and Russian competition, also required the acquisition of the Wei-hai-wei naval base in 1891. Balfour defended the leasing of Wei-hai-wei 'not as a commercial harbour, for which it is wholly unsuited, but as a naval base. It is not physically an island. . . . But in any case we wish to treat it as an island.'[11] Moreover, a threat to the naval base of Gibraltar prompted a positively bellicose statement from Balfour. During negotiations with Spain over Gibraltar in 1898, he said 'We shall have to send an ultimatum to the Spanish Government in the shape of a demand that one of our officers shall be allowed to inspect the works at Algeciras in southern Spain. If this is refused, I see nothing for it but to withdraw Wolff [the British ambassador to Spain] and blockade some Spanish port.'[12]

These fighting words reflected the unambiguous British insistence that her sea routes to Asia must be protected – if necessary by force. But if a jealous eye had to be kept on Gibraltar, and Malta and Cyprus, the need to control the Suez Canal was of overwhelming importance.

3

Egypt was the gateway to the East. Napoleon's abortive invasion in 1798 had not only threatened the security of Britain's Indian possessions but had emphasised Anglo-French rivalry for the control of the vital short route to the East. British interests in the eastern Mediterranean by the 1850s required not only that Russia should be kept from devouring Constantinople but also that French influence should not become paramount in Egypt. If the Crimean War satisfied the first requirement, the building of the Suez Canal by the French seemed to endanger the second. But after 1869 Britain and France co-operated to a remarkable degree in dominating Egyptian politics, finance and commerce. If fear of Russia, British naval supremacy, and the defeat of France by Prussia in the war of 1870–1 helped to produce this amity, the basic fact remained unchanged. Even Disraeli's purchase of the Khedive's shares in the Canal Company in 1875 did not destroy this balance, but sought rather to perpetuate it.

But the Khedive reeled from one financial crisis to another. In 1876 a dual Anglo-French control was established over the Khedive's finances. In this way it would be possible to prevent his defaulting over credit repayments to foreign bankers. In 1881, however, an Egyptian army revolt led by Colonel Arabi, threatened to sweep away both Khedive and foreign influence. Faced with the prospect of forcible exclusion from Egypt, and with France dragging her feet, Gladstone's ministry decided to intervene alone against Arabi and his nationalist forces. Sir Garnet Wolseley's conquest of Arabi in 1882 only posed more problems. The British government did not want to remain in Egypt indefinitely. Ideally, they would have liked to withdraw after the establishment of a purified, efficient and preferably solvent Egyptian administration. Then mere influence could resume its sway. Lord Cromer's rule in Egypt was meant to bring this about. Unfortunately, the Suez Canal became more vital to British interests, not less. British administrators and troops were there to stay.[13]

Justifications for the occupation came from Balfour in March 1885. He told the Commons that in intervening in Egypt, 'England was influenced by the desire to preserve the route to India, to improve the position of Egypt and to stimulate its internal prosperity and its external commerce. Our interests in that county were not financial, they were commercial; and the commercial interests of England were coincident with the interests of the Fellaheen. It might suit other powers to grind down the unhappy people, but it would not suit us; our interests were best served in bringing back prosperity to the Nile.'[14] Clearly the restoration of prosperity would assist an early British withdrawal, but Balfour underplayed the strategic importance of the Suez Canal. Nor, if he believed so firmly in British commercial interests in Egypt, was he altogether justified in attacking Gladstone's government for its hypocrisy in taking on extra administrative burdens. 'Egypt,' Balfour said, 'was as great a responsibility as if it belonged to us, and as small a gain as if it belonged to the French.'[15] Despite this rhetoric and despite his high-minded championing of the fellahin (the Egyptian peasantry) Balfour's later utterances on Egypt rested more frankly on the need to preserve Britain's strategic and commercial interests.

Of course, Balfour was right to doubt the advantages of occupation. For one thing, the Suez Canal was an international waterway. Some concession would have to be made over this. For another, France could hardly be expected to surrender completely her long-standing interest in Egypt. The Suez Canal Convention of 1888 solved some of these problems. All nations were guaranteed free passage through the Canal. But the Egyptian government was left to uphold this freedom, and the British government retained the right to ignore the Convention while they remained in occupation or if the security of Egypt was threatened. In effect, this meant that Britain controlled the Suez route to the East.[16]

Although in theory Britain could never blockade the Canal, this did not allay foreign hostility. In 1900, amid open French and German criticism of British activities in South Africa, Balfour confided privately to Goschen, the First Lord of the Admiralty, that 'from an international point of view our occupation of Egypt would assume quite a new complexion if it carried with it the enormous powers involved in the complete control of the Canal in time of war.' Balfour felt that 'The whole of the civilized world . . . dislike our occupation of Egypt chiefly because they dislike *us*. They would have, in my judgement, most substantial ground for disliking and if possible terminating it if amongst its perquisites was the complete control of one of the world's great waterways.'[17]

In practice, Britain did control the Suez Canal in both World Wars and was glad to be able to do so. But at the turn of the century there was some doubt as to the value of Egypt in the event of a war with France or Russia. In 1902 Sanderson (later Lord Sanderson) told Balfour that in 1894 Kitchener had disputed Egypt's value with the local military intelligence officers. Sanderson thought the latter had argued successfully 'that Egypt would be of no assistance'.[18] However by 1904 Britain and France were drawing closer together. During negotiations in April 1904, the French government asked for a time limit to be set on the British occupation of Egypt, while at the same time revealing their interest in Morocco.[19] But this was mere bargaining. The Anglo-French entente of the same year confirmed British supremacy in Egypt while allowing French interests free play in the rest of North Africa.

These negotiations caused the government to consider afresh the defence of Egypt. In April 1904 Balfour argued in a paper submitted to the C.I.D. that an 'overseas invasion of Egypt, say by 5,000 or 10,000 men, is not probable, in view of our naval forces in the Mediterranean.' This placed high confidence in the navy, especially when Balfour admitted that if such an invasion occurred the British garrison would be inadequate. But he did not propose to have in Egypt more troops than were needed to preserve internal order. Furthermore, since these troops were to keep order, not to further imperial defence, Balfour insisted that the Egyptian government should pay for them.[20]

This was a curious argument, but no more curious than the revelation contained in a Cabinet paper of July 1904 that: 'At present there is no defence scheme for Egypt and prior to last year the situation of British troops in that country and the protection of British interests in the event of war does not appear to have been considered by H.M.'s Government.'[21] Although it was becoming increasingly unlikely that France, or even Russia, would invade Egypt, the British government displayed a surprising degree of nonchalance in 1904 over the prize which had taken no little effort to win.

4

The occupation of Egypt involved Britain in the Sudan as well. After Gordon's self-sacrifice to the Mahdi's forces in 1885, the Sudan had been abandoned by the British and Egyptian governments. This was perfectly satisfactory as long as other European powers kept out of the Sudan. Once such a threat materialised, however, Britain would be forced to take action. Above all, no foreign power could be allowed to blackmail Egypt by manipulating the waters of the upper Nile – so vital to Egyptian survival. Between 1885 and 1896, Britain's policy towards the Sudan was based on the hope that the rule of the Khalifa (the Mahdi's successor) would decay sufficiently to allow an easy reconquest, and on the acquisition of Uganda as a possible southern base for an invasion.[22]

But on 1 March 1896 Italian forces attempting the conquest of Abyssinia were overwhelmed at a great battle at Adowa. There was evidence of French and Russian military advice and assistance. Moreover, the victorious King Menelek seemed ready to link up with the dervishes in the Sudan. This threw all previous British calculations to the winds, and on 12 March Salisbury announced the invasion of the Sudan from the north.

Initially, it was claimed that the invasion was to save the besieged Italian garrison at Kassala. But the Anglo-Egyptian forces made for Dongola, over 500 miles from Kassala. Sympathy for fellow-Europeans did not stretch very far in practice. In the Commons on 5 June Balfour defended the invasion. Dismissing accusations that the government had suppressed relevant information, he claimed that there was no correspondence with the Khalifa to lay before the House because: 'He is not in the position of a civilised ruler with whom we have been in negotiation for a long period and with whom negotiations have broken down.'[23] Balfour also denied that the expedition 'was based solely on European interests in general, and Italian interests in particular', although admitting 'that most undoubtedly the battle of Adowa, the Italian difficulties, and the siege and possible fall of Kassala were all circumstances which had great weight . . . in determining the period at which the expedition should take place.' Having paid this lip-service to the plight of the Italian army, Balfour stated quite candidly that the advance towards Dongola was 'necessitated by Egyptian interests, and by Egyptian interests alone – and that, even if the Italians had never been heard of in that part of Africa, that advance would sooner or later have had to be undertaken.'[24]

In 1896 Balfour's justifications for British intervention in the Sudan ran parallel to those advanced by Salisbury, Lansdowne and other members of the Cabinet.[25] But three years later, after

Kitchener had fought his way down the Nile and destroyed the dervishes at the battle of Omdurman, Balfour failed to mention the Italian disaster at all when he again defended the government's policy in the Sudan. Rather, he insisted that, 'being in Egypt, and having for the present to stay there, the Sudan question had to be settled sooner or later, and that the time of its settlement depended on many circumstances, of which perhaps the most important was the possibility of any Power other than Egypt occupying a position in the Nile Valley.' Moreover, Balfour accused Campbell-Bannerman of wanting to control the Nile valley and yet condemning 'an expedition to preserve that valley at a moment when that expedition could take place without bringing us into direct collision with a great neighbour.'[26]

This was a curious statement. It showed how profoundly government action had been affected by the fear of French control over the upper Nile. On the other hand, the confrontation at Fashoda between the victorious Kitchener and Captain Marchand, who had already hoisted the tricolor and threatened to deny the British the rewards of victory, was certainly a 'collision'. Indeed, Britain and France had subsequently stumbled to the brink of war. But in the diplomatic showdown, Britain possessed all the trump cards. Perhaps it was in this sense less of a trauma for Britain than for France, who felt the humiliation keenly.

If Kitchener's campaign aroused strong feelings in France, there were indignant complaints in Britain too. Although Balfour asked the Commons on 5 June 1899 for a grant of £30,000 for Kitchener, Liberal members had different questions to ask. For one thing, they did not accept Balfour's eulogy of Kitchener as having won 'great triumphs for Egypt, for England, and for civilization'.[27] There were rumours of atrocities and acts of barbarism committed by the Anglo-Egyptian forces after Omdurman. Had wounded dervishes been shot where they lay? Had the Mahdi's tomb been desecrated? Had Kitchener planned to use the Mahdi's large and handsome skull as an inkstand? Where, in all this, was the triumph of civilisation?

Balfour did his best to set such doubts at rest. He admitted to John Morley that 'as a matter of fact, there was a mere collection of bones which had fallen to pieces by natural processes before exhumation took place.' But he denied that the Mahdi's remains had been scattered due to any 'element of vengeance' on Kitchener's part. It had been necessary, however, to prove to the Sudanese that the Mahdi was no heaven-sent prophet but belonged 'to a temporary, false and dying creed'. There was but one step, Balfour claimed, 'from the recrudescence of Mahdism to the absolute destruction of every white man from north to south of the Soudan.' But he agreed with Morley that after proof of the Mahdi's mortality, the remains should have been reburied and not cast into the Nile.[28]

Three days later on June 8, Balfour answered charges in the Commons that wounded dervishes had been massacred. He denied that any of the wounded enemy had been killed except in self-defence. If a wounded man acted as a combatant, he must be treated as one.[29] It was clear, however, that wounded dervishes had been shot, and Kitchener had been heard to call repeatedly, 'Cease fire! Cease fire! Cease fire! Oh, what a dreadful waste of ammunition!'[30] Considering Kitchener's well-known hatred of waste, it is probable that the virtue of economy triumphed over that of humanity on the field of Omdurman.

Kitchener visited Balfour and his sister Alice in June 1899. After explaining how he was combating slavery in the Sudan, he 'repudiated with derision the idea that our troops looted and murdered . . . after the battle. On the contrary they were so exhausted . . . that many fell asleep where they stood.'[31] This was, at least, another explanation. But an unpleasant impression remained. Balfour was not wholly satisfied. Indeed, Alice Balfour wrote that 'I believe he thinks the Mahdi's tomb affair was mismanaged and the good effects could have been obtained without the unfortunate shocking of the taste of some people. I don't think Ld. Kitchener is a model of good taste.'[32]

However, Kitchener's job was to win battles, not to exhibit good taste. Not that the conquest of the Sudan ended Britain's problems in East Africa. Balfour had previously supported the Rosebery government's decision to establish a protectorate over Uganda in 1894.[33] But the defence of Egypt and the Sudan also required the maintenance of stability in Abyssinia and Somaliland. In 1900, the British government had made military arrangements to help King Menelek of Abyssinia suppress a fanatical Mullah, a religious leader who had been disturbing tribesmen on the border between Abyssinia and British Somaliland.[34] Balfour returned to the subject in 1903, and while deploring the expenditure involved, insisted that since Somaliland was a British protectorate the government must fulfil its obligations and help put down the Mullah and his followers.[35] The spectre of another Mahdist revolt was sufficient to send the army into action. For the sake of stability and the Suez Canal the British soldier attempted once more to scatter the forces of militant Islam.

5

It is clear that considerations of strategy and defence were largely responsible for the territorial acquisitions of late-Victorian Britain. But what part did the need to secure markets and raw materials play? To an enormous extent, of course, the protection of the route to India and Asia and Australasia can be seen in economic terms. British exports and investments flowed physically and metaphorically through the Suez Canal and round the Cape, and were met with food, raw materials, gold and luxuries from India, Australasia, South Africa and China. But what of territories in Africa? Egypt played an increasingly important commercial role. Few doubted the value of southern Africa. But for the rest the statistics show that 'The main streams of British trade, investment and migration continued to leave tropical Africa virtually untouched.'[36]

Joseph Chamberlain, however, was anxious to develop those estates of the realm that languished for lack of investment and attention. Nor was Balfour by any means pessimistic on this score. In 1895, the two men discussed how a £22,000,000 dividend from Britain's Suez Canal shares should be spent. Chamberlain wanted the money spent on the crown colonies. But Balfour suggested that expenditure should be limited 'not merely to

Crown colonies, but to Colonies, which, from the very nature of the case, so far as we can foresee, must always remain Crown Colonies. In this class I suppose may be included those tropical possessions of the Crown which, though very important to us commercially, are not likely for climatic and other reasons, ever to support a large native-born white population.' Balfour wanted this limitation because of 'the objection that may reasonably be felt to "improving an estate" which we do not hold upon a perpetual tenure.'[37]

Balfour clearly felt that some tropical possessions were of considerable commercial importance, and among these he would probably have included the West African colonies and the West Indies. He also envisaged that only colonies which lacked a substantial white settler population could be relied upon to have a long-term commercial relationship with Britain – or, at least, could be dominated by British interests. But Balfour was hardly ardent in his suggestions. Indeed, he also proposed that up to a third of the £22,000,000 should go towards developing public works in Britain, such as light railways in Ireland and the Scottish Highlands. This was hardly a proposal which would exhilarate the businessman in Chamberlain, and Balfour acknowledged that 'whereas *your* Colonial enterprises would, if properly managed, be probably remunerative, the kind of public work which I contemplate would bring in a small return, if any.'[38]

Balfour was no more radical when he considered the plight of the West Indies, where by the 1890s the decay of the sugar industry had created massive economic and social problems. The report of the West Indian Royal Commission of 1897 recommended that nearly £600,000 should be loaned and granted to the West Indies. Chamberlain also encouraged the establishment of the Department of Tropical Agriculture and Schools of Tropical Medicine in London and Liverpool.[39] In 1898 the Colonial Secretary proposed 'a five year plan for West Indian reconstruction'.[40] Balfour, however, feared that the government would be attacked 'for bolstering up with public money a particular industry'. This was chiefly a reference to the report of the Royal Commission, but perhaps also referred to Chamberlain's plan to subsidise the West Indies' fruit industry in face of fierce competition from the vast American United Fruit Company. Balfour, however, wanted the government's justification for this assistance to be that the object 'was *not* to alleviate the condition of a *suffering industry* but of *suffering communities*, – communities which, on historic grounds, have a special claim to the consideration and assistance of the mother country.'[41]

A case could certainly be made out for trying to revive the economy of the West Indies, although it is interesting that Balfour felt safer using humanitarian rather than commercial arguments. But what could be realistically hoped for from the new possessions in tropical Africa? In 1899 Campbell-Bannerman complained that Britain was neglecting markets elsewhere by 'running after this will-o'-the-wisp of markets in tropical Africa.'[42] Balfour called this 'a complete delusion', and denied 'that we fail in Crete because we open markets in the East, South or West of Africa, or that our energy in China is diminished by the fact that we think more of Africa than we did'. But as to complaints that British salesmanship was defective, Balfour significantly did not claim 'that the commercial education of those classes [of British merchants] is as highly developed as it is in some foreign countries'.[43]

But despite the undoubted expertise of German and American exporters and salesmen, and despite the growth of protection towards the end of the nineteenth century, Balfour stuck firmly to the principles of free trade for Britain's new African possessions. 'Wherever our flag flies,' he said, 'Frenchmen and Germans are allowed to go in on the same terms as our own merchants.' Believing that it was better to raise the quality of manufactures than embark on protection, Balfour insisted that Britain would keep at least part of Africa free from 'hostile and prohibitory tariffs'.[44]

Nor did he despair of the profitability of the protectorates, despite the fact that expenditure was increasing at a faster rate than revenue. Speaking chiefly of Somaliland, Uganda and Zanzibar, Balfour did not claim that 'next year, or the year after, or the year after that, we are going to have large favourable balances to show; but I do say that in this period of our commercial history more than any other it is urgent that we should develop markets that cannot be wrested from us by the hostile tariff action of any foreign Power.'[45]

If it was possible to reap only hypothetical profits from East Africa, there were moral and humanitarian claims to be made for British control. Balfour assured the Commons in 1903 that the recent establishment of rubber estates in Uganda would not lead to the same sort of cruelty and abuse of forced labour that had made the Congo a disgrace. As for slavery in Zanzibar and Pemba, it was 'in a fair way of settlement', while on the mainland it was dying 'as fast as it can well die.' For one who doubted the desirability of extending spheres of influence, Balfour could perhaps draw some comfort by stating, 'As our influence extends slavery disappears. I believe in a few years the whole question will be a matter merely of historical interest.'[46]

But Britain had not taken part in the partition of Africa simply to deal slavery a mortal blow. Nor had she extended her control elsewhere for objects so ephemeral. If the colonial exploits of the army sometimes caught the imagination of the British public, they left Balfour and his uncle Salisbury quite unmoved. Possibly the cold Cecil temperament explains this. But it is much more likely that Balfour's realistic mind, rejecting crude aggression, could only be influenced by vital, long-term factors. And of these, it is evident that the defence of the Empire and the protection of its trade ranked foremost in his mind.

18 British Interests Preserved

Let me, therefore, say that . . . the question of Egypt, the question of the Sudan, and the question of the Canal, form an organic and indissoluble whole . . . British supremacy exists, British supremacy is going to be maintained.

BALFOUR, 1919

I

By the beginning of the twentieth century the immense colonial empire acquired by Britain begged certain awkward questions. How essential to Britain's welfare and security were these possessions? Above all, how should they be governed, and what prospects of advancement awaited their native peoples?

These questions were all the more difficult to answer in view of the wide variety of the dependencies themselves. The West Indies were characterised by a long history of impoverishment and unemployment. The once-prosperous sugar islands now offered problems rather than profits. In the Mediterranean, Gibraltar, Malta and Cyprus bore witness to strategic needs, while Egypt, the Sudan, Uganda, Kenya and Somaliland on the one flank, and Aden and the Persian Gulf protectorates on the other, further marked out the route to India. Ceylon, with its naval base at Trincomalee, was an essential staging-post on the run to the Far East and Australasia.

Elsewhere there was not even the coherent justification of strategy. The West African colonies were either remnants from the slave trade or the products of commercial and humanitarian enterprise. Central Africa contained Rhodesia and Nyasaland. Rhodesia was ruled by the British South Africa Company but was hardly a boon to investors, although more satisfying for white colonists. Nyasaland served no fundamental British interest. In the Far East, Malaya and Borneo were becoming more valuable for their products of tin and rubber than for their strategic positions. Singapore, Hong Kong and Shanghai rested on commerce. In the Pacific there were colonies by no means vital to British security. Indeed, Australian and New Zealand anxieties had been responsible for the acquisition, for example, of South-Eastern New Guinea and the Cook Islands.

In the early 1900s these territories were hardly more divergent than the methods by which they were governed. Chartered companies ruled Rhodesia and North Borneo. Crown colony government predominated in the West Indies. Ceylon, too, was a crown colony. Protectorates abounded: East Africa, Somaliland, Northern and Southern Nigeria, Nyasaland, Bechuanaland, Aden. Then there were the protected states, such as Brunei, Zanzibar, the Malay states and Tonga, where local rulers remained, but were subject to the advice of British Residents. Egypt was a protected state also – and the one most vital to British imperial strategy. Yet another form of government was found in the Sudan and the New Hebrides, which Britain ruled jointly with Egypt and France respectively. But the Anglo-Egyptian condominium of the Sudan was a transparent device, and the Sudan was effectively a British dependency.

Regardless of the prevailing influence of Britain in all these territories, their administrations presented little consistency. The Colonial Office ruled the crown colonies, but the Foreign Office governed the protectorates and the condominiums. The chartered territories ruled themselves, although their charters could be revoked from London.

During the first thirty years of the twentieth century, successive British governments sought to impose a greater degree of order on the dependent empire. Protectorates were given crown colony status; in 1923 Southern Rhodesia became a self-governing colony, although not a fully-fledged Dominion. The remaining protectorates were administered through the Foreign Jurisdiction Acts as if they were British colonies.[1] At the same time, the peace treaties of 1919 brought Britain several mandated territories, and the need to categorise them. Palestine, Iraq and Jordan, being 'A' mandates, were treated as protected states. Tanganyika, Togoland and the Cameroons were 'B' mandates, and treated as protectorates – although the latter two were attached to the Gold Coast and Nigeria respectively.[2] In this way, a considerable measure of uniformity was retained.

Moreover, the work of Lord Lugard in Nigeria established the precedent for 'indirect rule'. Lugard's formula combined firm supervision from the central colonial government with the delegation of local administration to African chieftains. This eased the burden on the Colonial Service while associating traditional native rulers with British authority. Although 'indirect rule' tended to perpetuate the power of unenlightened hereditary chieftains, it seemed to accord indigenous people appropriate respect. In the 1920s variants spread to East and Central Africa. Unfortunately, 'indirect rule' served to obscure nationalist stirrings in Africa, a movement which only became fully evident after 1945. Nonetheless it had served its purpose, and had lent some sort of pattern to British rule in Africa.

2

These administrative problems brought little response from Balfour. Although the first half of his political life had seen so many additions to the colonial empire, the second half was characterised by a fundamental lack of involvement in its future. A few exceptions can be found to this statement: Egypt, with its continuing strategic significance; the mandated territories; and Kenya, where the 1920s were marked by a clash between white settler and African interests.

Commercial justifications for empire hardly entered into Balfour's calculations. In March 1909 he gave the Commons a revealing assessment of Britain's role in the protectorate of Somaliland. Balfour did not believe that Somaliland would undergo a great development in agriculture, or reveal vast mineral wealth, or provide an important market for British goods. But nor did he believe that it was possible for Britain to divest herself of her responsibility there:

We have got it and we must keep it, if for no other reason, because there is a large number of those tribes especially along the coast who believe in us, who have framed their policy because they know we can defend them, and whose fate would be disastrous indeed if we were to leave them in the lurch. No such policy is possible to any responsible government.[3]

Certainly Somaliland had few resources to gladden the hearts of British exporters and investors. In these circumstances, it was convenient that Balfour could emphasise Britain's moral obligations to tribesmen whose territory so neatly served Imperial strategic needs. Equally in the case of Egypt, morality and self-interest could be indulged on the grand scale.

In 1907 Lord Cromer, the Egyptian Consul General, retired after twenty-five years of service. During this time Cromer had been the effective ruler of Egypt. On 30 July, in the Commons, Balfour warmly supported a grant of money to Cromer, laying great stress on the value of the Consul General's work in Egypt:

Everything he has touched he has succeeded in . . . Lord Cromer's services during the past quarter of a century have raised Egypt from the lowest pitch of social and economic depredation until it now stands among Oriental nations, I believe, absolutely alone in its prosperity, financial and moral.[4]

Although Cromer's rule had undoubtedly revitalised and reformed many branches of the Egyptian administration, Balfour's claims were somewhat sweeping. Nor did they recognise the fact that Britain controlled Egypt for reasons other than the improvement of its people. The Suez Canal remained the artery of trade to India and the East. Moreover, as the oilfields of Mesopotamia and the Persian Gulf grew in importance, the Suez Canal became more vital to British interests, not less. Commercially, too, Egypt was of no small value to Britain. Between 1894 and 1913 British imports from Egypt rose from an average of £10,000,000 a year to £13,000,000 a year. Exports to Egypt in the same period increased from £4,000,000 to £6,000,000 a year. This meant that between 1890 and 1913 Egypt took, on average, roughly the same amount of British exports as the whole of tropical Africa, and supplied Britain with nearly three times as many imports.[5] These were comforting foundations for the high-minded policy of British administrators in Egypt.

Nonetheless, it was understandable that Balfour, like Cromer,[6] should justify British involvement in Egypt in terms of beneficent rule. Imperialism was thus most happily compounded of practical advantage and moral purpose. On 13 June 1910 Balfour treated the Commons to a lengthy discourse on the problems of governing Egypt, or, indeed, of governing any nation with a history and culture alien from British traditions. Balfour emphasised, somewhat heavily perhaps, that 'you cannot treat the problems with which we have to deal in Egypt or elsewhere as if they were problems affecting the Isle of Wight or the West Riding of Yorkshire. They belong to a wholly different category.'[7]

Balfour asked the Commons to appreciate the situation with which British statesmen had to deal when they were 'put in a position of supremacy over great races like the inhabitants of Egypt and countries in the East. We know the civilisation of Egypt better than we know the civilisation of any other country.... It goes far beyond the petty span of the history of our own race. . . . Look at all the Oriental countries. Do not talk about superiority or inferiority.' But, Balfour pointed out, despite the depth of Eastern civilisation 'you never find traces of self-government. All their great centuries . . . have been passed under absolute government.' In attempting to remedy some of the results of this absolute rule, Balfour recognised that British administrators had taken on an arduous labour:

I suppose a true Eastern sage would say that the working government which we have taken upon ourselves in Egypt and elsewhere is not a work worthy of a philosopher – that it is the dirty work, the inferior work, of carrying on the necessary labour. Do let us put this question of superiority and inferiority out of our minds. It is wholly out of place.[8]

Next, Balfour dealt with the stirrings of Egyptian nationalism. Basically his arguments were similar to those he had advanced in 1909 on the subject of Indian demands for a greater degree of self-government. Balfour believed that 'oriental' nations had never had, nor apparently desired, free institutions or self-government. Indeed, there was 'no evidence that until we indoctrinated them with the political philosophy, not always very profound, which has been the fashion in this country, they ever had the desire or the ambition.' This did not mean that at some time in the distant future such nations would not adopt British political principles and practice. Nonetheless, Balfour considered that after thousands of years of recorded history 'it is not thirty years of British rule which is going to alter the character bred into them by this immemorial tradition'.[9]

What, then, did Balfour consider to be the best form of government for India and Egypt? In a word, absolute government exercised by Britain:

I think experience shows that they have got under it a far better government than in the whole history of the world they ever had before, and which not only is a benefit to them, but is undoubtedly a benefit to the whole of the civilised West. . . . We are in Egypt not merely for the sake of the Egyptians, though we are there for their sake; we are there for the sake of Europe at large. If this be the task which, as it has been thrown upon us we ought to take up, as it is a task which . . . is of infinite benefit to the races with whom we deal, what are the special difficulties attaching to it?[10]

Lack of gratitude from the beneficiaries of British rule was one such difficulty. Balfour was certain that the fellahin, if they had been consulted 'immediately following the period when we relieved them from the abominable treatment to which they were subjected before we went into Egypt' would have expressed great and genuine gratitude. But:

Generations pass. New men arise. Old memories vanish. Under a policy which casts pain and inconvenience on some members of the community ancient wrongs are forgotten, ancient benefits are forgotten likewise. All that remains are those complaints, sometimes just, most commonly, I believe, unjust, on which the agitator can work when he wishes to raise difficulties in his own interest or in the interest of some, as I think, impossible ideal.[11]

However, Balfour thought that Britain's clear duty was to govern regardless of gratitude or recrimination. He then painted a sympathetic picture of the white administrator's burden:

We send out our very best to these countries. They work and strive, not for great remuneration, not under very easy or very luxurious circumstances, to carry out what they conceive to be their duty both to the country to which they belong and the populations which they serve.[12]

Owing to these difficulties, Balfour appealed for whole-hearted support from Britain for her administrators in Egypt. Unless this was forthcoming, he claimed that the local population would instinctively realise that their rulers were inadequately supported, and would 'lose all that sense of order which is the very basis of their civilisation.' If this were to happen, Balfour felt that Britain's 'civilising work in Egypt' would become impossible.[13] While there is no reason to doubt the genuineness of Balfour's belief in Britain's civilising mission in Egypt, it is still remarkable that in his entire speech of 13 June 1910 there was no mention of the vital importance of the Suez Canal.

The outbreak of war in 1914, however, clearly illustrated the priorities of British policy in Egypt. In order to secure the Suez route, and to help protect the increasingly valuable Near East, Egypt was made a British protectorate. At the very least, this move rationalised the situation whereby the Turkish sultan claimed suzerainty over Egypt while at the same time waging war against Britain.

The Great War brought new territorial responsibilities to Britain, even though it had been declared that the annexation of enemy possessions was not a British war aim. British and South African troops overran the German Empire in Africa. In the Near East the Ottoman Empire was dismembered mainly by British, Indian and Dominion forces. In the South Pacific, Australians and New Zealanders at last laid hands on coveted German islands. It was not easy to surrender these territories once they had been acquired.

Balfour was adamant that Germany's ex-colonies in Africa should be retained. In December 1917, when Foreign Secretary, he let the Cabinet know that he would 'regard the retrocession of Togoland and the Kamerouns as disastrous: – not because I have the least desire to increase our Colonial Empire, but because I am unwilling to give Germany a naval base on the flank of our trade routes.'[14] In August 1918 he poured scorn on suggestions that the restoration of Germany's African colonies would aid a peace settlement. Balfour argued that this would mean 'giving Germany submarine bases on all the great trade routes of the world, and putting, therefore, the world's commerce at Germany's disposal ... it means the tyrannical government of the native Africans. ... It means ... that Germany will deliberately set to work and create a great black army in Central Africa.'[15]

These arguments, though alarmist, were powerful. In the event, Britain maintained control of the more desirable of her conquests through the League of Nations' mandates. In December 1917 Balfour had professed no objection to Togoland and the German Cameroons being 'internationalised'.[16] The mandate system provided, in theory, something like 'internationalisation' for the former possessions of Germany and Turkey. Under the League of Nations, the victorious allies parcelled out these territories according to their own national interests. None fared better than Britain. In Africa, Togoland and part of the Cameroons were tacked on to the Gold Coast and Nigeria. Tanganyika became in effect a British colony.[17]

Britain's mandates in the Near East marked out new interests. Mesopotamia, renamed Iraq, brought the Mosul oil-fields under British control. Palestine had no oil-fields, but offered moral advantages instead. In November 1917 Balfour had declared on behalf of the British government that Palestine would become a national homeland for the Jews. The Balfour Declaration won its author the passionate support of world Jewry. More practically, it had been a timely gesture to Zionist opinion in the now belligerent United States. It was also an infinitely more acceptable offer than that of Uganda – which had been made originally in 1903 during Balfour's premiership.[18] It was, however, wholly appropriate that the declaration of 1917 should have borne Balfour's name. His long sympathy for the Zionist cause and his equally long friendship with Chaim Weizmann owed nothing to political expediency.

But the Palestine mandate faced Britain with the apparently impossible task of reconciling the Arab population to the influx of Jewish immigrants. In Palestine, the British got the problem they deserved. They had created a Jewish homeland, while encouraging their Arab allies to hope for national self-determination when Turkish overlordship was destroyed. The dilemma was all the more embarrassing since the role of the Arab forces in the war had won widespread respect in Britain. Balfour indeed, in November 1919, called the Arab troops 'faithful, brave and efficient'. He added, 'The prestige of the Arab race has greatly risen in consequence of this, and I have every hope ... that we shall see a resuscitation of the Arab civilisation.'[19]

But if Arab nationalism had been conveniently mobilised against the Turks, Britain did not welcome Egyptian demands for an end to occupation. In November 1919 Balfour acknowledged that 'Egypt has suffered, as so many parts of the world have suffered ... from the spirit of unrest which the world catastrophe has brought upon us all.' Balfour's response to this agitation was a plain restatement of British interests in Egypt and the Sudan:

Let me, therefore, say that ... the question of Egypt, the question of the Sudan, and the question of the Canal, form an organic and indissoluble whole, and that neither in Egypt nor in the Sudan, nor in connection with Egypt, is England going to give up any of her responsibilities. British supremacy exists, British supremacy is going to be maintained.[20]

To sugar this pill, Balfour stated that the government desired 'in every way we can to associate the Egyptians, the Egyptian native population, with the Government of the country. We desire further ... the prosperity of that ancient land.' As for recent dissension in Egypt, Balfour argued that if certain 'unrealisable expectations' were fulfilled, they would 'damage Great Britain, would damage the world, and would damage most of all the Egyptian population itself.'[21]

These benevolent justifications for the maintenance of British supremacy in Egypt were less in evidence than national self-interest when, in 1922, Egypt became a theoretically independent kingdom. Egyptian independence was meaningless unless Britain withdrew her garrisons. This she refused to do, even though there was no Anglo-Egyptian treaty allowing her the privilege of military occupation. Instead of a treaty, Britain had troops. Not until 1936 was an agreement signed which secured the withdrawal of the Nile valley garrison, while maintaining British forces in the canal zone.[22] British interests were thus revealed at their most fundamental.

In July 1926, Balfour spoke in the House of Lords on the subject of Egyptian and Iraqi independence. Of Egypt, where the British garrisons remained without permission, Balfour insisted that 'certainly and beyond question Egypt is a self-governing country.' He admitted, however, that there were limitations on Egyptian independence.[23] These reservations included the continuing presence of British troops, the protection of foreigners and minorities through the mixed courts, the retention of the old Ottoman 'capitulations' which accorded special privileges to Europeans,[24] and the maintenance of the Anglo–Egyptian condominium over the Sudan. Despite this formidable list, Balfour chose to set it aside and to regard Egypt as 'an independent country.... I hope that what I have said, which I think is the substantial truth, is also the formal truth as regards international law. I think substantially it is.'[25]

Balfour also considered Iraq, whose oil-fields were yearly increasing in importance, to be 'an independent State'. He claimed furthermore that the British government desired Iraq 'gradually to develop into a condition in which it requires assistance from no one and leans on no one.' But Balfour thought this fulfilment of the League of Nations' mandate far away. In the meantime, it was clear to him that 'reluctantly . . . we must carry on the process of assisting, supporting and advising the Government of Iraq.'[26] In fact Iraq, like Egypt, was too valuable to be given real independence. Far from Britain 'reluctantly' maintaining her influence in these countries, it is evident that she only reluctantly, and under pressure, surrendered it. Balfour was guilty of a certain amount of special pleading in this respect.

3

In the 1920s events in the colony of Kenya focused attention sharply on the relations between European and non-European. By 1923 there were some 18,000 white settlers in Kenya. Many of them farmed on the salubrious 'white highlands', which had become virtually a tribal reserve for Britons fleeing from high taxation and the advance of democracy. Under the vigorous leadership of the wealthy Lord Delamere, the settlers claimed that the control of the colony should be placed in their hands.[27] This disregarded the rights of the Indian community, which outnumbered the Europeans by several thousand. Above all, there were close on 3,000,000 Africans to consider.[28]

Despite the precedent of South Africa, and developments in Southern Rhodesia, the British government did not surrender to the Kenyan settlers. In 1923, the same year as it apparently confirmed white minority rule in the newly acceded colony of Southern Rhodesia, the British government made clear its priorities in Kenya. The Colonial Secretary, the Duke of Devonshire, declared that 'Primarily, Kenya is *African* territory', and told the whites that the grant of responsible government was out of the question for the foreseeable future.[29] A year later, the Kenya Legislative Council included five Indians and one Arab, elected, like the eleven Europeans, on a communal vote.[30] Although the settlers continued to agitate for responsible government and to cast longing eyes on southern Africa, the election of the second Labour administration in 1929 blunted such aspirations. Sidney Webb, translated to the House of Lords as Baron Passfield, and Labour's Colonial Secretary, declared in June 1930 that the paramountcy of native interests was a trust which could not be devolved.[31]

Balfour was by no means unsympathetic to settler interests. In May 1925 he described Lord Delamere as 'a man who intended to devote, and did devote, great ability, great capital, great energy and great enterprise' to the development of Kenya. Balfour also denied that the settlers had been guilty of exploitation, believing them to be 'enterprising, patriotic, honest and humane'.[32] At the same time, he asked the House of Lords to 'assume that our mission, which we have deliberately undertaken, is that of benefitting the natives by civilising the country in which they live and by making them sharers in that civilisation.'[33]

It was evident, however, that Balfour considered that 'If you want to have native welfare, you must use European methods, you must get a certain European population, you must get European capital . . . if you want to do that, you must give these settlers reasonable security for themselves, for their profits and for their capital.'[34] Balfour was aware that 'however much benefit we do the natives, we do certainly inflict some penalties upon them', but he did not believe that they should 'better be left in their native barbarism than go through the stage of contact with the white man, education by the white man, with all its attendant benefits and, let us fairly admit, with its attendant dangers and evils.'[35]

While it appeared reasonable to argue, as Balfour did, that it was mistaken to look at events in Kenya 'either from the native side or from the white man's side',[36] such impartiality was difficult to practise. The settlers already possessed sufficient power and advantages. To demand that the British government should be colour-blind in its policy towards Kenyan development, was to ignore the fact that the political and economic scales were already weighted against the African. There is, of course, no need to question Balfour's desire for 'native welfare'. But it is also probable that, as in South Africa, he did not envisage black men obtaining political equality with Europeans. His paternalism did not stretch that far.

4

When Balfour died in 1930, certain British colonial interests differed markedly in emphasis to those of half a century before. Whereas the route to India and the Far East had once been of paramount importance, the Near East itself now offered prizes of incalculable value. Most of Britain's oil came from Iraq and the Persian Gulf via the Suez Canal. Hence, although Egypt in 1922 and Iraq in 1930 were declared independent states, British influence and British bases remained.[37] Aden also increased in importance.

Correspondingly, many African colonies, acquired to counter or exclude German and French expansion in the late nineteenth century, lost their original significance. Worse still, they proved to be economic liabilities rather than assets. Even where this was not true (as in Northern Rhodesia, with its copper mines, and in Kenya) the pressure of permanent white minorities complicated Colonial Office policies – not that such policies as existed were particularly dynamic. The majority of African colonies lacked consistent and planned investment and development.

Elsewhere, the West Indies saw no great economic recovery, but remained dependent on British markets and charity, neither of which were over-abundant. Malayan tin and rubber, however, boomed. This meant that the poor colonies stayed poor, and the rich ones became richer. This reflected no credit on the Colonial Office nor on successive British governments.

On the other hand a certain amount of pride could be taken in constitutional advances. But even these varied strikingly in pace. In 1931 Ceylon was given responsible government and adult suffrage under the Donoughmore constitution – the first non-European colony to receive such privileges. In the Caribbean, too, coloured West Indians played an increasingly important part in local Legislative Councils. But Africans fared less well. By the early 1930s African political progress was negligible. The panacea of 'indirect rule' had been generally applied, and had generally succeeded in shelving the fundamental problem of African self-determination. In any case, nationalist stirrings were not yet coherent enough to force a readjustment of British policy. The African Empire seemed permanent, though generally unpromising.

Yet in the space of two decades, Britain was dismantling her Empire, and rushing her African colonies through the essential stages to self-rule. Despite the misgivings of conservatives, this process inflicted little harm on Britain. National needs had changed since the 1880s. Now, where essential, military and naval bases stayed in British hands. Equally important, most financial and commercial links remained intact. In these circumstances the instruments of government could be surrendered without compunction. Just as the colonial empire had been acquired for strategic and commercial reasons, these interests were by no means neglected at its downfall.

PART FIVE

The Colonies of White Settlement

[The King] is now the great constitutional bond uniting together in a single Empire communities of freemen separated by half the circumference of the globe.

BALFOUR, 1901

None of us conceive that of this conglomeration of free States one is above the other. One may have more responsibility than another . . . but all are on an equality.

BALFOUR, 1926

19 Anglo-Saxon Harmonies and Discords

A nation spoke to a Nation,
A Queen sent word to a throne:
'Daughter am I in my mother's house,
But mistress in my own'.
                    KIPLING, *Our Lady of the Snows*,
                    on the Canadian Preferential Tariff, 1897

The idea of war with the United States carries with it some of the unnatural horror of a civil war.
                                        BALFOUR, 1896

I

COMPARED to the firm though unavailing hold that Britain had maintained upon her American colonies, her grip upon the remaining colonies of white settlement grew progressively more relaxed. Despite the fact that the younger Pitt had reformed and tightened Imperial control over Canada in 1791 and Ireland in 1800, the 1840s saw major steps taken towards colonial self-government. The Durham Report of 1839, prompted by civil disturbances in Canada, had recognised the acceptable limits of British authority. Moreover, without specifically defining it as such, the Report had argued that responsible colonial government would best ensure a continuing connection between Canada and Britain. By 1850 not only Canada, but also New South Wales, Victoria, South Australia and Tasmania had representative institutions. Also by 1850, the repeal of the Corn Laws (in 1846) and the Navigation Laws (in 1849) had cut the major fiscal bonds between mother country and colonies. Free trade and free institutions flourished side by side.

By the time Balfour entered Parliament in 1874 a further revolution had been completed. All the Australian and New

Zealand colonies enjoyed responsible government. Canada had been given federation and full responsible government in 1867. The Cape had become self-governing in 1872. Natal seemed set on the same path. However, none of these self-governing colonies had severed their constitutional links with Britain. It is true that in a hard economic climate some colonies had put heavy tariffs on British goods. But after all it had been Britain herself who had scrapped protection in the 1840s. In any case, business interests and patriotic sentiment were not necessarily good partners.

The self-governing colonies, by 1874, also bore the responsibility for their own land defences. Britain had been glad to shift this burden onto colonial shoulders. Less willingly perhaps, the British government financed the Royal Navy's watch over Canadian, Australasian and South African shores. This division of responsibilities reflected the situation whereby the colonies of white settlement enjoyed almost complete domestic autonomy, while Britain controlled the Empire's foreign policy single-handed. Even when in 1887 the Australian colonies and New Zealand began annual contributions to the upkeep of the Royal Navy, foreign policy-making remained a British preserve.

Despite their self-governing institutions, despite their responsibilities for local defence, despite the lack of imperial reciprocal tariffs, the colonies of white settlement did not secede from the Empire. The English-speaking republics which the Cobdenites had anticipated in Australasia and Canada refused to materialise. Balfour, for one, was relieved. In January 1882 he reviewed John Morley's *Life* of Cobden. Balfour claimed that Cobden 'would have seen India go with pleasure and the colonies without regret', adding: 'I do not mean to discuss the effect which the loss of our Indian and colonial possessions would have on our trade, though I think Cobden ... greatly underrated it; nor yet the evil consequences of severance to the dependencies themselves.'[1]

Significantly, Balfour criticised Cobden for ignoring and misinterpreting 'every view of the Empire which was not exclusively commercial', and for regarding 'the motives which induce ordinary Englishmen obstinately to cling to the responsibilities of Empire as consisting of an uninstructed love of gain or

a vulgar greed of territory.' Balfour rejected such sordid material-
ism. He acknowledged the possibility that 'the sceptre of dominion
is doomed at no distant date to slide from our failing grasp.'
Moreover he thought it possible, though improbable, that even
in these circumstances 'our Board of Trade Returns may be such
as to delight the heart of a Chancellor of the Exchequer.'[2] But,
high-mindedly, Balfour struck other imperial attitudes:

The sentiments with which an Englishman regards the English
Empire are neither a small nor an ignoble part of the feelings
which belong to him as a member of the commonwealth. If
therefore the Empire is destined to dissolve ... if we ... are
henceforth to turn our gaze solely inwards upon ourselves and
our local affairs; if we are to have no relations with foreigners, or
with men of our own race living on other continents, except those
which may be adequately expressed by double entry and ex-
hibited in a ledger; – we may be richer or poorer for the change,
but it is folly to suppose that we shall be richer or poorer only. An
element will have been withdrawn from our national life which,
if not wholly free from base alloy, we can yet ill afford to spare;
and which none, at all events, can be competent to criticise
unless, unlike Mr. Cobden, they first show themselves capable
of understanding it.[3]

Balfour here provided an early, yet revealing, glimpse of his
feelings towards the Empire, and particularly towards the self-
governing colonies. Unhesitatingly, he rejected a materialistic
or solely commercial view of the Empire. In this he was at one
with his uncle Salisbury, and his cousins Robert and Hugh Cecil.
Moreover, in the article in *Nineteenth Century* he made interesting
use of the word 'commonwealth', employing it in close juxta-
position to a description of the 'sentiments with which an
Englishman regards the English Empire'. This was a relatively
unusual use of the word 'commonwealth' in 1882, and, although
Balfour employed the term somewhat vaguely, perhaps it marked
a minor step in the evolution of the word towards the meaning it
was to have in the first half of the twentieth century.

The 1880s, indeed, saw sophisticated attention given to the
possibilities of greater co-operation between the self-governing
colonies and Britain. The writings of academic propagandists like

Seeley in his *Expansion of England*, and Froude in his *Oceana*, echoed Dilke's wistful advocacy in 1869 of a *Greater Britain*. In 1884 the Imperial Federation League was formed, and aimed at drawing the self-governing units of the Empire closer together through constitutional innovation. Paradoxically, as the colonies of white settlement grew in independence, theorists in Britain argued for imperial unity. But, chary of theory, the British stumbled on empirical solutions instead. In 1887 Queen Victoria's Golden Jubilee gathered colonial statesmen in London. Seizing the opportunity, the British government convened the first Colonial Conference. Valuable though the Conference proved, particularly in the field of defence, the next full Colonial Conference had to wait until Victoria's Diamond Jubilee of 1897. In no way did Queen Victoria contribute more practically to the co-operation of the Empire than in her accumulation of years.

Not that constructive and energetic statesmen were nowhere to be found. After 1895, Joseph Chamberlain in particular was the inspiration of those who dreamed of a more united Empire. But Chamberlain's three great themes of an imperial *zollverein*, a council of defence, and an imperial parliament, came to nothing. The self-governing colonies were suspicious of firm ties, and reluctant to indulge in prior commitments. Ironically, even when after 1897 Canada showed consistent interest in reciprocal trade preferences, the British government found itself unable to make an effective and favourable response.

What bonds, therefore, would be the best for achieving greater imperial unity? Balfour, at least, was quick to recognise in the monarchy one such bond. In September 1900, the Colonial Office announced that the Duke and Duchess of York (the future King George V and Queen Mary) would visit Australia and open the first Parliament of the new Commonwealth, in Spring 1901.[4] When, following the funeral of Queen Victoria in February 1901, the proposal was revived, King Edward objected.

In reply Balfour wrote, on 6 February, a frank and cogent letter:

Mr. Balfour recognizes the force of all the objections which may justly be urged against the visit at the present moment. The recent death of the Queen; the general mourning which it has occasioned; the natural reluctance which Your Majesty and Your Majesty's subjects may well feel at seeing Your Majesty's only son leave the country at such a time and on so distant an expedition, are considerations which cannot be, and ought not to be, ignored. If, in Mr. Balfour's judgement, they have not conclusive weight, it is because he cannot help feeling that there are on the other side reasons to be urged which touch the deepest interests of the monarchy. The King is no longer merely King of Great Britain and Ireland, and of a few dependencies whose whole value consists of ministering to the wealth and security of Great Britain and Ireland. He is now the great constitutional bond uniting together in a single Empire communities of freemen separated by half the circumference of the globe. All the patriotic sentiment which makes such an Empire possible centres in him, or centres chiefly in him; and everything which emphasises his personality to our kinsmen across the sea must be a gain both to the Monarchy and to the Empire.

Now the present opportunity for furthering the policy thus suggested is unique. It can in the nature of things never be repeated. A great Commonwealth is to be brought into existence, after infinite trouble and with the fairest prospects of success. Its citizens know little and care little for British ministries and British Party politics. But they know and care for the Empire of which they are members, and for the Sovereign who rules it. Surely it is in the highest interests of the State that he should visibly, and, so to speak corporeally, associate his family with the final act which brings this new community into being: so that, in the eyes of all who see it, the chief actor in the ceremony, and its central figure, should be the King's heir, and that in the history of this great event the Monarchy of Britain and the Commonwealth of Australia should be inseparably united.[5]

Faced with this reasoned document, and believing that Balfour's views were shared by the whole Cabinet, the King reluctantly gave his consent to the visit.[6] Subsequently, the Duke and Duchess visited not only Australia, but Gibraltar, Malta, Aden, Ceylon, Singapore, New Zealand, Natal, the Cape and Canada as well.[7] It is important not to exaggerate the effect of this visit. Nonetheless, the identification of the monarchy with the creation of the Australian Commonwealth conveniently symbolised a fusion of the self-governing colonies' nationalism with loyalty to a distant throne.

Appropriately, in April 1901 the King's title was altered to include a reference to the Dominions, and now read, 'Edward VII, by the Grace of God, of Great Britain and Ireland, and of the British Dominions beyond the Seas, King, Defender of the Faith, Emperor of India.' Joseph Chamberlain was pleased with the new title and told the King that the reference to the self-governing colonies would 'recognize the loyal wishes of Your Majesty's Colonial subjects, to be referred to in the Royal Title.'[8]

Writing from Australia in November 1904, Northcote, the Governor-General, reinforced Balfour's belief in the unifying role of the monarchy. Northcote was convinced that the 'Chamberlain-ites are wrong in making so much of the loyalty to Empire cry. This does not enter in here. There is a strong feeling of devotion to the Throne, rather than to Great Britain, which is odd, since the King is personally unknown.'[9] Balfour, however, may well have felt that his insistence on the value of the Duke of York's trip to Australia was amply justified by Northcote's remarks.

2

The monarchy was, at best, a light and unrestrictive bond of Empire. But the introduction of more substantial measures was beset with difficulties. One of the most fundamental of these was the very independence of the self-governing colonies. British statesmen were thus confined to persuasion and advice when seeking to implement schemes for greater unity.

In defence matters, despite the annual naval subsidies from Australia, New Zealand, the Cape and Natal, the self-governing colonies had refused to give Britain any prior commitment as to the use of their land forces. Brodrick had complained in September 1903 that before the Boer War the British government had found itself obstructed by the determination of the self-governing colonies only to supply troops according to the circumstances under which war had arisen.[10] The post-war period had seen no advances made in this respect. Shaped by similar pressures was Balfour's adamant denial, in July 1903, that the self-governing colonies would be called upon to surrender some of their legislative independence in fiscal and industrial matters as a condition of their enjoying preferential treatment by Britain.[11]

Quite apart from these technical difficulties, relations between Britain and the self-governing colonies were by no means always free from strain. The 1903 Alaska boundary award, for instance, convinced many Canadians that Britain had surrendered their interests to the United States. In October 1903 Lansdowne, the Foreign Secretary, told Balfour that the Canadians felt betrayed by the agreement, and added, 'The conduct of the Canadians has been very undignified, and I am assured that they behaved badly throughout. . . . If serious charges are made in the Dominion Parliament, a rejoinder may be inevitable.'[12]

Nor is it difficult to find British statesmen who doubted the value or achievements of the self-governing colonies. Northcote thought that 'the best service [Australia] can render to the Empire is by developing her population and resources.' At present, in her half-developed state, he considered Australia, 'a positive source of weakness to the Empire'.[13] On another occasion Balfour's cousin Robert Cecil remarked, having seen the 'evidence' for himself: 'The really remarkable thing about Canada is the incompetence of the Canadians. There they have been for 150 years in a country of exceptional richness and look how little they've done with it . . . the English out here seem to be for the most part purely money-makers and the rest idolators of Empire.'[14]

Balfour himself was much more tolerant. He showed interest in the Labour Party's activities in Australia, telling Northcote comfortingly in June 1904 that the Australasians would 'prove themselves to be possessed of the Anglo-Saxon gift of "muddling through".'[15] Moreover, in the delicate and involved problems of imperial defence and tariff reform, Balfour displayed an acute awareness of the susceptibilities of the self-governing colonies. He made it clear that while he was at one with Joseph Chamberlain as to the object of imperial unity, he differed with him over the means. In essence, Balfour believed in long-term and permissive attitudes towards the self-governing colonies.

It could be argued, however, that Balfour's policy, though

permissive, was essentially negative. Certainly he only showed interest in what seemed to him to be practical proposals for achieving greater imperial co-operation. But, in the case of the C.I.D., Balfour's sense of the practical paid rich dividends. Furthermore, his appraisal of the feasibility of schemes for imperial unity was consistently accurate.

In June 1900 Balfour was asked in the Commons by Drage, the member for Derby, whether there could be a unification of the criminal law of the Empire. Balfour replied that 'it seems to me that the circumstances of the various parts of the Empire are so different that a universal criminal law applicable to all is almost illusory.'[16] This was a realistic assessment. Even though it was possible to argue that English law provided a natural and permanent inter-imperial bond, the self-governing colonies were not anxious to consider radical proposals in this field. Indeed when in 1901 Joseph Chamberlain, the Lord Chancellor, the Attorney- and Solicitor-Generals, and some colonial representatives had met to discuss the establishment of a Final Court of Appeal for the Empire, the results had been disappointing. In 1904 Alfred Lyttelton reminded Balfour that the colonies had on this occasion proved apathetic, and that Canada and Australia had taken no notice of the conference.[17] In any case, the Judicial Committee of the Privy Council served as a final court of appeal for the Empire. The self-governing colonies were, for the present, sufficiently satisfied with this arrangement.

By the time Balfour became Prime Minister in 1902, the Colonial Conference had proved itself an acceptable meeting-place for the representatives of the self-governing colonies and Britain. Indeed so useful was it that in December 1904 Alfred Lyttelton, Chamberlain's successor at the Colonial Office, pre-pared the first draft of his famous dispatch to the Governors of the self-governing colonies. An amended and final version of the dispatch was issued on 20 April 1905.[18] But before this Lyttelton sent the first draft of the dispatch to Balfour, and other members of the Cabinet, on 7 December 1904.[19]

Lyttelton argued that since 1887 the Colonial Conferences had assumed a more definite shape and acquired a more definite nature.

He claimed, moreover, that 'an Imperial Council for the discussion of matters which concern alike the United Kingdom and the self-governing Colonies has grown into existence by a natural process.' Lyttelton therefore proposed that the title 'Colonial Conference' should be discarded in favour of 'Imperial Council'. In addition he felt that the British Prime Minister should be the *ex officio* President of the 'Council', assisted by the Colonial Secretary. The permanent members of the 'Council' would be the Prime Ministers of Canada (who would also represent Newfoundland), Australia and New Zealand. The Prime Minister of Cape Colony would represent all the South African colonies until such time as federation had been achieved. To these permanent members could be added, when necessary, British or colonial ministers.[20]

This latter suggestion of Lyttelton's provided a striking parallel to the constitution of Balfour's C.I.D. Equally, perhaps, it reflected Lyttelton's political dependence on Balfour. The two men were friends of long standing, and Lyttelton's tenure of the Colonial Office between 1903 and 1905 was to be his only taste of ministerial office. After Chamberlain, Lyttelton provided Balfour with a vastly more pliable and respectful colleague. Moreover Lyttelton's belief that his proposed Imperial Council should not be defined precisely was in accord with Balfour's own inclinations for loose imperial bonds; and the Colonial Secretary's justification for his attitude could well have been Balfour's: 'The history of Anglo-Saxon institutions, such as Parliament or the Cabinet system, seem to show that an institution may often be wisely left to develop in accordance with circumstances, and . . . of its own accord, and that it is well not to sacrifice elasticity of power of adaptation to premature definiteness of form.'[21] From Salisbury, to Balfour, to Lyttelton ran this theme of permissiveness.

But Lyttelton went on to propose a permanent Commission to serve the 'Imperial Council'. This Commission was to be 'purely consultative and advisory'. It would be based in London, and its secretarial staff would be paid for by the British government. Its function would be to prepare subjects for discussion at the Colonial Conferences. The topics for discussion would be referred to the permanent Commission either by the Colonial Conference, or by two or more self-governing colonies. The Commission would then ensure that the topics were presented in as concise and clear a form as possible, and would periodically review the progress achieved. Lyttelton suggested that the permanent members of the Commission would be nominated by the Prime Ministers of Britain and the self-governing colonies, but that additional members could be appointed where this was appropriate.[22]

Lyttelton doubted whether, without such a Commission, 'the Colonial Conferences will ever mean real business.' His biographer has described the dispatch as 'Perhaps the most important action which Alfred took in his two years of office.'[23] At any rate, Lyttelton was quick to put his plans before Balfour for approval. Balfour's approval was qualified, and his criticisms telling.

While agreeing with Lyttelton's broad aims, Balfour pointed out certain difficulties. To begin with, he felt it would be impossible to exclude any self-governing colony from the Conference, or accord representation on the basis of population. Balfour agreed that 'It may seem absurd to give Newfoundland the same representations as Canada; but ... since the Imperial Council will be consultative, and not executive, and will, in its earlier phase ... not work by majorities, no injustice will be done to Canada by this inequality of treatment.'[24] Balfour also recognised that the principle of proportional representation would give substance to the fear of the self-governing colonies that, under such a system, their representatives would be swamped by a massive British delegation.

Balfour's second major criticism centred on the proposed permanent Commission. He found it difficult to imagine how it would function:

It is to be set in motion ... by the Governments of any two Colonies. You do not say whether the Home Government is to have the same power as two Colonies: but I suppose you intend that it should. Now, how would such a body ... deal with ... the Tariff problem? Who is to settle the 'Reference'? Or, are there to be as many possible 'References' as there are pairs of Colonies? Again, who is to appoint the Imperial representatives upon this permanent Commission? It can only be the Prime Minister of the day; and ... it is probable that I should appoint very different men from those who would be selected by Sir H. Campbell-

Bannerman. This, of course, is true of all temporary Commissions: but, then, they *are* temporary.[25]

Balfour was also alarmed at the prospect of a collision between the permanent Commission and the British government on some strictly party issue. Such a clash would be sufficiently inconvenient if domestic interests only were concerned, but Balfour felt that 'it might become really serious if the whole Empire were involved.' Despite these doubts, Balfour told Lyttelton that it was 'hard to see how the Imperial Council is to be effective unless *some* machinery can be devised for carrying out your idea.'

Personally, Balfour thought it better to develop the permanent Civil Service aspect of the scheme at the expense of the proposed Commission. He felt that an office in London 'in which each of the Colonies, if they desired it, might have a small staff . . . who might act together, or separately, according as they or their employers thought fit, would supply an organisation which, from its looseness of structure, might suit the needs of our loosely compacted Empire.'[26] Certainly, under this system, the Prime Ministers of the self-governing colonies could come to Colonial Conferences armed with any information they themselves required, and which had moreover been supplied by their own officials.

Lyttelton replied to these criticisms on 1 February 1905, agreeing, to begin with, that it would be impossible to exclude any self-governing colony from future Colonial Conferences. He also tried to clarify the nature of his proposed permanent Commission. Lyttelton confirmed that the Commission would act on references supplied by any two colonies normally attending Colonial Conferences. However, he envisaged that the Commission's chief use would be to examine questions actually referred to it at sessions of the Colonial Conference. Lyttelton wanted the British representatives on the Commission to be appointed by the British Prime Minister for terms of a few years. As to the possibility that changes of government in Britain would endanger the continuity of the Commission's work, Lyttelton hoped that 'when one Government had agreed upon a principle with the Colonial Governments its successors would do their best to carry it out, even if they did not approve of it, at least as much as they would a treaty made with a foreign Power.' While Lyttelton went out of his way to reassure Balfour on these points, he did not agree with the latter's suggestion that the permanent Civil Service side of the scheme should be developed at the expense of the joint Commission.[27]

Basically, Lyttelton's proposals were profoundly affected by the example of the C.I.D. Indeed, he told Balfour of his hope that the permanent joint Commission 'might become a kind of Imperial thinking Department corresponding on the Civil side to that which the Imperial Defence Committee is becoming on the Military and Naval side.' The C.I.D. was meant to provide the Empire with defence co-ordination and guidance after hearing the views of the relevant departments and governments. Lyttelton now wished 'to move in a similar direction in the region of those civil affairs which have a wider range than the boundaries of any single State in the Empire. On this side the Colonial Conference or 'Imperial Council' would (in a sense) stand to the Commission in the relation which the Cabinet bears to the Defence Committee.'[28]

Thus vetted and amended, Lyttelton's Circular Dispatch was issued on 20 April 1905. Lyttelton had entertained sufficient optimism as to its fate to tell Balfour, on 1 February, that 'Canada will probably fall in with such a modest scheme as that proposed.'[29] In fact, in the correspondence resulting from the dispatch, 'The Government of Canada maintained an attitude of reserve, and in particular expressed doubts as to whether the scheme would not conflict with the working of responsible government.'[30]

Reactions from the other self-governing colonies were mixed. Generally favourable replies were received from the Australian government, led by Alfred Deakin, an unashamed imperial patriot and Chamberlainite; from loyalist Natal; and from the Cape, where Dr Jameson had risen phoenix-like from the ashes of the Raid to hold the premiership from 1904–8. Newfoundland, however, accepted the principle of a permanent joint Commission reluctantly, and only after further correspondence. New Zealand sent no reply at all to the Circular Dispatch.[31]

When the self-governing colonies discussed Lyttelton's proposals at the Colonial Conference of 1907, these differences were once more revealed. Deakin's enthusiasm for the scheme was doused by the opposition of Laurier of Canada, supported by Botha of the Transvaal and the Newfoundland delegation.[32] At the same time, the Conference did accept a plan to establish a department dealing exclusively with the self-governing colonies and to which would be attached a permanent Conference secretariat.[33] This was the Dominions Department of the Colonial Office, which thus provided the nucleus of the Dominions Office – established in 1925. The Dominions Office was in turn to evolve into the Commonwealth Office.

Despite the eventual rejection of Lyttelton's proposals, they initially aroused a considerable degree of interest in the House of Commons. In June 1905 Balfour was able to remind Haldane that the government had been considering, for some time past, plans for improving the efficiency and continuity of Colonial Conferences.[34] More to the point, Balfour had in April 1905 told Black, the member for Banffshire, that 'the Colonial Conference is in itself . . . a Council of the Empire, and I think that this definition of it is a very good one.' Balfour went on to deny that Lyttelton's proposed scheme was meant to be a path to imperial unity alternative to tariff reform.[35] Despite this denial, there is little doubt that Balfour preferred Lyttelton's modest path to the grand and slippery road marked out by Joseph Chamberlain's tariff reform campaign.

Indeed, Balfour continued to believe in the lasting value of loose imperial ties, saying in May 1906, 'If a great Empire is to be kept together, sentiment and loyalty must enter into the emotions by which its component parts are animated.'[36] Loyalty to a common monarch was one unifying factor, and so was common experience and a common stock of ideas.

3

If Balfour had a family-like concept of the Empire, it is clear that he considered the United States of America to be a relative too.

Anglo-American relations, for long marked by mutual distrust and antipathy, took a distinct turn for the better over the Venezuelan border dispute of 1895-6. They were improved even further by the Alaska boundary award of 1903, which, while it infuriated the Canadians, gratified the Americans. In both cases American goodwill was purchased by the surrender of disputed land. But, in her 'splendid isolation', Britain needed goodwill. Hence the embarrassing aftermath of the Jameson Raid was partly alleviated by the simultaneous growth of Anglo-American friendship. Moreover, between 1895-7 the United States increased her number of modern capital ships fourfold. Admittedly this only brought the total to four, but the portent remained.[37]

The Venezuelan border dispute flared up in 1895 largely because the United States, after a decade of inactivity on this score, supported Venezuela's claim for a readjustment of the boundary between herself and British Guiana. Two factors above all prompted this renewal of American involvement. Firstly, the Monroe doctrine seemed threatened by British territorial encroachments on the disputed border. Secondly, the land allegedly devoured by Britain was supposed to be rich in minerals. Principle and commercial advantage were both persuasive advocates. Hence in a special message to Congress in December 1895, the Republican President Grover Cleveland adopted a positively bellicose attitude towards Britain.

But Britain could ill afford American hostility at the precise moment when the Kaiser's telegram, congratulating Kruger on his defeat of the Jameson Raid, revealed deeper hostilities on the part of European nations. Early in 1896 therefore, the British government sought to relax tension over the Venezuelan border question. No minister played a more positive part in this process than Balfour. On 15 January 1896 in a speech at Manchester, Balfour spoke in favour of arbitration, and insisted that Britain coveted no territory in the Americas. Furthermore, he said 'The idea of war with the United States carries with it some of the unnatural horror of a civil war. . . . The time will come . . . when . . . some statesmen of authority, more fortunate even than President Monroe, will lay down the doctrine that between English-speaking people war is impossible.'[38]

Subsequent speeches by Hicks Beach, the Chancellor, and Salisbury reinforced these attitudes, in particular making it clear that Britain had no objections to the appointment of an all-American boundary commission to settle the dispute. Balfour also backed this policy with a speech in the Commons. Henry Cabot Lodge, the Republican statesman, was warmly appreciative of Balfour's moderating influence throughout the crisis, and wrote to him on 1 February to congratulate him on his speech at Manchester of 15 January:

I feel as you do about a war between the two great English-speaking peoples, and should regard it as a terrible calamity to civilization. . . . I readily accept your statement that you do not desire to extend your possessions in the Americas. . . . There is no nation on earth which England could so easily make her fast friend as the United States. Every consideration of sentiment and interest alike point to this as the right policy . . . we have always had friends among English public men from the time of Chatham to the days of Bright, and still later of yourself.[39]

Although Salisbury moved only cautiously towards a détente with the United States, Balfour had no such hesitations. On 28 February 1896 he told his uncle that he had written a letter 'in response to a very earnest appeal from the Anglo-American Arbitration Committee of the National Social Union, to send them a line of sympathy.'[40] Later, in August 1896, Balfour told Salisbury that 'there is some evidence of importance going to show that there is *not* the desire, even in the West, to pick a quarrel with England on the first occasion, which many observers would have us believe in.'[41]

From 1896 onwards Balfour placed a strong emphasis on Anglo-American relations, which which were to him similar to the most enduring bonds between Britain and the self-governing colonies. Of course, the monarch could play no comparable part in the United States. But Balfour believed that there were other unifying factors. He did not believe that physical descent was the only circumstance which had to be taken into account:

Yet the fact that [the United States'] laws, its language, its literature, and its religion, to say nothing of its constitution are essentially the same as those of English-speaking peoples elsewhere,
ought surely to produce a fundamental harmony – a permanent
sympathy – compared to which all merely political alliances with
other states should prove to be the evanescent result of temporary
diplomatic convenience.[42]

This 'fundamental harmony' was further stimulated by the
United States' overt accession to the ranks of active imperialist
powers after her defeat of Spain in the war of 1898. Cuba and the
Philippines came under the rule of Washington, and it was to his
American kinsmen that Rudyard Kipling a year later dedicated
his exhortation to take up *The White Man's Burden*. Moreover, so
marked was the friendship for Britain of Secretary of State Hay,
that Balfour was even asked in the Commons in April 1902, by
J. O'Kelly, the member for Roscommon North, if the government would invite John Hay to the impending Colonial Conference. Inevitably, Balfour replied that foreign nations could not
be invited to the Conference.[43]

However other methods of consolidating Anglo-American
accord lay at hand. The Klondike gold strike of 1896, and the
subsequent rush to the Yukon, raised the question of the Alaskan
boundary between Canada and the United States. Balfour's
government, admittedly under some pressure from the Americans,
surrendered even the most reasonable of Canada's claims in 1903.[44]
Canadian resentment proved no deterrent. Britain still controlled
the making of foreign treaties by the self-governing colonies. In
any case, temporary Canadian hostility was a small price to pay
for American friendship. Canada's feeling of betrayal, on the other
hand, encouraged her desire to control her own foreign policy,
even though the effective consummation of that desire was over
two decades away.

Balfour apparently felt little remorse over the Alaskan boundary
award. In the same year he assured Andrew Carnegie, the outstandingly successful American steel-master, and an avowed
race patriot, that he in no sense regarded the United States as a

foreign community.[45] Balfour also envisaged a 'special relationship' between Britain and the United States, telling Carnegie on 30 January 1903 that he believed all British political parties desired 'that our relations with your Great Republic should be based on that foundation of mutual comprehension, affection and esteem which form stronger links than the most formal treaties. This, at all events, has been throughout my political life my most fondly cherished hope.'[46]

Pan-Anglo-Saxon sentiment, however, carried little weight in the isolationist Mid-West or in the large Irish-American community. Nonetheless, it was a theme to which Balfour was to return six years later. Early in 1909 he composed a paper entitled 'The Possibility of an Anglo-Saxon Confederation'. This speculative document was meant for the attention of President Theodore Roosevelt, with whom Balfour had begun corresponding in 1908. Whether Roosevelt ever saw it is in fact doubtful.[47] At any rate, the document provides a revealing insight into Balfour's view of future political developments.

Basically, Balfour saw the world divided between great federations. Russian power would extend from Vladivostok to Germany, possibly incorporating Norway and Sweden as well. Germany would dominate central Europe and perhaps even Denmark and Holland. Balfour also prophesied a loose 'Latin' federation, comprising Spain, Portugal, Italy, Belgium, France, French Switzerland and Greece. In Asia he expected Japanese or Chinese domination. Africa north of the Zambesi would in effect be abandoned by the Europeans.[48]

What role awaited the English-speaking people in such a world? Balfour believed that the British Empire and the United States should federate, and he hoped that the dynamic Theodore Roosevelt could help prepare the way for such a dramatic development. Federation, Balfour argued, would be beneficial to both major partners. The under-populated Dominions could only be made secure by British immigration and an invincible navy. On the other hand, 'America can only expand at the expense of Britain. England already possesses all the thinly populated areas on the earth fit for white settlement. She already holds practically all the strategic points. . . . Have England and America anything to gain by refusing to pursue their destinies together and electing to be in opposition?'[49]

Balfour clearly thought Anglo-American co-operation essential. The best form of co-operation could be achieved through a loose federation which would leave 'Each state to manage its own affairs exactly as it liked', but which would have common foreign and defence policies. Such a confederation 'would be practically unassailable and would dominate the world. . . . It would practically dictate peace by sea to the rest of the world.' Australia would be saved from the 'yellow peril'; other Dominions would grow in population and security; the Anglo-American navy would rule the waves.[50]

This was a sophisticated and by no means unrealistic extension of the *Pax Britannica*. At the same time, an American reader of Balfour's proposals might have considered that the United States was merely being offered a status somewhat superior to that of a self-governing colony. Indeed, Balfour seems to have cast the United States in the role of Britain's junior partner in the proposed federation. In 1909 there was some excuse for this, despite America's remarkable and persistent industrial advance. However, Balfour's speculations had no immediate political application. Consistent Anglo-American co-operation in foreign policy was not yet in sight, even though in 1917 the United States was to enter briefly, though decisively, into a warlike partnership with Britain. Nonetheless, Balfour was right to emphasise the links of tradition, kinship and self-interest which were ultimately to form the basis of the 'special relationship'.

4

In the meantime it was essential to achieve a satisfactory relationship within the Empire between Britain and the Dominions. The latter had developed by 1914 distinct identities and needs. Since federation in 1867 Canadian nationalism had thrived on increasing prosperity and the need for domestic compromise. In 1901 the creation of the Commonwealth of Australia had federated, in the pattern they themselves desired, the six self-governing colonies of Australia. The Colonial Conference of 1907 had adopted the title of Dominion to describe the self-governing colonies of Canada, Australia and New Zealand. However, it had been agreed that the Cape and the Transvaal, for instance, were not Dominions since they were single states, not the products of federation.[51] But by 1910 the Union of South Africa saw not only an essay in reconciliation, but the establishment of the fourth great Dominion.

The formal bonds between the Dominions and Britain in 1914 were hardly oppressive. The monarch provided a practical constitutional link, and was represented on the spot by the Governors-General who were, without exception, sent out from Britain rather than recruited in the Dominions. In theory, though hardly ever in practice, the British monarch and Parliament could disallow and obstruct such Dominion legislation which ran counter to constitutional practice or English common law. The Judicial Committee of the Privy Council served as a Final Court of Appeal for the Dominions. The Dominions Department of the Colonial Office maintained contact between Whitehall and the Dominions. The Committee of Imperial Defence functioned as a permissive and advisory body. Even the Imperial Conference provided merely a forum for discussion, disclaiming wider powers. It was true that Britain ran the Empire's foreign policy. But after all it was she who footed almost the entire bill. In any case, nothing could compel a Dominion to give practical support to any aspect of British foreign policy of which it disapproved.

The main foundation of mutual co-operation, therefore, was simply the *will* to co-operate. Pan-Anglo-Saxon sentiment, while a useful aid, was not an exclusively satisfactory formula for an Empire in which Laurier, Botha and Smuts were playing sub-stantial parts, and which included India and the dependencies. Nonetheless as regards the Dominions Balfour sought, with his customary realism, for acceptable bonds. Ultimately these bonds – a common sovereign, membership of the same imperial group, a

L

common law, common institutions – could be worn with few qualms simply because they were already part of the fabric of those 'communities of freemen separated by half the circumference of the globe.'[52] United by these common institutions, loyalties and interests, the Empire went to war in 1914.

20 Dominion Status, 1914-31

Of course if one has someone like Lord Balfour to explain things they become easy to understand.

Remark attributed to GENERAL HERTZOG, 1926

I

ON 4 August 1914 the British government, belatedly and to the relief of France, declared war on Germany. Britain's declaration of war also automatically committed the entire Empire to hostilities – the last time this was to happen. Despite their legal involvement in the war, there was no practical way of enforcing Dominion, or indeed Indian, participation in the fighting. Flanders was far from Ottawa and Auckland, and the defence of Ypres did not necessarily render Melbourne or Bombay or Johannesburg more secure. Moreover, there were French Canadian extremists, Afrikaner die-hards and Irish and Indian nationalists ready to rejoice at the Empire's discomfiture. Nor was the British Labour movement traditionally enthusiastic for imperialistic wars.

In the event, the Empire's contribution to the war effort was immense. Its citizens fought in every theatre of war. The infant navies of Canada and Australia were put at the disposal of the Admiralty. Food and essential raw materials crossed the high seas to sustain the British people and British industry. Over 200,000 men from the overseas Empire lost their lives. More than two thirds of these were Indians, for whom the territorial integrity of Belgium can have meant little (if, indeed, it had profound or permanent meaning for the majority of British citizens).

But, despite the evident loyalty and the sacrifice, some dissonant notes were struck. In South Africa, Afrikaner rebellion flared, only to be stamped out by loyalist Afrikaners. French Canadians were slow to volunteer for active service, and bitterly contested the introduction of conscription in 1917. Kitchener's curt rejection of southern Irish volunteers in 1914 did not, fortunately, prevent thousands of them from joining the colours anyway.[1] But 1916 saw the Dublin Easter rising and heralded civil war and dis-affection.

In less dramatic ways, the Great War stimulated nationalism throughout the Dominions and India to an extent which forced Britain to adjust her policies accordingly. Paradoxically, as nation-alism gathered strength the British Empire achieved, in the Imperial War Cabinet, a centralising body of unprecedented effectiveness. The Imperial War Cabinet was a by-product of Lloyd George's revolutionary War Cabinet, and ancillary to the Imperial War Conference which met in London early in 1917. The Imperial War Cabinet was chaired by the Prime Minister and consisted of the British War Cabinet and representatives of the Dominions and India. It dealt with the conduct and administra-tion of the war. The Imperial War Conference alternated with the Imperial War Cabinet and was presided over by the Colonial Secretary. At its meetings the respresentatives of the Dominions and India discussed miscellaneous problems.

This meant that the representatives of the Dominions and India had a dual function as members of both the Imperial War Conference and the Imperial War Cabinet. When the Imperial War Conference was in session the British War Cabinet met separately. From the overseas delegates' point of view, the Imperial War Cabinet provided them with a real chance to share in decision-making. This was Lloyd George's avowed intention.[2] It also provided a unique opportunity for the imperial statesmen involved.

Perhaps more was intended to flow from the precedent thus established. Lloyd George certainly seems to have cherished long-term plans for continuing imperial co-operation on these lines. The Imperial War Cabinet and the Imperial War Conference met again in 1918. In effect the British Empire delegation to the Versailles Peace Conference also played the part of the Imperial

War Cabinet. Later, when it was announced in November 1920 that an Imperial Conference was to meet in June 1921, *The Times* optimistically foresaw 'the beginning of a definite system of Empire Government in peace by an Imperial Peace Cabinet'.[3]

This proved to be a woefully mistaken prediction. Leopold Amery was right simply to claim that the 'Imperial War Cabinet registered the high water mark in the evolution of effective Commonwealth co-operation in our time'.[4] Subsequent events, of which the 1922 Chanak incident was the most dramatic, forcibly illustrated the impossibility of permanent imperial centralisation. Neither the Dominions nor Britain were able to submerge their identities in common policymaking. After the achievements of the Imperial War Cabinet, peacetime Imperial Conferences were useful reunions rather than assemblies with executive powers. Ultimately, every conclusion of the Conferences could be rejected by the legislatures of the respective participants. Dominion nationalism had jibbed predictably and finally at centralisation.

Even during the palmy days of the Imperial War Cabinet there had been manifest signs that the Dominions wanted a clear definition of their status to be produced after the war. On 16 March 1917, Smuts had drafted and carried through the Imperial War Conference a resolution calling for a special Imperial Conference after the war to readjust 'the constitutional relations of the component parts of the Empire'. The resolution placed on record the Dominions' desire that any such readjustment 'while thoroughly preserving all existing powers of self-government and complete control of domestic affairs, should be based upon a full recognition of the Dominions as autonomous nations of an Imperial Commonwealth'. The Dominions and India also claimed an 'adequate voice in foreign policy', and wanted provision made for 'continuous consultation in all important matters of common Imperial concern'.[5]

Despite a last desperate heave by Lionel Curtis and the Round Table group, the resolution of 16 March 1917 spelt the end to dreams of imperial federation and marked out the path which was to run to the Statute of Westminster of 1931, and beyond. Nor was this all. At the Versailles Peace Conference the Dominions and India claimed, and were granted, separate diplomatic representation in addition to enjoying membership of the British Empire delegation. They were also allowed to sign the peace treaties in their own right.

During these signally important developments, Balfour was Foreign Secretary. When Lloyd George overthrew Asquith's coalition government in December 1916, Balfour was the first of the Unionist leaders to accept office under the inspired yet devious 'Welsh wizard'. Although Asquith may have hoped that friends like Balfour would refuse to serve Lloyd George, the temptation of high office proved irresistible. Bonar Law was Lloyd George's advocate in wooing Balfour, who 'saw no alternative but to accept. But I did so with a sinking heart, due, I hope, as much to influenza as to other causes.'[6]

Balfour remained Foreign Secretary until replaced by Curzon in October 1919. It was the last major office he was to hold, but the tenure was a fruitful one. Not only was Balfour able to satisfy Jewry with his famous Declaration of November 1917, but he was also able to give practical expression to his long-standing belief in the necessity of Anglo-American co-operation, for on 2 April the United States declared war on Germany, spurred on by the Zimmerman telegram and unrestricted submarine warfare.

Doubts have remained as to the authenticity of the Zimmerman telegram (which the British intelligence service had decoded, and in which the German government apparently offered Mexico an offensive alliance against the United States). But submarine warfare was real enough, and so was Britain's need of American assistance. Balfour was immediately dispatched to the United States to further military, diplomatic and technical co-operation. He proved an ideal ambassador, creating and exploiting goodwill in private and in public. On the point of Balfour's return, Robert Lansing the Secretary of State wrote, 'We have always believed that you were peculiarly a friend of the United States and now we know it.'[7]

With the vast human and industrial resources of the United States thrown behind Britain and her allies, the war was virtually won. But when in November 1918 the peace became a reality, the Dominions pressed for separate representation at the ensuing conferences. This demand, while perfectly acceptable, posed certain delicate problems. In effect the Dominions were asking for a public acknowledgment of their independence, and an announcement that they possessed real diplomatic autonomy. Much could flow from this. The Dominions might subsequently draw further apart from each other and from Britain. On the other hand, Leopold Amery was optimistic. He argued in a memorandum of 14 November 1918 that 'The extent to which the Dominions are given a really effective voice in the Peace settlement will determine their whole outlook on Imperial questions in future.' Amery felt that if treated as equals 'they will be prepared to accept the idea of a single foreign policy for the British Commonwealth directed by the machinery of an Imperial Cabinet.' Amery was also aware of the advantages of having Botha requesting that the British Empire should retain conquered German colonies in Africa, or of Sir Satyendra Sinha proposing that Asian peoples (in the Near East) should come under British trusteeship.[8]

In the event the Dominions and India had the best of both worlds. Their representatives filled, by rotation, two places on the five-strong British Empire delegation. Moreover, in Lloyd George's absence it was Borden of Canada, not Balfour, who presided over the delegation.[9] Canada, Australia, South Africa and India in addition enjoyed separate diplomatic representation equivalent to powers like China, Greece, Poland and Portugal. New Zealand, however, had only one plenipotentiary delegate. The Dominions and India were also able to avail themselves of the diplomatic machinery which served the main British Empire delegation.

President Wilson at first objected to the double representation of the Dominions and India.[10] Fears were expressed that the British Empire would carry undue weight in the negotiations. President Wilson's objections were overcome, although the doubts of others may have lingered. In fact, the Dominion and British delegates by no means always saw eye to eye. Botha and Smuts thought the Versailles peace treaty too severe, and submitted a memorandum of protest even though they also signed the treaty. On the other hand Hughes of Australia was determined to wring the last concession out of Germany. He was contemptuous of President Wilson and the League of Nations, and only agreed that German New Guinea should be made a mandate on the understanding that the mandate system had little real meaning. Borden, however, seems to have played a moderating role throughout.[11]

The independent status of the Dominions was confirmed further by their membership of the League of Nations. India also belonged to the League. Furthermore, in 1920 the British government allowed Canada the right to appoint her own ambassador to Washington. However there seems to have been no intention that this example should be followed by other Dominions. It was argued that the Canadian relationship with the United States was unique, and that the Canadian ambassador should, in any case, work closely with the British ambassador. As it happened Canada did not make use of her new privilege until 1926, by which time the Irish Free State had already appointed an ambassador to the United States.[12]

But the precedent for a Dominion to appoint an ambassador now existed. Other demands were evident. In June 1919, Balfour told Curzon that 'There is, as you know, a growing feeling in the Dominions that they should appoint their own Governor-Generals.'[13] Balfour deprecated this sentiment, but it was clear that the function and identity of the post of Governor-General needed reassessment and possibly reform.

To these firm, though loyal, requests for a greater degree of independence was added a more strident voice. In December 1922 the Irish Free State formally came into existence, completing the process begun a year before by the fiercely controversial Anglo-Irish treaty. The Irish were in no mood to mince their words or subdue their grievances. Although the British King appointed the Irish Governor-General, and the members of the Irish parliament (the Dail) were obliged to swear an oath of allegiance to George V 'in virtue of the common citizenship of Ireland with Great Britain and her adherence to and membership of the group of nations forming the British Commonwealth of

Nations',[14] such bonds were paper-thin. The Irish Free State had the same status as Canada, the senior Dominion, but little of her Oedipus complex. The British Commonwealth had acquired its sixth Dominion, but also its most disloyal.

2

The early 1920s were crucial years for Britain and the Dominions. By 1922 Lloyd George's attempt to maintain the high level of centralised co-operation achieved during and immediately after the Great War had foundered, crippled by the Chanak incident. In September 1922 Lloyd George had publicly, and without prior consultation, invited the Dominions to send troops to defend Constantinople against the revolutionary forces of Kemal Ataturk, and to guarantee freedom of passage through the Dardanelles. Although Australia and New Zealand replied promptly and favourably, Canada and South Africa were distinctly cool in their response and, in fact, eventually offered nothing.

Hopes that the Empire could pursue a joint foreign policy were now practically in ruins. Britain had taken the unprecedented step of calling for assistance from her Dominions, and two of them had rebuffed her. The Imperial Conference of 1923 met under the shadow of the Chanak affair. Moreover, a few months previously Canada had negotiated and signed the Halibut Fisheries Treaty with the United States. The senior Dominion had thus won the right to conclude an international agreement without any participation in the treaty-making by the British government.[15] The 1923 Conference explicitly recognised the implications of the Halibut Fisheries Treaty. Less explicitly, grandiose assumptions that a common imperial foreign policy existed were jettisoned. The periodic Imperial Conference was to resume its sway, reinforced, in theory, by ample consultation between the mother country and the Dominions.

Unfortunately successive British governments seemed unable, or unwilling, to consult the Dominions over vital foreign policy decisions. Ramsay MacDonald's first Labour government recognised the Soviet Union in 1924 without consulting the Dominions in any way. In 1922, following the Chanak incident, Britain had failed to invite the Dominions to the subsequent peace conference at Lausanne between Turkey and the allied powers. When in 1924 the British government wished Canada formally to signify her concurrence to the ratification of the treaty, Canada refused. Indeed, when Britain ratified the treaty in the name of the Empire, both Canada and the Irish Free State declined to accept any definite responsibility for it.[16]

The treaty of Locarno in 1925 revealed further divergences between Britain and the Dominions. At Locarno an attempt was made to guarantee Germany's western frontier and to ensure the demilitarisation of the Rhineland. Britain, France, Germany, Italy, Belgium, Poland and Czechoslovakia signed the treaty. The Dominions, however, could not be expected to involve themselves in this peculiarly European situation. Neither they nor India wished to become parties to the treaty. Significantly, the British government, having learnt its lesson over Lausanne, specifically exempted the Dominions from the conference and the treaty, unless they particularly desired to accept its provisions.[17]

This was Britain's public acknowledgment that a common foreign policy for the Empire was an impossibility. In the Upper House, Balfour, now Lord President of the Council in Baldwin's government, allowed himself some speculation on the subject. Speaking on 24 November 1925, Balfour admitted that the Empire as a whole had not been involved in the Locarno agreements, but he trusted 'that in the evolution of the British Empire we shall find a remedy.' He continued, however:

I do not know that the remedy will be complete. I do not know that it is possible to get the sort of unity in the British Empire which is possible in other great States whose geographical conditions are different, whose constitutional position is different, who live under centralised governments. ... But though it is a matter for regret it is not a matter for shame that our Empire is less closely knit, less formally organised than the Empires of other States. We are engaged in an entirely new experiment in the world's history in empire building. We have slid into the position

... by dealing with the difficulties and problems as they have arisen, until one day we awoke and said: 'This is quite a new thing that we have instinctively created. How are we to turn it to the best account?'[18]

Having recognised the strength of Dominion separatism and, indeed, having paid some tribute to it, Balfour then drew the only optimistic conclusion available to him. This was simply to insist that if the Locarno treaty was broken, the Dominions would rally to Britain's side.[19] In this way, Balfour exemplified that empiricism which he believed was so central to the evolution of the Empire. Although he claimed the Empire to be an 'entirely new experiment', he had fallen back upon the traditional assumptions that, faced with a supreme crisis, divergences would disappear and common values assert themselves.

In the event, he was right. All the Dominions (save the Irish Free State) went to war in 1939 of their own volition, although with a heavier step than in 1914. But they *did* go to war. However, in 1925 Balfour's speech acknowledged the end of dreams of imperial centralisation. A year later he was to play an outstanding part in rationalising the independent status of the Dominions within the Empire.

3

The Imperial Conference of 1926 marked the end of an era. Its main achievement was that it brought imperial constitutional theory into line with practice. In theory, the Dominions were denied full nationhood by certain prerogatives and reserved powers possessed by the British monarch and parliament. These restrictions included the right of the Crown, under the 1865 Colonial Laws Validity Act, to 'disallow' such Dominion legislation as conflicted with that of Britain. Governors-General also had the right to withhold their consent to Dominion legislation and to 'reserve' this consent for the monarch himself. In addition, Dominion parliaments were denied the right to make laws 'repugnant' to the laws of Britain; nor could they pass laws having extra-territorial effect. Finally, Dominion citizens were able to appeal against the decisions of the highest courts in their own land to the Judicial Committee of the Privy Council in London.

In practice the British Crown and parliament had hardly ever since 1865 exercised their rights of 'disallowance', 'reservation', or 'repugnancy' – and even then, only in trifling matters. Certainly there was no intention of doing so in 1926. Nonetheless, the existence of these reserved powers provided 'essentially psychological stumbling blocks'[20] between Britain and the Dominions – particularly between Britain and Canada, South Africa and the Irish Free State. It was also expedient to allow the Dominions to legislate extra-territorially, and the question of appeals to the Judicial Committee of the Privy Council needed review.

At the same time, it is unlikely that the British government, if left to itself, would have initiated a precise analysis of the relationship between the mother country and the Dominions. Baldwin, the Prime Minister, was hardly possessed with the dynamic energies of a constitutional reformer. Indeed according to Leopold Amery (his Colonial and Dominions Secretary) Baldwin's main contribution to an early meeting with General Hertzog before the 1926 Conference was to smoke his pipe and, like Brer Rabbit, lie 'low' and say 'nuffin'.[21]

Dominion statesmen, however, brought more radical convictions to the Conference. Hertzog, since 1924 head of the Afrikaner-dominated Nationalist and Labour government in South Africa, wanted the Dominions' status defined and clarified. Leopold Amery has described Hertzog as being 'on a hair trigger where any suggestion, however unintentional, of English racial superiority or South African subordination seemed to him implied.'[22] Certainly Hertzog's contention that 'Unless our status is acknowledged by foreign nations we simply do not exist as a nation',[23] found ready acceptance in other Dominions. W. T. Cosgrave and Kevin O'Higgins of the Irish Free State came to the Conference to press for the removal of the lingering limitations on their country's sovereignty.[24]

The Liberal government of Canada also wanted a precise statement of the constitutional rights of the Dominions. This determination had been stimulated further by the disturbing, though histrionic, clash between Prime Minister Mackenzie King and the Governor-General, Lord Byng. In June 1926 Mackenzie King had been refused a dissolution by Lord Byng, who had subsequently acceded to a similar request from Meighen, the Conservative leader whose government had fleetingly replaced the Liberal administration. Despite Lord Byng's justifications for his action, Mackenzie King was able to present to the Canadian electorate a dark, though largely imaginary, picture of attempted subordination from Government House – if not from Whitehall itself.

Canada, therefore, particularly wanted to discuss the functions of the Governors-General and the method of their appointment. The Irish Free State wanted a rewording of the Royal Title which in its present form referred to the 'United Kingdom of Great Britain and Ireland' – hardly an accurate description since Ireland itself was divided between Ulster and the Free State. The South African government urgently required a definition of Dominion status. Australia, New Zealand and Newfoundland were more prepared to muddle along, and to deal with constitutional problems as they occurred. However, all the Dominions had profound misgivings over the British government's legal capacity to formulate foreign policy and to sign treaties on behalf of the Empire.

The most important work of the 1926 Conference was that undertaken by the Inter-Imperial Relations Committee. Although Balfour's name is indissolubly linked with this Committee and its report, he was not from the first marked out as its chairman. Amery had originally considered him to be the obvious chairman of the special Sub-Committee on Research.[25] It is true that in August 1926 Baldwin had written to Balfour expressing the hope that he would be able to take part in the impending Conference. But the letter had been couched in extremely vague terms.[26] By the time the Conference opened on 19 October, however, Amery had persuaded Baldwin that the pressures of the Prime Minister-ship necessitated his surrendering the chairmanship of the Inter-Imperial Relations Committee. Amery then suggested that Balfour, the Lord President of the Council, should take Baldwin's place. Balfour brought conviction and authority to a Committee composed of the Prime Ministers of the Dominions and the representatives of the Indian government, as well as Amery (the Colonial and Dominions Secretary) and Austen Chamberlain (the Foreign Secretary). Amery felt confident in his choice:

Balfour I knew to be entirely in sympathy with the newer conception of Commonwealth equality, while his immense personal authority would not only hold the Committee together, but commend its conclusions to the British Cabinet where, I felt, the greatest difficulty might have to be encountered.[27]

At the first meeting of the Inter-Imperial Relations Committee on 27 October, it was unanimously decided to attempt to define the present constitutional position, and to make whatever adjustments seemed necessary to that position. Balfour then spoke of the difference between status and function, and of the double loyalty involved in the separate yet common historical traditions of the Dominions and Britain. To illustrate this point, he told the Committee that as a Scot he was not prepared, because of Bannockburn and Flodden, to surrender his share in Magna Carta and Shakespeare.[28]

This type of masterly scholastic display was dear to Balfour's heart. Hertzog followed him and insisted on getting down to business. To further this purpose he later produced his own somewhat lengthy formula for a precise definition of Dominion status. Hertzog's formula referred to the Dominions as independent states 'equal in status and separately entitled to international recognition', but also 'united by the common bond of allegiance to the Crown and freely associated as members of the British Commonwealth of Nations'.[29]

Thus the basis of the famous Balfour definition of Dominion status already existed before Balfour himself had uttered a phrase of it. Hertzog's formula was then discussed. Mackenzie King disliked the word independence since it smacked too much of the Declaration of Independence of Canada's great neighbour. Next Balfour produced an alternative version of Hertzog's formula, but included in it the word Empire.[30] Hertzog's subsequent objections to the use of the word were overcome on the grounds that it was the only appropriate term to describe the miscellaneous collection of territories owing allegiance to the British monarch.

Both Balfour and Amery could take pleasure in the fact that even Hertzog had emphasised the common bond of allegiance to the Crown. On 19 October, the day the Conference had opened, Amery had written to Austen Chamberlain that he wanted 'great stress laid on the indissoluble unity of all parts of the Empire under King and Crown.'[31] Balfour also had long been convinced that loyalty to the Crown was the strongest bond between Britain and the Dominions. The formal recognition of this bond thus seemed assured from the first meeting of the Committee.

However, other difficulties remained. On 1 November, Amery told Balfour that Coates of New Zealand and Monroe of Newfoundland were 'anything but happy. . . . We must be careful not to alienate the people who really matter in the Empire for the sake of the representatives of the extreme section of South Africa or of the Irish.'[32] Nonetheless, Amery wrote Balfour a second letter on 1 November suggesting a compromise over Hertzog's phrase 'freely associated'. Balfour had objected to this phrase because it seemed equally to imply freedom to 'dissociate'. Amery felt that 'associated in equal freedom' would be an acceptable substitute.[33]

Evidently neither Balfour nor Amery wished to surrender too much to Hertzog. Despite this, 'freely associated' remained part of the basic definition of the relationship between Britain and the Dominions. After a fortnight of intermittent re-examination, the following formula was approved as a description of this relationship:

They are autonomous communities within the British Empire, equal in status, in no way subordinate one to another in any aspect of their domestic or external affairs, though united by a common allegiance to the Crown, and freely associated as members of the British Commonwealth of Nations.[34]

This was an extension and formalisation of opinions which Balfour had put before the House of Lords on 27 July 1926, three months before the Imperial Conference met. On 27 July, Balfour had anticipated a discussion of the Dominion's relations with Britain and had said:

My own personal view is that [these] relations are those necessarily of equality. None of us conceive that of this conglomeration of free States one is above the other. One may have more responsibility than another, one may be in more dangers than another. . . but all are on an equality. That is the very essence, as I understand it, of the British Empire.[35]

The Imperial Conference had thus afforded Balfour the opportunity of putting these convictions to practical purpose. The Inter-Imperial Relations Committee, however, had other achievements to record. The more militant Dominion delegates found the British representatives accommodating. Consequently, the Committee quickly agreed to sweep away those constitutional anomalies which some Dominions found objectionable. Disallowance, reservation and repugnancy were to be destroyed. The need of the Dominions to legislate extra-territorially was acknowledged, and subsequently investigated in detail. The Committee also recorded that it was constitutional practice that legislation by the British parliament applying to a Dominion could only be passed with the consent of the Dominion concerned. The British government furthermore stated that it had no desire that appeals to the Judicial Committee of the Privy Council should be determined contrary to the wishes of the Dominion primarily affected.[36]

On the controversial question of the duties of the Governors-General it was agreed that in future a Governor-General's functions were to be similar in all essentials to those of the monarch in Britain. In addition, although the Governors-General would be kept fully informed by both British and Dominion governments, they were no longer to act as a direct channel of communication between Whitehall and the Dominions. This at least meant that it would be more difficult to suspect the Governors-General of conspiring with the government in London. Mackenzie King was thus placated. However, more was to follow. In Amery's words it had become 'inevitable, and constitutionally right' that the appointment of Governors-General should be a matter for the exclusive initiative of the Dominions.[37] This, too, the Inter-Imperial Relations Committee approved. Finally, Amery agreed with Mackenzie King's suggestion that consultation and communications would be improved if the British government appointed High Commissioners to the Dominions, just as several Dominion High Commissions had already been established in London. Although the Committee did not bind itself to this policy, the first British High Commissioner to Canada was appointed soon after the Conference.[38] This example was then followed in regard to other Dominions, and eventually between the Dominions themselves.

The Irish representatives had also argued that the Royal Title should be altered from the form established by the Act of 1901: 'George V, by the Grace of God, of the United Kingdom of Great Britain and Ireland and of the British Dominions beyond the Seas King, Defender of the Faith, Emperor of India.' Kevin O'Higgins felt that this formula was inapt in view of the Irish Free State's new constitutional status. The Inter-Imperial Relations Committee unanimously agreed to recommend a slight alteration to the title, and a vital comma now symbolised the Irish Free State's separateness from the United Kingdom. The amended title now began: 'George V, by the Grace of God, of Great Britain, Ireland and the British Dominions beyond the Seas King. . . .'[39] In May 1927 a royal proclamation altered the title accordingly. As for the future, in 1931 the Statute of Westminster declared that any further alteration in the law concerning the Royal Style or Titles, or the succession to the throne, would require the assent of all the Dominions as well as that of Great Britain.

While the Balfour Committee dealt with these matters, a sub-committee under Austen Chamberlain discussed problems connected with international relations. Central to this discussion was the urgent need to agree on a satisfactory formula for the making of international treaties. The memory of the confusion over the Treaty of Locarno provided an effective spur to these deliberations. It was finally agreed that treaties would continue to be made in the name of the British monarch (thus preserving the indivisibility of the Crown), but that individual Dominions were not bound by any such treaty unless they chose to be and had ratified the agreement in their own Parliaments.[40] The 1930 Imperial Conference confirmed these recommendations.

This compromise was a reasonable one. Britain was bound to play the major part in foreign policy-making for the Commonwealth and Empire for the foreseeable future. Yet the Dominions could not be expected to approve of all of Britain's aims, nor to share all her obligations. At any rate, there was now nothing to prevent a Dominion remaining neutral while Britain went to war – indeed, the Irish Free State availed itself of this right in 1939. Also one natural corollary of the recognition that the Dominions were free to conduct their own foreign policy was the acceptance that they would increasingly require separate diplomatic representation abroad. As an antidote to such separatist tendencies, the British government predictably emphasised its intention to consult the Dominions more fully over foreign policy-making. Equally predictably, it failed to live up to its promises.

The opening section of the report of the 1926 Imperial Conference was drafted by Balfour. It was the quintessence of his convictions on the subject of Dominion status and inter-imperial relations, and had been unanimously approved by his committee colleagues. On Balfour's insistence, the crucial definition of the relationship between Britain and the Dominions was incorporated in the first part of the report rather than serving as a preamble in itself.[41] The purpose of this was to balance the somewhat negative character of the definition against more positive affirmations. Unfortunately, owing to a printer's error, the definition appeared in italics in the official report thus partly thwarting Balfour's intention.[42] Despite this oversight, the opening section of the report remained a balanced and realistic statement:

The Committee are of opinion that nothing would be gained by attempting to lay down a Constitution for the British Empire. Its widely scattered parts have very different characteristics, very different histories, and are at very different stages of evolution; while, considered as a whole, it defies classification, and bears no real resemblance to any other political organization which now exists or has ever yet been tried.

There is, however, one most important element in it which, from a strictly constitutional point of view, has now, as regards all vital matters, reached its full development – we refer to the group of self-governing communities composed of Great Britain and the Dominions. Their position and mutual relation may be readily defined. They are autonomous Communities within the British Empire, equal in status, in no way subordinate one to another in any aspect of their domestic or external affairs, though united by a common allegiance to the Crown, and freely associated as members of the British Commonwealth of Nations.

A foreigner endeavouring to understand the true character of the British Empire by the aid of this formula alone would be tempted to think that it was devised rather to make mutual interference impossible than to make mutual co-operation easy.

Such a criticism, however, completely ignores the historic situation. The rapid evolution of the Overseas Dominions during the last fifty years has involved many complicated adjustments of old political machinery to changing conditions. The tendency towards equality of status was both right and inevitable. Geographical and other conditions made this impossible of attainment by the way of federation. The only alternative was by the way of autonomy; and along this road it has been steadily sought. Every self-governing member of the Empire is now the master of its destiny. In fact, if not always in form, it is subject to no compulsion whatever.

But no account, however accurate, of the negative relations in which Great Britain and the Dominions stand to each other can do more than express a portion of the truth. The British Empire is not founded upon negations. It depends essentially, if not formally, on positive ideals. Free institutions are its life-blood. Free co-operation is its instrument. Peace, security, and progress are among its objects. Aspects of all these great themes have been discussed at the present Conference; excellent results have been thereby obtained. And though every Dominion is now, and must always remain, the sole judge of the nature and extent of its co-operation, no common cause will, in our opinion, be thereby imperilled.

Equality of status, so far as Britain and the Dominions are concerned, is thus the root principle governing our Inter-Imperial Relations. But the principles of equality and similarity, appropriate

to status, do not universally extend to function. Here we require
something more than immutable dogmas. For example, to deal
with questions of diplomacy and questions of defence, we
require also flexible machinery – machinery which can, from
time to time, be adapted to the changing circumstances of the
world.[43]

4

In 1931 the Statute of Westminster enshrined the major constitutional changes recommended by the 1926 Conference. In the
meantime, various precedents were established in the fields of
Dominion diplomatic representation and treaty-making which
showed that the agreements of 1926 were no hollow sham. But
the report of the 1926 Conference, and the work of the Inter-
Imperial Relations Committee in particular, made an immediate
impact.

Amery professed delight at the Committee's 'intimate and
searching discussions'. He also paid special tribute to Balfour's
part in the preparation of the report. Balfour's work was all the
more remarkable in view of his age, which was then seventy-eight.
Rather like his uncle Salisbury a quarter of a century before,
Balfour 'often dozed off, but somehow rarely missed a point.' In
fact, Amery considered that Balfour's 'final contribution was
outstanding.'[44] Furthermore, in his diary for 23 November, as the
Conference was dispersing, Amery wrote that of all the delegates,
nobody stood out individually 'except, perhaps, old Balfour,
whose introductory setting to the status formula was a stroke of
genius.'[45]

Others were no less complimentary. The fearsome Hertzog was
reported as saying 'of course if one has someone like Lord
Balfour to explain things they become easy to understand.'[46]
While there is no doubt that Balfour had deeply impressed Hertzog,
the latter could afford magnaminity; he had, after all, largely got
his own way over the definition of Dominion status. For his part,
Balfour viewed Hertzog's 'conversion' with a mixture of satisfaction and caution, telling Esher on 24 November 1926:

Last night I took a tender farewell of General Hertzog, whose whole attitude has altered since the beginning of the Conference. I do not know whether this change of heart will survive the rough and tumble of South African politics; for, though a man of much charm, some of his friends say he has but little persistence. However we must see.[47]

But Balfour had aroused admiration in bosoms other than Hertzog's. On 23 November his old friend Esher wrote with typical flamboyance:

My Dear Arthur,
Of all your great and manifold services, the 'Report' which bears your imprimatur throughout is one of the greatest. A crowning achievement. You are really very splendid.[48]

A little more soberly, Stanley Bruce, the Australian Prime Minister requested on 21 December 1926 a photograph of Balfour, and added:

Some day in the future I believe that the Conference will be recognised as one of the great landmarks in our Imperial history. When that day comes I hope it will be equally realised how greatly what was accomplished was due to you individually.[49]

What was the significance of the 1926 Imperial Conference in terms of imperial evolution? Had the Empire been given a constitution? Evidently not, for the Balfour report was adamant on this point. Nor were comparisons to Magna Carta and the Declaration of Rights completely apt. Had the Balfour report, then, merely papered over the divisions between the Dominions and Britain? But what alternative was there? The British government, by putting the best possible gloss on the process of decentralisation, had at least purchased a measure of Dominion goodwill at the same time. Balfour claimed even more when writing to Esher on 24 November, a day after the Conference ended:

I have great hopes that my statement will really put an end to the efforts of the small but obstinate minority who, in each of our self-governing Dominions, persistently advocate the break-up of the Empire.[50]

Perhaps the euphoric aftermath of the Conference and the widespread acclaim for his achievements accounted for this optimistic statement from Balfour. In the sense that the Dominions continued to tread independent and in some instances divergent paths, the break-up of the British Empire was not halted. On the other hand, the Conference had demonstrated that men like Hertzog and O'Higgins could find a place within an organisation which was founded upon equality of status, and only remained an organisation as long as its members chose to make it one. The Commonwealth 'club' had been formally recognised. Membership involved countless opportunities to co-operate, but no obligation to do so. The British Empire had thus acknowledged more clearly than ever before the dichotomy between a Commonwealth of white-settled Dominions (which could secede if they wished, but as yet chose not to) and the non-European Empire (whose subjects could not secede even if they had passionately desired it).

The members of the Commonwealth formed an élite within the British Empire. They enjoyed appropriate privileges – free institutions, self-government, and now equality of status. Such bonds as existed were most powerful when incidental. In December 1926, Balfour attempted to describe these bonds, claiming that the British Empire was 'a more united organism' than ever before, held together 'far more effectually by the broad loyalties, by the common feelings and interests – in many cases of history – and by devotion to great world ideals of peace and freedom. A common interest in loyalty, in freedom, in ideals – that is the bond of Empire. If that is not enough, nothing else is enough.'[51]

These were brave words, and reflected Balfour's convictions of three decades or more. Yet universal loyalty to the Crown was demonstrably absent in the Irish Free State and South Africa. Nor did the latter Dominion extend the most elementary political freedoms to the vast majority of its non-European inhabitants. Nonetheless, a stock of common interests and experience was for the time being a sufficient bond between Britain and the Dominions.

Balfour welcomed the years after 1926 as a new era of 'unalter-able equality of status' which left to 'friendly arrangement the flexible distribution of function'.[52] Convinced that co-operation in handcuffs was impossible, Balfour felt that the settlement of 1926 accorded with his own ideals of freedom and association, loyalty and autonomy. Yet the Conference had merely matched constitutional theory with practice. Balfour saw this clearly, and relished the process. Writing in May 1927 to Sir George Foster, a Canadian senator, he said:

As regards the Imperial Conference . . . nothing *new* has been done; and I have for many years held and publicly expressed the views embodied in our Report. But though the facts are as they have long been, the result of the Report no doubt brings their true character home to many . . . who did not thoroughly realise the situation. . . . We have been making, at first half consciously, the most novel and the greatest experiment in Empire-building which the world has ever seen. It is vain to think that so great an undertaking can be carried to a successful issue without earnest effort.[53]

It was more than appropriate that, at the end of his long life, Balfour should have been given the opportunity to put his realistic mind to the service of that Empire whose evolution he had followed with so shrewd an eye.

References

The manuscript sources for the book are described in the Bibliography. One gap in the records of Balfour's political life should be mentioned for the benefit of those interested in his time as Chief Secretary of Ireland (1887–91). The gap was created by the destruction of a large number of the public records of Ireland in a fire in Dublin in June 1922. (See *Bulletin of the Institute of Historical Research*, vol. 2, no. 4, June 1924, pp. 8–9.)

The abbreviations for sources are as follows:

B.M. Add. Mss.	British Museum, Additional Manuscripts.
P.R.O.	Public Record Office.
I.O.L.	India Office Library.
P.P. Cd.	Parliamentary Papers Command Paper.
Whittingehame	Balfour Papers deposited at the Tower, Whittingehame, East Lothian, in the possession of the Earl of Balfour.
Birmingham	Birmingham University Library, Papers of Joseph and Austen Chamberlain.
Christ Church	Christ Church Library, Oxford. The Salisbury Papers.
Bodleian	The Bodleian Library Oxford.
Hansard	Hansard's Parliamentary Debates.

Chapter One

1. A. J. Balfour, *Chapters of Autobiography*, ed. Blanche Dugdale, p. 7.
2. K. Young, *Arthur James Balfour*, pp. 426–7.
3. R. Jenkins, *Asquith*, p. 79.
4. A. J. Balfour, *Autobiography*, p. 113.

Chapter Two

1. D. C. Gordon, *The Dominion Partnership in Imperial Defense, 1870–1914*, chapter 2, and *Cambridge History of the British Empire*, vol. 3, pp. 230–1.
2. F. A. Johnson, *Defence by Committee*, pp. 12–13.
3. Ibid., p. 17
4. Public Record office: Cabinet Papers 17/93. Note, this consists of a short history of the Committee
5. F. A. Johnson, p. 18
6. Ibid., pp. 28–30
7. B.M. Add. Mss. (British Museum Additional Manuscripts) 49689, Balfour to Salisbury, 18 Jan. 1889
8. Hansard, 4th series, vol. 22, 16 March 1894, col. 490
9. Ibid.
10. Ibid.
11. F. A. Johnson, p. 33
12. Blanche Dugdale, *Arthur James Balfour*, vol. 1, p. 365
13. B.M. Add. Mss. 49690, Salisbury to Balfour, Aug. 1895
14. P.R.O. Cab. 37/40.64. 24 Aug. 1895
15. Ibid.
16. Christ Church, Box 3, Wallet 1, Balfour to Salisbury, 29 Aug. 1895
17. Letter of 22 Jan. 1952, quoted in Johnson, p. 34
18. Hansard, 4th series, vol. 78, 1 Feb. 1900, col. 261
19. P.R.O. Cab.5/1/19C, 3 Dec. 1896
20. Hansard, 4th series, vol. 38, 13 March 1896, col. 922
21. *English Historical Review*, vol. 77, p. 492, J. P. Mackintosh, 'The Role of the Committee of Imperial Defence before 1914'
22. B.M. Add. Mss. 49718. Cabinet paper.
23. Proceedings of the Colonial Conference, 1897 (C. 8569), p. 5
24. F. A. Johnson, p. 37
25. Christ Church, Box 3, Wallet 1, Balfour to Salisbury, 19 Dec. 1899
26. Ibid.
27. B.M. Add. Mss. 49683, Bigge to Balfour, 30 Dec. 1899
28. Ibid., Bigge to Balfour, 2 Jan. 1900
29. Ibid.
30. Whittingehame, Violet Cecil to Balfour, 26 July 1899
31. Ibid.
32. Christ Church, Box 3, Wallet 1, 19 Dec. 1899
33. Whittingehame, Wyndham to Balfour, 7 Oct. 1899
34. Ibid., Portland to Balfour, 17 Jan. 1900
35. Ibid., Violet Cecil to Balfour, 23 Jan. 1900
36. Ibid., Violet Cecil to Balfour, 9 May 1900
37. Ibid., Brodrick to Alice Balfour, 12 March 1900
38. Ibid., Balfour to Alice Balfour, 16 Dec. 1899
39. B.M. Add. Mss. 49891, Salisbury to Balfour, 29 Dec. 1899
40. Christ Church, Box 3, Wallet 1, Balfour to Salisbury, 19 Dec. 1899
41. *The Times*, 9 Jan. 1900
42. Hansard, 4th ser., vol. 78, 30 Jan. 1900, col. 24

43. F. A. Johnson, p. 44
44. B.M. Add. Mss. 49742, Balfour to H. White, 12 Dec. 1900
45. *The Times History of the War in South Africa, 1899–1902*, vol.1, p. 9
46. B.M. Add. Mss. 49717. Cabinet paper
47. A. P. Thornton, *The Imperial Idea and Its Enemies*, p. 143
48. Colonial Conference 1902, papers relating to the Conference (Cd. 1299), App. 4, p. 28, pp. 54–5.
49. B. Dugdale, vol. 1, p. 365
50. P.R.O. Cab. 38/1/13
51. Hansard, 4th ser., vol. 118, 5 March 1903, col. 1579
52. Ibid.
53. Ibid.
54. B.M. Add. Mss. 49691, Salisbury to Balfour, 19 April 1900
55. F. A. Johnson, p. 56. Quotation from a letter from Lord Hankey of 22 Jan. 1952
56. Hansard, 4th ser., vol. 118, 5 March 1903, col. 1582
57. Ibid., col. 1584
58. India Office Library, Mss. Eur. 111, 162, Godley to Curzon, 13 March 1903
59. Hansard, 4th ser., vol. 118, 5 March 1903, col. 1584
60. Ibid., cols. 1585–6

Chapter Three

1. F. A. Johnson, p. 51
2. P. Magnus, *King Edward VII*, pp. 283–4
3. D. C. Gordon, pp. 176–7
4. Kenneth Young, *Arthur James Balfour*, pp. 224–5
5. P.R.O. Cab. 37/69/33
6. P.R.O. Cab. 6/1/34D
7. P.R.O. Cab. 4/1/11B
8. P.R.O. Cab. 3/1/18A
9. F. A. Johnson, pp. 58–9
10. B.M. Add. Mss. 49710, Fisher to Balfour, 19(?) Oct. 1903
11. Ibid.
12. Ibid., Fisher to Sandars, 10 Jan. 1904
13. Ibid., Fisher to Balfour, 19(?) Oct. 1903
14. F. A. Johnson, p. 62
15. B.M. Add. Mss. 49718, note on War Office Reform, 20 Dec. 1903
16. Ibid.
17. B.M. Add. Mss. 49718, 2nd note on War Office Reform, 20 Dec. 1903
18. Hansard, 4th ser., vol. 22, 16 Mar. 1894, col. 490
19. B.M. Add. Mss. 49718, Balfour to Esher, 14 Jan. 1904
20. Ibid., Esher to Balfour, 16 Jan. 1904
21. Ibid.
22. B.M. Add. Mss. 49718, *National Strategy*, Esher, 27 Mar. 1904
23. Hansard, 4th ser., vol. 139, 2 Aug. 1904, col. 602
24. B.M. Add. Mss. 49722, Fisher to Arnold-Forster, 18 Oct. 1903
25. B.M. Add. Mss. 49718, Esher to Balfour, 30 Dec. 1903
26. P.R.O. Cab. 37/69/33, 29 Feb. 1904
27. Ibid.

28. Hansard, 4th ser., vol. 139, 2 Aug. 1904, col. 602
29. P.R.O. Cab. 37/69/33
30. Hansard, 4th ser., vol. 139, 2 Aug. 1904, col. 617
31. Ibid., vol. 131, 9 March 1904, col. 624
32. Ibid., vol. 139, 2 Aug. 1904, col. 619
33. P.R.O. Cab. 37/69/33
34. K. Young, pp. 224–5
35. D. C. Gordon, p. 95
36. Ibid., p. 91
37. Ibid., pp. 133–5
38. Ibid., pp. 135–6
39. B.M. Add. Mss. 49695, Hicks Beach to Salisbury, 13 Sept. 1901
40. Ibid., 49720, note by Brodrick, Sept. 1903
41. D. C. Gordon, pp. 158–63
42. B.M. Add. Mss. 49698, Feb. 1904
43. P.R.O. Cab. 37/69/33
44. Hansard, 4th ser., vol. 139, 2 Aug. 1904, cols. 618–19
45. P.R.O. Cab. 37/69/33
46. Ibid.

Chapter Four

1. Whittingehame, Balfour Papers, Wyndham to Balfour, 7 Oct. 1899
2. Hansard, 4th ser., vol. 139, 2 Aug. 1904, col. 620
3. P.R.O. Cab. 4/1/26B
4. P.R.O. Cab. 3/1/28A
5. P.R.O. Cab. 4/1/26B
6. B. Semmel, *Imperialism and Social Reform*, pp. 216–17
7. B.M. Add. Mss. 49698, Roberts to Balfour, 9 Nov. 1905
8. Hansard, 4th ser., vol. 146, 11 May 1905, col. 73
9. Ibid., cols. 76–7
10. M. Edwardes, *High Noon of Empire*, pp. 26–7. Curzon's book was called *Russia in Central Asia in 1889*
11. P.R.O. Cab. 6/1/7D, Paper reprinted for the C.I.D. in 1903
12. B.M. Add. Mss. 49732, Curzon to Balfour, 30 May 1892
13. P.R.O. Cab. 37/70/57
14. B.M. Add. Mss. 49729, Balfour to Lansdowne, 31 Dec. 1904
15. Christ Church, Box 1, Balfour to Salisbury, 19 April 1885
16. B.M. Add. Mss. 49728, Balfour to Lansdowne, 9 Jan. 1902
17. P.R.O. Cab. 6/2/62D
18. P.R.O. Cab. 37/79/154.6 Sept. 1905
19. Hansard, 4th ser., vol. 139, 2 Aug. 1904, col. 621
20. Hansard, 4th ser., vol. 146, 11 May 1905, col. 79
21. B.M. Add. Mss. 49728, Balfour to Lansdowne
22. Ibid.
23. Hansard, 4th ser., vol. 146, 11 May 1905, cols. 81–2
24. P.R.O. Cab. 4/1/26B. C.I.D. Paper, *The Military Needs of the Empire*
25. P.R.O. Cab. 3/1/28A
26. P.R.O. Cab. 6/1/32D
27. I.O.L., Mss. Eur. F. 111, Balfour to Curzon, 3 Nov. 1904

28. Ibid., Mss. Eur. F. 111, Balfour to Curzon, 23 June 1904
29. P.R.O. Cab. 6/1/34D
30. Ibid.
31. Hansard, 4th ser., vol. 146, 11 May 1905, col. 82
32. P.R.O. Cab. 6/1/34D
33. P. Magnus, *Kitchener, Portrait of an Imperialist*, pp. 197–8
34. M. Edwardes, pp. 222–3
35. I.O.L., Mss. Eur. F. 111, Balfour to Curzon, 23 June 1904
36. Ibid.
37. B.M. Add. Mss. 49691, Balfour to Salisbury, 14 April 1898
38. Dugdale, vol. 1, p. 371
39. Hansard, 4th ser., vol. 102, 13 Feb. 1902, cols. 1295–7
40. Hansard. 4th ser., vol. 110, 7 July 1902, col. 942. Also see C. D. H. Howard, 'Splendid Isolation', *History*, 1962, pp. 40–1.
41. P.R.O. Cab. 37/67/99, 22 Dec. 1903
42. Ibid.
43. B.M. Add. Mss. 49684, Balfour to Edward VII, 28 Dec. 1903
44. P.R.O. Cab. 4/1/11B
45. B.M. Add. Mss. 49728, Balfour to Lansdowne, 31 Dec. 1903
46. B.M. Add. Mss. 49735, Austen Chamberlain to Balfour, 6 Jan. 1904
47. K. Young, p. 235
48. B.M. Add. Mss. 49735, Austen Chamberlain to Balfour, 24 Aug. 1905
49. P.R.O. Cab. 37/77/98. 27 May 1905
50. Whittingehame, Clarke to Balfour, 11 June 1905
51. B.M. Add. Mss. 49685, Balfour to Edward VII, 9 June 1905
52. Hansard, 4th ser., vol. 137, 6 July 1904, col. 37
53. Ibid., vol. 138, 21 July 1904, col. 786
54. Ibid., 28 July, col. 1479
55. Ibid., vol. 144, 4 April 1905, col. 330
56. Ibid., 11 April 1905, col. 1280
57. Johnson, p. 79
58. B.M. Add. Mss. 49697, Balfour to Milner, 23 Feb. 1905
59. B.M. Add. Mss. 49698, Balfour to Roberts, 20 Nov. 1905
60. Hansard, 4th ser., vol. 139, 2 Aug. 1904, cols. 633–4
61. M. Hankey, *Diplomacy by Conference*, p. 86
62. I.O.L., Mss. Eur. 111, 162, Godley to Curzon, 13 March 1903
63. Ibid., Mss. Eur. 111, 162, Hamilton to Curzon, 11 June 1903
64. Ibid., Mss. Eur. 11, 162, Godley to Curzon, 24 April 1903
65. Ibid., Mss. Eur. 11, 163, Brodrick to Curzon, 18 March 1904
66. B.M. Add. Mss. 49718, Esher, Note on War Office Reform, 20 Dec. 1903
67. I.O.L., Mss. Eur. 11, 162, Curzon to Godley, 1 April 1903
68. Ibid., Mss. Eur. 11, 162, Brodrick to Curzon, 15 Oct. 1903
69. Hansard, 4th ser., vol. 146, 11 May 1905, col. 63

Chapter Five

1. A. J. Marder, *From the Dreadnought to Scapa Flow*, vol. 1, pp. 3–13
2. R. Ensor, *England 1870–1914*, p. 522
3. Hansard, 4th ser., vol. 156, 9 May 1906, col. 1410
4. Ibid., vol. 162, 2 Aug. 1906, cols. 1395–1397

5. B.M. Add. Mss. 49719, Notes of a conversation between Esher and Sandars, 15 March 1909

6. Ibid., 49697, Milner to Balfour, 6 April 1909

7. Ibid., 49694, Balfour to Winston Churchill, 9 Jan. 1912

8. Ibid., 49832, Balfour to Alice Balfour, 10 Nov. 1914

9. K. Young, p. 361

10. Hansard, 4th ser., vol. 156, 9 May 1906, col. 1410

11. F. A. Johnson, pp. 79–80

12. B.M. Add. Mss. 49719, Balfour to Esher, 6 Oct. 1906

13. Ibid., Balfour to Esher, 25 May 1908

14. Hansard, 4th ser., vol. 160, 12 July 1906, col. 1158

15. Ibid., vol. 162, 2 Aug. 1906, cols. 1389–94

16. K. Young, p. 269

17. Ibid., p. 270

18. Hansard, 5th ser., vol. 62, 19 May 1914, col. 1766

19. Ibid., 5th ser., vol. 8, 29 July 1909, col. 1391

20. B.M. Add. Mss. 49719, Memorandum by Sandars of a conversation with Esher, 9 Nov. 1911

21. Ibid., Balfour to Esher, 12 Jan. 1912

22. Hansard, 4th ser., vol. 162, 2 Aug. 1906, cols. 1392–3

23. Ibid.

24. Ibid., vol. 169, 15 Feb. 1907, cols. 464–5

25. Ibid., cols. 467–9

26. Minutes of Proceedings of the Colonial Conference, 1907 (Cd. 3523)

27. F. A. Johnson, pp. 87–8

28. Hansard, 5th ser., vol. 8, 29 July 1909, cols. 1396–7

29. D. C. Gordon, pp. 238–43

30. Hansard, 5th ser., vol. 41, 22 July 1912, col. 860

31. F. A. Johnson, pp. 150–1, and A. J. P. Taylor, *English History 1914–1945*, p. 82

32. F. A. Johnson, p. 150

33. Ibid., p. 213, and *Documents on British Foreign Policy 1919–39*. Ed. R. Butler and J. P. T. Bury, 1st ser., vol. 14

34. B.M. Add. Mss. 49719, Balfour to Esher, 4 Feb. 1910

35. B. Dugdale, vol. 2, pp. 234–5, and 243–4, and Butler and Bury, *Documents*, 1st ser., vol. 14

36. Butler and Bury, pp. 643–5

37. Ibid.

38. B.M. Add. Mss. 49697, R. Borden to Professor Stewart, 9 Jan. 1929

39. Hansard, 5th ser., vol. 56, 13 March 1924, col. 766

40. Ibid., col. 767

41. Ibid., vol. 58, 24 July 1924, col. 1001

42. Ibid., 5th ser., vol. 62, 24 Nov. 1925, col. 847

43. B.M. Add. Mss. 49694, Balfour to Baldwin, 12 March 1925

44. Hansard, 5th ser., vol. 61, 16 June 1926, col. 437

45. P.R.O. Cab. 32/46, 2 Oct. 1926. See Appendix 1

46. B.M. Add. Mss. 49694, Baldwin to Balfour, 25 May 1929

Chapter Six

1. K. Young, *Arthur James Balfour*, p. 77

2. B.M. Add. Mss. 49688, Balfour to Salisbury, 23 Dec. 1885

3. Birmingham, JC 5/5/1, Balfour to Joseph Chamberlain, 7 July 1892
4. A. J. Balfour, *Autobiography*, p. 221
5. J. L. Garvin, *Life of Joseph Chamberlain*, vol. 3, p. 5
6. Ibid., p. 11
7. J. Amery, *Life of Joseph Chamberlain*, vol. 4, p. 463
8. Birmingham, JC 5/5/70, Joseph Chamberlain to Balfour, 3 Feb. 1898
9. Whittingehame, Joseph Chamberlain to Balfour, 23 Aug. 1898
10. B.M. Add. Mss. 49691, Balfour to Salisbury, 14 April 1898
11. Ibid., Salisbury to Balfour, 9 April 1898
12. Ibid., Balfour to Salisbury, 14 April 1898
13. Birmingham, JC 5/5/34 and JC 5/5/35, Balfour to Joseph Chamberlain, 22 and 23 Aug. 1898
14. Birmingham, Joseph Chamberlain to Balfour, 27 Dec. 1899
15. J. Amery, p. 256
16. K. Young, pp. 461–2
17. A. M. Gollin, *Balfour's Burden*, pp. 243–4
18. B.M. Add. Mss. 49773, extract from a private letter, 6 June 1898
19. Ibid., Balfour to Harry White, 12 Dec. 1900
20. Ibid., Balfour to Choate, 1 June 1905
21. Midleton, *Records and Reaction*, p. 111
22. *The African Review*, 15 March 1902
23. B. Dugdale, vol. 1, pp. 336–7
24. Birmingham, JC 11/30 Joseph Chamberlain to Salisbury, 11 July 1902
25. J. Amery, vol. 4, p. 453
26. B. Semmel, pp. 87–90
27. P. Fraser, *Joseph Chamberlain*, pp. 230–1
28. A. M. Gollin, *Balfour's Burden*, p. 24
29. *The Times*, 12 May 1902
30. Ibid., 17 May 1902
31. P.R.O. Cab. 37/62/120
32. R. H. Wilde, 'Canada, the 1902 Conference and Chamberlain's Preference Campaign', Paper presented to the Institute of Commonwealth Studies, London, 28 Oct. 1965
33. B. Dugdale, vol. 1, pp. 339–40
34. J. Amery, vol. 4, pp. 527–8
35. Ibid., p. 475
36. Birmingham, JC 11/5/12, Balfour to Joseph Chamberlain, 4 Oct. 1902
37. P. Fraser, p. 235
38. *The Times*, 19 Nov. 1903
39. B. Dugdale, vol. 1, p. 345
40. Ibid., pp. 342–6
41. J. Amery, p. 436

Chapter Seven

1. *The Times*, 16 May 1903
2. A. M. Gollin, *Balfour's Burden*, p. 38
3. R. Jenkins, *Asquith*, p. 137
4. Hansard, 4th ser., vol. 122, 22 May 1903, col. 1553
5. B.M. Add. Mss. 49694, Balfour to Winston Churchill, 26 May 1903

6. Hansard, vol. 123, 28 May 1903, cols. 156–185
7. A. M. Gollin, pp. 63–4
8. B. Dugdale, vol. 1, p. 349, letter to Devonshire, 27 Aug. 1903
9. B.M. Add. Mss. 49759, Balfour to Hugh Cecil, 16 July 1903
10. B. Semmel, pp. 100–9
11. P.R.O. Cab. 37/65/47, 1 Aug. 1903
12. Ibid.
13. Ibid.
14. Ibid.
15. B. Dugdale, vol. 1, p. 351
16. Ibid., p. 352
17. P.R.O. Cab. 37/65/54 for Balfour of Burleigh's account, and Lord George Hamilton, *Parliamentary Reminiscences and Reflections*, p. 321. Treasury memorandum, P.R.O. Cab. 37/65/45
18. *The Times*, 18 Sept. 1903. Letter of resignation
19. P.R.O. Cab. 37/66/60
20. A. M. Gollin, chapter 9
21. Birmingham, AC 17/60, Arnold Forster to Austen Chamberlain, 21 Sept. 1903
22. B.M. Add. Mss. 49735, Austen Chamberlain to Balfour, 24 Aug. 1904
23. Whittingehame, Mary Chamberlain to Alice Balfour, 11 Oct. 1903
24. *The Times*, 2 Oct. 1903
25. Ibid., 7 Oct. 1903
26. Ibid., 2 and 7 Oct. 1903
27. P.R.O. Cab. 37/66/64
28. B.M. Add. Mss. 49737, Robert Cecil to Sandars, 5 Nov. 1903
29. Ibid., 49721, Brodrick to Balfour, 1 Jan. 1904
30. A. M. Gollin, *Balfour's Burden*, pp. 226–7
31. B.M. Add. Mss. 41214, Campbell-Bannerman to John Ellis, 10 Nov. 1903
32. Hansard, 4th ser., vol. 131, 9 March 1904, cols. 674–5, 685
33. Ibid., vol. 132, cols. 283–7
34. B.M. Add. Mss. 49735, Austen Chamberlain to Balfour, 24 Aug. 1904
35. Ibid.
36. B.M. Add. Mss. 49761, Sandars to Balfour, 14 (?) Sept. 1904
37. Ibid., 49735, Balfour to Austen Chamberlain, 10 Sept. 1904
38. Ibid.
39. Ibid., Austen Chamberlain to Balfour, 12 Sept. 1904
40. Ibid., Balfour to Austen Chamberlain, 22 Sept. 1904
41. Ibid., 49737, Robert Cecil to Balfour, 7 Dec. 1904
42. P. Fraser, *Joseph Chamberlain*, p. 257

Chapter Eight

1. B. Semmel, pp. 110–11
2. B.M. Add. Mss. 49831, Balfour to Gerald Balfour, 10 Nov. 1905
3. Ibid. 49737, Robert Cecil to Balfour, 25 Jan. 1906
4. P. Fraser, p. 258
5. B.M. Add. Mss. 49735, Balfour to Austen Chamberlain, 10 Sept. 1904
6. Hansard, 4th ser., vol. 125, 16 July 1903, col. 864
7. Ibid., 49774, Joseph Chamberlain to Balfour, 24 Feb. 1905
8. B.M. Add. Mss. 49697, Northcote to Balfour, 21 Aug. 1904

9. Ibid., 22 Nov. 1904
10. Bodleian, Monk Bretton Papers, Robert Roberts to Monk Bretton, 7 April 1904
11. S. R. Mehrotra, *Imperial Federation and India, 1868–1917*, p. 33, University of London Institute of Commonwealth Studies, Reprint series no. 13
12. Hansard, 4th ser., vol. 124, 24 June 1903, col. 397
13. B.M. Add. Mss. 49697, Balfour to Northcote, 1 Jan. 1905
14. Ibid., 49774, Balfour to Joseph Chamberlain, 18 Feb. 1905
15. Hansard, 4th ser., vol. 141, 14 Feb. 1905, cols. 156–66
16. Ibid., vol. 143, 22 March 1905, col. 888
17. Ibid., 29 March 1905, col. 1542
18. Ibid., vol. 146, 22 May 1905, cols. 1067–70
19. P. Fraser, pp. 263–4
20. Birmingham, AC 17/60, Austen to Joseph Chamberlain, 26 May 1905
21. B.M. Add. Mss. 49775, Lyttelton to Balfour, 27 May 1905
22. Ibid., 49735, Austen Chamberlain to Balfour, 27 May 1905
23. Ibid., 49775, Balfour to Lyttelton, 27 May 1905
24. Ibid., Lyttelton to Austen Chamberlain, 28 May 1905
25. Ibid., 49735, Austen Chamberlain to Balfour, 24 Aug. 1905
26. P. Fraser, pp. 271–2
27. Birmingham, AC 17/60, Balfour to Austen Chamberlain, 3 Nov. 1905
28. B.M. Add. Mss. 49697, Northcote to Balfour, 5 Dec. 1905
29. Birmingham, AC 17/60, Lady Edward Cecil to Lord Hugh Cecil, 30 March 1905
30. B.M. Add. Mss. 49737, Balfour to Robert Cecil, 8 Jan. 1906
31. Ibid., Robert Cecil to Balfour, 10 Jan. 1906
32. P. Fraser, p. 273
33. B.M. Add. Mss. 49697, Balfour to Northcote, 24 Jan. 1906
34. Ibid., 49685, Balfour to Knollys, 17 Jan. 1906
35. Ibid., 49729, Lansdowne to Balfour, 20 Jan. 1906
36. Whittingehame, Mary Chamberlain to Alice Balfour, 14 Jan. 1906
37. B.M. Add. Mss. 49764, Sandars to Balfour, 29 Jan. 1906
38. Whittingehame, Betty Balfour to Alice Balfour, 4 Feb. 1906
39. P. Fraser, p. 275
40. *The Times*, 15 Feb. 1906
41. Ibid.
42. B. Dugdale, vol. 2, p. 33
43. Birmingham, AC 17/60, Balfour to Austen Chamberlain, 23 Oct. 1907
44. B.M. Add. Mss. 49765, Sandars to W. Short, 4 March 1907

Chapter Nine

1. A. J. P. Taylor, *English History 1914–45*, p. 68
2. B.M. Add. Mss. 49765, Sandars to Balfour, 22 Jan. 1907
3. Ibid., 49779, W. A. S. Hewins to Balfour, 11 Feb. 1907
4. Hansard, 4th ser., vol. 169, 20 Feb. 1907, cols. 865–73
5. Ibid., cols. 872–4
6. Ibid., vol. 178, 15 July 1907, col. 453
7. B. Dugdale, vol. 2, p. 35

8. P. Fraser, p. 285
9. Colin Cross, *Philip Snowden*, p. 85
10. Philip Snowden, *The Chamberlain Bubble*, a tract published by the Independent Labour Party, 1903
11. B.M. Add. Mss. 49736, Austen Chamberlain to Balfour, 24 Oct. 1907, and Dugdale, vol. 2, p. 34
12. B. Dugdale, vol. 2, p. 35
13. Ibid., pp. 35–6
14. A. M. Gollin, *The Observer and J. L. Garvin*, p. 95
15. B.M. Add. Mss. 49832, Sandars to Alice Balfour, 20 March 1908
16. A. M. Gollin, *The Observer and J. L. Garvin*, p. 95
17. Hansard, 5th ser., vol. 1, 19 Feb. 1909, col. 390
18. A. M. Gollin, *The Observer and J. L. Garvin*, p. 96
19. Ibid., p. 96, and *Daily News*, 14 Jan. 1909
20. Ibid., pp. 97 and 100
21. P. Fraser, p. 292
22. B.M. Add. Mss. 49769, Balfour to Milner, 20 April 1910
23. P. Fraser, p. 299
24. A. M. Gollin, *The Observer and J. L. Garvin*, p. 287
25. Hansard, 5th ser., vol. 21, 6 Feb. 1911, col. 57
26. Ibid., 9 Feb. 1911, col. 480
27. K. Young, *Arthur James Balfour*, p. 313
28. B.M. Add. Mss. 49832, W. S. Short to Alice Balfour, 13 Nov. 1911
29. A. J. P. Taylor, p. 197
30. E. A. Walker, *The British Empire, Its Structure and Spirit 1497–1953*, p. 199
31. A. J. P. Taylor, pp. 339–40

Chapter Ten

1. F. A. van Jaarsveld, *The Awakening of Afrikaner Nationalism*, pp. 13–14
2. A. J. Balfour, *Chapters of Autobiography*, pp. 113–14
3. Birmingham, JC 11/30/152, Salisbury to Joseph Chamberlain, 14 Jan. 1899, and JC 11/30/144, Joseph Chamberlain to Salisbury, 15 Jan. 1899
4. Hansard, 4th ser., vol. 18, 9 Nov. 1893, col. 592–3
5. J. S. Marais, *The Fall of Kruger's Republic*, pp. 70–2
6. Blanche Dugdale, *Arthur James Balfour*, vol. 1, p. 224
7. Ibid., p. 225
8. P. Fraser, *Joseph Chamberlain*, pp. 171–3
9. J. S. Marais, chapter 4
10. P. Fraser, p. 172; Marais, pp. 132–5
11. Birmingham, JC 5/5/65, Joseph Chamberlain to Balfour, 2 Feb. 1896
12. Ibid.
13. Ibid., Joseph Chamberlain to Balfour, 2 Feb. 1896
14. J. S. Marais, p. 73
15. Christ Church, Box 3, Wallet 1, Balfour to Salisbury, 10 April 1897
16. Ibid.
17. J. S. Marais, pp. 79–87
18. Ibid., pp. 204–10
19. B.M. Add. Mss. 49691, Balfour to Salisbury, 14 April 1898

20. Birmingham, JC 5/5/32, Balfour to Joseph Chamberlain, 18 Aug. 1898

21. Birmingham, JC 5/5/34 and JC 5/5/35, Balfour to Joseph Chamberlain, 22 and 23 Aug. 1898

22. J. S. Marais, p. 215 and J. A. S. Grenville, *Lord Salisbury and Foreign Policy*, pp. 194–8

23. P.R.O. Cab. 37/48/71

24. P. Fraser, pp. 176–8

25. P.R.O. Cab. 37/49/29

26. Ibid.

27. Ibid. On 29 April 1899, Chamberlain had put his proposed draft dispatch before the Cabinet. The dispatch emphasised that *uitlander* grievances could not be allowed to continue. The Colonial Secretary also claimed that he meant the draft dispatch to be a protest not a threat, and an appeal to public opinion (P.R.O. Cab. 47/49/28). On 6 May, 1899, the revised dispatch, although re-emphasising Britain's paramountcy in the Transvaal and stressing that the British government could not permanently ignore the 'arbitrary treatment' of its fellow-countrymen, stated that Britain did not want to interfere in the internal affairs of the Transvaal. (P.R.O. Cab. 37/49/33).

28. Birmingham, JC 5/5/39, Balfour to Joseph Chamberlain, 6 May 1899

29. Ibid.

30. C[ambridge] H[istory] of the B[ritish] E[mpire], vol. 3, p. 363

31. P. Fraser, pp. 181–2

32. Ibid., p. 185

33. Whittinghame, Violet Cecil to Balfour, 26 July 1899

34. Ibid.

35. Ibid.

36. B.M. Add. Mss. 49717, Rhodes to Rothschild, 8 Sept. 1899

37. Whittingehame, Memorandum from Lansdowne to Salisbury, 4 Oct. 1899

38. Birmingham, JC 5/15/83, Joseph Chamberlain to Balfour, 3 Oct. 1899

39. Whittingehame, Wyndham to Balfour, 7 Oct. 1899

40. Birmingham, JC 5/5/40, Balfour to Joseph Chamberlain, 2 Oct. 1899

41. K. Young, *Arthur James Balfour*, p. 185

42. Hansard, 4th ser., vol. 97, 19 Oct. 1899, cols. 357–61

43. Bodleian, Bryce Papers, Balfour to Bryce, 2 Oct. 1899

Chapter Eleven

1. K. Young, p. 186

2. G. H. L. Le May, *British Supremacy in South Africa, 1899–1907*, chapter 2

3. B.M. Add. Mss. 49691, Balfour to Salisbury, 28 Nov. 1899

4. B. Dugdale, *Arthur James Balfour*, vol. 1, p. 295

5. Ibid., p. 300

6. K. Young, p. 188

7. Christ Church, Box 3, Wallet 1, Balfour to Salisbury, 19 Dec. 1899

8. *The Times*, 9 Jan. 1900

9. Birmingham, JC 5/15/83, Joseph Chamberlain to Balfour, 3 Oct. 1899

10. *The Times*, 9 Jan. 1900

11. *The Times*, 10 Jan. 1900

12. *The Times*, 11 Jan. 1900
13. I.O.L., Mss. Eur. F. 111, 159, Hamilton to Curzon, 1 Feb. 1900
14. B.M. Add. Mss. 49832, Balfour to Sidgwick, 15 Jan. 1900
15. B. Dugdale, vol. 1, pp. 306–7
16. B.M. Add. Mss. 49685, Balfour to Knollys, 5 June 1905
17. Ibid., 49684, Knollys to Sandars, 7 Nov. 1904
18. Birmingham, JC 11/30/144, Joseph Chamberlain to Salisbury, 15 Jan. 1899
19. Whittingehame, Joseph Chamberlain to Balfour, 11 April 1900
20. Ibid., Violet Cecil to Balfour, 9 May 1900
21. G. H. L. Le May, p. 96
22. A. M. Gollin, *Proconsul in Politics*, p. 36
23. Whittingehame, Joseph Chamberlain to Balfour, 21 Oct. 1900
24. Ibid., Salisbury to Balfour, 9 Oct. 1900
25. Hansard, 4th ser., vol. 88, 6 Dec. 1900, cols. 128–9
26. Ibid., 10 Dec. 1900, cols. 164–7
27. Ibid., 6 Dec. 1900, cols. 125–7
28. G. H. L. Le May, p. 90
29. Hansard, 4th ser., vol. 101, 16 Jan. 1902, col. 115
30. Ibid., vol. 99, 15 Aug. 1901, col. 1043
31. B.M. Add. Mss. 49774, Memorandum by Chamberlain, 6 Nov. 1902
32. G. H. L. Le May, p. 107
33. Hansard, 4th ser., vol. 99, 15 Aug. 1901, col. 1050
34. Ibid., vol. 101, 16 Jan. 1902, col. 117
35. Ibid., vol. 88, 6 Dec. 1900, col. 136
36. Ibid., vol. 89, 14 Feb. 1901, cols. 105–7
37. Ibid.
38. G. H. L. Le May, p. 97
39. Hansard, 4th ser., vol. 89, 14 Feb. 1901, cols. 196–7
40. P.R.O. Cab. 37/52/3
41. Ibid.
42. Hansard, 4th ser., vol. 88, 6 Dec. 1900, cols. 136–7
43. Ibid., vol. 86, 25 July 1900, col. 1241
44. Ibid., vol. 101, 16 Jan. 1902, cols. 114–15
45. Whittingehame, Joseph Chamberlain to Balfour, 21 Oct. 1900
46. Christ Church, Box 3, Wallet 2, Balfour to Salisbury, 5 Jan. 1901
47. Hansard, 4th ser., vol. 89, 25 Feb. 1901, col. 1099
48. Ibid., vol. 101, 21 Jan. 1902, cols. 549–50
49. Ibid., vol. 108, 2 June 1902, cols. 1104–6

Chapter Twelve

1. Christ Church, Box 3, Wallet 2, Balfour to Salisbury, 5 Jan. 1901
2. Hansard, 4th ser., vol. 98, 1 Aug. 1901, col. 838
3. Ibid., vol. 105, 10 April 1902, col. 1456
4. B.M. Add. Mss. 49683, Balfour to Edward VII, 23 Oct. 1903
5. B.M. Add. Mss. 49720, Cabinet paper, September 1903
6. Hansard, 4th ser., vol. 148, 26 June 1905, cols. 191–202
7. Ibid., vol. 147, 20 June 1905, col. 1110
8. Ibid., vol. 108, 5 June 1902, cols. 1587–9
9. C.H.B.E., vol. 3, p. 366, and J. Schull, *Laurier*, p. 383

10. B.M. Add. Mss. 49727, copy of a speech by Lansdowne, 13 Feb. 1902
11. A. M. Gollin, *Proconsul in Politics*, pp. 46–7
12. B.M. Add. Mss. 49774, Balfour to Joseph Chamberlain, 3 Sept. 1902
13. Ibid., Joseph Chamberlain to Balfour, 9 Sept. 1902
14. Ibid., Balfour to Joseph Chamberlain, 3 Sept. 1902
15. Ibid., Joseph Chamberlain to Balfour, 9 Sept. 1902
16. Ibid., 49684, Roberts to Knollys, 30 Oct. 1904
17. Ibid., 49685, Knollys to Balfour, 24 Jan. 1905
18. Ibid., 49775, Selborne to Lyttelton, 24 May 1905
19. Hansard, 4th ser., vol. 139, 2 Aug. 1904, cols. 524–6
20. Ibid., vol. 142, 6 March 1905, cols. 498–9
21. Birmingham, JC 11/30/209, copy of speech sent to Lord Salisbury, 25 May 1901
22. Birmingham, JC 11/7/3, Joseph Chamberlain to Balfour of Burleigh, 1902
23. B.M. Ad. Mss. 49697, Milner to Balfour, 2 Oct. 1904
24. Ibid., Balfour to Milner, 1904
25. Ibid., Milner to Balfour, 19 Dec. 1904
26. Ibid., 49775, Lyttelton to Balfour, 20 Jan. 1905
27. E. A. Walker, *A History of Southern Africa*, p. 515
28. B.M. Add. Mss. 49697, Balfour to Milner, 23 Feb. 1905
29. Hansard, 4th ser., vol. 142, 6 March 1905, cols. 495–502
30. Ibid., cols. 499–502
31. Whittingehame, Maud Selborne to Alice Balfour, 10 Aug. 1906
32. Hansard, 4th ser., vol. 98, 31 July 1901, col. 700
33. Ibid., vol. 99, 15 Aug. 1901, cols. 1043–5
34. Ibid., cols. 1049–50
35. Ibid., vol. 118, 19 Feb. 1903, col. 481
36. Ibid., vol. 99, 15 Aug. 1901, cols. 1043–5
37. Ibid., vol. 132, 21 March 1904, col. 354
38. Dugdale, vol. 1, p. 326
39. Hansard, 4th ser., vol. 132, 21 March 1904, col. 354
40. Ibid., cols. 343–52
41. Ibid., col. 353
42. E. A. Walker, *A History of Southern Africa*, pp. 509 and 511
43. B.M. Add. Mss. 49684, Roberts to Knollys, 30 Oct. 1904
44. Whittingehame, Maud Selborne to Alice Balfour, 10 Aug. 1906
45. Hansard, 4th ser., vol. 132, 21 March 1904, col. 353
46. G. H. L. Le May, p. 158
47. A. H. Gollin, *Proconsul in Politics*, p. 61
48. E. A. Walker, *A History of Southern Africa*, p. 512
49. Hansard, 4th ser., vol. 134, 5 May 1904, col. 549
50. Ibid., vol. 132, 21 March 1904, cols. 345–51
51. Ibid., cols. 353–6
52. Ibid.
53. B.M. Add. Mss. 49692, Balfour to Northcote, 15 June 1904
54. Ibid., 49697, Balfour to Milner, 24 Nov. 1904
55. Ibid.
56. Ibid., 49708, Balfour to Selborne, 21 Sept. 1905
57. A. M. Gollin, *Proconsul in Politics*, p. 79
58. B.M. Add. Mss. 49775, Balfour to Lyttelton, 20 Oct. 1905
59. R. Jenkins, *Asquith*, pp. 162–3

Chapter Thirteen

1. G. H. L. Le May, pp. 184–5, and J. C. Smuts, *Jan Christian Smuts*, pp. 97–8
2. E. A. Walker, *A History of Southern Africa*, pp. 516–17
3. Hansard, 4th ser., vol. 153, 14 March 1906, col. 1286
4. Ibid., cols. 1286–7
5. Ibid., col. 1281
6. Ibid., vol. 154, 21 March 1906, cols. 447–8
7. Ibid., cols. 449–50
8. Ibid., cols. 499–505
9. Ibid., vol. 170, 11 March 1907, col. 1367
10. Ibid., vol. 186, 23 March 1908, cols. 1138–44
11. E. A. Walker, *A History of Southern Africa*, p. 518
12. G. H. L. Le May, pp. 198–202
13. Ibid., pp. 202–4
14. Hansard, 4th ser., vol. 162, 31 July 1906, cols. 798–800
15. Ibid., col. 800
16. Ibid., cols. 801–4
17. G. H. L. Le May, p. 211
18. F. V. Engelenburg, *General Louis Botha*, p. 148
19. Minutes of Proceedings of Colonial Conference, Aug. 1907, Cd. 3523
20. F. V. Engelenburg, p. 142
21. G. H. L. Le May, p. 214
22. B.M. Add. Mss. 49697, Milner to Balfour, 19 Aug. 1907
23. W. K. Hancock, *Smuts: The Sanguine Years, 1870–1919*, p. 250
24. Ibid., p. 252
25. B.M. Add. Mss. 49697, Balfour to Fitzpatrick, 12 Nov. 1908
26. Hansard, 5th ser., vol. 1, 16 Feb. 1909, cols. 25–6
27. Ibid., vol. 9, 16 Aug. 1909, cols. 1007–8
28. Ibid., col. 1007
29. Ibid., cols. 1001–2
30. Ibid., cols. 1002–4
31. Ibid., col. 1008
32. Ibid., col. 1009
33. B.M. Add. Mss. 49697, Botha to Balfour, 23 Aug. 1909
34. Ibid., Balfour to Botha, 3 Sept. 1909
35. W. K. Hancock, *Smuts: The Sanguine Years*, pp. 242–3
36. Ibid., p. 272
37. E. A. Walker, *A History of Southern Africa*, p. 591
38. B. Dugdale, vol. 2, p. 282
39. A. J. P. Taylor, p. 82
40. G. H. L. Le May, p. 215

Chapter Fourteen

1. F. Madden, *Imperial Constitutional Documents, 1765–1952*, p. 6
2. S. Gopal, *British Policy in India, 1858–1905*, pp. 1–2
3. R. Robinson and J. Gallagher, *Africa and the Victorians*, p. 11

4. *Transactions of the Royal Historical Society*, Feb. 1962, I. M. Cumpston, 'The Discussions of Imperial Problems in the British Parliament, 1880–85', pp. 36–7

5. S. Gopal, pp. 145–7
6. A. J. Balfour, *Chapters of Autobiography*, pp. 93–4
7. Hansard, 4th ser., vol. 13, 8 June 1893, col. 536
8. Ibid., vol. 86, 26 July 1900, cols. 1428–30
9. Ibid., cols. 1428–31
10. M. Edwardes, *High Noon of Empire*, p. 92
11. Hansard, 4th ser., vol. 86, 26 July 1900, cols. 1431–2
12. Ibid., cols. 1432–3
13. Ibid., col. 1434
14. Lord Midleton (Brodrick), *Records and Reactions*, p. 109
15. I.O.L., Mss. Eur. F 111, 159, Curzon to Hamilton, 15 Aug. 1900
16. B.M. Add. Mss. 49732, Curzon to Balfour, 31 March 1901
17. Ibid., Curzon to Balfour, 16 July 1902
18. Ibid., Curzon to Balfour, 31 March 1901
19. S. R. Mehrotra, *India and the Commonwealth, 1885–1929*, p. 31
20. S. Gopal, pp. 261–3
21. B.M. Add. Mss. 49732, Curzon to Balfour, 31 March 1901
22. Ibid.
23. Ibid.
24. I.O.L., Mss. Eur. F 111, 161, Curzon to Balfour, 16 July 1902
25. Ibid., Curzon to Balfour, 3 Sept. 1902
26. B.M. Add. Mss. 49732, Curzon to Balfour, 20 Nov. 1902
27. Ibid., 49683, Knollys to Sandars, 24 Nov. 1902
28. Ibid., Knollys to Sandars, 27 Nov. 1902
29. Ibid., 49732, Curzon to Balfour, 10 Dec. 1902
30. Ibid., Balfour to Curzon, 12 Dec. 1902
31. Ibid.
32. Ibid., Curzon to Balfour, 29 Dec. 1902
33. Ibid., 49683, Edward VII to Balfour, 14 Dec. 1902
34. Ibid., Knollys to Sandars, 6 Jan. 1903
35. Ibid., 39732, Balfour to Curzon, 31 Jan. 1903
36. Ibid., Curzon to Balfour, 5 Feb. 1903
37. Ibid., Balfour to Curzon, March 1903
38. Ibid., 49683, Curzon to Edward VII, 29 April 1903
39. Ibid., Balfour to Knollys, 29 May 1903
40. Ibid., 49732, Curzon to Balfour, 30 April 1903
41. I.O.L., Mss. Eur. F 111, Balfour to Curzon, 10 June 1903
42. B.M. Add. Mss. 49732, Balfour to Curzon, 18 June 1903
43. Ibid., Curzon to Balfour, 8 July 1903
44. I.O.L., Mss. Eur. F 111, 233, Balfour to Curzon, 28 May 1904
45. B.M. Add. Mss. 49684, Ampthill to Edward VII, 7 Nov. 1904

Chapter Fifteen

1. M. Edwardes, p. 113
2. S. Gopal, pp. 242–6

3. B.M. Add. Mss. 49733, Curzon to Balfour, 23 Aug. 1905
4. B.M. Add. Mss. 49720, Balfour to Brodrick, 28 Oct. 1903
5. Ibid.
6. Ibid., Brodrick to Curzon, 29 Oct. 1903
7. M. Edwardes, pp. 217–18
8. Hansard, 4th ser., vol. 133, 13 April 1904, col. 126
9. Ibid., col. 127
10. Ibid., col. 131
11. P.R.O. Cab. 37/71/100
12. P.R.O. Cab. 37/73/149
13. B.M. Add. Mss. 49684, Ampthill to Edward VII, 7 Nov. 1904
14. Ibid., Balfour to Knollys, 6 Oct. 1904
15. P.R.O. Cab. 37/79/154. Memorandum. A Peerage for Lord Curzon, 6 Sept. 1905
16. P. Magnus, *Kitchener*, p. 144
17. B.M. Add. Mss. 49732, Curzon to Balfour, 5 Feb. 1903
18. Midleton, p. 201
19. Ibid., p. 202
20. Ibid., p. 203
21. I.O.L., Mss. Eur. F 111, Balfour to Curzon, 3 Nov. 1904
22. Midleton, p. 204
23. I.O.L., Mss. Eur. F 111, Balfour to Curzon, 1 Jan. 1905
24. P.R.O. Cab. 3/1/28A, 18 Dec. 1904
25. P. Magnus, *Kitchener*, p. 211
26. B.M. Add. Mss. 49733, Curzon to Balfour, 30 March 1905
27. Midleton, p. 206, and Cd. 2572
28. B.M. Add. Mss. 49733, Curzon to Balfour, 18 May 1905
29. Ibid., Balfour to Curzon, 9 June 1905
30. Midleton, pp. 205–6
31. B.M. Add. Mss. 49684, Balfour to Edward VIII, 19 or 20 July 1905
32. Ibid., Curzon to Edward VII, 6 July 1905
33. Ibid., 49733, Curzon to Balfour, 19 July 1905
34. Ibid.
35. Ibid.
36. Ibid., 49684, Curzon to Edward VII, 6 July 1905
37. Ibid., 49733, Curzon to Balfour, 19 July 1905
38. M. Edwardes, p. 236
39. Midleton, p. 207
40. Whittingehame, Balfour Papers, Lord Salisbury to Balfour, 8 Aug. 1905
41. B.M. Add. Mss. 49685, Knollys to Balfour, 10 Aug. 1905
42. Ibid., 49733, Balfour to Curzon, 23 Aug. 1905
43. I.O.L. Mss. Eur. 111. 162, Curzon to Godley, 1 April 1903
44. B.M. Add. Mss. 49685, Knollys to Balfour, 1 Sept. 1905
45. Ibid., Knollys to Sandars, 4 Sept. 1905
46. P.R.O. Cab. 37/79/154
47. Ibid.
48. Midleton, p. 198
49. P.R.O. Cab. 37/79/154
50. Ibid.
51. B.M. Add. Mss. 49685, Balfour to Knollys, 7 Oct. 1905
52. Midleton, p. 204

Chapter Sixteen

1. I.O.L., Eur. Mss. F 111/159/72, Curzon to Hamilton, 18 Nov. 1900
2. S. R. Mehrotra, pp. 35-7
3. Ibid.
4. *The Times*, 18 May 1906
5. Ibid.
6. Ibid.
7. S. R. Mehrotra, pp. 43-5
8. Ibid., pp. 48-9
9. Hansard, 5th ser., vol. 3, 1 April 1909, cols. 552-3
10. Ibid., cols. 555-6
11. Ibid., col. 557
12. Ibid., vol. 14, 21 Feb. 1910, cols. 42-3
13. S. R. Mehrotra, pp. 58-9
14. P. P. 1911 (Cd. 5979)
15. S. R. Mehrotra, pp. 60-2
16. Ibid., p. 96
17. Ibid., pp. 97-9
18. P.R.O. Cab. 21/68, 7 Aug. 1917
19. Ibid.
20. Ibid.
21. Ibid.
22. Ibid.
23. Lord Ronaldshay, *The Life of Lord Curzon*, vol. 3, p. 168.
24. E. A. Walker, *The British Empire*, pp. 157-8
25. S. R. Mehrotra, pp. 110 and 113
26. Ibid., pp. 113-14
27. Hansard, 5th ser., vol. 56, 27 Feb. 1924, cols. 416-17
28. Ibid., col. 417
29. Ibid., col. 420
30. Ibid., col. 422
31. S. R. Mehrotra, pp. 137-9
32. Hansard, 5th ser., vol. 231, 7 Nov. 1929, col. 1312
33. B. Dugdale, vol. 2, p. 296
34. A. P. Thornton, *The Imperial Idea and Its Enemies*, p. 234
35. B. Dugdale, vol. 2, p. 295

Chapter Seventeen

1. Sir Llewellyn Woodward, *The Age of Reform, 1815-1870*, p. 350
2. Robinson and Gallagher, p. 14 and pp. 29-30
3. Ibid., p. 6
4. Hansard, 4th ser., vol. 64, 10 Aug. 1898, col. 22
5. Ibid., col. 826
6. B.M. Add. Mss. 49728, Balfour to Lansdowne, 21 Dec. 1903
7. Ibid., 49688, Balfour's account of a conversation with Salisbury, 8 May 1880
8. P.R.O. Cab. 37/49/29

9. Birmingham, AC 16/55/353, Balfour to Austen Chamberlain, 31 Dec. 1902
10. B.M. Add. Mss. 49746, Balfour to Eric Barrington, 28 Jan. 1896
11. Hansard, 4th ser., vol. 64, 10 Aug. 1898, col. 830
12. B.M. Add. Mss. 49706, Balfour to Goschen, 30 Aug. 1898
13. See Robinson and Gallagher, chapters 4 and 5
14. Hansard, 3rd ser., vol. 296, 26 March 1885, cols. 726–31
15. Ibid.
16. C.H.B.E., vol. 3, p. 686
17. B.M. Add. Mss. 49706, Balfour to Goschen, 5 April 1900
18. Ibid., 49739, Sanderson to Balfour, 20 Aug. 1902
19. Ibid., 49728, Lansdowne to Balfour, 7 April 1904
20. P.R.O. Cab. 4/1/20B, 26 April 1904
21. B.M. Add. Mss. 49717, Cabinet Paper, July 1904
22. Robinson and Gallagher, pp. 348–50
23. Hansard, 4th ser., vol. 41, 5 June 1896, cols. 535–6
24. Ibid., col. 537
25. Robinson and Gallagher, pp. 348–349
26. Hansard, 4th ser., vol. 67, 24 Feb. 1899, col. 518
27. Ibid., 4th ser., vol. 72, 5 June 1899, cols. 327–32
28. Ibid., cols. 343–9
29. Ibid., 8 June, cols. 681–2
30. P. Magnus, *Kitchener*, p. 130
31. Whittingehame, Alice Balfour's Diary, 6 June 1899
32. Ibid.
33. Hansard, 4th ser., vol. 25, 4 June 1894, col. 312
34. Ibid., 4th ser., vol. 90, 14 March 1901, col. 1557
35. Ibid., 4th ser., vol. 127, 10 Aug. 1903, col. 716
36. Robinson and Gallagher, pp. 6 and 17
37. Birmingham, JC 5/5/24, Balfour to Joseph Chamberlain, 27 Nov. 1895
38. Ibid.
39. P.P. 1897, C. 8655, and W. M. Macmillan, *The Road to Self-Rule*, pp. 186–7
40. C.H.B.E., vol. 3, p. 395
41. Birmingham, JC 5/5/72, Memorandum by Balfour, Feb. 1898
42. Hansard, 4th ser., vol. 67, 24 Feb. 1899, col. 517
43. Ibid., cols. 517–18
44. Ibid., col. 518
45. Ibid., 4th ser., vol. 127, 10 Aug. 1903, col. 717
46. Ibid., cols. 719–20

Chapter Eighteen

1. D. K. Fieldhouse, *The Colonial Empires*, p. 292
2. Ibid.
3. Hansard, 5th ser., vol. 2, 15 March 1909, cols. 772–3
4. Hansard, 4th ser., vol. 179, 30 July 1907, col. 840
5. Robinson and Gallagher, p. 6
6. A. P. Thornton, p. 212
7. Hansard, 5th ser., vol. 17, 13 June 1910, col. 1140
8. Ibid., cols. 1140–1
9. Ibid., col. 1142

10. Ibid., cols. 1142–3
11. Ibid., col. 1143
12. Ibid., cols. 1143–4
13. Ibid., cols. 1144–6
14. B.M. Add. Mss. 49697, memorandum by Balfour on peace proposals by Smuts, 15 Dec. 1917
15. Hansard, 5th ser., vol. 109, 8 Aug. 1918, col. 1633
16. B.M. Add. Mss. 49697, memorandum by Balfour on peace proposals by Smuts, 15 Dec. 1917
17. D. K. Fieldhouse, p. 292
18. K. Young, *Arthur James Balfour*, p. 388
19. Hansard, 5th ser., vol. 121, 17 Nov. 1919, col. 770
20. Ibid., col. 771
21. Ibid.
22. E. A. Walker, *The British Empire*, pp. 175–6
23. Hansard, 5th ser., vol. 65, 27 July 1926, col. 285
24. P. M. Holt, *A Modern History of the Sudan*, pp. 110–11
25. Hansard, 5th ser., vol. 65, 27 July 1926, col. 285
26. Ibid., cols. 284–5
27. W. M. Macmillan, p. 179
28. Ibid.
29. W. M. Macmillan, p. 180
30. E. A. Walker, *The British Empire*, p. 163
31. W. M. Macmillan, p. 182
32. Hansard, 5th ser., vol. 61, 20 May 1925, cols. 408–12
33. Ibid., col. 409
34. Ibid., cols. 410–11
35. Ibid., col. 409
36. Ibid.
37. Hugh Thomas, *The Suez Affair*, pp. 10–12

Chapter Nineteen

1. A. J. Balfour, *Cobden and the Manchester School, Nineteenth Century*, Jan. 1882
2. Ibid.
3. Ibid.
4. H. Nicolson, *King George V*, pp. 66–7
5. B.M. Add. Mss. 49683, Balfour to Edward VII, 6 Feb. 1901
6. Ibid., Knollys to Balfour, 6 Feb. 1901
7. H. Nicolson, p. 68
8. B.M. Add. Mss. 49683, Joseph Chamberlain to Edward VII, 15 April 1901
9. Ibid., 49697, Northcote to Balfour, 22 Nov. 1904
10. Ibid., 49720, report presumably the work of Brodrick, Sept. 1903
11. Hansard, 4th ser., vol. 126, 23 July 1903, col. 84
12. B.M. Add. Mss. 49728, Lansdowne to Balfour, 20 Oct. 1903
13. Ibid., 49697, Northcote to Balfour, 21 May 1905
14. Whittingehame, Robert Cecil to Hugh Cecil, 8 Oct. 1905
15. B.M. Add. Mss. 49697, Balfour to Northcote, 15 June 1904
16. Hansard, 4th ser., vol. 85, 29 June 1900, col. 86
17. B.M. Add. Mss. 49885, Lyttelton to Balfour, 30 Nov. 1904

18. Final Dispatch on the Future Organisation of Colonial Conferences, 20 April 1905 (Cd. 2785)

19. B.M. Add. Mss. 49698, proposed draft of Circular Dispatch of the Governors of the Self-Governing Colonies

20. Ibid.

21. Ibid.

22. Ibid.

23. Edith Lyttelton, *Alfred Lyttelton*, p. 310

24. B.M. Add. Mss. 49775, Balfour to Lyttelton, 13 Jan. 1905

25. Ibid.

26. Ibid.

27. Ibid., Lyttelton to Balfour, 1 Feb. 1905

28. Ibid.

29. Ibid.

30. Correspondence *re* Future Organisation of Colonial Conferences, 1905 (Cd. 2785).

31. Ibid.

32. Minutes of Proceedings of Colonial Conference, 1907 (Cd. 3523)

33. Ibid., and J. A. Cross, 'The Dominions Department of the Colonial Office; origins and early years 1905–14'. London Ph.D. (External) 1965, pp. 35–6.

34. Hansard, 4th ser., vol. 147, 7 June 1905, col. 960

35. Ibid., vol. 145, 18 April 1905, col. 457

36. *The Times*, 18 May 1906.

37. C.H.B.E., vol. 3, p. 310.

38. *The Times*, 16 Jan. 1896.

39. Whittingehame, Henry Cabot Lodge to Balfour, 1 Feb. 1896

40. Christ Church, Box 3, Wallet 1, Balfour to Salisbury, 28 Feb. 1896

41. Ibid., Aug. 1896

42. B.M. Add. Mss. 49742, Balfour to Henry White, 12 Dec. 1900

43. Hansard, 4th ser., vol. 105, 10 April 1902, col. 1456

44. C.H.B.E., vol. 3, p. 320

45. B.M. Add. Mss. 49742, Balfour to Carnegie, 28 July 1903.

46. Ibid., Balfour to Carnegie, 30 Jan. 1903

47. K. Young, *Arthur James Balfour*, p. 277

48. Ibid., pp. 279–81

49. Ibid., pp. 281–3

50. Ibid.

51. Minutes of Proceedings of the Colonial Conference of 1907 (Cd. 3523)

52. B.M. Add. Mss. 49683, Balfour to Edward VII, 15 April 1901

Chapter Twenty

1. P. Magnus, *Kitchener*, p. 288

2. W. K. Hancock, *Smuts, The Sanguine Years*, p. 427

3. *The Times*, 18 Nov. 1920

4. L. S. Amery, *My Political Life*, vol. 2, p. 110

5. P.P. 1917, Cd. 8566, Resolution 9

6. B.M. Add. Mss. 49697, Balfour to Devonshire, 8 Dec. 1916

7. Ibid. 49742, Paulus Lansing to Balfour, 25 May 1917

8. Ibid. 49775, Memorandum by Leopold Amery, 14 Nov. 1918

9. L. S. Amery, p. 177
10. Ibid.
11. Ibid., p. 178
12. R. M. Dawson, *The Development of Dominion Status*, p. 36
13. B.M. Add. Mss. 49734, Balfour to Curzon, 9 June 1919
14. R. M. Dawson, p. 230
15. Ibid., pp. 67–72
16. Ibid., p. 74
17. Ibid., p. 101
18. Hansard, 5th ser., vol. 62, 24 Nov. 1925, cols. 844–5
19. Ibid., col. 846
20. L. S. Amery, p. 380
21. Ibid., p. 381
22. Ibid.
23. *The Times*, 29 May 1926
24. R. M. Dawson, p. 104
25. L. S. Amery, p. 382
26. B.M. Add. Mss. 49694, Baldwin to Balfour, 21 Aug. 1926
27. L. S. Amery, p. 384
28. P.R.O. Cab. 32/56. See Appendix 2
29. Ibid.
30. B.M. Add. Mss. 49704. See Appendix 2
31. B.M. Add. Mss. 49775, L. S. Amery to Austen Chamberlain, 19 Oct. 1926
32. Ibid., L. S. Amery to Balfour, 1 Nov. 1926
33. Ibid., L. S. Amery to Balfour, 1 Nov. 1926 (2nd letter of 1 Nov. 1926 to Balfour)
34. P.P. 1926, Cd. 2768
35. Hansard, 5th ser., vol. 65, 27 July 1926, col. 286
36. P.P. 1926, Cd. 2768
37. L. S. Amery, p. 387
38. Ibid., p. 388
39. P.P. 1926, Cd. 2768
40. Ibid.
41. L. S. Amery, p. 390
42. Ibid., p. 392
43. P.P. 1926, Cmd. 2768
44. L. S. Amery, p. 395
45. Ibid.
46. B.M. Add. Mss. 49868, letter to Balfour, 30 Nov. 1926
47. Ibid., 49719, Balfour to Esher, 24 Nov. 1926
48. Ibid., Esher to Balfour, 23 Nov. 1926
49. Ibid., 49797, S. Bruce to Balfour, 21 Dec. 1926
50. Ibid., 49719, Balfour to Esher, 24 Nov. 1926
51. Hansard, 5th ser., vol. 65, 8 Dec. 1926, col. 1334
52. Foreword by Balfour to L. S. Amery's *The Empire in the New Era*, p. xi
53. B.M. Add. Mss. 49697, Balfour to Sir George Foster, 4 May 1927

Bibliography

I Manuscript Sources

(a) Balfour Papers
   (i) The main collection of Balfour's papers are at the British Museum. None are now reserved.
   (ii) A small collection of Balfour's papers, containing a good many documents of public interest, are deposited at The Tower, Whittingehame, Haddington, East Lothian, in the possession of the Earl of Balfour.

(b) Salisbury Papers
   The papers of the 3rd Marquis of Salisbury, deposited at Christ Church, Oxford.

(c) Chamberlain Papers
   The papers of Joseph and Austen Chamberlain, deposited at the Library, Birmingham University.

(d) India Office Library. Mainly papers relating to Lord Curzon.

(e) The Asquith, Bryce, and Monk Bretton Papers, deposited at the Bodleian Library, Oxford.

(f) The Campbell-Bannerman Papers, deposited at the British Museum.

(g) The Milner Papers, deposited at New College, Oxford.

II Parliamentary Papers and Official Documents

(a) The Public Record Office's collection of Cabinet papers and C.I.D. papers.

(b) Hansard's Parliamentary Debates.

(c) Proceedings of the Colonial and Imperial Conferences of 1887, 1897, 1902, 1907, 1911, 1917, 1921, 1923, 1926, 1930, 1932. Also proceedings of the Colonial Defence Conference of 1909, of the Imperial War Conference of 1918, and of the 1929

Conference on the Operation of Dominion Legislation and Merchant Shipping Legislation.
(d) Reports of Royal Commissions and Government Committees
  (i) The Royal West India Commission, P.P. 1897 (C 8655).
  (ii) The Royal Commission on the War in South Africa (Elgin Report), P.P. 1904 (Cd. 1789).
  (iii) Report of the War Office (Reconstitution) Committee, P.P. 1904 (Cd. 1932, 1968, 2002). Chairman Lord Esher.
  (iv) Circular re the Future Organisation of Colonial Conferences, and Correspondence, P.P. 1906 (Cd. 2785, 2975).

III JOURNALS AND NEWSPAPERS

(a) *The Times*
(b) *The Daily News*
(c) *The African Review*

IV ARTICLES IN LEARNED JOURNALS

(a) *Bulletin of the Institute of Historical Research*, vol. 27, E. Drus: 'Select Documents ... concerning Anglo-Transvaal Relations, 1896–9.'
(b) *Economic History Review*, vol. 6 (2nd ser., 1953), J. Gallagher and R. Robinson: 'The Imperialism of Free Trade.'
(c) *Transactions of the Royal Historical Society*, 10 Feb. 1962, I. M. Cumpston: 'The Discussion of Imperial Problems in the British Parliament, 1880–5.'
(d) *History*, vol. 47, 1962, C. H. D. Howard: 'Splendid Isolation.'
(e) *English Historical Review*, vol. 77, J. P. Mackintosh: 'The Role of the Committee of Imperial Defence before 1914.'

V UNPUBLISHED THESES, SCHOLARLY PAPERS, AND TRACTS

(a) Cross, J. A. 'The Dominions Department of the Colonial Office: origins and early years, 1905–14.' Ph.D. thesis, London External, 1965.

(b) Lydgate, J. E. 'Curzon, Kitchener and the problems of Indian army administration, 1899–1909.' Ph.D. thesis, London, 1965.

(c) Mehrotra, S. R. 'Imperial Federation and India, 1868–1917,' University of London Institute of Commonwealth Studies, Reprint series no. 13.

(d) Wilde, R. H. 'Canada, the 1902 Conference and Chamberlain's Preference Campaign.' Paper presented at the Institute of Commonwealth Studies, London, 28 Oct. 1965.

(e) Snowden, Philip. *The Chamberlain Bubble*. Tract published by the Independent Labour Party, 1903.

VI Books

(All books are published in London unless otherwise specified)

Amery, J. *The Life of Joseph Chamberlain*, vol. 4 (1951).

Amery, L. S. *The Empire in the New Era* (1928).

— *My Political Life*, vols. 1 and 2 (1953), vol. 3 (1955).

Balfour, A. J. (Earl of Balfour) *Essays and Addresses* (1893) (Edinburgh).

— *Economic Notes on Insular Free Trade* (1903).

— *Speeches on Fiscal Reform* (1906).

— *Arthur James Balfour as Philosopher and Thinker, a collection . . . of his non-political writings, speeches and addresses, 1879–1912*, ed. Wilfrid M. Short (1912).

— *Opinions and Argument from Speeches and Addresses* (1927).

— *Chapters of Autobiography* (incomplete), ed. Blanche Dugdale (1930).

Bennett, G. (ed.) *The Concept of Empire* (1953).

Burns, A. C. *History of the British West Indies* (1954).

Butler, R. and Bury, J. P. T. (eds.) *Documents on British Foreign Policy 1919–39*, 1st ser., vol. 14 (1966).

Cambridge History of the British Empire, vol. 3 (1959), vol. 6 (1930), vol. 7 (i) (1933), vol. 8, 2nd ed. (1963) (Cambridge).

Chamberlain, A. *Down the Years* (1935).

— *Politics from the Inside, 1906–14* (1936).

Creighton, D. G. *Dominion of the North* (2nd ed., 1958).

Cross, C. *Philip Snowden* (1966).

Dawson, R. M. *The Development of Dominion Status, 1900–36* (1937).

— *William Lyon Mackenzie King* (1959).

Dugdale, Blanche E. *Arthur James Balfour*, vols. 1 and 2 (1936).

Edwardes, M. *High Noon of Empire: Curzon* (1965).

— *The West in Asia, 1850–1914* (1967).

Engelenburg, F. V. *General Louis Botha* (1928) (Pretoria).

Ensor, R. *England 1870–1914* (1936) (Oxford).

Esher (Viscount) *Journals and Letters of Viscount Esher*, ed. M. V. Brett, 2 vols. (1934).

Faber, R. *The Vision and the Need* (1966).

Fage, J. D. *An Introduction to the History of West Africa* (1955) (Cambridge).

Fieldhouse, D. K. *The Colonial Empires* (English ed., 1966).

Fraser, P. *Joseph Chamberlain* (1966).

Gandhi, M. *An Autobiography* (1949).

Garvin, J. L. *The Life of Joseph Chamberlain*, vols. 1–3 (1932–4).

Gollin, A. M. *The Observer and J. L. Garvin* (1960).

— *Proconsul in Politics: Study of Lord Milner* (1964).

— *Balfour's Burden* (1965).

Gopal, S. *British Policy in India, 1858–1905* (1965).

Gordon, D. C. *The Dominion Partnership in Imperial Defense, 1870–1914* (1965) (Baltimore).

Graham, G. S. *The Politics of Naval Supremacy* (1965) (Cambridge).

Grenville, J. A. S. *Lord Salisbury and Foreign Policy* (1964).

Gwynn, S. and Tuckwell, G. *The Life of the Rt. Hon. Sir Charles Dilke*, vol. 2 (1917).

Hailey (Lord) *An African Survey* (2nd rev. ed., 1957).

Hall, H. D. *Mandates, Dependencies and Trusteeship* (1958).

Hamilton (Lord George) *Parliamentary Reminiscences and Reflections*, vol. 2 (1922).

Hancock, W. K. *Smuts*. vol. i, *The Sanguine Years, 1870–1919* (1962), and vol. ii, *The Fields of Force, 1919–50* (1968) (Cambridge).

— *Survey of British Commonwealth Affairs*, vol. i, Problems of Nationality 1918–36 (1937).

Hankey, M. (Lord Hankey) *Diplomacy by Conference* (1946).

Harrison, H. *Ireland and the British Empire* (1939).

Hobson, J. A. *Imperialism: A Study* (1902).

Holt, P. M. *A Modern History of the Sudan* (1961).

— *Egypt and The Fertile Crescent, 1516–1922* (1966).

Jenkins, R. *Mr. Balfour's Poodle* (1954).

— *Asquith* (1964).

Johnson, F. A. *Defence by Committee* (1960).

Kipling, R. *The Definitive Edition of Rudyard Kipling's Verse* (1940).

Keith, A. B. *Selected Speeches and Documents on British Colonial Policy, 1763–1917* (1918).

— *Speeches and Documents on the British Dominions, 1918–31* (1932).

Knaplund, P. *Britain, Commonwealth and Empire, 1901–55* (1956).

La Nauze, J. A. *Alfred Deakin* (1965) (Melbourne).

Le May, G. H. L. *British Supremacy in South Africa, 1899–1907* (1965).

Lockhart, J. G. and Woodhouse, C. M. *Rhodes* (1963).

Lloyd George, D. *War Memoirs*, vols. 1–6 (1933–6).

Lugard (Lord) *The Dual Mandate in British Tropical Africa* (1936).

Lyttelton, Edith *Alfred Lyttelton* (1917).

Macmillan, W. M. *The Road to Self-Rule* (1959).

Madden, F. (ed.) *Imperial Constitutional Documents, 1765–1965; a supplement* (1967) (Oxford).

Magnus, P. *Kitchener* (1958).

— *King Edward VII* (1964).

Mansergh, N. *The Name and Nature of the British Commonwealth* (1954) (Cambridge).

Marais, J. S. *The Fall of Kruger's Republic* (1961) (Oxford).

Marder, A. J. *From the Dreadnought to Scapa Flow*, vol. 1 (1961).

Mehrotra, S. R. *India and the Commonwealth, 1885–1929* (1965).

Midleton (Earl of Midleton; St John Brodrick) *Records and Reactions* (1939).

Nicolson, H. *King George V* (1952).

Oliver, R. A. and Fage, J. D. *A Short History of Africa* (1962).

Pakenham, E. *The Jameson Raid* (1960).

Parry, J. H. and Sherlock, P. M. *A Short History of the West Indies* (1956).

Preston, R. A. *Canada and 'Imperial Defense'* (Duke U.P.: Durham, North Carolina).

Pyrah, G. B. *Imperial Policy in South Africa, 1902–10* (1955).

Robinson, R. and Gallagher, J. *Africa and the Victorians* (1961).

Ronaldshay (Lord; Dundas, L. J. L.) *The Life of Lord Curzon*, vol. 3 (1928).

Sanderson, G. N. *England, Europe and the Upper Nile, 1882–99* (1965) (Edinburgh).

Saul, S. B. *Studies in British Overseas Trade, 1870–1914* (1960) (Liverpool).

Schull, J. *Laurier* (1965) (Toronto).

Semmel, B. *Imperialism and Social Reform* (1960).

Shaw, A. G. L. *The Story of Australia* (1955).

Sinclair, K. *A History of New Zealand* (1959).

Smuts, J. C. (junr.) *Jan Christian Smuts* (1952).

Spear, T. G. P. (ed.) *The Oxford History of India* (3rd ed., 1961) (Oxford).

— *A History of India*, vol. 2 (1966).

Taylor, A. J. P. *English History 1914–45* (1965) (Oxford).

Thomas, H. *The Suez Affair* (1967).

Thornton, A. P. *The Imperial Idea and Its Enemies* (1959).

The Times History of the War in South Africa, ed. L. S. Amery, vol. 1 (1900).

Tyler, J. E. *The Struggle for Imperial Unity, 1868–95* (1938).

Van Jaarsveld, F. A. *The Awakening of Afrikaner Nationalism* (1961) (Cape Town).

Walker, E. A. *The British Empire; Its Structure and Spirit* (1956).

— *A History of Southern Africa* (1957).

Wheare, K. C. *The Statute of Westminster and Dominion Status* (5th ed., 1953) (Oxford).

— *The Constitutional Structure of the Commonwealth* (1960) (Oxford).

Woodward, Sir Llewellyn *The Age of Reform, 1815–1870* (1938; 2nd ed., 1962) (Oxford).

Wrench, J. E. *Alfred Lord Milner* (1958).

Young, G. M. *Portrait of an Age: Victorian England* (2nd ed., 1953).

Young, K. *Arthur James Balfour* (1965).

Appendix 1

THE COMMITTEE OF IMPERIAL DEFENCE

Statement by Baldwin at Imperial Conference, 1926 (P.R.O. Cab. 32/46)

STATEMENT BY THE PRIME MINISTER OF GREAT BRITAIN

Foreign Affairs the Basis of Great Britain's Defence Policy

Mr. Baldwin: We have already heard from the Secretary of State for Foreign Affairs an account of our foreign relations, and have had an interesting discussion on the subject. The dominant note of that statement was that our watch-word is the maintenance of peace. It is only in the last resort, and after every means of preserving peace has been exhausted, that we can contemplate the possibility of war. We might perhaps describe our policy in the words of the philosopher Thomas Hobbes, who speaks of—

" The first and fundamental law of Nature which is to seek Peace and follow it.
" The second the summe of right of Nature; which is by all means we can to defend ourselves."

Close to the northern entrance of Whitehall Gardens there stands a statue to the late Duke of Devonshire, who was Chairman of the Defence Committee of the Cabinet in the late Lord Salisbury's last administration. Behind the plinth will be found the following motto:

" Cavendo Tutus " (" Safe by taking precautions ").

These words might well form the motto of the Committee of Imperial Defence, which is our principal organ for the co-ordination of all activities in the sphere of defence.

The Committee of Imperial Defence

The Committee of Imperial Defence, whose records date from December, 1902, was brought into existence in its present form by Lord Balfour in 1904. He conceived it as a purely advisory body, as shown by the following words he used in the House of Commons as far back as the 2nd August, 1904:

" I think that my Honourable Friend need not fear that the Defence Committee will in any sense trench upon the responsibilities which properly lie, in the first instance, with the Admiralty or the Army Department, and, in the second remove, with the Cabinet as a whole. In truth, I think that one of the great merits of the Defence Committee is that it has no executive authority at all. It has no power to give an order to the humblest soldier in His Majesty's Army or the most powerless sloop under the control of the Admiralty."

That Mr. Balfour recognised the special importance of the advisory status of the Committee from the point of view of the Dominions (or " Self-Governing Colonies " as in those days they were termed) is shown by his very next sentence:

" I think that it is especially valuable from a point of view not yet touched upon—namely, the relations between the Defence Committee and those Self-Governing Colonies of the Empire over which no Office in this country has any control at all. I hope that when any problem of defence, which touches them nearly, comes up, and even when they take a closer interest in the problems of Imperial Defence as a whole, we may have the advantage of their assistance in our councils. But I am certain that the Self-Governing Colonies will never allow any representative of theirs to come to the Defence Committee if the Defence Committee, with that addition, has the smallest authority to impose obligations, financial, political, military, or naval, on the Colonies which they represent."

The advisory and consultative character of the Committee of Imperial Defence has been rigidly adhered to by successive Governments throughout all the developments of that organisation. I must again quote Mr. Balfour's words:

" It is quite true that, so far as the Home Departments are concerned, advice from a Committee which contains the Prime

Minister and which practically never meets without having the
assistance of the Secretary of State for War, the First Lord of
the Admiralty, the Head of the Army Staff, the Head of the
Army Intelligence Department, the First Sea Lord, and the
Head of the Naval Intelligence Department—it is, I say,
practically certain that a Committee so constituted is likely to
have its advice taken by the Departments."

Broadly speaking, this is true, but the power of decision has
always rested with the Cabinet, and I could, if need be, give
instances from the records of successive Governments where the
Home Cabinet, reviewing a question from a broader standpoint,
has modified or even rejected the recommendations of the Committee of Imperial Defence. So far as the Dominions are concerned,
as Mr. Balfour laid down twenty-two years ago, the Committee
of Imperial Defence has not " the smallest authority to impose
obligations, financial, political, military, or naval."

Before proceeding further, therefore, I wish to emphasise as
strongly as I can the purely advisory and consultative character of
the Committee.

Its Composition

Now as to membership. The Committee consists, and always
has consisted, only of the Prime Minister of this country and any
person whom he chooses to invite to attend. In the ordinary
course the instructions to the Secretary are to invite the following
Ministers and Officials to attend the meetings:

> The Lord President of the Council.
> The Lord Privy Seal.
> The Secretary of State for Foreign Affairs.
> The Chancellor of the Exchequer.
> The Secretary of State for Dominion Affairs.
> The Secretary of State for the Colonies.
> The Secretary of State for War.
> The Secretary of State for India.
> The First Lord of the Admiralty.
> The Secretary of State for Air.
> The Chiefs of Staff of the three Fighting Services.
> The Permanent Secretary to the Treasury.

But other Ministers, Officers, Officials or experts of the Home
Government, the Dominions, and India, are invited as the

occasion offers. This elasticity of organisation has proved of the greatest value and is made use of extensively, particularly in the case of the Sub-Committees to which questions are referred for detailed examination and report. This is proved by the fact that in the year ended the 31st March, 1926, the Committee and its Sub-Committees were attended by no less than 430 different persons, including 19 Ministers of the Crown, 6 representatives of the Overseas Empire, 142 Service Officers, 157 Civil Servants, and 48 outside experts.

It will be seen that this elasticity of membership enables the Dominions and India to take advantage of the facilities of this advisory and consultative Committee to any extent which they may desire. They can refer particular questions for advice—as they have done up to the most recent times: they can be represented to such degree as they may themselves desire by Ministers Officers, or Officials on the main Committee or on its Sub-Committees, as to a limited extent they have done and are doing. They can accept, modify, or reject its advice.

Connection of the Dominions and India with the Committee

I will now touch briefly on the question of how far the Dominions and India have used the Committee of Imperial Defence. India, let me say at once, has always been closely associated with the Committee. The Secretary of State is, and from almost the earliest days has been, one of those regularly summoned to its meetings, and the Military Secretary and other officials of the India Office are also frequently present. One of the Assistant Secretaries of the Committee has always been an Officer of the Indian Army. Officers of the Indian Army and Officials of the Indian Government have been associated in many of its large enquiries into questions affecting the defence of India in which the Indian and Home Governments are both concerned.

The first instance of the presence of a Dominion representative was in December, 1903, when Sir Frederick Borden, the Canadian Minister of Militia, attended a meeting to discuss various questions connected with the defence of Canada. In 1909 the representatives of the Dominions at the Imperial Conference on Defence attended a meeting. In 1911, during the Imperial Conference, representatives of all the Dominions attended a series of very important meetings, to which I referred in my opening speech.

Among the conclusions reached at these meetings were the following:

" 1. That one or more representatives appointed by the respective Governments of the Dominions should be invited to attend meetings of the Committee of Imperial Defence when questions of naval and military defence affecting the Oversea Dominions are under consideration.

" 2. The proposal that a Defence Committee should be established in each Dominion is accepted in principle. The constitution of these Defence Committees is a matter for each Dominion to decide."

Considerable effect was given to both these resolutions before the war.

In 1912, meetings of the Committee were attended by Sir Robert Borden (who had succeeded Sir Wilfrid Laurier as Prime Minister) and a number of his colleagues who had come to England for purposes of consultation.

Between that time and the outbreak of war, meetings were attended in 1913 by Sir James Allen on behalf of New Zealand, and later in the same year by Mr. (now Sir Thomas) White and Mr. Burrell on behalf of Canada, and in 1914 by Sir Edward (now Lord) Morris, representing Newfoundland, and later by Sir George Perley. Just before the outbreak of war, Sir George Perley, a Minister of the Canadian Government without portfolio, had become High Commissioner for Canada, with authority to attend meetings of the Committee of Imperial Defence.

The War, of course, involved considerable changes in our defensive system, and I need only mention that the machinery of the Committee of Imperial Defence, tuned up and intensified, was adapted successively to the purposes of the War Committee, the War Cabinet, and the Imperial War Cabinet.

Since the War the opportunities of personal association of representatives of the Dominions with the Committee of Imperial Defence have not been numerous. Owing, perhaps, to the more frequent meetings of the Imperial Conference, there have been very few, if any, visits from individual Dominion Ministers concerned in Defence matters. At the meetings of the Imperial Conference, however, the question of Imperial Defence has been discussed in the greatest detail, and the material prepared as the basis of those discussions, as well as the technical memoranda on Defence prepared for the use of the British Empire Delegation at the Washington Conference, has been organised by the Committee of Imperial Defence. The Imperial Conferences have, indeed, provided an opportunity for a stocktaking of the work of the Committee.

Apart from the personal attendance of Ministers, however, the association of the Dominions with the Committee since the War has been considerable. Australia, New Zealand, and South Africa, for example, are represented on its Sub-Committee on Reduction and Limitation of Armaments. During the last year or two, one of its Sub-Committees has been engaged on a review of coast defences under post-war conditions. The late Prime Minister of Australia (Mr. Hughes) invited the Committee to advise at the same time on the defences of Australian ports, and other Dominions subsequently invited similar reviews. Detailed reports have been forwarded to Australia and New Zealand. In the case of the Australian ports the Committee had the great advantage of the co-operation of several Australian officers. It is hoped to furnish reports to the other Dominions shortly, but for the moment the Committee is fully occupied with the Home and Mediterranean ports. Also, we understand that it would be in accordance with the wish of the Dominion Governments that the Oversea Defence Committee, which is studying the question of reserves of ammunition, should make recommendations for the Dominions.

In addition, a considerable number of reports approved by the Committee of Imperial Defence have been forwarded confidentially to the Dominions, and in some cases technical suggestions have been received from them, and adopted. Some of these reports have resulted in corresponding arrangements being made in the Dominions and India, and we hope this process will continue. When action is taken on one of our reports it is useful to the Committee of Imperial Defence to know what that action is.

Appendix 2

IMPERIAL CONFERENCE 1926. Documents from the Committee on Inter-Imperial Relations

(*a*) Opening statement by Balfour, 27 October 1926 (P.R.O. Cab./32 56)

AFTER a brief preliminary discussion concerning procedure and publicity, LORD BALFOUR read the following statement:

" Since the shock of the Great War has, for good or for evil, hastened so many movements which were, in any case, inevitable, it is no matter for surprise that men ask themselves how the structure of the constitution of the British Empire has fared in this changing world. Before 1914 it seemed to alien observers the frailest of political structures. A State which (so far as its western elements were concerned) consisted in the main of six self-governing communities, bound together by no central authority, not competent to enlist a single recruit or impose a shilling of taxation, might look well painted on the map, but as fighting machine is surely negligible.

" The war refuted this plausible conjecture: but it left the Empire unexplained and undefined. Then came the Peace; and the constituent States took their full share in framing and signing the Treaty which they had done so much to secure. But this procedure, though it demonstrated the effective reality of the British Empire, did little to make its position clear to students of comparative politics.

" (ii)

" The difficulty which so many find in ' placing ' the British Empire arises largely from the fact that its character and constitution are entirely without precedent, and that, as a result, it does not comfortably fit into any familiar theories, nor can it be described by the ordinary concepts of international law. Yet its general character is not difficult to delineate.

" (iii)

" It may be conveniently divided into elements of four different kinds:

" (1.) The seven self-governing communities—Great Britain and the North of Ireland, Canada, Australia, New Zealand, South Africa, the Irish Free State and Newfoundland.
" (2.) India.
" (3.) The Dependencies of the self-governing State, namely, the Colonies, the Protectorates, and the Mandated Territories of Great Britain, Australia, New Zealand and the Union of South Africa.

" (iv)

" In what consists the unity of this varied assortment of communities, scattered over the whole globe, and differing from each other in language, race, religion and history?

" From a strictly juridical point of view, there are only two attributes which they all share with each other and with nobody else. They are all under one Crown; and their inhabitants are all citizens of one Empire. But juridical formulas, if they stand alone, are but a brittle bond. On what solid foundation of patriotic sentiment does the fabric of the Empire rest? It rests upon the well-founded conviction that the Empire makes for general peace, and for the security of its diverse portions. Whether in war or in peace, there is no constituent of the Empire which does not gain in consideration and status by being part of a greater whole; and what is gain to them is far from being any loss to others. For the very existence of this complex unity makes for the maintenance of world peace, and on the maintenance of world peace depends the future of civilisation.

" (v)

" It is true, no doubt, that, while in our knowledge of present needs and in our hopes of future security we may all of us find adequate ground for Imperial patriotism, the different parts of this varied whole cannot draw their strength from memories of a common history. Their history has been too diverse; their ancient differences have been too acute. Yet Imperial unity gives us all the right to a share in the glories of each other's past, and to claim an interest in each other's contributions to the wealth of the world in the spheres of literature, science, politics and war. I at least, as a Scotsman, am not going to surrender my share of Magna Charta and Shakespeare on account of Bannockburn and Flodden. This may seem fanciful; but I hope it is as real to others as it is to me.

" (vi)

" These general reflections are a necessary prelude to the more particular business of the Committee of Prime Ministers; and I turn to the problems raised by the most novel and yet most characteristic peculiarity of the British Empire—I mean the co-existence within its unity of seven autonomous communities. This statement of fact, though very simple, is barely intelligible to foreigners, and no doubt has among ourselves given rise to some secondary difficulties. It is with these secondary difficulties that the Committee has to deal; but in dealing with them it is vital to remember that they *are* secondary, and that the fundamental truth to which they are subordinate is the equality of status which is the essential foundation of this part of our imperial fabric.

" (vii)

" It is undoubtedly true that this equality of status is combined at present, and probably will always be combined in some form or other, with differences of function. For example, four out of the seven self-governing communities—Great Britain, Australia, New Zealand and South Africa—have Dependencies belonging to the Empire. Canada, the Irish Free State and Newfoundland have not. Great Britain has special relations with India, the Colonies, the Protectorates and the Channel Islands not directly shared by the Dominions. She also takes a leading part in the all-important and most burdensome task of Imperial Defence and in the direction of Foreign Affairs which has no exact parallel elsewhere.

" (viii)

" Her relations with these two great departments of Imperial activity are no doubt due in part to historic reasons. But there is a more fundamental explanation arising out of the actual conditions with which, as practical statesmen, we have all got to deal. The principles determining the general direction of Foreign Affairs may be, and ought to be, the product of consultation; and it will be among our chief duties to make that consultation more continuous and more effective. But there are always moments in the conduct of fleets, of armies, and of negotiations, when decisions, if they are to be of use, must be rapid, and when consultations, if they involve delay, are a danger rather than a strength. If this be so, it must be on one of the seven self-governing communities that the greatest weight of responsibility must be thrown; and so long as the centre of difficulty is Europe, and the present distribution of population in the Empire suffers no overwhelming change, it seems impossible to ask any other portion of the Empire to perform the major duties which now devolve upon Great Britain. We must content ourselves with improving to the utmost the machinery of imperial consultation, which, in any case, will work more rapidly and smoothly as the progress of invention enables us to overcome more effectually the obstacles presented by Time and Space."

(b) Hertzog's draft declaration (P.R.O. Cab. 32/56)

DRAFT DECLARATION PREPARED BY GENERAL HERTZOG

THE Prime Ministers of the—
  United Kingdom

and of the Dominions of—

  Canada,
  Australia,
  New Zealand,
  South Africa,
  Newfoundland and
  Ireland,

with their associated fellow Ministers assembled at the Imperial Conference, recognising that—

  they are respectively the representatives of independent States, equal in status and separately entitled to international recognition, with Governments and Parliaments independent of one another; united by the common bond of allegiance to the Crown and freely associated as members of the British Commonwealth of Nations,

    are agreed that—

(a) whatever surviving forms of inequality or subordination there may be in the mutual relations between the one and any other of the said States, whether in respect of legislature, executive or judiciary, such inequality or subordination is due to and dependent upon the voluntary consent of the associated State concerned,

and—

(b) that it is desirable that the constitutional relationship between Great Britain and the Dominions be properly known and recognised, and that the necessary steps be taken that the equal status of the associated States and their relations as above set forth be formally and authoritatively intimated to their own communities and to the world at large.

2, *Whitehall Gardens, S.W.* 1,
    October 28, 1926.

(c) Balfour's original draft defining the relationship between Britain and the Dominions (B.M. Add. Mss. 49704)

" Great Britain and the self-governing Dominions are autonomous communities of equal status, united by the common bond of allegiance to the Crown, but in no sort of subordination one to another.

All their inhabitants though under many governments are citizens of one Empire under one Crown.

To that Empire and Crown they have duties and obligations, but each is (through its own Parliament) the sole judge in its own case of the manner in which those duties and obligations may best be fulfilled.

Formal survivals from an earlier stage of development are matters of consent and can always be modified or eliminated by common agreement if they prove inconvenient."

(*d*) Final definition of the relationship between Britain and the Dominions (P.R.O. Cab. 32/56)

" They are autonomous communities within the British Empire, equal in status, in no way subordinate one to another in any aspect of their domestic or external affairs, though united by a common allegiance to the Crown, and freely associated as members of the British Commonwealth of Nations."

Index

Balfour is shown as AJB throughout the index. Sub-entries are arranged chronologically wherever possible.